Expertise and Skill
Impact of William G. Chase

MW01252941

The research on human expertise and complex skill acquisition that William G. Chase performed in the decade between the publication of the classic chess studies that he conducted with Herb Simon in 1973 and his untimely and tragic death, has proven profoundly influential and enduring. Its impact spans disciplines that include psychology, computer science, education, cognitive neuroscience, medicine, and human factors. It has contributed significantly to the emergence of cognitive engineering and has led to significant applications in the areas of training and instruction, and knowledge-based "intelligent" computational systems. Its influence can be seen in current discussions of intelligence, heritability, intellectual potential, and achievement found in the contemporary popular press.

The chapters in this volume document the enduring scientific contributions of William G. Chase to current knowledge and understanding of human expertise and skill acquisition, and applications that his work has supported. It will be of interest to those researching, studying, and working in the multiple fields that were greatly influenced by Chase's work.

James J. Staszewski is a Research Professor in the Psychology Department at Carnegie Mellon University, USA. He conducts use-inspired research focused on understanding human expertise and its development and applies the results to designing training programs and training technologies.

Carnegie Mellon Symposia on Cognition

David Klahr, Series Editor

Expertise and Skill Acquisition: The Impact of William G. Chase

Edited by

James J. Staszewski

Psychology Press
Taylor & Francis Group
NEW YORK AND LONDON

GUELPH HUMBER LIBRARY
205 Humber College Blvd
Toronto, ON   M9W 5L7

First published 2013
by Psychology Press
711 Third Avenue, New York, NY 10017

Simultaneously published in the UK
by Psychology Press
27 Church Road, Hove, East Sussex BN3 2FA

Psychology Press is an imprint of the Taylor & Francis Group, an informa business

© 2013 Taylor & Francis

The right of James J. Staszewski to be identified as the author of the editorial material, and of the authors for their individual chapters, has been asserted in accordance with sections 77 and 78 of the Copyright, Designs and Patents Act 1988.

All rights reserved. No part of this book may be reprinted or reproduced or utilised in any form or by any electronic, mechanical, or other means, now known or hereafter invented, including photocopying and recording, or in any information storage or retrieval system, without permission in writing from the publishers.

Trademark notice: Product or corporate names may be trademarks or registered trademarks, and are used only for identification and explanation without intent to infringe.

Library of Congress Cataloging in Publication Data
Expertise and skill acquisition: The Impact of William G. Chase/Edited by
James J. Staszewski.—1st Edition.
    pages cm.—(Carnegie Mellon symposia on cognition series; 32)
    1. Expertise. 2. Ability. I. Staszewski, James John.
    BF378.E94E97 2012
    153.1'5—dc23
    2012032580

ISBN: 978-1-84872-890-5 (hbk)
ISBN: 978-1-84872-627-7 (pbk)
ISBN: 978-0-203-07454-1 (ebk)

Typeset in New Caledonia LT Std
by Book Now Ltd, London

SUSTAINABLE
FORESTRY
INITIATIVE

Certified Sourcing
www.sfiprogram.org
SFI-00555
The SFI label applies to the text stock.

Printed and bound in the United States of America by
Walsworth Publishing Company, Marceline, MO.

William G. Chase

Contents

Figures

Tables

Contributors

John R. Anderson
Department of Psychology, Carnegie
Mellon University, Pittsburgh, PA,
USA

Daniel Ansari
Department of Psychology,
University of Western Ontario,
London, Canada

Sian L. Beilock
Department of Psychology, University
of Chicago, Chicago, IL, USA

Shawn Betts
Department of Psychology, Carnegie
Mellon University, Pittsburgh, PA,
USA

Neil Charness
Department of Psychology, Florida
State University, Tallahassee, FL,
USA

Catherine C. Chase
Department of Psychology and
Human Computer Interaction
Institute, Carnegie Mellon University,
Pittsburgh, PA, USA

Michelene T. H. Chi
Department of Psychology, Arizona
State University, Tempe, AZ, USA

Trevor A. Cohen
Center for Cognitive Informatics and
Decision Making, School of
Biomedical Informatics, University of
Texas at Houston, Houston, TX, USA

K. Anders Ericsson
Department of Psychology, Florida
State University, Tallahassee, FL,
USA

Jennifer L. Ferris
Department of Psychology, Carnegie
Mellon University, Pittsburgh, PA,
USA

Jon M. Fincham
Department of Psychology, Carnegie
Mellon University, Pittsburgh, PA,
USA

Fernand Gobet
Department of Psychology, Brunel
University, Uxbridge, UK

Ashley Kingon
The Earth Institute, Columbia
University, New York, NY, USA

Kenneth Kotovsky
Department of Psychology, Carnegie
Mellon University, Pittsburgh, PA,
USA

Michael I. Posner
Department of Psychology,
University of Oregon, Eugene,
OR, USA

Giulia Righi
Children's Hospital Boston,
Harvard Medical School, Boston,
MA, USA

David A. Rosenbaum
Department of Psychology,
Pennsylvania State University,
University Park, PA, USA

Roger W. Schvaneveldt
Applied Psychology Program,
College of Technology and
Innovation, Arizona State University,
Mesa, AZ, USA

Robert S. Siegler
Department of Psychology,
Carnegie Mellon University,
Pittsburgh, PA, USA

James J. Staszewski
Department of Psychology,
Carnegie Mellon University,
Pittsburgh, PA, USA

Michael J. Tarr
Department of Psychology,
Carnegie Mellon University,
Pittsburgh, PA, USA

G. Kerr Whitfield
Department of Basic Medical
Sciences, The University of Arizona
College of Medicine—Phoenix,
Phoenix, AZ, USA

Preface

The contents of this collected volume are based chiefly on presentations given at the 36th Carnegie Symposium on Cognition held in June 2009. The topic of the Symposium was "Expertise and Skill Acquisition: The Impact of William G. Chase." The variety of topics covered in this volume illustrates how research on expertise and its development has expanded in depth and breadth since Bill Chase and Herb Simon (Chase & Simon, 1973a, 1973b; Simon & Chase, 1973) conducted their seminal studies of chess expertise in the early 1970s.

Plans for the Symposium and this volume were hatched in a meeting of Carnegie Mellon University (CMU) Psychology Department faculty who serve on the Chase Memorial Award[1] Committee. Such was the professional and personal regard in which Bill Chase was held by the Psychology colleagues that, when he died suddenly at 43, this award was created as a memorial. Noting that 25 years had passed since Bill Chase's untimely death and 35 years since publication of the now classic papers on the cognitive bases of chess expertise, the committee decided to convene a Symposium to honor his contributions. That Chase and Simon first presented "The Mind's Eye in Chess" (Chase & Simon, 1973a), at the 8th Carnegie Symposium, which Bill organized, made this venue all the more fitting.

The scientific aims of this meeting and this volume were to examine the state of knowledge and understanding influenced by Bill's research on expertise and complex skill acquisition, frame issues for future investigation, and promote progress in these areas. By examining and documenting the scientific legacy of our late colleague and friend on contemporary research in cognitive science and the related areas, we would pay tribute to his contributions, and through dissemination of the products of this meeting, stimulate further inquiry and scientific contributions. Modest by nature and a bit shy, Bill might not have welcomed the spotlight that goes with the former, but without doubt would have appreciated the latter.

---

1 The Chase Memorial Award was established by the Department of Psychology at Carnegie Mellon in Bill Chase's memory. His friends and colleagues wished to honor Bill and the intellectual and personal values that he embodied: honesty, judgment, facility with experimental methods, an eye for interesting empirical phenomena, and theoretical vision. The award is traditionally given to a person within five years of receiving the Ph.D. who, in our opinion, best exemplifies these virtues. Recipients include: James Stigler (1985), Phillip J. Kellman (1987), Susan A. Gelman (1989), Eldar Shafir (1993), Robert L. Goldstone (1996), and Marvin Chun (2000).

The authors invited to participate were selected with two criteria in mind. First, all had done and were doing interesting and important research on the topics selected as this conference's foci. Second, their work was related clearly to topics in Bill's research portfolio. Many of the participants, but not all, were professional colleagues of Bill who had collaborated with Bill as well as personal friends. Among this group were Mike Posner, his graduate advisor, and Roger Schvaneveldt, a graduate school classmate. Most of the CMU-affiliated participants had known Bill for the entirety of their careers. No personal relations could be closer than his wife, Micki Chi, and his daughter, Catherine Chase. No claims to unbiased sampling can or will be made; the 36th Carnegie Symposium could rightfully be considered the academic equivalent of a gathering of the Chase Clan and this collection viewed as a *Liber amicorum*—a book of friends.

The chapters in this volume are organized loosely on the basis of three headings: (1) educational implications of expertise and skill acquisition; (2) mainstream cognitive research on human expertise; and (3) the biological bases of expertise. The sequence of chapters reflects the presentation order in the Symposium and includes commentaries on the chapters delivered by discussants, Bob Siegler, Ken Kotovsky, and Daniel Ansari.

The sampling of Bill Chase's scientific influence reflected by these chapters surely underestimates his intellectual contribution for several reasons. First, the range of topics covered in this volume is dwarfed by the number found in the *Cambridge Handbook of Expertise and Expert Performance* (Ericsson, Charness, Feltovich, & Hoffman, 2006). Chase's work represents a cornerstone on which this body of knowledge rests. Second, outside of the areas of expertise and skill acquisition but still within the field of cognitive psychology, Chase and Clark's studies of semantic representation in the comparison of sentences and pictures (Chase & Clark, 1971, 1972; Clark & Chase, 1972) remain influential, cited more than 100 times in the past decade, despite 40 years passing since their publication. Outside of psychology, Chase's expertise research has had broad influence in the field of education, especially in the areas of learning (Bransford, Brown, & Cocking, 1999) and assessment (Pellegrino, Chudowsky, & Glaser, 2001). Finally, Chase's work on expertise contributed heavily to the development of knowledge-based computer systems, e.g., expert systems, decision-support systems, etc. (Simon, 1989), spawning not only a large and active branch of study in Artificial Intelligence, but also applications for myriad domains[2]. Finally, contemporary popular interest in expertise and exceptional performance reflected in recent writings of Gladwell (2008), Brooks (2009) and

2 *Expert Systems with Applications*, an international journal, publishes papers in the areas of, but not limited to: finance, accounting, engineering, marketing, auditing, law, procurement and contracting, project management, risk assessment, information management, information retrieval, crisis management, stock trading, strategic management, network management, telecommunications, space education, intelligent front ends, intelligent database management systems, medicine, chemistry, human resources management, human capital, business, production management, archaeology, economics, energy, and defense.

Colvin (2008) focuses on Chase and Simon's (1973a) core claim that knowledge acquired through experience is the foundation of human expertise.

Gedenkschrifts[3] carry no small element of poignancy. This Symposium was no exception. What was exceptional, according to feedback from speakers and audience, was the quality of the presentations, the enthusiasm with which they were presented and received, and the engagement and interaction of speakers, Symposium fellows, and attendees in the meetings' formal and informal activities. In short, the atmosphere evoked the professional dedication, rigor, intense curiosity, infectious enthusiasm, humor, and vitality for which Bill Chase was so well known. Although print is hard pressed to convey such an atmosphere, the chapters in this volume show that research on expertise and its acquisition is a healthy, diverse, and growing enterprise owing greatly to his pioneering efforts.

REFERENCES

Bransford, J. D., Brown, A. L., & Cocking, R. R. (1999). *How people learn: Brain, mind, experience, and school*. Washington, DC: National Academy Press.

Brooks, D. (2009, April 30). Genius: The modern view. *The New York Times*, p. A23.

Chase, W. G., & Clark, H. H. (1971). Semantics in the perception of verticality. *British Journal of Psychology, 62*, 311–326.

Chase, W. G., & Clark, H. H. (1972). Mental operations in the comparison of sentences and pictures. In L. Gregg (Ed.), *Cognition in learning and memory*. New York: Wiley.

Chase, W.G., & Simon, H.A. (1973a). The mind's eye in chess. In W. G. Chase (Ed.), *Visual information processing* (pp. 215–281). New York: Academic Press.

Chase, W.G., & Simon, H.A. (1973b). Perception in chess. *Cognitive Psychology, 4*, 55–81.

Clark, H. H., & Chase, W. G. (1972). On the process of comparing sentences against pictures. *Cognitive Psychology, 3*, 472–517.

Colvin, G. (2008). *Talent is overrated: What really separates world-class performers from everybody else*. New York: Penguin Group.

Ericsson, K. A., Charness, N., Feltovich, P. J., & Hoffman, R. R. (2006). *The Cambridge handbook of expertise and performance*. New York, NY: Cambridge University Press.

Gladwell, M. (2008). *Outliers: The story of success*. New York: Little, Brown, and Co.

Pellegrino, J. W., Chudowsky, N., & Glaser, R. (2001). *Knowing what students know: The science and design of educational assessment*. Washington, DC: National Academy Press.

Simon, H. A. (1989). Human experts and knowledge-based systems. In M. Tokoro, Y. Anzai, & A. Yonezawa (Eds.), *Concepts and characteristics of knowledge-based systems* (pp. 1–21). Amsterdam: North Holland.

Simon, H. A., & Chase, W. G. (1973). Skill in chess. *American Scientist, 61*, 394–403. Reprinted in I. L. Janis (Ed.), *Current trends in psychology* (pp. 194–203). Los Altos, CA: William Kaufmann, 1977.

---

3 A Festschrift is a collection of writings honoring the scholarly contributions of a colleague, usually in academia. When the tribute is posthumous, such a volume is called a Gedenkschrift.

Acknowledgments

Partial funding for the 36th Carnegie Symposium on which this book is based was provided by generous grants from the U.S. Army Research Laboratory (W911NF-09-1-0048) and the National Science Foundation (BCS-0842617). The proposals were submitted in tough economic times and these agencies came through with much appreciated support. The views, opinions, and/or findings contained in this volume are those of the authors and should not be construed as an official Department of the Army position, policy, or decision, unless so designated by other documentation. Likewise, any opinions, findings, and conclusions or recommendations expressed in this material are those of the author(s) and do not necessarily reflect the views of the National Science Foundation.

Fernand Gobet, Christian Lebiere, David Reitter, David Rosenbaum, Bob Siegler, Mike Tarr, Connie Tompkins, and Matt Wood provided valuable reviews on various chapters in this volume. A reviewer's reward rarely approaches the time and effort careful reviewing demands, so the expertise and professional generosity that these people provided deserve special recognition.

Claudia Righi, Mike Tarr, Ashley Kingon and Daniel Ansari contributed chapters that were not presented in the symposium (regrettably), but clearly enhance this volume.

The assistance of Ginger Placone, Theresa Kurutz, Shellie Sherman, Rochelle Croom, Erin Donahoe, and Emilie Rendulic in the organization of the symposium contributed materially to its successful outcome. Their supporting efforts are deeply appreciated. Ginger Placone's outstanding administrative support is especially valued.

Thanks to David Klahr for his introductory symposium presentation and his dedicated support for continued publication of the proceedings of the Carnegie Symposia.

Finally, Diane Briars' encouragement and support of the symposium and this volume are especially valued and appreciated.

1

Learning from Observing an Expert's Demonstration, Explanations, and Dialogues[1]

MICHELENE T. H. CHI

Arizona State University, USA

INTRODUCTION

A teacher/mentor is sometimes an expert in the sense that they know the content domain in which they have to teach or mentor students, even though they may not be an expert at pedagogy. Nevertheless, as a content expert, s/he can teach in at least three different ways: (1) by modeling and demonstrating to a large number of students, in the context of a classroom, how a problem is solved or how a chemical reaction can be produced, without any verbal interactions with the students; (2) by explaining verbally some difficult concepts or how a problem is solved; and (3) by guiding and interacting with a specific student through extended dialogue to understand a concept or to solve a problem, with other students observing such interactions. In short, there are many ways that teachers/mentors can deliver instruction even though they may not be an expert at pedagogy. The question is, which method of instruction is best for students' learning?

This chapter is a tribute to my late husband, William G. Chase; I am indebted to him for all the ways (described above) that he had mentored me. Like other students, I had the opportunity of learning from him in formal settings, such as listening to his lectures at colloquia and explanations in classes.

1 This research was supported by a grant from the Spencer Foundation (200800196). I am indebted to Marguerite Roy for the new analyses reported in the last part of this chapter.

However, I had the additional privilege of learning from him in many informal settings. In undertaking his daily research tasks, Bill served as a role model to me by demonstrating how he asked critical questions, designed studies without a confound, analyzed data, and even more importantly, how he revised and repaired his designs and analyses. But most importantly, before we would go home each day, I would always sit in a corner in his office waiting for him to finish his day, often watching and listening-in to him explaining and guiding the many students who came in and out of his office daily asking how to modify their conceptual questions or analyze their data. I am forever grateful for those years of informal observations since it had a profound influence on my research style and methodology. Little did I realize then that the many years of observing him in these different ways would inspire me to now ask whether some ways of observing are more effective for learning than others.

This chapter discusses the advantages and potential limitations of observing each type of teaching/mentoring. Before doing so, this section will briefly clarify and differentiate what will be discussed here from related work on "vicarious learning." "Vicarious learning" is a term that was introduced in the 1960s to describe learning that results primarily from observing the *behaviors* of others and the consequences of those behaviors for their enactors (Bandura, 1989). The important aspect of Bandura's social learning experiments is that even though the observers did not execute the actions being observed or experience feedback from the consequences of those actions, learning still occurred. For example, if children watch other children behave aggressively, even on television, or if they are exposed, even briefly, to violent video games (Anderson & Bushman, 2001), then they are also more likely to exhibit aggressive behavior (Bandura, Ross & Ross, 1961). In this case, they have learned either the aggressive behaviors themselves or they have learned to lower their inhibitory thresholds to exhibit aggressive behavior. Many other studies have shown that people can learn a behavior by watching a demonstration, such as watching a video of how to tie nautical knots (Schwan & Riempp, 2004). The main difference between the kind of tasks vicarious learning studies use and the tasks in the studies to be described later in this chapter is that in many of the vicarious studies, the tasks tend to be physical behaviors whereas our work examines academic tasks such as solving mathematics or physics problems.

In the preceding paragraphs, learning from observing was described under three instructional contexts: (1) watching an expert *demonstrating* (e.g., solving a problem at the whiteboard); (2) watching and listening to an expert *demonstrating* and *explaining* (e.g., solving and explaining the solution steps beyond describing what was written down at the whiteboard); and (3) observing an expert *guiding* another student as s/he works out a problem or task (e.g., answering the student's questions or scaffolding him/her). (Henceforth, in this third context, this other student with whom the expert is directly interacting will be called a "tutee" and the task of problem-solving will be used as an example throughout the discussion in this chapter.) Although the chapter began with questions about whether there are differential learning advantages to each of these observing contexts, note that only the first two contexts (e.g., watching an expert solve a problem, and watching an expert solve and explain a solution) are prevalent in current classrooms (e.g., in math and physics classes). Thus, in these two contexts, the students are both observing and receiving instruction directly from the expert/teacher (in that the demonstrations and explanations are intended for the observing-students, and the students can have some minimal interactions with the expert). However, the third context, observing an expert guiding another student/tutee (e.g., while the tutee solves a problem at the whiteboard), is less conventional, but it is the only context (among the three) in which the observing-students and the tutees experience different instructional opportunities, in that the tutees get to interact directly with the expert whereas the observers do not. Thus, the central question raised in this chapter is whether the observing-students in the third context can learn as well as the tutees, and if so, under what circumstances.

But before addressing this last context, the limitations of the first two contexts will be reviewed. That is, in the first context, the following question will be considered: how much can students learn by observing an expert visually demonstrating a skill or perform a complex task such as solving a problem, without directly interacting with the expert? In the second context, the question is: how much can students learn by watching an expert demonstrate a skill or perform a complex task and listening to the expert's verbal explanations while demonstrating it? Finally, in the third context, some preliminary evidence will be provided regarding how much students can learn by observing an expert explaining, guiding, and dialoguing with a tutee. Potential interpretations for our results are offered. In authentic classrooms and other situations, a teacher/mentor may combine several of these methods of instruction. However, for research purposes, each of these contexts will be discussed separately.

EXPERTS MODELING WITH DEMONSTRATIONS ONLY

In many classroom and training contexts, experts typically can teach by visually demonstrating to students. This occurs often for many procedural skills, such as serving in tennis, detecting mines, cooking, or knitting. There are many reasons why a task is sometimes demonstrated without many verbal explanations. One practical reason, as in the case of mine detection (Staszewski, Chapter 2, this volume), is that the expert must demonstrate it from afar for safety reasons. A second reason is that the expert often has no accessible knowledge that s/he can articulate, or the articulated knowledge is essentially useless. For example, a tennis coach might explain that the student player should "pull his shoulders back when serving" but that description is too vague for the student to know exactly how that should be done. So there are many occasions when training occurs from demonstrations alone.

Do students learn from watching experts demonstrate a skill or a procedure? Certainly there has been abundant and consistent evidence suggesting that one can learn a great deal of physical skills from watching, such as anecdotal evidence from anthropology (in weaving, Lave, 1988), and laboratory evidence such as learning to tie nautical knots from watching a video only (without audio; Schwan & Riempp, 2004). The most compelling evidence comes from work in social psychology, as illustrated above, in the context of behaviors such as aggression (Bandura, 1989).

The fact that people can learn by watching physical behavior without direct interaction should not be surprising given that it is a form of imitation that both chimpanzees (Whiten, 1998) and young children undertake. For example, young children will spontaneously pick up books and imitate adults' reading after exposure to models who were reading aloud. These children were learning the behavior of reading, but not the content of what the adult models were reading (Haskett & Lenfestey, 1974). What about other cognitive behaviors such as learning and collaborating skills? Two studies have shown that observing-students can learn cognitive behaviors such as asking questions by watching an animated agent ask questions (Craig, Gholson, Ventura, Graesser, & the Tutoring Research Group, 2000) and by observing others collaborate (Rummel & Spada, 2005). Note that the observing-students were asked to learn the *skills* of asking questions and collaborating, which are observable overt behaviors, but they were not required to learn the specific content of the topics used in the studies. That is, they were not asked to learn the content of the questions asked, but only to learn to ask questions; and they were not asked to learn the content of the collaborative diagnosis of a clinical case, but only to learn how to collaborate.

For the kind of tasks illustrated above, such as acting aggressively and asking questions, the behavior to be mimicked is directly displayed so that it is observable. However, complex academic task performance often involves many covert inferences and reasoning steps before an overt step is taken, so that there is not a one-to-one correspondence between the actions displayed and the reasoning behind the displayed actions. For instance, suppose a teacher is solving a geometry problem on the whiteboard by writing down a sequence of six steps (some involving equations). Students can obviously "learn" this particular sequence of steps, in that they can reproduce these steps for solving similar problems (VanLehn, Graesser, Jackson, Jordan, Olney, & Rose, 2007). But can they solve other less similar problems? Abundant evidence in the literature shows that students generally cannot transfer what they have learned from studying or watching an example solution to a new, slightly different problem (Reed, Dempster, & Ettinger, 1985; Ross, 1987), because they have not learned the reasoning by which the original steps were derived. In short, the cognitive processes underlying the decision about what step to display (on the whiteboard, for instance) maps many to-one (the actual step displayed). Similarly, if a novice had to learn how to troubleshoot a complicated piece of equipment, watching an expert throw all the switches on a board does not tell the observing novice how the problem was diagnosed. Because there is a lack of one-to-one mapping between the cognitive processes underlying the decisions for which switches to throw and the observable actions of throwing switches, we concluded back in 1991 that one cannot learn by watching an expert perform a cognitively rich task (Chi & Bjork, 1991), unless the displayed steps of the task map one-to-one with the reasoning behind the steps (Carroll & Bandura, 1990).

In sum, watching an expert demonstrate a task is adequate for enabling the observing-students to learn how to perform that task to the extent that the task is a physical or behavioral one where each step is overtly displayed. However, if a task requires multiple deep reasoning steps before an overt step is displayed, then learning from watching an expert demonstrate some of the procedural or behavioral steps is more limited. An extreme example might be watching an attending physician inject a drug into a patient. An observing medical student will not learn much from watching this action unless s/he also understands the explanations for the injection. Similarly, students do not understand the solution steps a teacher writes on the whiteboard (because they typically just copy the steps from the whiteboard without knowing the reasoning behind each step), unless the students provide their own reasoning for each demonstrated step, as in self-explaining (Chi, Bassok, Lewis, Reimann, & Glaser, 1989). Thus, learning from watching a demonstration of a complex task is shallow with limited understanding.

EXPERTS MODELING WITH DEMONSTRATIONS PLUS GIVING MONOLOGUE EXPLANATIONS

What about the case of an expert modeling while providing explanations along with it, but without giving feedback to the student (thereby there is no direct interaction)? By *explaining* the steps of a problem, we mean explaining the reasoning that leads from one step to the other, as opposed to *describing* the steps of a problem, which is only uttering verbally what each step is or does. To use knitting as a contrast to a cognitively rich task, telling the student verbally to first put the needle through one loop, then another, is a *description* of the steps, corresponding almost to the student watching the steps. The verbal descriptions did not constitute *explanations* because they do not add any further clarification, justification, or information. One prevalent example of this context is teaching in a large lecture class. Typically, a teacher instructs a class by demonstrating and explaining. For instance, a math teacher can demonstrate how to solve problems by writing down the solution steps on the whiteboard, and explaining each step as s/he writes. Many instructional videos (in the market, or on television) also teach numerous everyday skills through demonstrating and explaining, such as in cooking. Unfortunately, in many of these cases, the explanations are merely descriptions of the demonstrated steps.

The question addressed in this section is: For a complex cognitive task, such as solving geometry and physics problems, in which there are many reasoning steps corresponding to one overt step, are experts' accompanying verbal explanations helpful to students' learning? That is, if instructors are asked to articulate the intervening reasoning for each step (sometimes referred to as making thinking visible, Linn, 1995), will hearing those explanations be helpful, especially for deep learning? Evidence across a variety of research contexts shows that in general, expert-articulated explanations do not always help students achieve a great deal of learning or transfer, whether it is in a classroom context (Deslauriers, Schelew & Wieman, 2011), or in a tutoring context (Chi, Roy, & Hausmann, 2008). For example, Deslauriers et al. (2011) compared students' learning in quantum mechanics classes that were either instructed by an expert faculty member (one who was motivated, had many years of experience teaching this quantum mechanics course, and had received high student evaluations) who lectured and demonstrated how to solve mechanics problems, with interactive classes that were instructed by a postdoctoral fellow in which students could ask questions and receive feedback, and worked in small dyad groups. A 2.5 standard deviation difference in learning was obtained between the two conditions, consistent with our interpretation that students do not learn very well by listening to an expert explain with demonstrations. Compatible with the minimal learning from listening to an expert's explanations is the finding from expert–novice research showing that learners perform significantly better when instructed by novices than by experts in an electronic wiring task (Hinds, Patterson, & Pfeffer, 2001), suggesting that answers and explanations are helpful to a questioner only if the answers are adjusted to the appropriate level of the question (Webb, 1989). This is also consistent with Feldman, Campbell and Lai's (1999) point that "Students of similar achievement levels may be more effective than teacher–student pairs because peers can discuss strategies at their own novice's zone of proximal development." In a similar vein, in the audience-design literature, it has been shown that experts underestimate the complexity of a subject and their explanations of it (Bromme, Jucks & Runde, 2005; Clark & Murphy, 1982). Thus, this body of evidence suggests that explanations have to be tailored to the level of the recipient's understanding in order for them to be effective, and since experts are not always accurate at gauging a novice's understanding (evidence for this to be presented below), this is one possible reason why experts' explanations, when they accompany demonstrations, may not be that helpful for deep learning.

One reason that experts cannot accurately gauge a novice's understanding (therefore making their explanations ineffective for novices' learning) is that there is usually a mismatch between the normative mental model from which the expert is generating an explanation of a concept, a problem step, or a system, and the naïve mental model to which a student has to assimilate that explanation. We have direct evidence showing that experts, while tutoring, are inaccurate at predicting their tutees' exact level of understanding (or mental model) of the circulatory system (Chi, Siler, & Jeong, 2004). For example, using the technique of categorizing a student's mental model of the circulatory system into six levels, with levels five and six as the most accurate, tutors tend to think that students have a mental model at a fifth or sixth level when, in fact, students have only a second or third level understanding. This finding was based on data collected from interrupting both tutors and their tutees at two points during tutoring to ask the tutors what they thought their respective tutees' mental model of the circulatory system was, as well as asking the tutees themselves what their current understanding was. The tutors seemed unaware of (or were inaccurate in predicting) the nature of their tutees' flawed mental models. This suggests that an expert's explanations cannot be targeted precisely at what a tutee misunderstands. Instead, a tutor generates feedback on the basis of a mismatch between a tutee's incorrect response as compared with the correct normative response, rather than tailoring the feedback to the tutee's naïve understanding. This finding of a mismatch between an expert's representation and a student's representation or understanding is consistent with the expert blind spot hypothesis, which states that greater content knowledge skews expert teachers' ideas of what students understand. For example, high school teachers assumed that verbal problems were more difficult for students to solve than symbolic problems, when, in fact, the reverse was true (Nathan & Koedinger, 2000). This is because high school math teachers take a domain-centered (or normative) view, reasoning that symbolic problems would be easiest for students to solve because they were written in "pure math."

A second reason for the ineffectiveness of watching and listening to an expert's demonstration along with monologue explanations for cognitive-rich tasks is that experts often cannot articulate all the intervening reasoning steps, because they are often not consciously available to them (Ericsson & Simon, 1984). This may be due to their having automatized or chunked the intervening steps, or alternatively, the intervening reasoning may be implicit (as illustrated in our tennis serving example described above). If the reasoning is not accessible to them, then their explanations often become a description of the procedural steps themselves, which are not a helpful sort of explanation since they do not add any information.

In sum, experts' monologue explanations, when they accompany demonstrations, may not be as helpful as one may think for two possible reasons. The first reason is the mismatch between a novice's and an expert's representations, making it difficult for students to understand experts' explanations when students' representations are naïve. The second reason is that experts' explanations may not be complete or accurate because experts' knowledge may be implicit or automatized, causing it to be inaccessible.

EXPERTS MODELING WITH DEMONSTRATIONS PLUS SCAFFOLDING DIALOGUES

The preceding sections described two common instructional contexts. In the first context, an expert demonstrates a skill or performs a procedure, while students watch the demonstration. Although students can learn in this context, it has its limitations for cognitively rich and complex tasks. The second instructional context involves an expert demonstrating while explaining. Students can learn in this context as well, but again there are limitations for cognitively rich tasks, such as learning to solve complicated problems. In both of these contexts, the students are observing with some minimal opportunities to interact with the expert/mentor. However, it has been well documented in the tutoring literature that when students have a large number of interactions with an expert, such as interacting with a tutor one-on-one, then learning is maximized. Although such interactions are obviously advantageous, one-to-one interactions with an expert/tutor are costly. However, there is a third possible instructional context, that is for students to observe the dialogue between a tutor and a tutee, without directly interacting with the tutor. In this context, the observing-students do not get to interact with the tutors; only the tutees get to interact directly with the tutors. For this context, the question is, can the observing-students learn from overhearing such dialogues without directly interacting with the experts? In other words, can students learn from watching others learn (Mayes, Dineen, McKendree, & Lee, 2001; McKendree, Stenning, Mayes, Lee, & Cox, 1998)? There are obvious advantages to knowing this answer because it means that one can scale up an expert's dialogue with a tutee by showing or reusing it with many other observing-students.

    There are many situations in which students are expected to learn by observing and listening-in to the dialogue that occurs between a teacher and a student (such as when one of the students is being called to solve a problem at the whiteboard, guided by the teacher while the rest of the students watch and listen); or a master cellist guides and demonstrates to a student while an audience watches and listens), or between an expert and a novice (such as a chef on a cooking show teaching a naïve cook how to prepare a dish; or an adult teaching a young student about science demonstrations in shows such as *The Wizzards* (Field, 1983–1990; 1991–1995). The most serious enterprise that takes advantage of this form of training is in the medical field, where interns go on rounds with an attending physician and a resident. In such clinical training settings, typically the attending physician either does the demonstrating (such as palpating the patient) or gives the resident feedback while s/he palpates the patient. Like a tutor, the attending physician focuses his/her attention and dialogues on the resident/tutee, while the rest of the interns simply listen and watch. They are given opportunities to ask questions, but the main dialogue is between the attending physician and the resident. Becoming more prevalent are related contexts, such as remote telemedicine. Suppose a nurse talks to a remote medical consultant about a child patient, and the child's mother is present and listens in. What can we assume that the mother has learned about the child's condition by overhearing the conversation between the nurse and the medical consultant? Can we assume that she has learned enough so that she can later monitor and treat her child appropriately? Thus, the same question applies in all these cases, that is, do the observers who overhear dialogues, learn anything and if so, what, how and how much?

Two Constructs Relevant to Observational Learning

Before describing the utility and prevalence of an instructional context in which students observe an expert guiding and dialoguing with a novice, we briefly clarify the kinds of "observers" we are interested in, and the issue of intentionality.

Types of Observers There are several nuances to the meaning of "observers," especially pertaining to the listening aspect of observing. According to Goffman (1976), there are three types of listeners in the context of a conversation or dialogue. A *side participant* is a participant recognized by both the speaker and addressee as a full member of the conversation. A *bystander* is a participant who both the speaker and addressee are aware can overhear them, but who is not participating in the conversation. Finally, an *eavesdropper* is an over-hearer of which neither the speaker nor the addressee is aware. In this chapter, by "observers," we mean it in an "eavesdropping" sense in that neither the speaker nor the addressee is necessarily aware of the presence of the observer. Therefore, there are no mutual obligations between the speaker and the observer to monitor and repair each other's understanding, in a process called "grounding" (Clark, 1996). With "grounding," individuals who are engaged directly in conversation with each other must make sure that they share common knowledge (such as to whom they are referring, or what event they are talking about) in order to be understood and have a meaningful conversation. However, an observer would not share grounding experiences with the speaker. Therefore, according to Clark's theory, an "eavesdropper-type" of over-hearer would not fare as well as the addressee in understanding what a speaker says, since the over-hearer did not participate in grounding with the speaker.

In summary, in this chapter, we focus on the "eavesdropper-type" of observers, also referred to by Rogoff, Paradise, Arauz, Correa-Chavez and Angelillo (2003) as "third-party observers". We refer to such observers as *observing-students*, and refer to the addressees as *tutees* since they are participating in a one-on-one dialogue with the tutors. The eavesdropper-type of observer is also prevalent in the context of online discussion (Sutton, 2001) and, in fact, they make up the majority of members in online groups, usually referred to as "lurkers" (Nonnecke & Preece, 2001). Because the term *overhearing* connotes passivity and *eavesdropping* connotes a forbidden nature, we agree with Rogoff et al. (2003) that the term *listening-in* is preferable. In short, in this chapter, the term *watching* will be used to refer to observing visual inputs such as gestures, diagrams, or overt behaviors of models; the term *listening* will be used to refer to hearing a monologue explanation; the term *listening-in* will be used to refer to accessing or hearing dialogue that was not meant for the listeners; whereas *observing* will be used as a general term to refer to both *watching* and *listening-in*.

Intentional Participation or Doing

A relevant question for vicarious learning is the sense of *intentionality*. Intentionality can be considered from two perspectives. From the perspective of the teacher/mentor, instruction is typically targeted either at a co-present interacting tutee or no student at all (such as in an online learning environment or even in a large lecture hall); but it is not intended for a listening-in observing-student. However, from the perspective of the observing-students, in many scenarios, they do intend to learn even though instruction is not targeted at them. For example, in many cultures in which children are integrated into mature community activities, children are expected to learn without direct guidance and monitoring from adults. Instead of directly interacting with adults as conversational partners, children in many cultures learn by *participating* in aspects of adult activities, while *observing* demonstrations and *eavesdropping* on adult talk in context, which includes questions and directives (Rogoff, 1990, p. 122). A key component of third-party observation in such a context is that children are actively and *intently participating in* or *doing* related chores while "keenly observing and listening," (Rogoff et al., 2003, p. 178) because they anticipate undertaking the activity that they are observing. The notion of *intent participation* implies that observational learning is not incidental or accidental, from the perspective of the observing-learners, but requires *actively doing a relevant task* that may lead to learning. Thus, borrowing from Rogoff et al. (2003), we define *intent participation* in a laboratory study as being required to undertake or *do the relevant task* for which the observers are asked to learn.

In this chapter, we focus on the first question, that is, can observing-students learn without directly interacting with the expert/mentor, if they have the goal of *intending-to-learn*? Our hypothesis, consistent with Rogoff et al.'s (2003), is that observational learning can be as beneficial as directly interacting with a tutor, if the observers are *intently* trying to learn by participating or doing the task. We focus on learning complex concepts and procedures, ones that are taught in school, rather than physical skills that can be directly displayed and mimicked.

Three Different Ways of Observing Tutorial Dialogues

There are three different ways of observing tutorial dialogues: (1) alone; (2) collaboratively in pairs; and (3) collaboratively in pairs with *intent participation* or doing. We consider relevant studies to each situation in turn, to see whether and how much students learn.

Watching and Listening-in on Dialogues in Solo   There is only scant and inconsistent evidence on how well observers can learn by overhearing instructional or tutorial dialogues, without direct interactions with the instructor or tutor. Three sets of relevant studies are described here. In Schober and Clark (1989), the target task used is the placement of a sequence of random shapes by a Matcher (analogous to a tutee) under the direction of a Director (analogous to a tutor) who tells the Matcher which shape to pick up and place next. Both the Matcher and the Director each have the same set of random shapes (or tangrams), and a screen blocks the views of each other's tangrams. The Director has to describe the shape of each tangram in such a way so that the Matcher will pick the correct one to place down. The Matcher may ask the Director for clarifications and other information. How successfully the Matcher placed the random shapes in the sequence requested by the Director was compared against how successfully a bystander (analogous to an observing-student) placed his/her own set of tangrams. The bystander could overhear the dialogues between the Director and Matcher, but could not see their tangrams. The results showed that Matchers were significantly more accurate than the solo bystander-observers. This suggested that being directly guided by and interacting with a Director, as in the case of a Matcher, was better than overhearing the dialogues as a solo bystander.

The Schober and Clark study did not measure learning; instead it measured the ability to correctly place the referred-to tangram in the sequence as instructed by the Director, which basically required coming to an agreement about how to refer to a tangram. For example, one ambiguous shape was first described by the Director as "a dancer or something really weird. Um, and has a square head...," and the Matcher followed with a clarification question of, "Which way is the head tilted?" and the Director said "The head is..eh..towards the left, and then th-an arm could be like up towards the right?..and It's-" At this point the Matcher said, "an a big fat leg?" They then settled on referring to this shape as "the dancer with the big fat leg." In short, in the Schober and Clark study, the task mainly consisted of linguistically finding ways to refer to a random shape that both the Director and the Matcher agreed upon, since placing the shape in a sequence is trivial once the correct one is identified.

A similar comparison, very much like the one in the Schober and Clark (1989) study, was carried out by Craig, Driscoll and Gholson (2004), with the exception that the latter study measured learning. Craig et al. (2004) compared how well students learned 12 computer literacy topics through either interacting directly with a tutoring system, or by observing recordings (screen captures of the voices) of the tutorial interactions between the computer tutor and a student. The results of Experiment 1 were consistent with the results of Schober and Clark (1989), in that the tutees who directly interacted with the tutor learned significantly more than students who merely observed the screen captures of tutoring.

One way to understand and interpret the results of these two studies is that in contrast to the tutees, the solo observers were not very generative or constructive. Being generative, in the traditional associative recall type of memory studies (Slamecka & Graf, 1978; Stein & Bransford, 1979), meant that the participants were able to generate their own elaborations or associations. The classic finding from the memory literature was that when participants generated their own associations between two words, they tended to have better recall of the words. This has been referred to as the generation effect. Similarly, being constructive (as in self-explaining) means that learners are constructing a relationship between two solution steps or generating an inference that ties two sentences together, and doing so enhances learning (Chi, et al., 1989; Chi, de Leeuw, Chiu, & LaVancher, 1994). Based on the snippet of negotiation on how to refer to a shape described in the above example, a simple interpretation for the advantage of the Matcher's performance over the observer's performance is that the Matcher was the one who was generating part of the referral label, especially the part of "the big fat leg." An observer in this task, however, was not at liberty to generate any references.

In sum, an interpretation for the advantage of the Matcher's performance is simply that s/he had opportunities to be generative, which has been shown to be advantageous in many memory studies and self-explanation studies, whereas the solo observers had no opportunities to be generative. Thus, an alternative interpretation for the poorer performance of the solo observers in the Schober and Clark (1989) study is their lack of opportunities to be generative, as opposed to the interpretation that the Matchers had opportunities to be inter- active with the Director. Of course, it is possible for observers to be covertly generative, but it is reasonable to assume that one is more likely to be genera- tive when participating in a conversation, as in the case of the Matchers, than when merely observing alone.

In the tangram-placing task, even though the solo observers did not perform as well as the Matchers, overhearing a dialogue between the Matcher and the Director was nevertheless better than overhearing just the Director explaining the placement and sequencing of the tangrams in a monologue (Tree, 1999). This finding, that listening to dialogues is more effective for performance than monologues, has now been supported by several other studies that did measure learning (Craig et al., 2000; Craig, Chi, & VanLehn, 2009; Muller, Sharma, & Reimann, 2008). The advantage of dialogues over monologues confirms our assumption in the prior section that students do not learn very much from listen- ing to an expert's monologue explanations with demonstrations.

In sum, the overall findings from both a matching tangram task and a learn- ing task show that listening to an expert dialoguing with a novice is not an effec- tive instructional method for solo observers. However, listening to a dialogue is superior to listening to a monologue, but neither is as good as directly interact- ing with an expert.

Watching and Listening-in on Dialogues in Pairs   As stated above, our interpretation for the ineffectiveness of an observing dialogue paradigm is that the solo observers were neither generative nor constructive. To increase active participation, Craig et al. (2004, Experiment 2) asked students to observe tutor- ing dialogues in pairs. However, the paired observers still did not learn as much as the tutees who had the opportunities to directly interact with the tutor, and the paired observers also did not learn any more than the solo observers. Given that collaboration typically improves learning over solo activity, this latter find- ing is surprising. Our interpretation for the equivalent learning of the paired and solo observers in the Craig et al. (2004) study is that the dyads did not inter- act much with each other; in fact, on average they each took only three con- versational turns in a 35-minute session. One reason that they were not very interactive could be that they were not motivated to learn, in the sense that they were not *intently participating* (i.e., they were not required to do a task while watching the video). Thus, even though the observers were paired up, because they were not very interactive with each other (Craig et al., 2004, Experiment 2), they essentially were observing alone. So, in essence, we can only conclude that observing without *intent participation* (even if in pairs) is not a very effective way to learn, and is comparable to observing alone.

To summarize, for the studies cited above, three hypotheses can explain the inferior learning of the observing-students. The first hypothesis, favored by Shober and Clark (1989), is simply that a student needs to interact directly with an instructor in order to learn. A second hypothesis, presented here and in Chi et al. (2008), is that the observing-students did not have opportunities to be generative (either with a tutor or with a peer-partner). A third related hypothesis, inspired by Rogoff's work, is that observing-students, even when paired up, may not be motivated to intently learn, and so are not very interactive. In contrast, tutees typically interact much more frequently with their tutors. For example, in our natural tutoring data with inexperienced tutors (Chi, Siler, Jeong, Yamauchi, & Hausmann, 2001), the tutors took on average 256 conversational turns whereas the tutees took 224 turns, over a span of around one-and-a-half to two hours. This suggests that in a 30-minute interval, the tutees took at minimum, over 60 turns, as compared with the three turns in Craig et al.'s (2004) data. Thus, there is no question that tutees have many opportunities to interact with a tutor and can thereby be constructive in their interactions. The observers in Craig et al.'s 2004 study, even though paired, were obviously not as interactive as tutees could be, as shown in the data of Chi et al. (2001). Thus, it seems that a scenario in which observing-students really have opportunities to be interactive (thereby constructive) and intently participate, is needed in order to test whether observers can, in fact, learn as effectively as tutees from listening-in on dialogues. The next section describes a study that created a situation in which observing-students had to *intently participate*, in the sense of doing the task at hand, and that doing may cause them to interact more frequently.

Watching and Listening-in on Dialogues in Pairs with Doing   In Chi et al. (2008), we asked pairs of students to solve physics problems collaboratively while simultaneously watching a video of a tutee being guided by a tutor in solving the same problem. Making the observing-students collaboratively solve the same problems while watching and listening to a video of tutorial dialogue likely forced them to participate more intently (as opposed to the Craig et. al. 2004 study, where the paired observers only had to listen/watch the video and were not required to do any other activity). Our study consisted of a tutoring condition (Tutoring), which served as the benchmark condition, since tutoring typically offers the largest learning gains in terms of effect size for students. The second condition (Pairs + Video) was the target condition consisting of dyads collaboratively observing a video of tutoring while doing a task, but without opportunities to interact directly with the tutor. These two conditions (Tutoring, and Pairs + Video) were compared in terms of the amount learned by the tutees and the paired observing-students. The learning gains of the tutees and the observing-students were also compared with three other conditions: pairs of students collaborating to solve problems with the aid of a

textbook (instead of a tutoring video; Pairs + Text); solos solving problems while studying a tutoring video alone (of the same videos used in the Pairs + Video condition; Solos + Video), and, finally, solos solving problems with the aid of a textbook (Solos + Text).

Ten students served as tutees, and so 10 videos were created from an expert instructor who tutored each individual student. The instructor was a 30-year veteran college physics professor and tutored each tutee in solving three mechanics problems. The 10 videos were then shown to pairs of collaborative observers (the target Pairs + Video condition), and to individual observers (in the Solos + Video condition). In the two text conditions, pairs or solos had access to the relevant portions of a physics textbook (Chapters 1–5) that contained worked examples similar to the problems that they had to learn to solve. All conditions received the same pre-test and post-test. In the four non-Tutoring conditions (whether studying the video or text, either alone or in pairs), all the students had to solve the same problems that the tutees in the Tutoring condition were learning to solve. Therefore, this manipulation should have required all students to participate intently.

Figure 1.1 shows the results expressed as the mean (and standard error) of post-test scores adjusted for pre-test scores in an ANCOVA. Scores were based on correctness of deep problem-solving steps. (Details of the scoring procedure are presented in Chi et al., 2008.) Foremost, consistent with the tutoring literature, the Tutoring benchmark condition (right-most bar) had the largest learning effect. This is not surprising especially given that our tutor was not only an expert physicist who had taught physics for over 30 years, but moreover, he was employed full-time by another project as a physics tutor, where his main job was to tutor students and then analyze transcripts of his tutoring to find ways to improve it.

What is amazing is that in our target condition (Pairs + Video – second column from the right in Figure 1.1), the paired observers learned about as well as the tutees in the Tutoring condition. (Figure 1.1 shows adjusted post-test

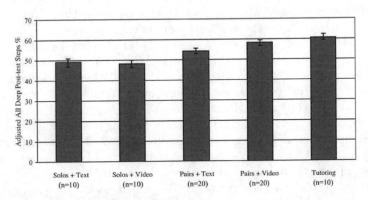

Figure 1.1   Adjusted mean proportion correct of all deep post-test steps, controlling for all deep pre-test steps for each condition. The error bars are standard errors.

scores; but to get a sense of the magnitude of gains, we report pure gain scores, which are 17% for the paired observers and 21% for the tutees.) Both of these conditions were significantly better than the other three conditions, as analyzed via pair-wise comparisons, which supports our assertion that students from the Pairs + Video condition learned about the same amount as those from the Tutoring condition, our benchmark. This equivalence of the Tutoring and Pairs + Video conditions suggests that pairs of observing-students can learn without directly interacting with a tutor.

The results of this study thus support the second and third hypotheses described above, that because students in the Pairs + Video condition had to participate intently (in solving the same problems), they had opportunities to be generative and interactive, resulting in learning gains equivalent to those of students in the Tutoring condition. Thus both factors (generative and inter-active), together, account for the superior learning of the paired observers (superior in the sense that they did learn as well as the tutees even though they had no opportunities to interact directly with the tutor). Although intent partici-pation (Rogoff, et al., 2003) or hands-on practice while observing (Shebilske, Jordan, Goettl, & Paulus, 1998) is an effective way to learn, this factor alone is not sufficient to enhance paired observers' learning. This is confirmed by the results from the Solos + Video condition, wherein the observing-students also had opportunities to intently solve problems, but they did not learn as well as the students in the Pairs + Video condition, suggesting that intently participat-ing alone is not a sufficient factor for learning from observing dialogues, but being interactive with a partner also seems to be critical.

If interacting with a peer-partner might have contributed to the paired observers' learning, is there evidence that they were, in fact, interacting? In our data, the paired observers (in the Pairs + Video condition) interacted, on aver-age, 121 conversational turns per 35-minute interval, as compared with three conversational turns per 35-minute interval in Craig et al.'s (2004) data. Thus, in our study, *intent participation* may have led to more interactions between the dyads, and greater collaborative interactions must have approximated the amount of interactions that tutees experience with tutors.

How Did the Paired Observing-students Learn?

In the preceding section, we showed that in a study described in Chi et al. (2008), observing-students can learn as well as tutees if they observed in pairs, because that allows them to be interactive with a peer-partner. In this section, we explain *how* students learned from observing a video of tutorial dialogues collaboratively.

In general, tutees learn because they usually have the benefit of: (1) being constructive while interacting with a tutor (such as opportunities to ask ques-tions, make suggestions, and attempt steps; Chi et al., 2001); (2) receiving cor-rective feedback in terms of whether a solution step or explanation is correct or incorrect; and (3) receiving a variety of scaffolding guidance from tutors that might elicit more constructive learning. Likewise, the paired observers in our study, as collaborators, can also learn by: (1) being constructive while interacting with each other; (2) receiving feedback from each other; and (3) receiving a variety of scaffolding guidance. However, paired observers, in contrast to tutees, do not receive corrective feedback or scaffolding from an expert/tutor. So, because tutees benefit from receiving direct feedback and guidance from the tutor, logically, observing-student pairs must have learned in a different way compared to the tutees. Is there any evidence to suggest that observing-student pairs learn via a different mechanism from the way tutees learn? In this section, we present new data and new analyses beyond the ones reported in Chi et al. (2008) in order to shed light on this question of how the paired observers might have learned.

One would assume that tutees typically pay attention to their tutors, especially when the tutors request responses from them, as dictated by Grice's conversational pragmatics. The natural tutoring data presented in Chi et al. (2001) showed this assumption to be true. In the tutoring protocols of that 2001 study, we identified three categories of tutor requests (such as asking questions, scaffolding tutees with a hint, and asking whether tutees understand). There were a total of 94 such requests and there were a corresponding 104 tutee responses. These approximately equivalent counts of the number of tutor and tutee statements point out that tutees typically respond to tutors' requests, confirming our assumption that tutees do pay attention to what their tutors ask and may have learned from the tutors' scaffoldings. If paired observers cannot interact with a tutor, will they still pay attention to the tutor?

To answer the last question, we analyzed the dialogues of the paired observers from the Chi et al. (2008) study in the following way. We segmented the paired observers' conversation into episodes, with each episode addressing only one concept or one problem solving step. We then narrowed down and focused only on episodes in which the paired observers were trying to resolve and make sense of what a segment in the video was explaining or doing. Within each of these resolving episodes, we coded whether the paired observers' discussion referred to what the tutee did and said, or what the tutor did and said (as well as referrals to the whiteboard or referrals to both the tutor and the tutee). The analysis of interest is to contrast referrals to the tutor versus the tutee. We found, surprisingly, that the paired observers referred significantly more frequently ($p < .02$) to what the tutees said (6.8 episodes per problem) than what the tutor said (1.8 episodes per problem). This result is counter-intuitive, as we expected more references to what the tutor said, consistent with the common assumption stated above that tutees do pay attention to (and presumably learn from) what tutors say. The fact that the paired observers referred more often to what the tutees said over what the tutor said, could be interpreted as undesirable, in that it was done out of necessity to understand what tutees said. For example, the paired observers could have attended to the tutor's comments, but possibly then had to spend more time assessing the tutees' understanding of what the tutor said, which may have been confusing and error-prone.

To disambiguate whether the paired observers simply *preferred* to attend more to what the tutees said, or *needed* to take more time understanding what the tutees did and said, we assessed whether attending to what tutees say is beneficial to learning. To assess learning, we divided the tutees into Good-learner versus Poor-learner tutees, based on how well the tutees learned on their own (as assessed by a pre-test that was administered *prior* to tutoring but *after* tutees learned some relevant background knowledge on their own). The results reported in Figure 3 of Chi et al. (2008, p. 316) showed that the Pairs + Video observing-students learned significantly more from Good than the Poor tutees (mean gain of 21.9% vs. 7.8%, $p < .01$); and they also referred to what Good tutees said in 9.75 episodes, but referred to what Poor-tutees said in only 3.8 episodes. Thus, this pattern of results suggests that when observers attend even more to what tutees say (in the case of Good tutees) than to what tutors say, they then learn significantly more. This confirms the interpretation that observers *prefer* to attend to what tutees say, and rejects the interpretation that observers *have to* attend to what tutees say in order to understand them better. If observers were attending simply because they *had to* understand tutees better, then one might expect them to have paid more attention to the Poor tutees, since poorer tutees made more errors and their tutorial dialogues were more confusing (for example, the Poor tutees expressed confusion twice as often as the Good tutees (Chi et al., 2008, p. 315). Instead the opposite was found – observers paid far more attention to Good-learner tutees.

Why did the paired observers overall prefer to pay more attention to the tutees over the tutor? Aside from the social reason that observers may prefer peer models (Davidson & Smith, 1982), we speculate on four possible cognitive reasons for why paired observers might find what the tutees say and do more learnable than what a tutor says and does.

Zone of Proximal Representational Match   One reason that paired observers may have preferred to pay attention to what the tutees said is because the observers' understanding (or representation) matches more closely with the tutees' understanding (since they are both novices), than with the tutor's norma-tive understanding. We might call this the "zone of proximal representational match." Chi, Feltovich and Glaser (1981) and Chi et al. (2004) have shown evi-dence for a *mismatch* between novices' naïve representation and experts' nor-mative representation. Thus, we suggest that the paired observers in our 2008 study paid more attention to the tutees perhaps for the same reason, i.e., that their naïve representation matched more closely with the naïve representation of the tutees, and therefore they could understand better what the tutees were asking and saying.

Explaining a Tutee's Errors   A second reason for why attending to tutees' contributions might help observers learn has to do with the errors that tutees make. Although there is a large body of evidence in several areas of literature showing that one can learn better from making "errors" (Ben-Zeev, 1995), "impasses" (VanLehn, 1988), "conflicts" (Dreyfus, Jungwirth, & Eliovitch, 1990; Piaget, 1952), and "productive failures" (Kapur, 2008), there is very little evidence showing that one can learn better by observing someone else make errors.

There is, however, suggestive evidence from three diverse sets of literature. From developmental literature, Siegler (2002, Figure 1.5), for example, has shown that asking children to explain an adult's correct and incorrect reasoning led to greater learning than explaining an adult's correct reasoning only. Given that tutors rarely, if ever, display errors, but that tutees, in general, do tend to make errors while being tutored, the observing pairs of students in our study might have preferred to attend to the tutees more than the tutor in order to explain (and learn from) the tutees' errors.

Related findings also occur in social psychology. For example, Schunk, Hanson, and Cox (1987) investigated how children learn by observing a model solve fraction problems. Children learn significantly better when they observed a model who had to cope (or struggle to solve the problem) versus a model who demonstrated a smooth master performance. A master model is like a tutor who performed all the operations in the problem correctly without any hesitations or uncertainties, stating confidently that, "I can do this one" or "I'm good at this." A coping model is analogous to a tutee who made errors, was hesitant, and made comments such as, "I'm not sure I can do that" or "I'm not very good at these." The observing-students not only learned better by watching the coping model, but they had significantly enhanced self-efficacy.

Finally, there is also suggestive evidence in the vicarious learning literature. In particular, Monaghan and Stenning (1998, Study 1) found that students who watched a video of a model struggling to solve syllogism problems learned slightly more than students who watched a model sailing through the problem solving, although the difference was not significant.

If observers learn from watching tutees struggle, one might wonder then, why did the paired observers learn less from the Poor-learner tutees, since the Poor tutees made many more errors? We can provide an explanation based only on informal analyses of both the Good and the Poor tutees' video tapes. The informal analyses of the videos suggest that the dialogues with the Poor tutees were very disorganized and confusing. Although we had reported that the Poor tutees gained 15.6% from the pre-test to the post-test (whereas the Good tutees gained 24.6%), we failed to emphasize in the 2008 study (Chi et al., 2008, p. 315) that the Poor tutees' pre-test scores were around 30%, whereas the Good-learner tutees' pre-test scores were around 50%. After tutoring, the Poor tutees' post-test scores were still below 50%. Therefore, one could argue that the Poor tutees' performance was below a critical threshold, and therefore their dialogues could not serve as good learning materials.

In sum, there are various findings from disparate literature showing that there is some benefit to observing and explaining a tutee's errors, accounting for why observing-students might learn via a mechanism that requires them to focus on the tutees. The benefit of doing so may overcome the limitation of not being able to interact directly with a tutor.

Abstract versus Grounded Descriptions   In reading and studying the tutorial protocols, we noticed an intriguing and prominent difference between the way the tutor talked about a concept or a principle and the way a tutee talked about it. We characterize this difference as being *abstract* versus *grounded*. That is, when a concept/principle is discussed in an abstract way, the description involves context-general information about characteristics or definitions that are not specific to the current problem situation, whereas when it is discussed in a grounded way, the description relates to specific features of the problem situation at hand. Here are two examples of comments coded as abstract; the first one made by the tutor and the second one made by a tutee, taken from our data (Chi et al., 2008):

Tutor: Normal force is always normal and is perpendicular to the surface in contact.
Tutee: The acceleration is due to gravity?

In contrast, grounded comments are ones that are context-dependent, such as these following two examples:

Tutor: This normal force . . . first look at the weight . . . uh, weight force. Is there any other force acting downward?
Tutee: There, weight is pushing down. [Gesturing pushing down]

Context-sensitive comments can be identified easily by deitic references such as, "this," "there," "look at," and so forth.

   To reduce the amount of data we had to code, we examined only the "critical nodes." A problem solving node, as defined in the original coding in Chi et al. (2008, see Figure 1 on p. 310), corresponded to a state in a problem space. Each node defined a subgoal, such as "draw a free-body diagram of forces on Mass A in the X direction." Critical nodes were a subset of all the nodes, and they were the more important ones, defined as involving sub-procedures for which critical parts of the problem solution were generated, or for which important physics principles were applied to attain each of the main goals stated in the target problem.

   For each critical node, we further determined whether the substantive contributions to solving that node (segmented into "statement" size units) were made primarily by the tutor, the tutee, or jointly by both (the term "substantive" refers to content-relevant contributions). Jointly covered meant that both the tutor and a tutee made substantive contributions to the node. Table 1.1 shows the number of statements made when a critical node was covered or contributed either by the tutor alone, the tutee alone, or jointly by both. When a node is covered only by the tutor, the tutor made, on average, 33.8 statements, and when it was covered primarily by a tutee, the tutee made on average, 13.6 statements. This difference makes sense since the tutor obviously could say more about how to solve a critical node.

TABLE 1.1   Number of Statements Contributed in Discussing a Critical Node and Correlations with Paired Observers' Deep Learning

	Frequency	Observers' Learning
Tutor Alone	33.8	N.S.
Abstract	12.8	N.S.
Grounded	21.0	N.S.
Tutor and Tutee	77.9	N.S.
Abstract	14.7	N.S.
Grounded	63.2	$r = .416, p = .068$
Tutees Alone	13.6	N.S.
Abstract	2.2	N.S.
Grounded	11.3	$r = .544, p = .013$

However, we further coded each of the tutor and tutee critical node statements to see whether the contributions were more abstract or grounded. The results confirm only half of our intuitive impression, in that the tutees did tended to discuss the situation of each node in a more grounded way versus an abstract way (11.3 grounded statements vs. 2.2 abstract statements), a five-to-one difference. However, the tutor also described the critical nodes in a more grounded way than in an abstract way, although the difference was more modest (21.0 grounded vs. 12.8 abstract statements). But what is interesting is that there were no significant correlations between the tutor's descriptions (related to these nodes) and the paired observers' learning, regardless of whether the tutor described them in an abstract or grounded way. This is consistent with the overall lack of correlation found earlier (see Chi et al., 2008, Table 3) between the tutor's explanations and both the tutees and observers' learning, using either the entire set of protocols coded at a statement level or at a node level (see Chi et al., 2008, Table 6). However, when a critical node is covered either by the tutees alone or between the tutor and tutee jointly, then the frequency of such coverage correlates with observers' learning, but only when the node is discussed in a grounded way, either by the tutees alone (shown by the significant correlation between tutees' grounded discussion and observers' learning, $r = .544$, $p = .013$), or approaches significance when a node is discussed jointly by the tutor and tutees in a grounded way ($r = .416$, $p = .068$). This pattern of correlations confirms our prior analyses showing that observers paid more attention to what the tutees said over what the tutor said, and supports our conjecture that observers may have preferred to pay attention to the tutees' statements because they were more grounded, thereby making them more understandable (see Table 1.1).

Learning the Skills of How-to-Interact-with-an-Expert to Learn   The fourth possible reason for why paired observers might learn by paying more attention to tutees than a tutor (in a tutorial dialogue tape) is the conjecture that an observer might be acquiring *how-to-interact-with-an-expert* learning skills from the tutees. Although a great deal of research (Chi, 2009; Webb & Palincsar, 1996), along with practices in a classroom setting, have focused on student learning when interacting with another peer, little work has addressed understanding what *interacting-with-an-expert* learning skills are, and how we can optimize students' acquisition of such skills. There are increasingly more settings that require students or trainees to interact with an expert, such as other team members who have different expertise, a knowledgeable animated agent, or an older and more knowledgeable peer (Roscoe & Chi, 2007).

We conceive of *interacting-with-an-expert* learning skills as a form of 21st-Century skills that are different from *interacting* skills *per se* in a collaborative learning sense. *Interacting-with-an-expert* learning skills are also different from the burgeoning literature on team interactions and coordination. That literature, by and large, focuses more on understanding team communication, such as effective communication strategies for calling attention to problems and getting action and attention from the other team members (Fischer & Orasanu, 2000), or effective communication related to sharing critical information (Fisher, McDonnell, & Orasanu, 2007). The ideas of *interacting-with-an-expert* learning skills proposed here are also different from the traditional learning-to-learn skills introduced by Ann Brown (Brown, Campione, & Day, 1981) over two decades ago. Much of the early learning-to-learn skills involved monitoring one's own understanding, such as acknowledging that one does not understand, gauging that one needs to spend more time on a specific concept, and so forth. In short, they involve self-reflection and self-regulation skills (Butler & Winne, 1995; Schraw, Crippen & Hartley, 2006; Zimmerman, 2000).

What might be considered *interacting-with-an-expert* learning skills? Several examples can be considered productive *interacting-with-an-expert* learning skills, such as asking questions, initiating new topics for discussion, and so forth. Such tutee behaviors, if exhibited, would demonstrate to observers that the tutees are actively taking control of their own learning, and that they are not merely responding to a tutor's leads and scaffoldings. Essentially such behaviors would illustrate that the tutees are equal partners in the tutorial dialogues. We hypothesize that Good-learner tutees (previously defined as tutees who were more successful at learning on their own prior to tutoring) would engage in these types of *interacting-with-an-expert* learning skills more often than Poor-learner tutees, thus enabling observing-students to learn more from the Good-learner tutees' dialogues.

To test this hypothesis, we re-examined our tutorial dialogues (Chi et al., 2008). We again focused strictly on the critical nodes, but this time we focused on those nodes that were jointly covered, since we were interested in why the paired observers paid more attention to the tutees, it seemed only fair to focus on nodes for which there was joint coverage, so that we could understand why there was a bias towards attending to the tutees. We coded the frequency of tutees' overall initiated comments, questions and meta-comments when tutees jointly covered a critical node with the tutor. On average, among the 27.8 critical nodes that were jointly covered, 20.8 of them had comments initiated by the tutees, which were comments not elicited by the tutor. This is in stark contrast to the number of questions that students typically initiate in class, which is 0.11 per hour (Graesser, Person, & Magliano, 1995). Although we know in general that tutorial dialogues often involve tutees *responding* to a tutor's elicitations, such as answering a tutor's questions and scaffolding hints, as shown by the equivalent number of tutor requests (94) and tutee responses (104) described above (from data reported in Chi et al., 2001), what we did not know is that the tutees also do *initiate* many comments, questions, and meta-comments. Furthermore, across all the critical nodes, the Good-learner tutees initiated comments in 27.5% of the nodes on average, compared to 6.43% for the Poor-learner tutees, and the difference was significant ($F(1,7) = 29.851$, $p = .011$). This contrast confirms our interpretation that perhaps the paired observers learn more from the Good-learner tutees' dialogues because those dialogues illustrate *interacting-with-an-expert* learning skill (such as initiating) more often than the dialogues with Poor-learner tutees.

Another *interacting-with-an-expert* learning skill might relate to a tutee making joint contributions with the Tutor, as explained above. A tutee contributing jointly with the Tutor implies that the tutee has the confidence to assume that what s/he has to say is important and meaningful, whereas students in a classroom may often be timid and more reluctant to make contributions. Although in a tutoring context, the majority of the critical nodes were covered jointly by both the tutor and the tutees (consistent with the statement data shown in Table 1.1 above, indicating that 77.9 statements were made jointly in the context of covering critical nodes, vs. 33.8 statements for the tutor's primary coverage and 13.55 for the tutees' primary coverage), nevertheless, for dialogues with the Good tutees, 90% of the critical nodes were covered jointly, whereas for dialogues with the Poor tutees, only 50% of the critical nodes were covered jointly. This difference provides some support that Good-learner tutees were more skillful at making joint contributions.

Behaviors such as initiating new comments and jointly contributing to solving a critical node imply that a tutee is treating himself/herself as an equal to the tutor, and that the tutee can take control of the learning task. If our interpretation that observing-students acquire *interacting-with-an-expert* learning skills is correct, then there ought to be a correlation between the display of such behaviors from the tutees and the observers' behaviors. We did, in fact, find a very strong correlation ($r = .662$, $p = .003$) between the number of joint explanations that tutees made with the tutor, and the number of joint explanations paired observers made with each other. Such correlations further support our hypothesis that paired observers may have acquired *interacting-with-an-expert* learning skills. In sum, this fourth conjecture postulates that by paying more attention to the tutees rather than the tutor, the observing-students might have benefitted from observing displays of these *how-to-interact-with-an-expert* learning skills.

Summary of How Paired Observers Might Have Learned

We have provided preliminary evidence supporting the hypothesis that observers of tutees learned to solve physics problems in ways different from the tutees themselves. Observers might learn by paying attention to what the tutees said because what they said was more grounded and understandable as compared to the tutor. Doing so may mean that observers might be explaining the tutees' errors, and may be picking up other *interacting-with-an-expert* learning skills, such as taking initiative and making joint explanations. In addition, observers might understand a tutee's initiations because they have a closer zone of proximal representational match with a tutee than with a tutor. Thus, interacting with a partner and observing tutoring, for various reasons, can compensate for the lack of opportunities to interact directly with a tutor.

CONCLUSION

In this chapter, we address the broad question of whether students can learn from experts or teachers/mentors without directly interacting with them, since experts are a costly resource with regard to one-on-one instruction. We analyzed three ways that experts could impart their knowledge to novices without directly interacting with them: (1) by demonstrating their expertise in terms of overtly performing the task(s) for which they are skilled; (2) by accompanying their demonstrations with monologue explanations; or (3) by guiding a novice's problem-solving through dialogues and letting other novices observe. The first method (demonstrating expertise from overt performance only—such as a math professor standing at the board and writing out the solution steps) is not an effective educational practice, and moreover, difficult academic tasks cannot be easily demonstrated overtly. So we will ignore this method as a viable approach to academic instruction. Educational practices often involve the second method, which is for experts to demonstrate while explaining. Although this is a common practice, its effectiveness is limited. The third way is to have an expert (e.g. a tutor) guide and interact with a novice (e.g. a tutee) while students observe. Our finding that the paired observing-students were able to learn as well as the tutees, even though they were not directly interacting with a tutor but they could interact with a peer partner, suggests a way of multiplying the benefits of investments in tutoring (which we know is extremely effective for the students being tutored; however, one-on-one tutoring is expensive and labor-intensive).

How did paired observers learn from watching and listening-in to tutoring dialogues? We postulated that the observing-students must have learned in a way that was different from the tutees, since the observing-students could not interact with the tutor. Although there was also likely some benefit of interacting with each other, we confirmed this difference by showing that the observers paid more attention to what the tutees said and did (especially the Good-learner tutees), rather than what the tutor said and did. We hypothesized several reasons for why observers had a biased preference to attend to the tutees' comments over the tutor's comments. One reason is that the observers, being novices, might have had representations that more closely matched those of the tutees (who are also novices) than the tutor's. Such a closer zone of proximal representational match would have made the tutees' comments and questions more understandable to the observers, as compared to the tutor's normative comments and explanations. Related to this mismatch idea, tutees' comments are also most often more grounded than a tutor's comments, and therefore, observers might be able to understand tutees' comments better. Third, there is evidence in the literature that by explaining tutees' errors, the observers might learn. Since tutees often make errors, the observers might be intrigued or challenged to explain and resolve the tutees' errors, and such effort might have caused the observers to learn. Fourth, observers might be able to acquire *interacting-with-an-expert* learning skills from tutees, since tutees tend to display these skills when interacting with a tutor. One interacting-learning skill might be in initiating new comments and ideas, and this contrasts with the typical tutorial dialogue pattern in which the tutor initiates and the tutee responds. In sum, these reasons might account for our most counterintuitive finding that observers are biased to attend to the tutees more than to the tutor.

In summary, this chapter suggests that a teacher/mentor's instructional expertise can be amplified for other student observers by having the expert interact with a novice (tutee). Aside from the advantages of learning, watching a video of someone else learn also has scale-up economic advantages, such as amortizing the expense of one-to-one tutoring over a multitude of learners, as with the concept of re-usable instructional dialogues (McKendree et al., 1998; Stenning et al., 2000). This suggests that creating instructional videos of an expert tutoring a novice student might have exciting applications in distributed and networked environments, and in online discussion boards, in which direct discussion with an expert is limited.

REFERENCES

Anderson, C. A., & Bushman, B. J. (2001). Effects of violent video games on aggressive behavior, aggressive cognition, aggressive affect, physiological arousal, and prosocial behavior: A meta-analytic review of the scientific literature. *Psychological Science*, 12(5), 353–359.

Bandura, A. (1989). Social cognitive theory. In R. Vasta (Ed.), *Annals of child development. Vol. 6. Six theories of child development* (pp. 1–60). Greenwich, CT: JAI Press.

Bandura, A., Ross, D., & Ross, S. A. (1961). Transmission of aggression through imitation of aggressive models. *The Journal of Abnormal and Social Psychology*, 63(3), 575–582.

Ben-Zeev, T. (1995). The nature and origin of rational errors in arithmetic thinking: Induction from examples and prior knowledge. *Cognitive Science*, 19(3), 341–376.

Bromme, R., Jucks, R., & Runde, A. (2005). Barriers and biases in computer-mediated expert-layperson-communication. In R. Bromme, F. W. Hesse, & H. Spada (Eds.), *Barriers, biases and opportunities of communication and cooperation with computers – and how they may be overcome* (pp. 89–118). New York, NY: Springer.

Brown, A. L., Campione, J. C., & Day, J. D. (1981). Learning to learn: On training students to learn from texts. *Educational Researcher, 10*(2), 14–21.

Butler, D. L., & Winne, P. H. (1995). Feedback and self-regulated learning: A theoretical synthesis. *Review of Educational Research, 65*(3), 245–281.

Carroll, W. R., & Bandura, A. (1990). Representational guidance of action production in observational learning: A causal analysis. *Journal of Motor Behavior, 22*(1), 85–97.

Chi, M. T. H. (2009). Active-constructive-interactive: A conceptual framework for differentiating learning activities. *Topics in Cognitive Science, 1*, 73–105.

Chi, M. T. H., Bassok, M., Lewis, M., Reimann, P., & Glaser, R. (1989). Self-explanations: How students study and use examples in learning to solve problems. *Cognitive Science, 13*, 145–182.

Chi, M. T. H., & Bjork, R. A. (1991). Modeling expertise. In D. Druckman, & R. Bjork (Eds.), *In the mind's eye: Enhancing human performance* (pp. 57–79). Washington, DC: National Academy Press.

Chi, M. T. H., de Leeuw, N., Chiu, M. H., & LaVancher, C. (1994). Eliciting self-explanations improves understanding. *Cognitive Science, 18*, 439–477.

Chi, M. T. H., Feltovich, P., & Glaser, R. (1981). Categorization and representation of physics problems by experts and novices. *Cognitive Science, 5*, 121–152.

Chi, M. T. H., Roy, M. & Hausmann, R. G. M. (2008). Observing tutoring collaboratively: Insights about tutoring effectiveness from vicarious learning. *Cognitive Science, 32*(2), 301–341.

Chi, M. T. H., Siler, S. A., & Jeong, H. (2004). Can tutors monitor students' understanding accurately? *Cognition and Instruction, 22*(3), 363–387.

Chi, M. T. H., Siler, S., Jeong, H., Yamauchi, T., & Hausmann, R. G. (2001). Learning from tutoring. *Cognitive Science, 25*, 471–533.

Clark, H. H. (1996). *Using language*. Cambridge: Cambridge University Press.

Clark, H. H., & Murphy, G. L. (1982). Audience design in meaning and reference. In J. F. Le Ny, & W. Kintsch (Eds.), *Language and comprehension*. Amsterdam: North-Holland.

Craig, S. D., Chi, M. T. H., & VanLehn, K. A. (2009). Improving classroom learning by collaboratively observing human tutoring videos while problem solving. *Journal of Educational Psychology, 101*(4), 779–789.

Craig, S. D., Driscoll, D. M., & Gholson, B. (2004). Constructing knowledge from dialog in an intelligent tutoring system: Interactive learning, vicarious learning, and pedagogical agents. *Journal of Educational Multimedia and Hypermedia, 13*, 163–183.

Craig, S. D., Gholson, B., Ventura, M., Graesser, A. C., & Tutoring Research Group. (2000). Overhearing dialogues and monologues in virtual tutoring sessions: Effects on questioning and vicarious learning. *International Journal of Artificial Intelligence in Education, 11*, 242–253.

Davidson, E. S., & Smith, W. P. (1982). Imitation, social comparison, and self-reward. *Child Development, 53*, 928–932.

Deslauriers, L., Schelew, E., & Wieman, C. (2011). Improving learning in a large-enrollment physics class. *Science, 332*, 861–864.

Dreyfus, A., Jungwirth, E., & Eliovitch, R. (1990). Applying the "cognitive conflict" strategy for conceptual change: Some implications, difficulties, and problems. *Science Education, 74*, 555–569.

Ericsson, K. A., & Simon, H. A. (1984). *Protocol analysis: Verbal reports as data*. Cambridge, MA: MIT Press.

Feldman, A. I., Campbell, R. L., & Lai, M. K. (1999). Improving elementary school science teaching by cross-level mentoring. *Journal of Science Teacher Education*, *10*(1), 55–67.

Field, F. (1983–1990/1991–1995). *Mr. Wizard's World*. Calgary: Nickelodeon.

Fischer, U., McDonnell, L., & Orasanu, J. (2007). Linguistic correlates of team performance: Toward a tool for monitoring team functioning during space missions. *Aviation, Space, and Environmental Medicine*, *78*, B86–B95.

Fischer, U., & Orasanu, J. (2000). Error-challenging strategies: Their role in preventing and correcting errors. In Proceedings of the International Ergonomics Association 14th Triennial Congress and Human Factors and Ergonomics Society, 44th Annual Meeting, San Diego, CA, August.

Goffman, E. (1976). Replies and responses. *Language in Society*, *5*, 257–313.

Graesser, A. C., Person, N., & Magliano, J. (1995). Collaborative dialog patterns in naturalistic one-on-one tutoring. *Applied Cognitive Psychology*, *9*, 359–387.

Haskett, G. J., & Lenfestey, W. (1974). Reading-related behavior in an open classroom: Effects of novelty and modeling on preschoolers. *Journal of Applied Behavior Analysis*, *7*(2), 233–241.

Hinds, P. J., Patterson, M., & Pfeffer, J. (2001). Bothered by abstraction: The effect of expertise on knowledge transfer and subsequent novice performance. *Journal of Applied Psychology*, *86*, 1232–1243.

Kapur, M. (2008). Productive failure. *Cognition and Instruction*, *26*, 379–424.

Lave, J. (1988). *Cognition in practice*. New York: Cambridge University Press.

Linn, M. C. (1995). Designing computer learning environments for engineering and computer science: The scaffolded knowledge integration framework. *Journal of Science Education and Technology*, *4*(2), 103.

Mayes, J. T., Dineen, F., McKendree, J., & Lee, J. (2001). Learning from watching others learn. In C. Steeples, & C. Jones (Eds.), *Networked learning: Perspectives and issues* (pp. 1–16). London: Springer.

McKendree, J., Stenning, K., Mayes, T., Lee, J., & Cox, R. (1998). Why observing a dialogue may benefit learning: The vicarious learner. *Journal of Computer Assisted Learning*, *14*, 110–119.

Monaghan, P., & Stenning, K. (1998). Learning to solve syllogisms by watching others' learning. Research Paper HCRC/RP-98. Human Communication Research Centre, University of Edinburgh.

Muller, D. A., Sharma, M. D., & Reimann, P. (2008). Raising cognitive load with linear multimedia to promote conceptual change. *Science Education*, *92*(2), 278–296.

Nathan, M. J., & Koedinger, K. R. (2000). An investigation of teachers' beliefs of students' algebra development. *Cognition and Instruction*, *18*, 207–235.

Nonnecke, B., & Preece, J. (2001). Why lurkers lurk. *America Conference on Information Systems*, 1–10.

Piaget, J. (1952). *The child's concept of number*. New York: W.W. Norton.

Reed, S. K., Dempster, A., & Ettinger, M. (1985). Usefulness of analogous solutions for solving algebra word problems. *Journal of Experimental Psychology: Learning, Memory and Cognition*, *11*, 106–125.

Rogoff, B. (1990). *Apprenticeship in thinking: Cognitive development in sociocultural activity*. New York: Oxford University Press.

Rogoff, B., Paradise, R., Arauz, R. M., Correa-Chavez, M., & Angelillo, C. (2003). Firsthand learning though intent participation. *Annual Review of Psychology*, *54*, 175–203.

Roscoe, R. D., & Chi, M. T. H. (2007). Understanding tutor learning: Knowledge-building and knowledge-telling in peer tutors' explanations and questions. *Review of Educational Research, 77,* 534–574.

Ross, B. H. (1987). This is like that: The use of earlier problems and the separation of similarity effects. *Journal of Experimental Psychology: Learning, Memory and Cognition, 13,* 629–639.

Rummel, N., & Spada, H. (2005). Learning to collaborate: An instructional approach to promoting collaborative problem solving in computer-mediated settings. *The Journal of the Learning Sciences, 14,* 201–241.

Schober, M. F., & Clark, H. H. (1989). Understanding by addressees and overhearers. *Cognitive Psychology, 21,* 211–232.

Schraw, G., Crippen, K. J., & Hartley, K. (2006). Promoting self-regulation in science education: Metacognition as part of a broader perspective in learning. *Research in Science Education, 36*(1), 111–139.

Schunk, D. H., Hanson, A. R., & Cox, P. D. (1987). Peer-model attributes and children's achievement behaviors. *Journal of Educational Psychology, 79,* 54–61.

Schwan, S., & Riempp, R. (2004). The cognitive benefits of interactive videos: Learning to tie nautical knots. *Learning and Instruction, 14,* 293–305.

Shebilske, W. L., Jordan, J. A., Goettl, B. P., & Paulus, L. E. (1998). Observation versus hands-on practice of complex skills in dyadic, triadic, and tetradic training-teams. *Human Factors, 40,* 525–540.

Siegler, R. S. (2002). Microgenetic studies of self-explanation. In N. Granott, & J. Parziale (Eds.), *Microdevelopment: Transition processes in development and learning* (pp. 31–58). Cambridge: Cambridge University Press.

Slamecka, N. J., & Graf, P. (1978). The generation effect: Delineation of a phenomenon. *Journal of Experimental Psychology: Human Learning and Memory, 4,* 592–604.

Stein, B. S., & Bransford, J. D. (1979). Constraints on effective elaboration: Effects of precision and subject generation. *Journal of Verbal Learning and Verbal Behavior, 18,* 769–777.

Stenning, K., McKendree, J., Lee, J., Cox, R., Dineen, F., & Mayes, T. (2000). Various learning from educational dialogue. *Proceedings of Computer-Supported Cooperative Learning (CSCL, '99),* 341–347.

Sutton, L. A. (2001). The principles of vicarious interaction in computer-mediated communications. *International Journal of Educational Telecommunication, 7,* 223–242.

Tree, J. E. F. (1999). Listening in on monologues and dialogues. *Discourse Processes, 27*(1), 35.

VanLehn, K. (1988). Toward a theory of impasse-driven learning. In H. Mandl, & A. Lesgold (Eds.), *Learning issues for intelligent tutoring systems* (pp. 19–41). New York, NY: Springer.

VanLehn, K., Graesser, A., Jackson, G., Jordan, P., Olney, A., & Rose, C. (2007). When are tutorial dialogues more effective than reading? *Cognitive Science, 31,* 3–62.

Webb, N. M. (1989). Peer instruction, problem-solving, and cognition: Multidisciplinary perspectives. *International Journal of Educational Research, 13,* 21–39.

Webb, N. M., & Palincsar, A. S. (1996). Group processes in the classroom. In D. C. Berliner, & R. C. Calfee (Eds.), *Handbook of educational psychology* (pp. 841–873). New York, NY: Prentice Hall.

Whiten, A. (1998). Imitation of the sequential structure of actions by chimpanzees (Pan troglodytes). *Journal of Comparative Psychology, 112,* 270–281.

Zimmerman, B. (2000). Self-efficacy: An essential motive to learn. *Contemporary Educational Psychology, 25,* 82–91.

2

Cognitive Engineering Based on Expert Skill

JAMES J. STASZEWSKI

Department of Psychology, Carnegie Mellon University, USA

INTRODUCTION

*L*andmines are a major military threat (Hambric & Schneck, 1996; LaMoe & Read, 2002) that all too often remain lethal or capable of maiming for years after the conflicts that led to their use have ended. Hidden and still armed, mines remain for years as a serious and long-lasting humanitarian hazard in lands where these weapons have been placed (MacDonald *et al.*, 2003). Typically, individuals operate handheld equipment in close proximity to these hidden hazards to detect and subsequently disarm and dispose of them (Figures 2.1a, 2.1b).

Development and deployment of relatively inexpensive landmines containing minimal amounts of metal (designated LM and illustrated in rows 2 and 4 of Figure 2.2) in the 1990s considerably escalated the difficulty and the danger involved in their detection. This reduction of metallic content dramatically increased the problem of detecting mines with then current technologies, including the Army/Navy Portable Special Search-12 (PSS-12), which, until the deployment of the new Army/Navy Portable Special Search-14 (PSS-14) detector, depended on electromagnetic induction (EMI) sensors to detect mines' metal parts (MacDonald et al., 2003). A test of the PSS-12 shortly before it was fielded revealed the severity of the problem. Results showed that only 3.8% of M14 targets—very small, low metal anti-personnel mines—were detected (U.S. Army Test and Evaluation Command, 1991). This ominous finding motivated the search for new, more effective detection technologies, and included the development of the PSS-14.

Figure 2.1 (a) The PSS-12 remains U.S. Army standard equipment for landmine detection. Manufactured by Scheibel Corp., this system uses electromagnetic induction to sense the metallic content of landmines. (b) The PSS-14 is an innovative dual-sensor detection system that uses both electromagnetic induction and ground-penetrating radar. A U.S. Army combat engineer is shown using the PSS-14 in a live countermine operation.

Landmines

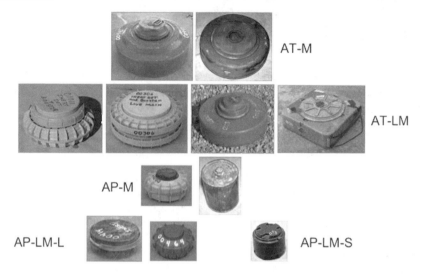

Figure 2.2   Mine targets used in testing. Top row: left to right, shows anti-tank mines with metal bodies and firing mechanisms, the TM62M and M15. Second row: low metallic, anti-tank mines with plastic body shells, VS1.6, VS2.2, TM62P3, and M16. Third row: anti-personnel mines with high metallic content, VS-50, Valmara 69 (a bounding mine). Bottom row: anti-personnel mines with low metallic content: PMA3, TS-50, M14. The latter are divided into two subgroups on the basis of physical size and are distinguished in HSTAMIDS test results. For size reference, the larger circular AT mines are roughly 12 inches in diameter, whereas the M14, which contains but 0.6 grams of metal, is 2.2 inches in diameter.

FROM CHESSBOARDS IN THE LAB TO MINEFIELDS

Landmine detection presented a fascinating and challenging area in which to investigate human expertise. Along with the possibility of contributing to mitigation of a problem of considerable scope as well as humanitarian and military significance, part of the motivation to study landmine expertise, starting with the study of a PSS-12 expert, was to test the prospective hypothesis expressed by the following analogy:

Genome: Genetic engineering:: Expert model: Cognitive engineering

Essentially, this analogy asserts that just as molecular biology possesses sufficient principles, theory, and methods to understand the structure of a species genome and use that knowledge to solve practical biological problems, indeed, replicate organisms with desirable properties and capabilities, so too does cognitive science know enough about human expertise to propagate more of it in a scientifically-principled manner. In short, the studies reported here tested the viability of cognitive engineering based on expert skill (CEBES) as an approach to designing instruction and training.

The bases for this assertion came from two sources. Simon's (1980) arguments: (1) that learning and natural selection were both mechanisms of adaptation, although they operated on different time scales; and (2) that expertise reflected the adaptation of an organism with bounded-rationality to a particular task environment and provided a conceptual framework. Discoveries about expertise by Chase and his collaborators gave the above hypothesis empirical credibility, four of which were particularly influential and are discussed below.

First, Chase and Simon's (1973a, 1973b) studies of chess expertise linked superior performance to knowledge acquired through prior chess experience, confirmed the findings of de Groot (1965) and led to the bold claim that "practice is the major independent variable in the acquisition of skill" (Chase & Simon, 1973a, p. 279). The indirect evidence for this claim was later generalized by numerous studies of skilled memory effect in additional domains (Chase, 1986). More direct support for the relation between task practice and expertise came from a longitudinal study of memory skill acquisition conducted by Chase and Ericsson (1981; Ericsson, Chase, & Faloon, 1980) in which an undergraduate subject (SF) of otherwise normal abilities increased his digit-span by roughly an order of magnitude under laboratory observation by practicing a mnemonic strategy he invented. The growth of his span as a function of practice is shown in Figure 2.3. Further confirmation as well as generality came

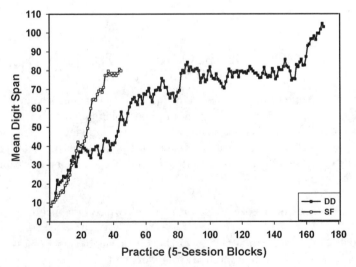

Figure 2.3   Learning curves for two expert mnemonists who expanded their digit-spans to prodigious lengths through laboratory practice. Data points represent mean list length for trials presented in five consecutive practice sessions.

from subsequent longitudinal studies that also tracked the transition from novice to expert in the lab (Chase & Ericsson, 1982; Staszewski, 1988; Wenger & Payne, 1995). By showing that levels of practice and the environment(s) in which practice occurred represented core determinants of skill acquisition, variables that could be manipulated by learners or instructors, these studies implied that expertise could be purposefully built rather than bestowed naturally.

Showing that expert knowledge could be described in detail was a second major contribution. Chase and Simon's (1973a) clever application of theory and chronometric methods identified patterns of chess pieces that their novice, intermediate player, and expert perceived and recalled as chunks in the chessboard displays presented in these studies. Investigations of digit-span expertise (Chase & Ericsson, 1981, 1982; Staszewski, 1990; Wenger & Payne, 1995), expert mental calculation (Chase & Ericsson, 1982; Staszewski, 1988), and a waiter with exceptional memory for restaurant orders (Ericsson & Polson, 1988) further confirmed that it was possible to successfully analyze expert knowledge to identify component mechanisms, also finding that chunks and retrieval structures were mechanisms employed by experts in tasks from the above domains that impose heavy memory demands. In short, Chase and his colleagues' work led the way in delineating not only the content of experts' knowledge but also its organization in memory, analogous to the way in which Crick and Watson were able to characterize the "structure of life" by their analysis of DNA (Watson, 1968). Later computer simulation models of expert performance further confirmed that the methods applied to analyze expert knowledge and thought processes were capable of describing these mechanisms and their interaction in fine detail and comprehensively enough to reproduce expert performance with a high degree of fidelity (Gobet, de Voogt, & Retschitzki, 2004; Richman, Staszewski, & Simon, 1995).

Third, Chase and Ericsson (1982) introduced training experiments as a way to test process theories of expert performance. With an understanding of the cognitive strategy that SF used to expand his digit-span and the evidence that the knowledge and processes implementing that strategy developed with task practice, they recruited a new trainee (DD) with a background and knowledge base suitable for implementing SF's mnemonic strategy for a training experiment. Starting with a digit-span in the normal range, DD was given SF's mnemonic strategy with instructions to use it on subsequent digit-span practice trials. DD's daily practice regimen mirrored that of SF and continued for over four years. The effects of this practice on his digit-span are shown along with those for SF in Figure 2.3. Later training experiments in other skill domains further showed how identification of the mechanisms producing expert performance provided blueprints for reproducing the capabilities of interest (Biederman & Schiffrar, 1987; Schafstaal & Schraagen, 2000; Staszewski, 1988; Staszewski & Chase, 1984; Wenger & Payne, 1995).

Finally, Chase's (1983) study of expert taxi cab drivers' navigational skills made the prospects of using models of expertise for engineering human skills plausible in another important way. This work contrasted the skills of experts at terrestrial navigation—operationally defined as highly experienced Pittsburgh taxi drivers—with the skills of intermediates and novices who had fewer years of driving experience in this particular environment. Glossing over findings that linked group differences in spatial representations of the environment to navigational performance, Chase (1983) showed how data collected *in the field* about practical skills that developed in the natural, external environment could yield sound inferences about the representation of expert knowledge and the ways it contributed to superior performance.

In short, a body of principles and theory about human expertise and its development had accumulated in the decade after Chase and Simon's studies of chess expertise that made it plausible to hypothesize that expertise could be engineered.

ANALYSIS OF PSS-12 MINE DETECTION EXPERTISE

An operator with extensive experience and an impressive record of achievement (RR) volunteered to participate in a study of PSS-12 operational expertise (Staszewski, 1999; Webster, 1996). Data collection involved capturing multimodal records of RR's activities while his skills were tested against a representative sample of landmines buried at an Army test facility.[1] Observations included continuous viewpoint video of RR's movements of the PSS-12's search head over the ground surface accompanied by sounds captured synchronously on two channels. One recorded all output signals of the PSS-12. The other channel recorded concurrent verbal reports given by RR, as per instructions, as he applied his routine techniques to find mines and mark their suspected locations.

Analysis of the audio/video records involved coding over 200 events identified in roughly 30 hours of recording. The events consisted of activity sequences that ended in successful detections, those related to missed targets, those that produced false alarms, and either aborted investigations or investigations resulting in correct rejections. Coding focused on identifying movements of the detector head, audible responses of the PSS-12, and the locations of both relative to the positions of mine targets.

Findings

Several procedural regularities appeared in what, upon initial observation, appeared complex and confusing. Except for procedures that RR used to check for drift in the equipment's sensitivity, the relatively few macro-processes

---

1 Details on simulated mine targets used in testing and the training environment can be found in Staszewski (1999) and Davison and Staszewski (2002).

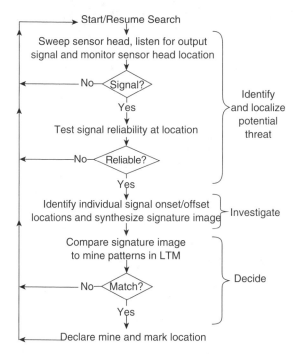

Figure 2.4   Model of the PSS-12 expert's detection procedures showing his three basic macroprocesses.

composing the model shown in Figure 2.4 accounted almost completely for his activities on test trials.

RR's successful detection of mines involved three sequential stages illustrated in Figure 2.4. The first stage, search, involved RR placing the sensor head on the ground on one side of the 1.5m-wide lane[2] to be searched and gliding it lightly over the surface at a rate of about 1 ft. per sec on a trajectory perpendicular to his heading to the opposite side of the lane. If no output signals were produced on this sweep, RR then raised the search head just enough to keep it in contact with the ground surface and advanced it forward about 15 cm—about the radius of the search head. He would continue with a second sweep in the opposite direction with a trajectory parallel to the previous cross-lane sweep, making sure that the search head's path overlapped the area covered by the previous sweep by roughly half, thus ensuring exhaustive surface coverage. Cross-lane sweeps in alternating directions would continue until either the detector produced an output signal, or RR paused to check the sensitivity

---

2 Areas designated for clearance in testing and in live operations are referred to as lanes. Lanes are roughly the width needed to extract casualties. Army doctrine sets lane width at 1.5 m. This lane width is used at all training and testing sites described here.

setting, which had a known tendency to drift, or he completed his search of a designated area.

When an output signal sounded during search, RR typically directed his gaze to the location of the sensor head and completed his cross-lane sweep. He would then move the sensor head back over the area where the alert had occurred. With movements shorter and slower than those used in the cross-lane search, he would try to reproduce the output in the same spot. If the signal could not be reproduced in the same location after several attempts, search forward would resume with successive cross-lane sweeps. If a signal reliably sounded in the same location, search head movements marking the beginning of investigation would follow, immediately adjacent to the alerting signal's location.

In the investigation phase, RR would explore the vicinity of the alerting signal location with sensor head movements like those used to confirm the alerting signal's reliability. Movement on specific trajectories would stop when an ongoing signal stopped and remained off for a few more inches of the sensor head's movement. A backtracking movement would occur on the same trajectory to make the opposite signal transition occur at the point it had stopped on the previous movement. If the locations of such "edge" or signal transition points varied on different search movements, a further search of the area continued to establish a reliable edge location.

Once RR had located an edge point, the process was repeated a few inches away to locate another. These operations continued until edge points defined a region within whose boundary the PSS-12 sang and outside of which no signals sounded. Occasionally, RR physically marked edge points on the ground surface (on bare soil lanes, where such marking was possible, versus lanes with crushed stone surfaces) using the point of the trowel he carried.[3] In other instances, his verbal reports sometimes contained references to distinctive surface features like a stone for edge landmarks. Although his use of physical landmarks was infrequent, RR's occasional marking activities and landmark references were the clues that prompted spatial analysis of the auditory signals he used the PSS-12 to generate.

The area covered with such investigatory actions varied, first as a function of whether the signals were coming from landmines or clutter. Clutter is the umbrella term for conductive objects or materials in the lanes that produce responses from the PSS-12 but are not mines. If the investigation occurred where a low-metal LM mine was buried, signal on–off points tended to cluster within a foot or less of one another. Alternatively, if a high-metal mine was investigated, the area circumscribed by edge points would form a semi-circle, called the metallic (MD) halo, sometimes more than a meter in diameter. If the signals were produced by clutter, the halos they defined varied much more in size and shape than the halos of mines, showing far less symmetry.

---

3 RR used the trowel for checking his equipment for drift from the set sensitivity in the context of testing, as described in Staszewski (1999). He also used this tool to excavate suspected mines in live operations—thus providing timely and valuable feedback for detection and discrimination learning.

When RR's investigation ended, he would pause and scan the area examined. If he decided the halo had been produced by a mine, he would move the sensor head to its center and direct the experimenter to mark the spot. Otherwise, he resumed cross-lane sweeps searching for another alert.

A non-intuitive regularity emerged from analysis of the audio/video records of RR's investigations, which involved mapping the locations at which signal onsets or offsets occurred relative to the locations of targets that RR accurately and confidently marked. The contours created by connecting onset–offset or "edge" points formed semi-circular halos with mines at the center. The length of the radii for these arcs covaried with the metallic mass of the target. Although any single edge point could be obscured and moved outward by the presence of nearby metallic clutter, in the absence of clutter, mine halos showed "good" form as described by Garner (1974). Some examples of the spatial patterns produced by RR are shown in Figure 2.5.

These regularities in RR's successful detection episodes led to the inference that he located mines by sequentially finding landmarks identified by the offset or onset of the detector's auditory signals, holding these locations in memory, and linking them to form spatial contours in his mind's eye in a process resembling the phenomenon of visual pattern synthesis (Finke, 1990; Klatzky & Thompson, 1975; Palmer, 1977). RR presumably then matched these patterns against patterns held in his memory of previously detected mines. Spatial pattern recognition thus appeared to support his skill in landmine detection, consistent with findings from laboratory studies of expertise in a variety of visuospatial task-domains (Chase, 1986), including chess.

ANALYSIS OF PSS-14 EXPERTISE

The PSS-12 project led to the study of expert operation of a new, technologically innovative piece of detection equipment developed to replace the PSS-12. While the PSS-12 project was in progress, the intended successor to the PSS-12, the Handheld Standoff Mine Detection System (HSTAMIDS) prototype (later renamed the PSS-14) was undergoing operational testing. After nine years and $38 million had been invested in its development, the results, shown in Figure 2.13 on p. 51, revealed substandard performance that cast doubt upon the new system's capability. The government project sponsor therefore convened a "Red Team" to review the development program and the results it produced. The Red Team included the author, due to the relevance of the PSS-12 effort. The review identified the training operators were perceived as a contributory factor to the system's disappointing performance (Guckert, 2000). As part of the "second chance" development effort that followed, the CEBES approach was applied to develop training for operators.

The prototype HSTAMIDS system developed by CyTerra Corporation and illustrated in Figure 2.6 consists of two main physical components. Its search head houses the system's EMI and ground-penetrating radar (GPR) antennae in a plastic case. The head is attached to an adjustable-length wand that has a

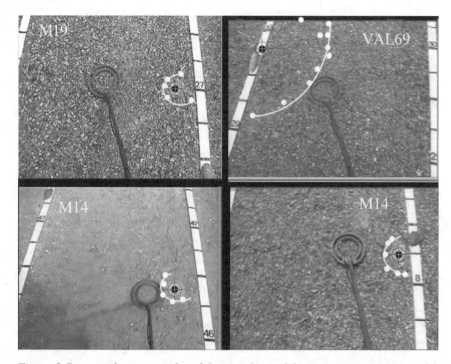

Figure 2.5   Spatial patterns inferred from analyses of the PSS-12 expert's successful detection of mines in performance testing. Cross-hair marks indicate the approximate locations of the centers of the buried targets; solid white circles indicate the "edge" locations defined by either onset–offset or offset–onset of the PSS-12's auditory output signal; the white arcs shown are fitted by hand to the edge points to show pattern contours. Note the difference between the pattern sizes produced by the Valmara 69, an anti-personnel mine with very high metallic content, and the patterns of the M14, a low-metal, anti-personnel mine, and the M19, a low-metal anti-tank mine. These mines are illustrated in Figure 2.2.

set of controls at its opposite end. Here, on a panel just above the pistol grip used by the operator to hold the unit, are switches that power the system up or down, adjust sensitivity levels of the GPR subsystem, and adjust the volume of the unit's auditory outputs. Cabling runs along the shaft, linking the sensors to the controls. Another cable connects the wand's components to a rectangular metal-cased unit weighing about 35 lbs. and worn like a backpack by the operator. This unit housed electronics circuitry for processing raw signals from the EMI and GPR sensors independently, using sensor-specific algorithms, and generating auditory outputs based on the inputs.

The operator controls movements of the search head by grasping a head pistol grip attached to the wand and cinching his forearm at the end opposite to the search head, thus making the wand an extension of his arm. This arrangement enables the operator to move the search head laterally above the ground about a meter forward of his feet, providing a small, but important buffer from threats ahead.

Figure 2.6   The HSTAMIDS prototype shown in the configuration used for training development and testing in its extended product development risk reduction or "second chance" phase.

Fortunately, the operational test results identified one participant whose detection performance far exceeded that of all other test participants. He (KJ) was an employee of the manufacturer who also had the most experience with the detector. As both the most experienced and most proficient operator, he served as the expert for the project.

Because the HSTAMIDS, like the PSS-12, used EMI sensing, the expert's technique was expected to resemble RR's. Learning how information afforded by GPR sensing was acquired and used would be a matter of exploration, but the prior study of PSS-12 expertise provided guidance in analyzing and modeling the HSTAMIDS expert's skill.

The benefits of this prospective approach to analysis of HSTAMIDS expertise were magnified by factors limiting data collection opportunities. First, with only one prototype system available, observations of the expert's use of the system were limited to test sessions interleaving lengthy periods of hardware and software development. Development included continuous changes to system detection algorithms, with the software undergoing modifications up to the month before the first training test. Some enhancements proved less successful than intended. The system changes and less-than-optimal reliability, not unexpected with any complex technology under development, limited observation time and complicated interpretation.

Instrumentation used for data collection added further challenges to the analysis. A computer-controlled camera system being developed to give trainees feedback on sweep coverage (Herman & Inglesias, 1999) was also used to capture the expert's activities. Reliability issues limited the corpus of recorded observations available for off-line analysis. Thus, analysis of the expert's skill relied to a worrisome degree on direct, real-time observations of system operation as the empirical basis for abstracting regularities. These observations covered an estimated 90–120 hours of testing spread over five developmental test sessions at three different test locations. Some 850 encounters with mine targets like those shown in Figure 2.2 were observed, but a much smaller, unsystematic sample of these observations, totaling roughly 10 hours of audio/video recording, was captured and available for detailed examination. These video records were used to test hypotheses about the expert's techniques and thought processes based on the live field observations and hand-recorded notations.

Findings

Observations of the HSTAMIDS expert's detection procedures showed that the model of RR's procedures generalized surprisingly well.[4] The model shown in

---

4 RR and his techniques were unknown to KJ until similarities were pointed out to him by the author, at which point this knowledge had no influence on his technique.

Figure 2.7 with its procedural sequence of search, investigation, and decision operations provided an excellent characterization of his detection activities. An alerting signal encountered during search sweep, received as an output from either the MD or GPR subsystem, would trigger investigation in the area where the alert occurred. KJ then typically started investigation with the metal detection system, using it in a way that was functionally similar to RR's procedures for investigating alerts. That is, he used the MD to locate MD edges and build, in a piecemeal fashion, the contours of the patterns that constitute the metallic halos of mines. His MD investigation was characterized by relatively slow continuous movements of the sensor head (roughly 2–8 cm/sec) in scallop-shaped trajectories producing consistent changes in the frequency of the MD output signal. These changes allowed him to continuously trace the edges of an MD halo, first working from the "six o'clock" position to the "three o'clock" and then back around to the "nine o'clock" position.

He would then use the established MD pattern, particularly if it described the semi-circular pattern produced by mines, along with his knowledge of the sizes and shapes of mines to guide investigation with GPR. If MD investigation produced a large semi-circular contour .75–1.5 m at its widest—characteristic of an AT-M or AP-M target—GPR investigation would be conducted inside the

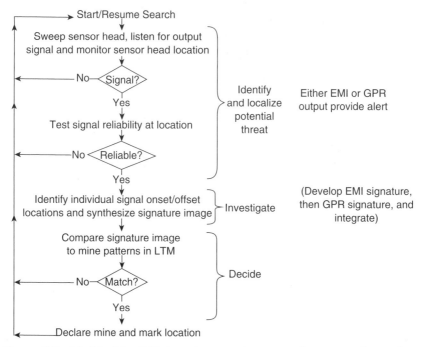

Figure 2.7   Model of the HSTAMIDS expert's basic procedures. Note the similarity to that of the PSS-12 expert model in Figure 2.4.

metal halo. If the MD halo was small (~ 2.5–8 cm), suggesting a low-metal target, investigation would start outside the halo, especially if the alerting signal came via GPR followed by an MD signal as detector head sweeps advanced beyond the GPR alert. If the alert occurred first via MD, GPR investigation proceeded either inside or over the edges of the MD halo, depending upon its size. GPR investigation involved movements that were typically performed at a speed 1–5 cm per second faster than head velocities in MD. The sensor head trajectories for GPR investigation involved back-and-forth movements on a path anywhere from 10–20 cm in length running perpendicular to the six o'clock–twelve o'clock axis of the MD signature. For AP targets, the initial trajectories would carry the head back and forth over the three o'clock–nine o'clock axis with GPR outputs starting as the head passed over the edge of the mine and ceasing after the head passed over the far edge. Pulling back to the six o'clock position, KJ applied similar back-and-forth movements in a forward direction, producing GPR outputs as the head passed over the near edge of a mine target and continued toward the three o'clock–nine o'clock axis. Further "GPR short sweeps" that advanced forward would then produce GPR outputs that diminished in frequency (for mines with circular shape) until the sensor head passed over the far edge of the target and GPR outputs ceased. For the larger AT mines, GPR investigation would be performed first at the three o'clock position, then at the nine, then at the six, and finally at the twelve. Essentially, when a mine was present, GPR output signals occurred whenever the search head passed from off the body of the mine to over it, and continued until the head's sweep carried it off the body. Mapping where GPR outputs occurred made it possible to infer the shape of the buried target. From statements like "OK, we've got a M19. It's square," or "This looks small, maybe an M14," it appeared that KJ matched the contours produced by GPR investigation to his knowledge of the various sizes and shapes of mines. The spatial patterns of GPR onset and offset points for each of five generic mine types are shown in Figures 2.8(a–d).

KJ's decision process, like RR's, appeared to be based on pattern matching, with the combined MD and GPR patterns that the HSTAMIDS produced creating patterns of greater complexity. Comparisons of the spatial relations between the MD and GPR patterns, and possibly their fusion, appeared to inform his "mine/no mine" decisions. This was suggested by comments found in KJ's verbal protocols that commonly preceded successful mine declarations: "Got MD. Got solid GPR. MD and GPR are correlated." His explanation of "correlated" was that contours of the MD and GPR signatures produced by each mine investigation shared common axes of symmetry, whose intersections were spatially coincident. Thus, for mines with circular bodies, the MD halo and the GPR outline in his mind's eye would have to share the same center point for him to make a mine declaration. His declaration mark would also be placed precisely at that point.

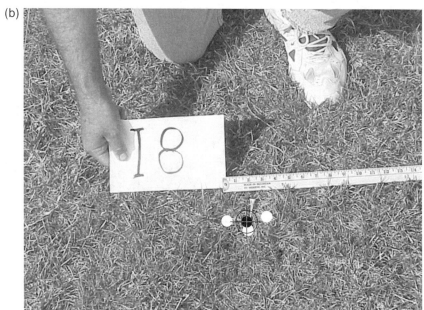

(Continued)

(c)

(d)

Figure 2.8 HSTAMIDS sensor output pattern for (a) an M16 (AP-M); (b) an M-14 (AP-LM-S); (c) an M15 (AT-M); and (d) a TM62P3 (AT-LM); buried in a training area at Aberdeen Proving Ground, MD. Target centers are marked with crosshairs. White circular markers indicate edges of metallic halo. Black markers show onset/offset locations of GPR signals. Signal processing algorithms for GPR signals detect changes in the returned radar signals produced by the different dielectric constant values of a mine's body and the surrounding soil.

A prospective test of this representational hypothesis was performed that sought to validate these inferences about KJ's coding of target patterns. The test environment contained multiple exemplars of each of the mines shown in Figure 2.2. Their center points were marked on the ground surface, but KJ was blind to their identities. His task was to locate the MD and GPR pattern edges on designated vectors radiating from each target's mark for each of 81 targets. Each edge point was marked as he declared it. Examples of the resulting patterns for specific targets are shown in Figures 2.8(a–d).

Analytic procedures adapted those used by Rosch, Mervis, Gray, Johnson, and Boyes-Braeme (1976) to identify prototypes of basic-level perceptual categories. Radial distances from the target centers to the same edge points of mines within five broad target groupings were measured and averaged. The spatial patterns shown in Figure 2.9 emerged. Despite local, mine-to-mine variability, stable signature prototypes emerged for each category, as seen by the relatively small standard errors associated with each mean distance. These results confirmed inferences about KJ's coding of mine patterns derived from observations taken during developmental tests.

To sum up, analyses of expert operators of the PSS-12 and PSS-14 suggested that like experts in other areas, both expert operators relied on recognition of visuo-spatial patterns created and held in memory to locate buried mines

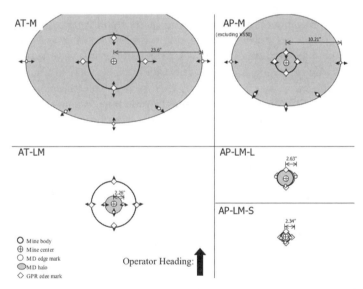

Figure 2.9   Prototypical HSTAMIDS signal patterns for mine categories shown in Figure 2.2. The patterns were produced by averaging the distances from target center point to edge markers for multiple exemplars from each of five mine categories. Sensor signal onset and offset points are illustrated relative to the target mine body (outlined in black with crosshairs marking the target center points). These markers shown represent the mean distances produced by aggregating the measurements taken from patterns like those illustrated in Figures 2.8a–d.

successfully. Both employ a search process, that is, search sweep, to identify the general area where mine patterns are located. The location of the sensor head at the time of an alerting signal marks the general area. The patterns that identify mines are not found whole at these locations. Instead, the experts appear to synthesize them serially using a process resembling mental synthesis (Finke, 1990; Klatzky and Thompson, 1975; Palmer, 1977). The pattern parts are acquired by iterative investigation routines that serially identify a series of locations held in the mind's eye where each system's auditory outputs define pattern boundary or edge points. Imaginary connection of adjacent edge points constructs contours (for both MD and GPR, in the case of the PSS-14), whose sizes and shapes are matched against those produced by the operators' previous investigations of mines. If the pattern produced by investigation is sufficiently similar to patterns of previously encountered mines, the operator declares a mine and marks its location.

TRAINING BASED ON EXPERT SKILL

The process analyses of the expert PSS-12 and PSS-14 operators had produced hypothetical explanation of how each achieved exemplary performance with his equipment. Each model described component processes at a high "macro" level of abstraction, far above the grain size of elementary cognitive processes. The models were nonetheless complete in the sense that each described a series of macroprocesses in which information was presumably acquired and used by each expert to identify locations where potential threats were buried and then classify them as mines or not. The validity and practical utility of each model were tested using the strategy that Chase and Ericsson had used to test their account of SF's digit span expertise—by examining each model's ability to reproduce the performance of interest. Training programs were designed using each model as a blueprint and then used to train novice operators.

Comprehensive description of the training, even for just one detector, is beyond the scope of this chapter, but it should be noted that implementing the above principles in a context in which multiple operators could be trained simultaneously required not only a training plan, but also a novel design for the physical training environment, and development of new training aids for performance assessment. Details about the training programs can be found in Davison and Staszewski (2002), Headquarters, Department of the Army (2002, 2006), and Staszewski and Davison (2000).

PSS-12 CEBES TRAINING

The initial test of PSS-12 training (Staszewski & Davison, 2000) was conducted at the U.S. Army Engineer School at Ft. Leonard Wood, MO, using combat engineers. All had just completed advanced individual training which included then-standard training on use of the PSS-12. After randomly assigning soldiers to treatment (n =10) and control groups (n = 10), all were pre-tested using the standard techniques. The groups' detection rates were indistinguishable, and those for low metal targets were dangerously low, especially for M14s, the targets with the least metal content. After the soldiers in the treatment group received instruction and 12–15 hours of practice with feedback each, both groups were again tested. The control group, which did not have the opportunity to practice, essentially replicated its pre-test performance. The treatment group's detection rates illustrated in Figure 2.10 showed unexpectedly strong gains against the LM targets.

The improvements of the first test seemed too good to be true so a second test was performed to investigate the reliability of the treatment group's gains. With a nod toward generalization and ecological validity, six soldiers from this group were tested three days after the first test concluded, now wearing cumbersome body armor that would be worn in an operational setting. Results replicated those observed in the initial test (Staszewski & Davison, 2000).

Because the targets used for testing thus far had been simulated mines instead of actual mines, further testing of generality and skill retention involved transporting the treatment group to another training site, where actual demilitarized landmines now served as targets, roughly a month after their original training. This test produced an aggregate detection rate of 0.97, which included a detection rate of 1.00 against real M14s (Staszewski & Davison, 2000).

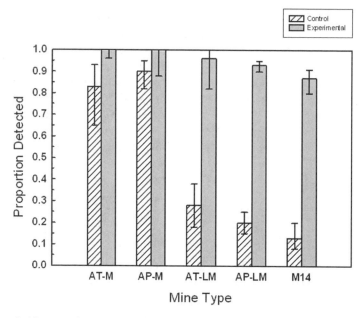

Figure 2.10   Initial PSS-12 test results produced by combat engineers who had received experimental training and controls showing proportion of targets detected as a function of target category. Error bars show 95% confidence intervals. Pre-testing of both groups showed equivalent performance for each mine category.

Two further tests of the PSS-12 training conducted prior to its official adoption by US Army showed its effects to be robust. The first was enabled by an invitation from combat engineer and military police units at the Joint Readiness Training Center (JRTC), Ft. Polk, LA. These units were scheduled for overseas deployment to areas where landmines were a major threat. The author and collaborator Davison were asked to build a permanent mine detection training site at JRTC and administer the still-experimental PSS-12 training. Non-commissioned officers (NCOs) would now participate as trainees, and the training (and training site design) could be extended to include training and testing in a forested environment. Plans for replicating the earlier tests were hampered by severe weather and unexpected last-minute reductions in the availability of troops. These factors reduced the time for instruction and practice to the range of 3–4 hours per soldier. Another unexpected event occurred in the midst of post-testing; Soldiers were informed that long holiday weekend leaves which would begin upon conclusion of their mine detection training were cancelled and that they would depart for two weeks of field training immediately. These orders negatively affected the motivation of some of the trainees still engaged in testing as indicated by test behaviors before and after word came through, test scores, and *very* explicit expressions of disappointment. Results showed post-training detection rates lower than those observed in training drills, but the gains from pre-test performance, shown in Figure 2.11, were greater than expected.

An unexpected test of the PSS-12 training program immediately followed the JRTC exercise, carried out by JRTC personnel responsible for training and assessment of combat engineer units. Two NCOs who had participated as trainees in the previous week's training served as trainers. These minimally experienced trainers trained six platoons of combat engineers (approximately 180 soldiers) who were scheduled for immediate overseas deployment. They used the materials and training aids from previous weeks' exercise provided by the author and his collaborator, although neither was present to oversee or advise. The procedures of the previous week were followed including pre-testing trainees who used the then-standard Army techniques and testing following the experimental instruction and related drills. There was one substantial modification: Schedule constraints limited instruction and practice time to approximately one hour per trainee. The resulting pre- and post-test detection rates are shown in Figure 2.12.

Across all tests, training effects remained relatively robust in spite of variation on several factors that seemed likely to impair learning. These factors included training time, ground surfaces, weather conditions, soil moisture and humidity levels, mine targets, equipment condition, trainee rank and military experience, military specialization, and instructor experience.

PSS-14 CEBES TRAINING

The first test of the prototype PSS-14 training program involved five operators; two Army NCOs serving as project liaisons and three civilians. Reliability issues with both the brand new prototype detectors and with instrumentation used for

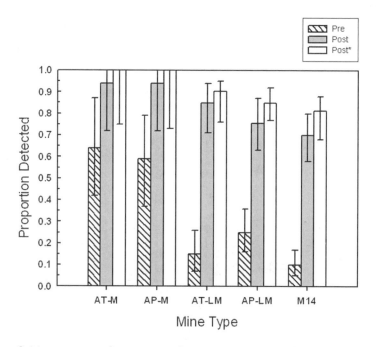

Figure 2.11   Pre-test and post-test performance as a function of mine type for non-commissioned officers trained at the Joint Readiness Training Center, Ft. Polk, LA. Results for group labeled Post* eliminate the data of two soldiers whose individual post-test detection rates were 5 and 7 standard errors below those which both had shown in earlier blind search drills. Both showed an apparent loss of motivation upon learning that a long holiday weekend leave, which had been scheduled to begin upon conclusion of the training exercise, was cancelled and that their unit would start two weeks of field training immediately.

delivering feedback and scoring introduced frequent interruptions and cut training time from the planned 40 hours per trainee. Even so, the roughly 28–32 hours of instruction and practice per trainee produced the CEBES results shown in Figure 2.13.

Because the trainees in the first CEBES test all had prior exposure to the system before the training, which might have inflated their performance, trainees selected for the second test were completely unfamiliar with the equipment. They also represented the military population most likely to use the system and thus need training—if the system showed sufficient potential to merit further development and deployment. Four combat engineers, two from the US Army and two from the US Marine Corps served as trainees. They received the same training content and amount of practice, however, improved system reliability diminished the frustrating delays encountered in the previous test. Detection rates for the second CEBES test, shown in Figure 2.13, were statistically indistinguishable from that of the first trainee group.

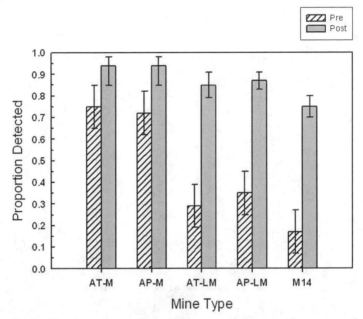

Figure 2.12   Pre-test and post-test performance as a function of target type for combat engineers from the 10th Mountain Division. Training was administered by JRTC NCOs who had participated in the previous week's training exercise, and time allowed for only 1 hour for drill and practice of the new expert detection techniques. Data were collected by JRTC training personnel and provided courtesy of then MAJ (now LTC) Tommy Mize.

The PSS-14 test results had three important effects. First, the improvement in detection rates achieved by CEBES-trained operators relative to the initial operational test results were sufficient to justify continued funding for PSS-14 development. Second, the pattern of results informed diagnosis of system shortcomings and thus guided subsequent and successful engineering refinements. Third, the results showed the importance of operator training to system performance. This latter realization led to a policy of distributing the system only to units whose soldiers had received CEBES training.

COMMON TRAINING EFFECTS

Several features of the CEBES training effects were common to both training programs and also unexpected. The first was the speed with which positive effects appeared. The prototype PSS-12 program provided between 12–15 hours of drill and practice per trainee. The prototype PSS-14 program provided roughly 28–32 hours, due to the system's operational complexity and the considerable cognitive and perceptual-motor demands it places upon operators. Despite the novelty of the techniques and the comparatively brief training

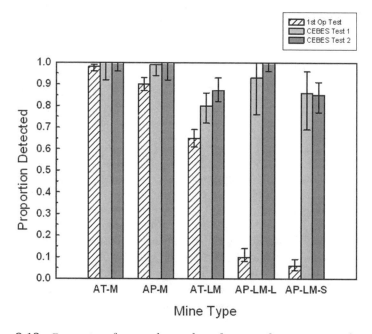

Figure 2.13   Proportion of targets detected as a function of target category for each of two tests of the HSTAMIDS training program. Results from original operational testing of the HSTAMIDS prototype are shown for reference. Error bars show 95% confidence intervals. Asymptotic performance shown for AT-LM and AP-LM-S targets served to diagnose equipment limitations of the prototype that were remedied by subsequent hardware/software modifications incorporated in the PSS-14.

periods for both of the CEBES mine detection training programs, both produced large improvements in detection capability.

Even more surprising were the effects observed well before operators had completed training. In each training session operators first received instruction and practice on subtasks before engaging in blind search drills, which require integration of the individual skill components that the part-task exercises were intended to develop. The trainee groups in each of the four initial training sessions (initial PSS-12 training, JRTC training, and both PSS-14 tests) achieved near-asymptotic detection rates on the first set of blind search exercises. That is, the first time trainees applied expert techniques in complete task trials, substantial improvements occurred that were reminiscent of the improvement shown by the mnemonist DD in Figure 2.3 on digit-span trials immediately following his adoption of SF's expert strategy.

The false alarm rates observed for both training programs were unexpectedly good. False alarms result from encounters with unknown buried materials that are not parts of target mines, but produce output signals from the detectors. Such clutter, especially metallic clutter, is remarkably omnipresent in the natural environment. The training/test areas used in these projects were no exceptions and some, but by no means all clutter was removed. Despite the absence of any explicit instruction or drills intended to develop operators' discrimination skills, false alarm rates were low for the clutter present. In PSS-12 training tests, aggregate false alarm rates (0.33 FA/m^2) nearly achieved the ambitious goal of 0.30 set for the PSS-14. The PSS-14 rates bettered this criterion with $.08$ FA/m^2 in training drills and 0.25 in subsequent testing. Figure 2.14 shows the receiver operating characteristic obtained for the soldiers who received the initial PSS-12 CEBES training and the military operators who participated in the second PSS-14 training exercise. The data points for PSS-12 and HSTAMIDS training exercises show detection and false alarms rates for a common test environment at Aberdeen Proving Ground.

Definitive evaluation of clutter discrimination capabilities requires a controlled manipulation of clutter, and an appropriately configured test was not available when these tests were conducted. The removal of some of the clutter originally found in the training and testing areas used in the studies reported here further complicates interpretation and generalization of the false alarm rates reported here. Nonetheless, observations of both programs' trainees during testing showed numerous instances in which operators encountered clutter, but did not make mine declaration. The discrimination capabilities that both

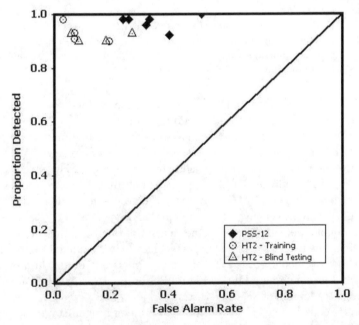

Figure 2.14   Relations between detection and false alarm rates for CEBES-trained PSS-12 operators and HSTAMIDS operators achieved in the same test environment. HSTAMIDS measures came from the second test of training using military operators previously unfamiliar with the HSTAMIDS.

programs produced were unexpected in the absence of any explicit discrimination training or practice. The training program's emphasis on positive identification of target patterns which included an explicit strategy to support abstraction of target pattern categories or prototypes (Posner & Keele, 1968) appears to have had the beneficial effect of supporting mine/clutter discrimination.

DISCUSSION

The results presented here support the hypothesis posed earlier, showing that the accumulated principles, theory, and methods used to understand human expertise are sufficiently mature to support engineering. Tests of the model-based PSS-12 and PSS-14 CEBES training development programs each substantially improved performance on a practical task of considerable difficulty, danger, and importance. The gains produced in operators' detection rates relative to extant levels were sufficiently compelling for military leaders to adopt, disseminate, and implement training programs. Both the PSS-12 and the PSS-14 training programs have been adapted also to the requirements of Humanitarian Demining operations as well (Saucedo, 2001; Ritter, 2007). Within the emerging discipline of cognitive engineering, these project outcomes along with the success that Schaafstal and Schraggen (2000) achieved using analyses of naval fire control experts to develop troubleshooting training suggest CEBES' greater potential utility (Cooke & Durso, 2007; Crandall, Klein, & Hoffman, 2006).

The general practical efficacy of CEBES is under investigation. Recently, an independent review of literature relevant to detecting improvised explosive devices (IEDs) has advocated adapting a CEBES approach to developing training to improve current capability (Vaughn, CuQlock-Knopp, Murphy, & Stanard, 2010). Ongoing CEBES investigations include analyzing expertise in detecting IEDs from unmanned aerial vehicles (Cooke et al., 2010) and refining current understanding of the PSS-14 expert's decision-making processes using computational modeling (Staszewski & Lebiere, 2009; Lebiere & Staszewski, 2010). The former has produced results and recommendations for training improvements that have led to changes in standard operating procedures in current theaters of operation that support soldiers and marines. The latter has produced a first approximation model that shows a good fit to the decision-making patterns of the expert. Further development testing is planned to produce a model with potential to inform training in a way expected to improve mine/clutter discrimination without compromising detection rates and to serve as an intelligent interpretive software component in a robotic mine detection system based on PSS-14 technology.

The studies described here link practical applications to basic science on expertise, particularly that of Bill Chase and his colleagues. Their analyses of experts' skills corroborate theoretical claims about the role of pattern recognition as a key general element of human expertise (Chase, 1986; Simon, 1979, 1990). They also showed, as Chase (1983) had, that human cognition can be studied in the natural environment (although no claims are made about the ease of doing so). Similar to the way in which Chase and colleagues successfully tested theoretical accounts of expert performance with training studies, the results of the mine detection training studies supported assumptions made about the representations and processes that the expert operators used.

The generalization of earlier laboratory research to the current CEBES results might be considered a pleasant surprise for at least two reasons. First, experts represent a relatively rare subject population, making their identification and recruitment considerably more expensive and difficult than recruitment of young college adults. Scarcity of this critical resource surely slows scientific progress. Second, this scarcity also engenders an opportunistic approach that has exploited expertise wherever it can be found for investigation. As a result, the database on human expertise is populated with studies of skills that some cognitive scientists regard as sufficiently esoteric or exotic, that they question their relevance to "real-world" expertise and, thus, the practical utility of current knowledge and understanding. Considering the fundamentally adaptive nature of human expertise, tapping seemingly disparate skill domains should increase the difficulty of integrating findings. The connections between the findings of prior basic research, particularly that of Bill Chase, and the outcomes reported here, testify to the reliability and generality of the fundamental principles and understanding accumulated under the constraints that expertise research entails.

Bill Chase was known for

> [his] powerful experimental skills, ingenuity in experimental design and analysis, [and] a strong sense for the theoretical relevance and implications of experimental findings...through an experimental program developed over more than a decade, Bill Chase provided an important base for understanding the nature of expert skills and the knowledge that underlies them.
>
> (Simon, 1985)

The influence of Chase's work on that described here should make it clear that whatever contributions the CEBES approach has made or will make should rightfully be considered a part of Chase's legacy as much as the products of genetic engineering are the legacy of Crick and Watson.

REFERENCES

Biederman, I., & Shiffrar, M. M. (1987). Sexing day-old chicks: A case study and expert systems analysis of a difficult perceptual-learning task. *Journal of Experimental Psychology Learning, Memory, and Cognition, 13*, 640–645.

Chase, W. G. (1983). Spatial representations of taxi drivers. In D. R. Rogers, & J. A. Sloboda (Eds.), *Acquisition of symbolic skills* (pp. 391–405). New York: Plenum Press.

Chase, W. G. (1986). *Visual information processing: Handbook of perception and human performance.* Ed. L. K. K. R. Boff, & J. P. Thomas (vol. 2, pp. 28–71.) New York: Wiley.

Chase, W. G., & Ericsson, K. A. (1981). Skilled memory. In J. R. Anderson (Ed.), *Cognitive skills and their acquisition* (pp. 141–190). Hillsdale, NJ: Erlbaum.

Chase, W. G., & Ericsson, K. A. (1982). Skill and working memory. In G. H. Bower (Ed.), *The psychology of learning and motivation* (vol. 16, pp. 1–58). New York: Academic Press.

Chase, W. G., & Simon, H. A. (1973a). The mind's eye in chess. In W. G. Chase (Ed.), *Visual information processing* (pp. 215–281). New York: Academic Press.

Chase, W. G., & Simon, H. A. (1973b). Perception in chess. *Cognitive Psychology, 4*, 55–81.

Cooke, N. J., & Durso, F. (2007). *Stories of modern technology failures and cognitive engineering successes*. Boca Raton, FL: Taylor & Francis.

Cooke, N. J., Hosch, C., Banas, S., Hunn, B. P., Staszewski, J., & Fensterer, J. (2010). Expert detection of improvised explosive device emplacement behavior. *Proceedings of the Human Factors and Ergonomics Society 54th Annual Meeting*. Santa Monica, CA: Human Factors and Ergonomics Society.

Crandall, B., Klein, G., & Hoffman, R. R. (2006). *Working minds: A practitioner's guide to cognitive task analysis*. Cambridge, MA: MIT Press.

Davison, A., & Staszewski, J. (2002). *Handheld mine detection based on expert skill: Reference guide for training plan design and training site development*. Aberdeen Proving Ground, MD: Army Research Laboratory Human Research and Engineering Directorate.

de Groot, A. D. (1965). *Thought and choice in chess*. The Hague: Mouton Publishers.

Ericsson, K. A., Chase, W. G., & Faloon, S. (1980). Acquisition of a memory skill. *Science, 208*(4448), 1181–1182.

Ericsson, K. A., & Polson, P. (1988). A cognitive analysis of exceptional memory for restaurant orders. In M. T. H. Chi, R. Glaser, & M. J. Farr (Eds.), *The nature of expertise* (pp. 23–70). Hillsdale, NJ: Lawrence Erlbaum Associates.

Finke, R. A. (1990). *Creative imagery: Discoveries and inventions in visualization*. Hillsdale, NJ: Erlbaum Associates.

Garner, W. R. (1974). *The processing of information and structure*. Potomac, MD: Erlbaum Associates.

Gobet, F., de Voogt, A. J., & Retschitzki, J. (2004). *Moves in mind: The psychology of board games*. Hove, UK: Psychology Press.

Guckert, R. (2000). HSTAMIDS Red Team experiences/Lessons learned. In *Proceedings of the UXO/countermine forum*, Anaheim, CA, 2–4 May.

Hambric, H. H., & Schneck, W. C. (1996). The antipersonnel mine threat. In *Proceedings of the technology and the mine problem symposium*, 1, Naval Postgraduate School, 18–21 November, 3–11–3–45.

Headquarters, Department of the Army. (2002). *Mine/countermine operations: FM20-32 C3*. Washington, DC: Department of the Army.

Headquarters, Department of the Army. (2006). *Operator's and unit maintenance manual for detecting set, mine AN/PSS-14: TM 5-6665-373-12&P*. Washington, DC: Department of the Army.

Herman, H., & Inglesias, D. (1999). Human-in-the-loop issues for demining. In T. Broach, A. C. Dubey, R. E. Dugan, & J. Harvey (Eds.), *Detection and remediation technologies for mines and minelike targets IV, proceedings of the Society for Photo-Optical Instrumentation Engineers, 13th annual meeting, 3710*, 797–805.

Klatzky, R. L., & Thompson, A. (1975). Integration of features in comparing multi-feature stimuli. *Perception and Psychophysics, 18*, 428–432.

LaMoe, J. P., & Read, T. (2002). Countermine operations in the contemporary operational environment. *Engineer, 32*, 21–23.

Lebiere, C. J., & Staszewski J. J. (2010). Expert decision making in landmine detection. *Proceedings of the Human Factors and Ergonomics Society 54th Annual Meeting.* Santa Monica, CA: Human Factors and Ergonomics Society.

MacDonald, J., Lockwood, J. R., McFee, J., Altshuler, T., Broach, T., Carin, L., Harmon, R., Rappaport, C., Scott, W., & Weaver, R. (2003). *Alternatives for landmine detection.* Santa Monica, CA: Rand Science and Technology Policy Institute.

Palmer, S. E. (1977). Hierarchical structure in perceptual representation. *Cognitive Psychology, 9*, 441–474.

Posner, M. I., & Keele, S. W. (1968). On the genesis of abstract ideas. *Journal of Experimental Psychology, 77*, 353–363.

Richman, H. B., Staszewski, J., & Simon, H. A. (1995). Simulation of expert memory using EPAM IV. *Psychological Review, 102*, 305–330.

Ritter, K. D. (2007). AN/PSS-14 mine detection system offers improved countermine capability. *Army Acquisition, Logistics, and Technology Magazine*, January–March, 54–59.

Rosch, E., Mervis, C. B., Gray, W., Johnson, D., & Boyes-Brame, P. (1976). Basic objects in natural categories. *Cognitive Psychology, 8*, 382–439.

Saucedo, J. (2001). The Jordanian humanitarian demining program: A model of optimism and persistence. *Journal of Mine Action*, Issue 5.3, December 2001. Retrieved from: http://maic.jmu.edu/journal/5.3/focus/Jose_Saucedo_Jordanian/Jose_Saucedo.htm.

Schaafstal, A. M., & Schraagen, J. M. (2000). Training of troubleshooting: A structured, task analytical approach. In J. M. Schraagen, S. F. Chipman, & V. L. Shalin (Eds.), *Cognitive task analysis* (pp. 57–70). Mahwah, NJ: Lawrence Erlbaum Associates.

Simon, H. A. (1979). Human information processing models of cognition. *Annual Review of Psychology, 30*, 363–396.

Simon, H. A. (1980). Cognitive science: The newest science of the artificial. *Cognitive Science, 4*, 33–46.

Simon, H. A. (1985). Obituary: William G. Chase (1940–1983). *American Psychologist, May*, p. 561.

Simon, H. A. (1990). Invariants of human behavior. *Annual Review of Psychology, 14*, 1–19.

Staszewski, J. (1988). Skilled memory in expert mental calculation, In M. T. H. Chi, R. Glaser, & M. J. Farr (Eds.), *The nature of expertise* (pp. 71–128). Hillsdale, NJ: Lawrence Erlbaum Associates.

Staszewski, J. (1990). Exceptional memory: The influence of practice and knowledge on the development of elaborative encoding strategies. In W. Schneider, & F. E. Weinert (Eds.), *Interactions among aptitudes, strategies, and knowledge in cognitive performance* (pp. 252–285). New York: Springer-Verlag.

Staszewski, J. (1999). Information processing analysis of human land mine detection skill. In T. Broach, A. C. Dubey, R. E. Dugan, & J. Harvey (Eds.), *Detection and remediation technologies for mines and minelike targets IV, proceedings of the Society for Photo-Optical Instrumentation Engineers, 13th annual meeting, SPIE, 3710*, 766–777.

Staszewski, J., & Chase, W. G. (1984). Skilled memory in mental calculation. *Bulletin of the Psychonomic Society, 22*(4), 289.

Staszewski, J., & Davison, A. (2000). Mine detection training based on expert skill. In A. C. Dubey, J. F. Harvey, J. T. Broach, & R. E. Dugan (Eds.), *Detection and remediation technologies for mines and mine-like targets V, proceedings of Society of Photo-Optical Instrumentation Engineers 14th annual meeting, SPIE, 4038,* 90–101.

Staszewski, J., & Lebiere, C. (2009). Applied cognitive models of frequency-based decision making. *Proceedings of the AAAI 2009 Fall Symposium Series* (FS-09-01), Biologically Inspired Cognitive Architectures-II. Technical Report FS-09-01. Available at: http://www.aaai.org/Press/Reports/Symposia/Fall/fall-reports.php#FS09.

U.S. Army Test and Experimentation Command (1991). *Expanded test report: AN/PSS12 metallic-mine detector. (Report EU-E/CS-1600).* Ft. Hood, TX: U.S. Army Test and Experimentation Command.

Vaughn, B., QuClock-Knopp, ZV. G., Murphy, J., & Stanard, T. (2010). *Improving IED detection through training and personnel selection: Lesson learned from basic and applied visual search.* (DTIC Publication #AFRL-RH-WP-TR-2010-0041). Wright Patterson AFB OH: Air Force Research Laboratory, 711th Human Performance Wing, Human Effectiveness Directorate.

Watson, J. D. (1968). *The double helix: A personal account of the discovery of the structure of DNA.* New York: Touchstone.

Webster, D. (1996). *Aftermath: The remnants of war.* New York: Pantheon Books.

Wenger, M., & Payne, D. (1995). On the acquisition of mnemonic skill: Application of skilled memory theory. *Journal of Experimental Psychology: Applied, 1,* 195–215.

3

Motivating Persistence in the Face of Failure[1]

Equipping Novice Learners with the Motivational Tools of Experts

CATHERINE C. CHASE

Carnegie Mellon University, USA

INTRODUCTION

Throughout their school careers, students encounter many challenging learning tasks where some degree of failure is inevitable. When doing a math problem, coming up with an idea for an essay, or writing a computer program, students' first attempts may fail. Oftentimes, students take the easy way out by giving up on the task entirely, which impedes learning. Ideally, students will persevere through these failures, learn from their mistakes, and eventually master the relevant concepts and skills. But rebounding from failure requires a sophisticated set of motivational behaviors that many novices, including children, often do not perform.

How can we foster student persistence in the face of failure during learning? In this chapter, I look to experts as models of tireless persistence in the face of failure. Presumably, this persistence has aided them in learning their domain of expertise and has eventually led them to become successful at what they do. In the research presented here, I examine the motivational tools that experts employ in the face of failure with an eye towards supplying them to

1 This material is based upon work supported by the National Science Foundation under grants EHR-0634044, SLC-0354453, and by the Department of Education under grant IES R305H060089. Any opinions, findings, and conclusions or recommendations expressed in this material are those of the authors and do not necessarily reflect the views of the granting agencies.

novice learners. I then discuss a technology-based classroom intervention called Teachable Agents, which, I argue, provides novice students with the motivational tools of experts, enabling them to persist after failure and learn from challenging tasks.

EXPERT PERSISTENCE IN THE FACE OF FAILURE

Experts have knowledge, skills, and mental representations that far surpass those of novices or even skilled practitioners. How do experts come to possess these superior cognitions and skills? When asked this question at a conference, Bill Chase responded with the adage "no pain, no gain." Experts become good at what they do through plain hard work. Indeed, the expert chess players that Chase studied had practiced approximately 10,000 hours before gaining international-level playing skills (Chase & Simon, 1973). Several studies have now shown that it takes ten or more years to become an expert across many domains such as music, medicine, and mathematics (Ericsson & Lehmann, 1996).

But not everyone becomes an expert after 10,000 hours of practice. True experts undertake "deliberate practice," where they systematically rehearse a particular skill (Ericsson, Krampe, & Clemens, 1993). For instance, chess players will re-enact famous games and attempt to predict their moves, and musicians will sustain hours of solitary practice on a single piece. While practicing deliberately, experts maintain intense levels of concentration and effort even though they often find it unpleasant (Ericsson, Krampe, & Clemens, 1993). In fact, many experts are unable to sustain deliberate practice for more than four hours a day because it requires such extreme physical and/or mental exertion (Ericsson, 2002).

During deliberate practice, experts push themselves to attempt challenges beyond their current level of ability. Bereiter and Scardamalia (1992) call this "progressive problem-solving," where individuals "work at the edge of their competence" by giving themselves progressively more difficult challenges. They studied expert writers who generated demanding writing problems for themselves. These problems pushed the experts to discover new knowledge and new styles of writing (Scardamalia & Bereiter, 1987).

But when experts work at the boundary of their abilities, attempting extremely difficult tasks, they are bound to experience failure. Even Michael Jordan, a basketball legend, has failed many times, as illustrated by this quote from a television commercial: "I've missed more than 9000 shots in my career. I've lost almost 300 games. 26 times, I've been trusted to take the game winning shot and missed. I've failed over and over and over again in my life. And that is why I succeed." If experts frequently work on tasks they have not yet mastered, failure along the way is inevitable.

But failures can lead to learning. John Dewey once wrote, "Failure . . . is instructive. The person who really thinks learns quite as much from his failures as from his successes" (Dewey, [1933] 1998, p. 142). The discrepancy between intended and actual outcomes provides information that fuels analysis (Wiener, 1948). New discoveries are often made when experiments come out differently than predicted. In a study of a molecular biology lab, Dunbar (1999) found that biologists paid particular attention to discrepant results. Asking why these results had occurred often pushed them to generate novel theories and innovations in their field. The same principle applies for children learning in school. For instance "struggling and making mistakes are believed to be essential parts of the learning process in Japan," where teachers let students make errors and learn from observing their consequences (Stigler & Hiebert, 1999, p. 91). So too experts must learn a great deal from failing at challenging tasks and then working through their mistakes.

But failure can be debilitating. Studies have linked the experience of repeated failure to low self-efficacy, learned helplessness, and even depression, conditions that strongly hinder motivation (Bandura, 1997; Peterson, Maier, & Seligman, 1993). Yet somehow, experts find ways to persist after failure, and presumably, these failures help them become the best at what they do. But exactly how do experts sustain the motivation to persevere in the face of constant failure?

In the remainder of this chapter I will address this question, with an eye towards designing interventions to help novices persist during challenging learning tasks. I begin with a summary of motivational theories that could explain experts' motivation in the face of failure, highlighting where they are relevant to an intervention for novices. I then describe a suite of motivational tools—an ego-protective buffer, acceptance of responsibility, and an actionable path—that appear to help experts persist and learn in the face of failure. A study of expert motivation presents suggestive evidence for these tools. I then go on to describe a computer-based intervention called Teachable Agents, where students learn by teaching a computer character. Finally, two studies suggest that the Teachable Agent software leads children to adopt the motivational tools of experts, persist at difficult learning tasks, and make significant learning gains.

WHAT MOTIVATES EXPERTS?

What motivates experts to persist for thousands of hours of deliberate practice, enduring frequent failure? Unfortunately, there is very little research on the motivation of experts, but there are two motivational constructs that seem intuitively applicable: self-efficacy and intrinsic motivation.

Self-efficacy is the belief that one is capable of performing a specific task. According to Bandura (1997), the most robust source of self-efficacy is accumulated past experiences of success with a particular task. Most experts are differentiated from novices and mere skilled individuals by their ability to perform extremely well in evaluative contexts like competitions, academic tests, or public presentations. So while experts often fail during deliberate practice, they experience a great deal of success in performance venues. These experiences of success lead experts to cultivate a strong sense of self-efficacy for tasks in their domain.

Bandura (1997) hypothesizes that high self-efficacy for a particular task leads individuals to persist in the face of difficulty, attribute failure to external or unstable causes, and rebound quickly from failure, because they believe that they can succeed (Kitsantas & Zimmerman, 2002; Silver, Mitchell, & Gist, 1995). A lack of this belief, demonstrated by low self-efficacy, leads individuals to persist for shorter periods of time, attribute failure to internal or stable causes, and give up after failure. According to Bandura, a well-developed sense of self-efficacy is important for generating a healthy response to failure.

There is some evidence that experts have high self-efficacy for tasks in their domain. In a study of expert, non-expert, and novice volleyball players, the experts rated their self-efficacy significantly higher than both non-experts and novices before executing a serve (Kitsantas & Zimmerman, 2002). Moreover, their self-efficacy rating did not change after missing a serve, while the self-efficacy rating of both non-experts and novices declined after failure. This stable sense of self-efficacy could help experts endure extended periods of failure during training.

Another obvious motivator for experts is their intense passion for their domain. If experts are willing to practice for thousands of hours, then they probably like what they do. That means experts almost certainly have a well-developed personal interest (Renninger, Hidi, & Krapp, 1992) and are intrinsically motivated in their area of expertise (Deci & Ryan, 1985). In the same study of volleyball players described above, experts rated their intrinsic interest in the overhand serve significantly higher than both non-experts and novices (Kitsantas & Zimmerman, 2002). Intrinsic motivation has been shown to predict people's choice in activities and how long they are willing to persist at those activities (Deci & Ryan, 1985). It seems likely that a strong interest in their topic of expertise could spur experts to initiate deliberate practice and persist when they encounter obstacles in their domain.

FROM EXPERIENCE-DRIVEN MOTIVATIONS TO MOTIVATIONAL TOOLS

When considering how to help novices persist after failure, it seems ill-advised to rely directly on the motivational constructs of self-efficacy and domain-specific intrinsic motivations, at least early on. With little knowledge and experience in a domain, novices cannot have attained the success necessary for high self-efficacy in domain-specific tasks, nor can they have the deep intrinsic motivations that drive experts to engage tasks at their "breaking point." Given the limitations of self-efficacy and interest for sustaining novices' persistence in the face of failure, a search for more practical, intervention-focused motivators is warranted. A study with experts suggested a confluence of three motivational tools that yield persistence after failure: (1) an ego-protective buffer; (2) acceptance of responsibility; and (3) actionable paths for making progress. I describe the motivational tools first, and then describe the relevant study.

A *motivational tool* supports and encourages motivation in a specific context; in this case, the context is failure. Like cognitive tools and physical tools, these motivational tools can be used and possessed by people, though not necessarily deliberately. Motivational tools differ from more general motivational constructs like self-efficacy or intrinsic interest, which rely on developed self-concepts and preferences. Motivational tools can be more easily manipulated. So while it can be difficult to increase student self-efficacy or sustain intrinsic interest in the face of failure, we can provide students with motivational tools. Another benefit of motivational tools is that they suggest specific design points for interventions, which I describe in a subsequent section.

An Ego-Protective Buffer

An *ego-protective buffer* lessens the impact of failure on one's psyche. Chemical buffers are substances that maintain a stable pH in a solution by neutralizing the effects of added acids or bases. An ego-protective buffer maintains a stable sense of competence by allowing the learner to place some of the blame for failure on an external agent like the situation or the difficulty of the task. This protects the learner from self-blame and its accompanying assumption— that the learner has poor ability or low intelligence.

The ego-protective buffer relates to attribution theory, which claims that individuals are motivated to find the causes of significant outcomes like failure so they can determine how to avoid failure in the future. One dimension of attributions is their locus; attributions can be internal or external to the individual. Attributing failure to some internal causes, like fixed ability or intelligence, can have a negative impact on expectations of future success, persistence and even performance (Anderson & Jennings, 1980; Weiner, 1985), whereas attributing failure to external causes can boost self-esteem (Weiner, 1979). By enabling attributions to external causes, the ego-protective buffer blocks unhealthy internal attributions and negative self-thoughts like "I simply don't have the ability to do this" or "I'm stupid."

This is important because negative self-thoughts pull cognitive resources away from the task at hand, making learning much less likely to occur. For instance, individuals with test anxiety often have a solid understanding of the concepts but simply do not perform well on tests. This is because during the test, they focus all their cognitive resources on the negative consequences of performing poorly (Wine, 1971). The ego-protective buffer can draw learners away from these negative self-thoughts so they can focus on the learning task.

Acceptance of Responsibility

Simply shielding learners from the negative self-thoughts inspired by failure may not be enough. Learners need to be motivated to do something about the failure, and not simply feel safe from it. Persistent learners *accept responsibility* for repairing the failure and preventing it from occurring again. This sense of responsibility implies that the learner cares about the task outcome. If one feels responsible, then one exercises a sense of ownership and investment in the task and feels a duty to succeed. For persistence to occur, learners must believe that the onus to remedy the failure is on the self, and they must believe that they themselves can control future progress in the task. If learners deem that fixing and preventing the failure are beyond their control, then they will not be motivated to take personal action. This belief can lead the learner to give up on the task, which curtails learning.

This relates to another dimension of attributions—controllability. Controllability refers to whether the individual has the power to change the source of the outcome. Failure due to bad luck is not controllable while failure due to poor effort is the kind of failure that the learner can take action to avoid. In fact, many attribution researchers advocate training students to attribute failure to effort because it boosts persistence (Schunk, 1982; Weiner, 1979). However, I argue that learners can make an external attribution for past performance while taking control over future failures. By accepting responsibility for remedying the failure or preventing it in the future, learners are exercising control over future failures even if they view past failures as dependent on external causes.

So the ego-protective buffer and acceptance of responsibility constructs do not contradict one another. The key distinction is that one can accept responsibility for the future action of remedying the situation without harping on the shame of a past failure. For example, after receiving negative reviews on a submitted journal article, an author might blame the idiosyncratic nature of the reviewers or the writing styles of the co-authors, but in the end, that author will often take personal responsibility for revising and resubmitting the paper. Likewise, experts are highly attuned to the external conditions that affect their performance, and they adapt their behaviors to deal with them (Ericsson, 2002). For instance, when a gust of wind blows a tennis player's serve out of the court, the player might chalk it up to bad luck. However, he might also believe that if he had aimed more conservatively, the ball would have stayed in. So he might conclude that the failure was caused by bad luck, but he can avoid misses in the future by playing more conservatively on windy days. There are many situations where people blame external sources for failure but take matters into their own hands when it comes to repairing or preventing future failures.

An Actionable Path

Buffering the psyche and intending to fix things may not be sufficient to pull the learner forward. Without a clear *actionable path* for moving forward, the learner can get stuck with no way of moving beyond the failure. Persistence is far more likely if the learner has a store of content-specific strategies or domain-specific knowledge that can be used to develop a new approach to the task. These new approaches are actionable if, in the mind of the learner, they create a potential avenue towards progress. If learners cannot find any actionable paths to take, then they are likely to quit the task, which inhibits learning.

While theories of self-regulated learning recognize that cognitive and motivational concepts are co-mingled (Boekarts, 1997; Pintrich & De Groot, 1990; Zimmerman, 2002), the concept of an actionable path is often overlooked in motivational theory. For instance, many attribution retraining studies teach learners to attribute failure to poor effort or ineffective strategies (Anderson & Jennings, 1980; Dweck, 1975). However, if students have no knowledge of other strategies or no direction for their efforts, this would be a futile approach. Merely trying harder, without knowing what to try, makes it difficult to persist. Interventions aimed at supporting student persistence need to focus on developing students' cognitive resources as well as their motivational ones.

One example of how these three components can come together to motivate persistence after failure is in how teachers are taught to reprimand children by first criticizing the behavior, not the child, and then explaining how the child can change her behavior. For instance, a teacher might start by saying "It's not *you* that I don't like, it's your *behavior*," making clear that the teacher does not have a personal dislike of the child, but rather the behavior is to blame. Then, the teacher might go on to say "Interrupting while others are speaking slows down the class conversation and frustrates everyone. Next time that you're bursting to say something, please write it down so you won't forget, then wait your turn to be called on." Here the teacher clearly places the burden of fixing the behavior on the student. Moreover, she explains a specific strategy the child can use to change her own behavior. Through a combination of these three mechanisms: (1) deflecting the blame away from the student while (2) assigning them personal responsibility for improvement, and (3) providing specific strategies for moving forward, the teacher equips her student with an excellent set of tools for persisting after a behavioral failure.

HOW DO EXPERTS SUSTAIN MOTIVATION AFTER FAILURE?

This chapter discusses two specific hypotheses. (1) Experts use a suite of motivational tools—an ego-protective buffer, acceptance of responsibility, and actionable paths—to help them move beyond failure. (2) If we provide these tools to novice students, they should be more likely to persist in the face of failure. I do not attempt to claim that these three tools are either necessary or sufficient for motivating persistence in the face of failure; the studies I present were not specifically designed to test this claim. However, I present suggestive evidence that these tools work effectively in concert.

These three motivational tools emerged from a study on expert motivation that was designed to test whether the motivations that help experts persist in the face of failure are confined to their areas of expertise. I contrasted relative experts in math and English as they performed extremely difficult math and English tasks. This cross-over design was created to compare the motivational behaviors of experts in two different domains: a domain where they are novices and a domain where they are experts. Verbal protocol data were carefully coded for attributions to failure and were also informally analyzed to determine how experts made progress in the tasks. Two measures of persistence were collected—time on task and whether participants chose to revisit the tasks in their spare time.

Study participants were 19 relative experts in either English (n = 9) or math (n = 10); they were upper-level undergraduate students and doctoral students pursuing degrees in either subject. During the study, all experts attempted two tasks—one in math and one in English. For the math task, participants were asked to do a proof involving prime numbers; for the English task, participants were expected to interpret a poem with very oblique language (see Appendix). The tasks were chosen for both their approachability and difficulty, to ensure that while everyone could attempt each task, they were likely to fail.

Participants were told they would have up to 12 minutes to work on each task but they could quit before the time was up, if they wanted. During the tasks, participants thought aloud and their voices were audio recorded. At the end of the session, participants were asked to return a few days later for a brief interview and were informed they would not have to work on the tasks again. However, during the second session, participants were indeed asked to revisit the tasks and think aloud again. This was done to determine whether subjects had chosen to work on the tasks in their spare time, outside the demands of the experiment. During their second attempt at the task, participants often stated whether they had worked on the task in between the two sessions or not. This was confirmed by a brief interview given afterwards.

Figure 3.1 shows that experts in both math and English spent significantly more time on the task in their domain, using almost the full 12 minutes.[2] Moreover, far more of the experts reported working on the task in their domain during the time between the two experimental sessions.[3] Of the math experts, 100% of them chose to work on the math task while only 30% worked on the English task. The English experts behaved similarly; while 56% of them revisited the English task, only 33% of them returned to the math task. So for tasks in their domain, the experts continued to persist even outside the demands of the experiment, in their free time.

---

2 Persistence times were entered into a repeated-measures ANOVA with one between-subjects factor of expert type (math or English) and one within-subjects factor of task type (math or English). Neither main effect was statistically significant, $F_{Expert\ Type}(1, 17) = 1.08$, $p = .31$, F_{Task} $(1, 17) = 0.90$, $p = .36$. However, there was a strong interaction effect of expert type by task type, $F(1, 17) = 30.34$, $p < .001$. This cross-over effect, displayed in Figure 3.1, shows that math experts persisted longer at the math task, while English experts persisted longer at the English task.

3 A log-linear model was fitted to the three crossed factors of expert type (math or English), task type (math or English), and persistence choice (yes or no). In the final fitted model, only the three-way interaction was significant, $\chi^2(1, n = 38) = 11.77$, $p < .001$, none of two-way interactions or main effects were significant. The percentage of subjects who chose to persist at each activity in their spare time demonstrates this interaction clearly. Experts were more likely to revisit the task in their domain of expertise.

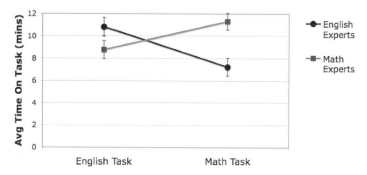

Figure 3.1   Persistence times broken down by task type and expert type.

Hints at why the experts persisted in their domains came from the verbal protocol data. Experts tended to make more external attributions for failure while working on the task in their domain while they made slightly more internal attributions during the task outside of their domain.[4] Figure 3.2 displays this pattern along with sample attributions. For instance, English experts often blamed the task ("This poem is all over the place—there is no way of connecting these ideas"), the situation ("It's weird to work on it in isolation. If I were doing the task outside of an experiment, there are people I would call, things I would Google"), or sometimes the method ("I need to try other things, try a different approach"), for their failure in interpreting the poem. However, when working on the math problem, English experts often blamed themselves, claiming either poor ability ("I'm not very good at things like this") or lack of knowledge ("If I knew more algebra, I'd be able to work it out. It's too complicated for my lame high school math"). Though the cross-over effect was slightly less prominent in the math experts (particularly on the English task), overall, math experts displayed a similar pattern of attributions, citing mostly external causes for failure on the math task ("This is a complicated theorem," "Talking out loud is really slowing me down and screwing me up," "This strategy's

4 A "locus" score was computed for each subject's attributions during each task by subtracting the total number of internal attributions from the total number of external attributions and then dividing by the total number of attributions made during the task. A positive score indicates a bias towards external attribution, while a negative score suggests an internal bias. The locus score became the dependent measure in a repeated-measures ANOVA with expert type (math or English) as a between-subjects factor and task type (math or English) as a within-subjects factor. The main effects of expert type, $F(1, 15) = 0.19$, $p = 0.67$, and task type, $F(1, 15) = 2.50$, $p = 0.14$, were not significant. However, a significant two-way interaction, $F(1, 15) = 6.07$, $p = 0.03$ indicated that both types of experts made more external attributions during the in-domain task and more internal attributions during the out-domain task. Two subjects were dropped from this analysis because they only made attributions during one of the tasks. However, the attributions they did make followed the same pattern as the other subjects. For the sake of simplicity, Figure 3.2 depicts the average proportion of internal and external attributions made by math and English experts during each type of task (rather than the locus score which is more difficult to interpret).

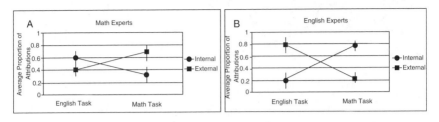

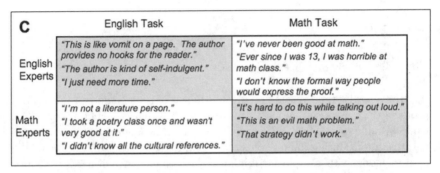

Figure 3.2   Average proportion of internal and external attributions made by (A) math experts and (B) English experts. Example attributions (C).

obviously not working very well") and slightly more internal causes for the English failure ("This is kind of over my head," "It seems very far removed from anything I have any idea about"). This ability to divert the blame for failure away from themselves and towards external sources is an ego-protective buffer that protects experts' sense of competence in their domain.

At the same time, experts accepted responsibility for repairing the failure. After making mistakes, the experts continued to take productive actions in the task, and they even initiated work on the tasks in their free time, outside the demands of the experiment. In contrast, when doing the out-domain task, in which participants were novices, they often stopped taking actions after a few failures and eventually gave up on the task entirely.

Further evidence of experts' acceptance of responsibility comes from the finding that not all of the experts' attributions for the task in their domain were external. About 30% of them were internal. While external attributions allowed experts to protect their egos, the few internal attributions they did make show that they held themselves accountable for remedying the situation. This is notable since most studies of attribution theory ask participants to select a single attribution for an outcome, when in reality, the participant may subscribe to several different attributions at once.

It is also interesting to note that experts later went on to alter the external causes of their failure by changing the conditions under which the task (in their domain) was performed. During the first session, many of the experts complained about these conditions, stating that they did not have enough time, found it difficult to talk aloud and think at the same time, or did not have access to resources. But by revisiting the task outside the demands of the experiment, the experts eliminated the time limit and the requirement of talking aloud. Many of the experts reported consulting other resources like the Internet or a knowledgeable friend. So the experts were motivated enough to change the external conditions they believed were contributing to the failure, thereby turning uncontrollable external causes into internally controllable ones.

Moreover, the experts had actionable paths for making progress in the task It was clear from the protocol that both types of experts made significantly more progress on the tasks in their domains. They did so by using specific knowledge and strategies that moved them closer to their ultimate goal of completing the task.[5] For instance, while interpreting the poem, English experts looked for patterns in the punctuation style, analyzed when and why the prose switched voice, and searched for clues to the context in which the poem was written. These methods for analyzing a poem come from experience and knowledge—something that the novice math experts did not have when approaching the poem. The math experts tended to apply very few specific strategies or essential information during work on the poem. However, during the math problem, math experts applied several pieces of knowledge about the distribution of prime numbers, the format of proofs, and logical assumptions towards solving it, which the English experts did not. So, both kinds of experts had strategies and knowledge that gave them further avenues to pursue when their first attempts at the task in their domain failed. Whereas, when working on tasks outside their domain, acting as novices, participants quit when they ran out of things to try, saying things like "I'm not making any more progress here. That's all I can do." Participants simply had more actionable paths available to them in their domain of expertise.

This study presents suggestive evidence that experts employ all three motivational tools in the face of failure—an ego-protective buffer, acceptance of responsibility, and actionable paths. While more direct evidence for this claim is warranted before stronger assertions can be made, my interpretation is as follows. Experts are able to divert the negative impact of failure towards external sources while still taking personal responsibility to move beyond the failure, and they do so by implementing practical strategies and useful knowledge that help them progress in the task.

Notice that experts' failure-coping mechanisms are domain-specific; the motivational behaviors that math experts displayed during the math task did not appear when they worked on the English task, and vice versa for the English experts. This provides evidence to refute the claim that experts possess some general trait-like characteristic of high motivation that pervades all their behavior

---

5 Given the high prior plausibility of this claim and the enormous literature that confirms it (Bédard & Chi, 1992; Ericsson & Charness, 1994; Ertmer & Newby, 1996), I chose not to code and count episodes of task progress and their accompanying strategies and actionable paths.

(Winner, 2000). Experts are not motivated to do everything; rather their expert-like motivational tools are reserved for their specific area of expertise.

PROVIDING NOVICE STUDENTS WITH THE TOOLS TO MOVE BEYOND FAILURE

Experts, who have accumulated years of experience in a domain, have tools for moving beyond failure, but can we encourage novices to show the same persistence in the face of failure? Unlike experts, novices have no prior knowledge, no special interest, and no well-developed sense of self-efficacy in a domain. But if given the right motivational tools, novices should be able to persist in the face of failure, just like the experts.

Software learning environments make compelling motivational interventions because of their affordances for scaffolding learning activities. For instance, cognitive tutors provide just-in-time hints during problem-solving. They also demonstrate specific problem-solving methods through worked examples (Koedinger, 2001). Likewise, scientific simulations provide students with the infrastructure for running experiments. They designate exactly which variables can change and encourage students to make their own changes and observe the consequences (De Jong & Van Joolingen, 1998). In this way, software learning environments can provide students with precise methods for moving forward in a task. If an initial simulated experiment fails, students can try manipulating a different variable. If their problem-solving strategy did not work, students can ask the cognitive tutor for a hint. Software learning environments are well suited to provide the third motivational component for moving beyond failure—a specific actionable path for making progress in the task.

But how can we provide students with an ego-protective buffer and a sense of responsibility? One way is to introduce another social entity—someone who acts on the student's behalf yet behaves independently. For example, coaches, who train their players, feel responsible for a lost game since the players were acting on their teachings. But the coach cannot be held solely responsible for the players' behaviors. The players themselves clearly had some hand in losing the game. Teachers often feel the same way about their students. Because teachers can have a profound effect on the beliefs, thoughts, and actions of their students, they have a duty to do their job well. At the same time, they realize that students have a will of their own and can easily divert from the teacher's prescribed path. A software learning environment that harnesses this particular kind of social situation could inspire a sense of responsibility while providing an ego-protective buffer to absorb some of the blame for failure.

A Teachable Agent (TA) is one such software learning environment. Based on the narrative of teaching and equipped with supports for specific learning activities, the Teachable Agent contains all the tools for moving beyond failure. A Teachable Agent is a graphical character on the computer that children teach, and in the process of teaching, the children learn themselves. As a product of the child's tutelage, the agent is a reflection of the child herself, but as an independent actor, it takes on a life of its own (Chase, Chin, Oppezzo, & Schwartz, 2009). Occupying the unique social space of part self, part other, the agent motivates students to feel partly responsible for its failures, while the agent itself can shoulder some of the blame. In addition, the software has built-in structures and scaffolds to support specific methods or actionable paths for improving performance.

A TEACHABLE AGENT CALLED BETTY'S BRAIN

Betty's Brain is a type of Teachable Agent (TA) software where students learn by teaching a graphical character on the computer (Biswas, Leelawong, Schwartz, Vye, & TAG-V, 2005; Schwartz, Blair, Biswas, Leelawong, & Davis, 2007). Each student creates her own agent by naming and designing its appearance and then populating its "brain" with knowledge. Students teach their agents by building concept maps of nodes connected by qualitative causal links; for example, 'heat production' increases 'body temperature'. Betty was designed to model chain-like mechanisms of cause and effect. For this reason, Betty is ideal for science domains that have long chains of causal relationships, like those found in many areas of biology.

A Teachable Agent (TA) is equipped with an artificial intelligence reasoning engine which enables it to reason about the information it has been taught. For instance, a TA can answer questions. Figure 3.3 demonstrates Betty's query feature. In response to a question, the TA will respond by successively highlighting each node and link in a causal chain as it reasons through them. This makes the TA's "thinking" visible to the student, who can revise her agent's knowledge by editing its concept map; meanwhile, the student herself learns along the way.

Betty comes with several kinds of feedback features which help students debug their maps and further their understanding of the content. In addition to the query feature discussed above, Betty also contains a quiz feature. When students submit their agents to take a quiz, the TA responds to a set of questions and receives right/wrong feedback, and students can observe the TA's performance. Betty also comes with the Triple-A Game Show displayed in Figure 3.4—a *Jeopardy*-like game where students' agents play against one another. During the game show, the host poses a series of questions. Students wager points on their agent's answer while the host provides right/wrong feedback and awards points. These various features are meant to engage students in the process of teaching while providing feedback on their maps and overall understanding.

Betty comes with two additional features. One is a chat feature which enables students to carry on a written conversation with one another while working in the Betty software. Another is a set of reading resources that students can access throughout the teaching process, to help clarify their understanding of the concepts.

Past studies have shown that Betty's Brain is an effective learning tool (Chin et al., 2010; Schwartz et al., 2009). In one study, 6th grade students were taught

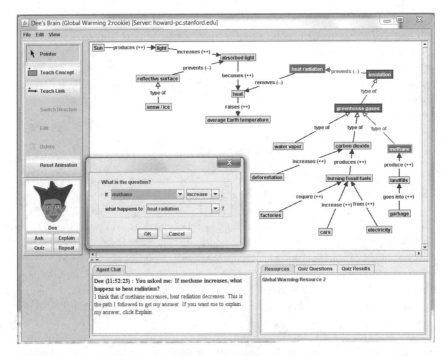

Figure 3.3   Screenshot of the Betty's Brain interface.

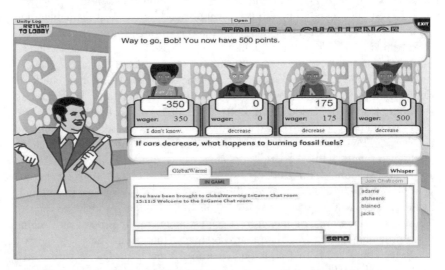

Figure 3.4   Screenshot of the Triple-A Game Show.

about global warming. In the TA condition, students worked with their TAs to structure what they had learned from various in-class activities and homework. In another condition, students learned the same material, but worked with a commercial concept mapping program called Inspiration. Students took three paper and pencil tests spread out over three weeks of curriculum. Over time, the gap between TA and Inspiration students' test scores widened. Compared to the Inspiration condition, TA students were able to reason about longer and longer causal chains as the unit progressed. These results indicate that Betty's Brain is a valuable classroom learning tool that can help students learn causal relations. The study described next focuses on the motivational benefits of the TA.

TAs seem to contain all the motivational tools for moving beyond failure. The agent can provide an ego-protective buffer—it can act as a scapegoat to take some of the blame. For instance, when a question is answered incorrectly in the game show, students can view it as the TA's fault, not their own. Yet students may still feel responsible for their agent's knowledge. After all, they did program its brain. The TA also provides a specific actionable path for fixing the failure. Correct the links in the agent's map and its performance will improve. Because these motivational elements are built into the TA system, it seems plausible to assume that the TA could help students move beyond failure. A protocol study examining student motivation in the context of the TA offers evidence for this assertion.

CAN A TEACHABLE AGENT HELP STUDENTS MOVE BEYOND FAILURE?

In this study, twenty-four 5th grade students were pulled from class for individual think-aloud sessions, while they worked with Betty's Brain (Chase et al., 2009). All students used nearly identical versions of the software that contained an on-screen computerized character. However, one group of students (the TA group) believed they were learning on behalf of their digital pupils while a second group (the Self group) believed they were learning for themselves. Students provided think-alouds while they worked, which were analyzed for evidence of affect and attributions for failure. Persistence times were collected and it was noted whether students chose to revise their agent's (or their own) knowledge following feedback. If the agent provides students with the motivational tools to move beyond failure, then greater persistence and choice of revision are expected from the TA students. Also, TA students' protocol data should reveal a significant percentage of failure attributions ascribed to the agent so that not all the blame falls on the student. However, TA students should accept personal responsibility for moving beyond the failure by ascribing some of the blame for failure to themselves and by taking specific actions to remedy the situation. Self students, on the other hand, should persist less and ascribe relatively more of the blame for failure to themselves.

Figure 3.5 shows an overview of the study and highlights differences between conditions. Each hour-long session was comprised of three phases: Study, Play, and Revise. During the Study phase, students read a passage about fever mechanisms then built concept maps to organize their knowledge on the topic. All students were familiar with concept mapping and had experience constructing maps in class as graphic organizers. However, the TA group was told that the purpose of building the map was to teach their agent, while for the Self group, the object of the concept mapping activity was to learn (for themselves).

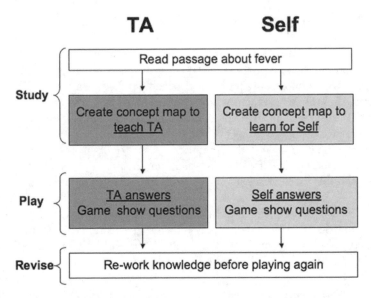

Figure 3.5   Outline of the TA study.

After students built their maps they moved on to the Play phase where they played one round of the game show alone. In the TA group, the agents answered the host's questions based on the maps, while in the Self group, the students themselves answered the questions by selecting answers from a drop-down menu. Game show questions were selected for their difficulty, ensuring that no student (or agent) would answer all questions correctly. As such, the game provided several opportunities for success and failure.

Students' think-aloud protocols during game show play revealed that TA students were much more likely to acknowledge failure than Self students. After getting a question wrong in the game show, TA students made far more statements of negative affect ("I'm sorry Diokiki" or "Uhgh!! Why does he keep answering large increase!?!"). They also made more attributions of blame for the failure ("I didn't know this one" or "He got it wrong") whereas the Self students rarely mentioned failure. Thus, TA students paid greater attention to failures by expressing negative affect and making attributions.

An examination of how the TA students apportioned blame for failure revealed an even spread of attributions across the student and the TA. On average 28% of attributions were made towards the TA ("He got it wrong"), 32% were directed to the self ("I didn't know this one"), and 40% were ascribed to some combination of both ("I, err . . . he didn't know this one"). In contrast, Self students, who did not have the luxury of an agent scapegoat to take the fall for them, made 100% of the attributions to themselves. Thus, the TA seemed to act as an ego-protective buffer by allowing another outlet for blame. However, not all of the blame fell to the TA; students did take some responsibility for the failure by making just as many self-attributions.

Furthermore, TA students acted on this sense of responsibility to their agents by choosing to revise their understanding. After receiving feedback in the game show, all students went on to the Revise phase where they were given the option of reworking their knowledge in preparation for a second, harder round of the game. During revision, students were allowed to review the passage, view and edit the concept map, or look over the game show feedback. A full 100% of the TA students chose to revise after the game show compared to only 64% of the Self students.

On the other hand, TA students' drive for revision is not surprising, given that the TA's performance is dependent on the maps. But this aspect of teaching a TA is an important part of moving beyond failure. For persistence to seem fruitful, there must be clear actionable paths or possible approaches for improvement. For the TA students, it is obvious how to increase the TA's knowledge—fix the links in its brain. For the Self students, it may not be so obvious how they can increase their own knowledge, especially for young children who do not have well-developed metacognitive skills. It is notable that 36% of Self students did not choose to revise at all; they did not even see the value in glancing at the reading again. Of the Self students who did choose to revise, they spent a mere 2.5 minutes doing so, compared to the TA students' average of 8.6 minutes. Perhaps by having the means for repairing the failure at their fingertips, TA students were motivated to persist longer at the task.

On the view advanced in this chapter, the following describes my interpretation of how students learning for the sake of a TA persisted longer than students who were learning for themselves. Presenting students with the narrative of teaching an agent provided them with the tools for moving beyond failure. Since the TA was the one performing, not the students themselves, the TA could absorb part of the blame for failure, sparing students' sense of competence. At the same time, students felt responsible to their agents. They owed it to their agents to do better. This spurred them to continue work on the task. However, increasing blind effort without knowing specific actions to take towards improvement can lead to floundering. But TA students had obvious actions for revision and clear paths towards improvement, which made revision seem fruitful. Thus, the three motivational tools for moving beyond failure—an ego-protective buffer, acceptance of responsibility, and actionable paths—were all present in the Teachable Agent environment. Perhaps it is these three elements that ultimately led the TA students to acknowledge failures and attend to those failures by persisting at the task.

In this study, novice students learning with a TA displayed the same motivational behaviors as experts working on a task in their domain. Relative to Self students, TA students persisted longer, were more likely to revise, and made more failure attributions to external causes. Moreover, the TA enabled students to make progress in the task using specific strategies (i.e., editing the map). I propose that the agent provides students with the same set of motivational tools that experts have built up over many years of experience. However, the motivational tools of the agents are born of different mechanisms. The agents use social motivators—another social being is there to take the blame and incite responsibility. The software provides the latter part—specific, well-structured ways to improve. For experts, the ability to move beyond failure may stem from a strong sense of self-efficacy, a well-developed personal interest, and domain-specific knowledge and skills. The students in this study did not have any of these qualities. Yet despite their lack of built-in motivational advantages, they were able to persist in the face of failure, with the support of the agent technology.

Nevertheless, getting students to persist in the face of failure is not always fruitful. For instance, perseverance on the same failing strategy is not a productive way to move towards success. This next study aimed to ascertain whether the failure-tackling environment created by the TA would lead to productive persistence that would enhance learning. From an interventionist standpoint, it was also important to know whether the TA's motivational tools would prove effective in a classroom setting.

DO THE MOTIVATIONAL TOOLS IN THE TA SYSTEM ENHANCE LEARNING?

In this study, 8th grade students were learning about how the body generates a fever (Chase et al., 2009). Sixty-two students from four different classes participated in the experiment; intact classes were randomly assigned to condition. The conditions were the same as in the prior study; either students were learning on behalf of their agents or learning for themselves. TA students were told: "Today you are going to teach your agent about how the body generates a fever." They were instructed to "teach" their agents by creating a concept map that would represent the "agent's brain." In contrast, the Self group was told: "Today you are going to learn about how the body generates a fever" by building concept maps, which was a fairly typical learning activity for these students. All classes were taught by the experimenters. Both groups used similar versions of the Betty software.

Students used Betty in the classroom over two days of instruction. Compared to the prior study, students had far more options in regulating their own learning. For the most part, students could choose how to spend their time in the system. They could read the resources, edit the map, take quizzes, query the map, play the game show, or use the chat tool whenever they wanted. Students tended to bounce back and forth between these activities. Every student action within the system was logged on the server, leaving a record of student behaviors and time spent using various Betty features.

Students in the TA group chose to spend more of their time on learning activities; about 50% of their time in the system was spent taking quizzes, asking questions, editing the map, and reading. In contrast, the Self group spent most of their time playing the game show and chatting; only 20% of their time was spent on learning activities. Looking at reading times alone, the TA group spent significantly more time reading ($M_{TA} = 13.4$ mins, $M_{Self} = 8.4$ mins), which is particularly impressive given the presence of other, more interactive attractors

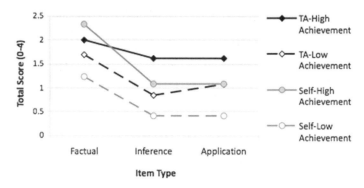

Figure 3.6   Post-test scores broken down by item type, achievement level, and condition. The low-achieving TA students performed similarly to the high-achieving Self students on inference and application questions.

Source: Adapted from Chase, Chin, Oppezzo, & Schwartz (2009).

in their environment. These results demonstrate that TA students persisted longer at Betty's learning activities.

Moreover, on a paper-and-pencil post-test of factual, integration, and application problems, the TA group significantly outperformed the Self group on the harder questions—the inference and application problems. In Figure 3.6, the groups are split into high and low achievers based on prior science grades, demonstrating that the TA was particularly effective for low-achieving students. In fact, on harder questions, the low-achieving TA students performed at the same level as the high-achieving Self students.

This second study confirms some of the findings of the prior study, that learning on behalf of a TA inspired persistence at learning-relevant activities, which surely contained some failure along the way. Moreover, this persistence seemed to provide significant learning gains, especially for low achievers. This makes sense since low achievers experience frequent failure and the motivational tools of the TA help students recover from mistakes. Moreover, the study provided initial evidence that the TA could work as an intervention in real-life classroom settings.

CONCLUSION

During their 10,000 hours of deliberate practice en route to mastery, experts have learned to cope with frequent experiences of failure. They have also managed to persevere through those failures, learning along the way. I examined experts as models of undying motivation, in an effort to design instructional interventions that would motivate students to get through difficult learning tasks where failure is likely.

A study with experts found suggestive evidence that they employ a suite of motivational tools while experiencing failure—an ego-protective buffer, acceptance of responsibility, and an actionable path for moving forward. However, experts' motivational skills are domain-specific; they do not display these three motivational mechanisms when working on a task outside of their domain. This domain-specificity makes sense, given that experts' extensive knowledge in their area provides them with content-specific methods for moving beyond failure. Moreover, their self-efficacy and personal interest are domain-specific as well.

A viable classroom intervention for encouraging novices to adopt expert-like motivation is the Teachable Agent. A protocol study suggested that the Teachable Agent encourages novice children to use the same set of motivational devices that experts employ following failure. A classroom study demonstrated that teaching an agent leads to substantial learning gains, presumably through motivational means. The learning benefits of the TA are particularly robust for low-achieving students, who stand to gain the most from the failure-coping mechanisms of the TA.

I argue that three motivational tools promote persistence in the face of failure. However, definitive support for this claim requires further evidence. Studies that relate the presence or absence of each of these three tools to persistence outcomes would provide more direct evidence for the tools' existence. For instance, in a study designed to test the ego-protective buffer, the agent could spontaneously generate attributions after failure. In one condition the agent might say, "Oops. I got that one wrong," attributing blame to the agent, while in another condition, the agent could say, "Oops. You got that one wrong," attributing blame to the student. One could imagine similar studies that manipulate the responsibility and actionable path tools. Moreover, studies that systematically add or remove one or more of the tools could determine whether all three tools must be used in combination or whether each works in isolation.

The proposed suite of motivational tools is comprised of both motivational and cognitive components. The motivational literature could benefit from a comprehensive exploration of the relationship between motivation and cognition, as it relates to learning. Specific domain-related knowledge and skills could have a strong impact on motivation. For instance, perhaps experts' knowledge of their domain enabled them to make external attributions. It takes a skilled eye to accurately assess the difficulty of a problem or to assess how external conditions precisely affect performance. When doing the math problem, some of the English experts naïvely assumed they were unsuccessful because they "didn't know the equation," thereby making internal attributions. Math experts, on the other hand, had the skill and knowledge to ascertain that no simple equation could be plugged in to the problem, rather, it would take some serious thinking and mulling over to generate the requisite proof. Given these circumstances, it makes sense that many math experts made external attributions to the conditions under which they were asked to perform, claiming they did not have enough time or access to external resources. This kind of interaction between knowledge and ego-protective mechanisms would be interesting to explore further. An important goal for future educational research should be to understand how motivation and cognition interact in the context of learning.

Another interesting question for further study is whether novices could learn, over time, to employ these motivational tools on their own, without needing an external support like the agent technology. There is some evidence that external social supports, such as encouraging parents and competent teachers, are often present during the initial stages of expertise development (Barron, 2006; Sloboda & Howe, 1991; Sosniak, 1985), but, eventually, experts are able to generate the motivational means for moving beyond failure by themselves. Many motivational theories address the phenomenon of how external motivators become internalized (Hidi & Renninger, 2006; Ryan & Deci, 2000) but not from the perspective of failure. Future research might examine whether students who have learned with the TA go on to self-generate the same suite of motivational tools when facing failure on learning tasks presented outside the TA environment.

In closing, I would like to share a brief story about my late father, Bill Chase, an eminent researcher in the field of expertise. My mother used to call him stubborn, but I believe his obstinacy was a testament to his unfailing persistence in the face of failure. For instance, one summer he ran 20 different variations on a single experiment until he finally got the materials just right, because he truly wanted to know the answer to his experimental question. I do not have evidence of the motivational tools that supported my father's dogged persistence, but I do know that his perseverance helped him to become an expert in expertise, making intellectual innovations that have changed the field of cognitive psychology. And so I hope my father can serve as an example to us all—an example of how tireless perseverance in the face of failure can lead one to develop expertise, make new discoveries, and leave a lasting impact on a field.

REFERENCES

Anderson, C.A., & Jennings, D.L. (1980). When experiences of failure promote expectations of success: The impact of attributing failure to ineffective strategies. *Journal of Personality, 48*(3), 393–407.

Bandura, A. (1997). *Self-efficacy: The exercise of control.* New York: W.H. Freeman.

Barron, B. (2006). Interest and self-sustained learning as catalysts of development: A learning ecology perspective. *Human Development, 49*, 193–224.

Bédard, J., & Chi, M. T. H. (1992). Expertise. *Current Directions in Psychological Science, 1*(4), 135–139.

Bereiter, C., & Scardamalia, M. (1992). *Surpassing ourselves: An inquiry into the nature and implications of expertise.* Chicago: Open Court.

Biswas, G., Leelawong, K., Schwartz, D. L., Vye, N., & TAG-V (2005). Learning by teaching: A new agent paradigm for educational software. *Applied Artificial Intelligence, 19*, 363–392.

Boekaerts, M. (1997). Self-regulated learning: A new concept embraced by researchers, policy makers, educators, teachers, and students. *Learning and Instruction, 7*(2), 161–186.

Chase, C. C., Chin, D. B., Oppezzo, M. A., & Schwartz, D. L. (2009). Teachable Agents and the Protégé Effect: Increasing the effort towards learning. *Journal of Science Education and Technology, 18*(4), 334–352.

Chase, W. G., & Simon, H. A. (1973). The mind's eye in chess. In W. G. Chase (Ed.), *Visual information processing* (pp. 215–281). New York: Academic Press.

Chin, D. B., Dohmen, I. M., Cheng, B. H., Oppezzo, M. A., Chase, C. C., & Schwartz, D. L. (2010). Preparing students for future learning with Teachable Agents. *Educational Technology Research and Development, 58*(6), 649–669.

Deci, E. L., & Ryan, R. M. (1985). *Intrinsic motivation and self-determination in human behavior.* New York: Plenum Press.

De Jong, T., & Van Joolingen, W. R. (1998). Scientific discovery learning with computer simulations of conceptual domains. *Review of Educational Research, 68*(2), 179–201.

Dewey, J. ([1933] 1998). Analysis of reflective thinking. In L. A. Hickman, & T. M. Alexander (Eds.), *The essential Dewey, Volume 2: Ethics, logic, psychology* (pp. 137–144). Bloomington: Indiana University Press.

Dunbar, K. (1999). How scientists build models: In vivo science as a window on the scientific mind. In L. Magnani, N. Nersessian, & P. Thagard (Eds.), *Model-based reasoning in scientific discovery* (pp. 89–98). New York: Plenum Publishers.

Dweck, C. S. (1975). The role of expectations and attributions in the alleviation of learned helplessness. *Journal of Personality and Social Psychology, 31*(4), 674–685.

Ericsson, K. A. (2002). Attaining excellence through deliberate practice: Insights from the study of expert performance. In M. Ferrari (Ed.), *The pursuit of excellence through education* (pp. 21–55). Mahwah, NJ: Lawrence Erlbaum Associates.

Ericsson, K. A., & Charness, N. (1994). Expert performance: Its structure and acquisition. *American Psychologist, 49*, 725–747.

Ericsson, K. A., Krampe, R. T., & Clemens, T-R. (1993). The role of deliberate practices in the acquisition of expert performance. *Psychological Review, 3*, 363–406.

Ericsson, K. A., & Lehmann, A. C. (1996). Expert and exceptional performance: Evidence of maximal adaptation to task constraints. *Annual Review of Psychology, 47*, 273–305.

Ertmer, P. A., & Newby, T. J. (1996). The expert learner: Strategic, self-regulated, and reflective. *Instructional Science, 24*(1), 1–24.

Hidi, S. & Renninger, K. A. (2006). The four-phase model of interest development. *Educational Psychologist, 41*(2), 111–127.

Kitsantas, A. & Zimmerman, B.J. (2002). Comparing self-regulatory processes among novice, non-expert, and expert volleyball players: A microanalytic study. *Journal of Applied Sport Psychology, 14*, 91–105.

Koedinger, K. (2001). Cognitive tutors as modeling tools and instructional models. In K. D. Forbus, & P. J. Feltovich (Eds.), *Smart machines in education* (pp. 145–167). Cambridge, MA: MIT Press.

Peterson, C., Maier, S. F., & Seligman, M. E. (1993). *Learned helplessness: A theory for the age of personal control.* New York: Oxford University Press.

Pintrich, P. R., & De Groot, E. V. (1990). Motivational and self-regulated learning components of classroom academic performance. *Journal of Educational Psychology, 82*(1), 33–40.

Renninger, K. A., Hidi, S., & Krapp, A. (1992). *The role of interest in learning and development.* Hillsdale, NJ: Lawrence Erlbaum Associates.

Ryan, R. M., & Deci, E. L. (2000). Self-determination theory and the facilitation of intrinsic motivation, social development, and well-being. *American Psychologist, 55*(1), 68–78.

Scardamalia, M., & Bereiter, C. (1987). Knowledge telling and knowledge transforming in written composition. In S. Rosenberg (Ed.), *Advances in applied psycholinguistics, Volume 2: Reading, writing, and language learning* (pp. 142–175). Cambridge: Cambridge University Press.

Schunk, D. H. (1982). Effects of effort attributional feedback on children's perceived self-efficacy and achievement. *Journal of Educational Psychology, 74*, 548–556.

Schwartz, D. L., Blair, K. P., Biswas, G., Leelawong, K., & Davis, J. (2007). Animations of thought: Interactivity in the teachable agents paradigm. In R. Lowe, & W. Schnotz (Eds.), *Learning with animation: Research and implications for design* (pp. 114–140). Cambridge: Cambridge University Press.

Schwartz, D. L., Chase, C., Chin, D. B., Oppezzo, M., Kwong, H., Okita, S., Biswas, G., Roscoe, R. D., Jeong, H., & Wagster, J. D. (2009). Interactive metacognition: Monitoring and regulating a Teachable Agent. In D. J. Hacker, J. Dunlosky, & A. C. Graesser (Eds.), *Handbook of metacognition in education* (pp. 340–358). New York: Taylor & Francis.

Silver, W. S., Mitchell, T. R., & Gist, M. E. (1995). Responses to successful and unsuccessful performance: The moderating effect of self-efficacy on the relationship between performance and attributions. *Organizational Behavior and Human Decision Processes, 62*(3), 286–299.

Sloboda, J. A., & Howe, M. J. A. (1991). Biographical precursors of musical excellence: An interview study. *Psychology of Music, 19*(1), 3–21.

Sosniak, L. A. (1985). Learning to be a concert pianist. In B. S. Bloom (Ed.), *Developing talent in young people* (pp. 19–67). New York: Ballantine.

Stigler, J. W., & Hiebert, J. (1999). *The teaching gap: Best ideas from the world's teachers for improving education in the classroom.* New York: The Free Press.

Weiner, B. (1979). A theory of motivation for some classroom experiences. *Journal of Educational Psychology, 71*(1), 3–25.

Weiner, B. (1985). An attributional theory of achievement motivation and emotion. *Psychological Review, 92*, 548–573.

Wiener, N. (1948). *Cybernetics: Control and communication in the animal and the machine.* Cambridge, MA: MIT Press.

Wine, J. (1971). Test anxiety and direction of attention. *Psychological Bulletin, 76*(2), 92–104.

Winner, E. (2000). The origins and ends of giftedness. *American Psychologist, 55*(1), 159–169.

Zimmerman, B. J. (2002). Becoming a self-regulated learner: An overview. *Theory into Practice, 41*(2), 64–70.

APPENDIX

Math Problem

Taken from the 2006 William Lowell Putnam Mathematical Competition (www.math.harvard.edu/putnam/2006/index.html).

Alice and Bob play a game in which they take turns removing stones from a heap that initially has n stones. The number of stones removed at each turn must be one less than a prime number. The winner is the player who takes the last stone.

Alice plays first. Prove that there are infinitely many n such that Bob has a winning strategy. (For example, if $n = 17$, then Alice might take 6 leaving 11; then Bob might take 1 leaving 10; then Alice can take the remaining stones to win.)

Poem

This poem is taken from *Mistaken Identity* by Bruce Andrews and reprinted with the author's permission (http://www.theeastvillage.com/t11/andrews/p1.htm).

1.

The situation has a situation
Electro-convulsive opinions eat us
Pig brink dollarization, the marriage of money gobble gobble money
Profit margin american cream dream cultures of vultures
A social predicament, the losers are self-preoccupied
Jellyfish FBI – are you a vending machine?
Who fights the free? – at least the exploited ones have a future
Dayglo ethics, corporate global chucksteak
Lose the flag, nightstick imitation value goosing me
Estados Unidos, suck o loaded pistol
Scale model blonde – zoloft, paxil, luvox, celexa
Need money? – it's easy, it's simple
Dot-commie foreskin arrevederci
Hot mark-up johnny on the spectacle
You as the human labor saving device
Culture, please – all very non-missionary
Massive doses of dog tranquilizer – to stop being reeducated
Hostess of the ecosystem
Subpoena the rocket so angsty
Self-catapulting PFC shimmy
Stiletto, spice it up – live & die for the hell of it
Viva las vegans
Future suture stipend stutter
Only your insecurities make you jealous
Nasty simulacra – you jerk, you forgot your pistol
Bunny potlatch – Slam Slam Happens
Integrabby glisses up
You're the cowboys, we're the cattle
And Scrooge McDuck
The non-oligarchical wisecracker irritainment
Listen honey, we call it passive regressive
Dirt at crime scene – cineplex moonshine foxtrot
White Collar Hairnet – Burn-outs for Christ
Culture dead codehead down, pre-rave accessorizing the wick
Wallet had icing
Cops money satan
So contextual it squirted

A spore with a scholarship – to reconcile the pre-ops
Bankroll some more pronouns bail to the chief
Contras got drug cash
Trustees in a world of pleat
The dotted line barks back to restooge our rights
PRISTINA – rub our jobs on it
Red army faction – well done, Society Members
The more reactionary & stupid, the more popular
Guillotine volunteers – delighted
Eat the free-for-all, ephemera on cruise control
Immersicans
We just want it easy
Fat cats & middlemen, too many pills
Money to bork, licky-splitty totalizing enough

4

Approaches to the Study of Life-Span Chess Expertise[1]

NEIL CHARNESS

Florida State University, USA

INTRODUCTION

*I*n preparing this chapter it was helpful to reflect back on my time as a graduate student from 1969–1974 at Carnegie Mellon University, working with Bill Chase from 1970 onward. Those were heady days in the development of the new field of cognitive psychology, with drafts of chapters of Newell and Simon's (1972) book *Human Problem Solving* circulating in the department and a new collaboration on determinants of chess skill developing between Bill Chase and Herb Simon. It was in fact that chess project, coupled with my interest in chess as an avid amateur player, which prompted me to make the fateful decision to shift supervisors and work with Bill. However, it was an accidental finding a few years after leaving CMU, age effects on memory but not on problem solving in bridge players (Charness, 1979), that started me on the path toward a life-span developmental perspective on cognition.

In their classic book, Newell and Simon (1972) noted that development was a dimension to consider when building theories about human information processing,[2] though they chose not to deal with development in that volume. When

1 This research was supported in part by NIA grant 5R01 AG13969.
2 According to Newell and Simon:

> The other source to which we must look for constraints upon human cognition, hence for commonalities across all human problem solvers, is the set of processes by which the contents of the LTM of the human adult are acquired: the processes of development and learning.
>
> (1972, p. 866)

Chase (1978) outlined the goal of understanding elementary information processes, he too was primarily concerned with normative performance rather than individual differences across the life span, though much of his work at the time was being devoted to understanding skill differences. There has been considerable progress in the intervening three decades in understanding the role that development plays in human performance, though not that much in the domain of expertise in chess that Chase and Simon (1973a, 1973b) made famous.

My goal here is to highlight some methodological approaches that seem useful in developing a rich description of life-span development of expertise. To try to provide an organizational structure, I rely mainly on a framework (Figure 4.1), first introduced in Charness, Krampe, and Mayr (1996) that was developed using chess as a "drosophila" (Simon & Chase, 1973), a model cognitive organism. Studies of skill in chess have had a small but significant impact in enriching our understanding of the role of knowledge in child development (e.g., Chi, 1978) and in adulthood and aging (Charness, 1981a; Charness & Krampe, 2008).

Figure 4.1 provides a framework for understanding the factors that may influence expertise, focusing on broad societal factors and individual

A Taxonomy of Skill Factors

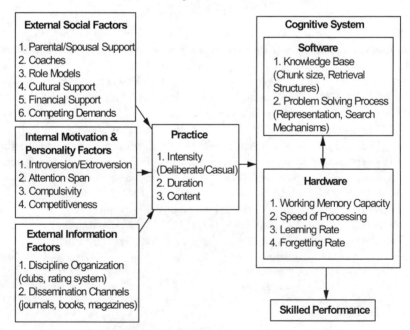

Figure 4.1   Framework for understanding factors influencing the trajectory of skill development.

Source: Charness, Krampe, & Mayr (1996).

motivational factors that influence the way in which people practice to acquire and maintain their skill, particularly what has been termed *deliberate practice* (Ericsson, 2006).

Practice can be seen as the mechanism that tunes the cognitive components that support expert performance. One reason for focusing on practice as the gating mechanism is that it appears to be the primary determinant of expertise (e.g., Charness et al., 2005) from adolescence (DeBruin, Smit, Rikers, & Schmidt, 2008) through old age (Krampe & Ericsson, 1996), although other factors such as engaging in tournament play seem to be important in the domain of chess (Gobet & Campitelli, 2007). See Gobet and Charness (2006) for a review of skill in chess. By taking an expansive view of factors that influence expertise, it becomes obvious that there is a need for multiple methods to identify the roles that these factors may play. I will focus in this chapter on four approaches that have proven particularly useful in investigations that my colleagues, students, and I have made of life-span expertise: (1) analysis of archival data sources; (2) survey studies; (3) experimental studies; and (4) simulation studies. The first two represent a "rough-cut" approach to identifying macro-level trends in expertise development. The latter two represent a "fine-cut" approach to identifying cognitive mechanisms that support skilled performance.

ARCHIVAL DATA ANALYSIS

An important first step in any investigation of a phenomenon, such as expert performance, is measuring the skill in question. One of the difficulties in understanding expertise has been in the definition and measurement of expertise (see the chapters in Ericsson, Charness, Hoffman, & Feltovich, 2006). Fortunately for studies of chess, Arpad Elo, a physicist by training, developed a wonderful tool for measuring skill, his chess rating scale, first introduced in the scientific literature to help understand aspects of the aging process (Elo, 1965, 1978, 1986). This scale has been adopted by the Fédération Internationale des Echecs (FIDE), the international chess body providing ratings to players around the world, and this rating method was also adopted by other organizations (e.g. Scrabble: Tuffiash, Roring, & Ericsson, 2007). Elo (1965) provided us with a longitudinal plot of the relation between a chess grandmaster's age and his rating (all the players in his sample were male), standardizing the plot to the player's performance at age 21, as seen in Figure 4.2.

The function comprises what has been termed an inverted J-shaped curve characteristic of many domains of human endeavor (Simonton, 1988). It was apparently first identified by Quetelet ([1842] 1969) and in the English language literature by Harvey Lehman (1953). Performance typically rises sharply in the teen years, peaks in the decade of the thirties and then starts to decline slowly, though performance at age 65 is no worse than that at age 21 for chess players. There were relatively few individuals in Elo's data set and the competitors represented the very top performers in the field, chess grandmasters. An important question to address, in the context of understanding societal factors

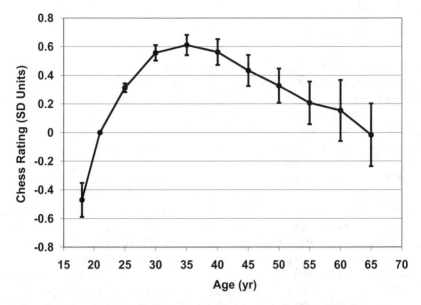

Figure 4.2   Figure derived from Elo's (1965) data set of longitudinal performance of a small set of chess grandmasters, with 95% confidence intervals added by the
author.

such as external information factors, is, how has this function changed across
time, particularly for peak performance?

As many researchers have noted, there are strong secular trends in peak
performance, particularly in the domain of sports where world record times in
the marathon in the 1890s are the required qualifying times for being eligible
to enter marathon competitions today (Charness & Krampe, 2008). This
increase over time in human performance is not restricted to athletic functioning. As Flynn (1987) pointed out, cognitive performance is also showing striking
increases in the last generation, with intelligence test performance advancing
about one standard deviation. In chess, a 2500 rating (roughly equivalent to the
grandmaster level) 30 years ago put you in 12th place in the list of United
States FIDE-rated players. In 2009, one needed a 2579 rating (standard deviation is about 200 rating points) to reach the same rank. But, it is somewhat
problematic to compare chess rating points at different times in history, given
changes in the rating system over time. An example is the rating deflation that
occurred in the United States rating pool following the boom in chess participation in 1972 when Fischer won the world championship. When a large number
of rated players abandoned the sport within a few years, they took their rating
points with them. Rating points are won by defeating players who have them,
so when a player retires, the rating points cannot be won back.

Roring (2008) made good use of the archive of games played in past world
championship matches to provide a direct test of improvement in chess

performance over the past century by analyzing tactical errors in world championship matches from 1886–2000 which he obtained from a commercially available database, Chessbase. He used a strong chess playing program, Fritz 8.0, to analyze every move of every game in these matches to 12 ply in depth in order to determine when a poor choice was made. He defined a tactical error as any move that changed the value of the position by 1.5 pawns (excluding clearly winning positions where the difference was already 3 pawns in value), a criterion first introduced by Chabris and Hearst (2003). Roring found a striking rise in quality when he correlated tactical errors with year of the championship, $r(35) = -.62$, $p < .001$. He ruled out other explanations such as the unregulated nature of early world championships before 1948 when FIDE took responsibility for their organization. Before that time, players who were considered to be the world champion chose their opponents for official matches. If those opponents were chosen because they were weak, the correlation might be expected to diminish if restricted to matches after 1948. However, on that subset of championship matches, the same relation holds: $r(12) = -.67$, $p < .01$. So there is strong evidence that world champions have become stronger tactically over time, making far fewer blunders in match play.

This rise in playing strength is probably partly due to increases in the population of tournament players with concomitant log-linear increase in the performance of the top echelon players (e.g., Charness & Gerchak, 1996; Chabris & Glickman, 2006) coupled with better external information resources (bottom left box of Figure 4.1) available to modern players, such as chess databases, strong computer chess programs, and readily available strong opponents through Internet chess clubs. Given these secular trends, it becomes difficult to determine whether the decline part of the function seen in Figure 4.2 represents a pure negative effect of physiological aging, or some mix of physiological decline, practice decline, or more effective training techniques adopted more readily by younger generations of players against whom mature players must compete.

Nonetheless, having archival data sources to trace tournament performance, rate players, and observe trends over time provides historiometric data (Simonton, 2006), that our theories of human performance need to account for. Given the very short time span for this improvement in human history, changes in the genome (mainly affecting the cognitive apparatus on the right side of Figure 4.1) appear to be an unlikely source for change in performance. Changes in the culture (factors listed on the left side of Figure 4.1) look to be a more promising explanation for these trends.

Lehman (1953, Chapter 18) suggested that the peak for performance in disciplines like physics was changing across successive birth cohorts with peak contributions coming earlier in life. However, given the need to accumulate a great deal of knowledge to perform at high levels, it may also be the case that a fixed and relatively slow learning rate for humans (Simon, 1974) sets some limits on how quickly peak performance can be achieved. Compare, for instance, the amount of formal schooling that people typically acquire to pursue careers in today's economy and the economy of a century ago.

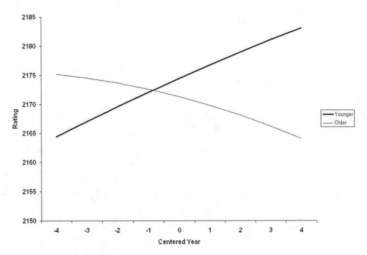

Figure 4.3   Longitudinal growth curve fits for younger (M = 25 years) and older (M = 55 years) chess players.

Source: Reproduced without permission from Roring and Charness (2007).

To investigate the shape of the chess development function, Roring and Charness (2007) explored the issue of peak performance in chess, making use of a new database on world class players tracked by FIDE, aggregated by Howard (2006). By using multi-level modeling techniques it was possible to estimate the shape of the growth and decline curve and to identify peak performance longitudinally for players. Similar to what Elo showed, young players showed a rising curve, whereas older players showed a declining one, as seen in Figure 4.3.

Contrary to finding the peak occurring in the decade of the thirties as shown in Elo (1965), we found that peak performance was centered in the early forties (43 years of age). This finding seems paradoxical in light of earlier and earlier achievement of the grandmaster title by successive cohorts of younger players.[3] It suggests the hypothesis that although there is easier access at this time to chess knowledge, the collection of information is still expanding rapidly. Players must still expend considerable time and effort to master it, leading to both earlier high achievement (ease of access), but a later peak (growing knowledge base).

Because the rating database also contained information about FIDE-rated tournament games it was possible to see whether the tournament influenced performance (though not all tournaments are FIDE-rated). Generally, higher

---

3 In 1958, future world champion Bobby Fischer achieved eligibility for the grandmaster title at age 15 years and 6 months, then the youngest age for doing so in history. Judit Polgar beat this record in 1991 at age 15 years and 5 months. In 2002, Sergey Karjakin became a grandmaster at 12 years, 7 months. At least a dozen players have reached this milestone in the last decade before their 15th birthday (http://en.wikipedia.org/wiki/Chess_prodigy#List_of_youngest_grandmasters).

FIDE-rated tournament activity predicted higher ratings in the overall sample, but did not interact with age or predict linear growth. Because the sample was partitioned a number of ways, based on age and initial chess rating when entering the FIDE pool, we could also assess whether tournament play influenced rating growth differentially for those player subsets. We found that in the initially more able sample, tournament activity positively predicted rating intercept and negatively predicted slope, implying that more active players tend to be higher rated, but also exhibit lower improvements in rating over time.

However, ratings tend to increase and decrease more slowly for higher rated players based on the mathematics of how ratings are calculated in FIDE, where the weighting factor for adjusting ratings is more conservative for higher-rated players, meaning that they gain or lose fewer rating points based on their current performance than do less skilled players. Thus, the higher rated players who are also more active may be improving at a slightly slower rate due to the mathematics of the ratings system. Or, tournament play is somewhat less valuable for those who are highly experienced chess players, a possibility explored below in the survey data to be discussed.

In summary, archival data on chess performance (Elo, 1965; Howard, 2009; Roring & Charness, 2007), suggests that we need to identify mechanisms (e.g., right-hand side of Figure 4.1) that explain the sharp rise in performance in young adulthood, the peak in the early part of the forties and then the slower but steady decline past the forties. I turn now to survey data that can also speak to some of the correlates of skill acquisition, particularly the middle box in Figure 4.1.

SURVEY DATA

Ericsson, Krampe, and Tesch-Römer (1993) were among the first to gather a combination of questionnaire and diary data, using a moderate-sized sample of musicians at an elite school in Berlin to examine the daily activities of individuals who were highly skilled (namely, their admission to the school). They found that "deliberate practice," that is, practice aimed at improving performance (see Ericsson, 2006, and Chapter 9 in this volume for a discussion) occupied a significant component of their daily activities. Many investigations into sports expertise have also shown that the amount of accumulated deliberate practice is a powerful correlate of current skill level (e.g., see chapters in Ericsson, Charness, Hoffman, & Feltovich, 2006). How well does this finding describe chess skill?

Charness, Tuffiash, Krampe, Reingold and Vasyukova (2005) reported on the results from two questionnaire studies of chess players in Europe and North America. Samples were large enough to ensure adequate power to detect relationships that might be weak: n = 239 for the 1993–1995 survey and n = 180 for the 1997–1999 survey. Participants were recruited from Canada, Germany, Russia, and the United States, with surveys translated from English to Russian and German and back-translated to ensure that questions were rendered properly in the foreign languages.

Questions were aimed at obtaining demographic information relevant to the left side of Figure 4.1 including the age when players first learned to play, when they joined a chess club, when they considered that they first started serious play, what type of instruction they received, extent of chess library, and questions about practice activities, tournament play, etc.

A variety of integrity checks were conducted to ensure that the same player did not fill out both questionnaires, as well as to cross-check the reported chess rating against official sources. The main focus was on the practice activities of the players, particularly, hours spent in serious study alone (deliberate practice) year by year. In the second sample there was an integrity check for reports of cumulative deliberate practice by asking the players to fill out the questionnaire in year 1 and in year 5 of the study (the study also involved experimental procedures). For those who remained in the study and who had complete data on both occasions, the test–retest reliability for accumulated practice estimates was $r(52) = .77$, suggesting that self-reports were consistent across occasions.

We used multiple regression procedures to assess which predictors of current chess rating made independent contributions. The results of one set of analyses can be seen in Table 4.1.

For the combined sample, which provides the most power to detect significant effects, the only significant positive predictors were deliberate practice (log total cumulated hours of serious study alone), years of private instruction, current hours/week of serious study alone and current hours/week of tournament play. These predictors accounted for about 33% of total variance in chess ratings.

TABLE 4.1   Predictors of Chess Rating for Two Samples and Combined

Current Rating	Sample 1 (n = 206)		Sample 2 (n = 169)		Combined (n = 375)	
Chess activity predictor variables	B (S.E.)	Beta	B (S.E.)	Beta	B (S.E.)	Beta
Constant	1037 (137)		1198 (141)		1145 (98.6)	
Total log hrs. serious study	185 (44.3)	.33*	198 (42.2)	.38*	195 (30.6)	.36*
Total log hrs. tournament play	83.9 (49.0)	.12	4.1 (38.6)	.00	32.7 (30.8)	.05
Total yrs. private instruction	20.8 (5.4)	.27*	5.5 (3.2)	.11	9.4 (2.8)	.15*
Total yrs. group instruction	−4.2 (4.2)	−.06	10.4 (4.8)	.14	4.3 (3.0)	.06
Current hrs./wk. serious study	6.6 (3.4)	.12	5.2 (3.3)	.11	6.3 (2.4)	.12*
Current hrs./wk. tournament play	16.0 (8.0)	.11	25.6 (13.5)	.12	20.3 (6.8)	.13*
Model summary	$R^2 = .41$ (adj. $R^2 = .39$) $F(6,199) = 23.06$ Std Error of estimate = 223		$R^2 = .31$ (adj. $R^2 = .28$) $F(6,162) = 12.16$ Std Error of estimate = 213		$R^2 = .34$ (adj. $R^2 = .33$) $F(6,368) = 32.13$ Std Error of estimate = 222	

Note: Significant predictors (Beta values) are shown with asterisks.

Source: (Charness et al., 2005).

To attempt to eliminate age as a significant (negative) factor for older players in the samples, we also estimated similar regression equations for a player's self-reported peak rating. In that regression log cumulative serious study alone was the only significant factor, accounting for about 37% of the variance in peak chess ratings. Not every questionnaire study about practice has replicated these findings. For instance, Gobet and Campitelli (2007) showed in their Argentinian sample that cumulative hours of tournament play were the strongest independent predictor of current chess rating. To the extent that their sample had younger players, this finding is consistent with one analysis from Charness et al. (2005) which found that for players with an age less than 40 years tournament play was the second strongest independent predictor of current rating, but only serious study alone was a significant predictor for those over the age of 40.

We also plotted the first ten years of cumulative serious study alone (to eliminate the potential confound of current age varying across the sample) for players in different current rating strata to examine how rating grew with deliberate practice. The results can be seen in Figure 4.4.

The range of rating groups is large, starting from the average rating of a serious chess tournament competitor of about 1700 points to that for those near to grandmaster strength, 2400+points. What Figure 4.4 illustrates is that players more or less started from the same point in year 1 but began to diverge by the second year for the strongest players and diverged by about year 4 for all the other skill levels, with the exception that those in the 2000–2199 group mirrored

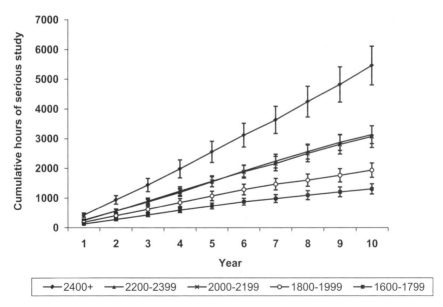

Figure 4.4   Growth in hours of deliberate practice by current chess rating category group (1600–1799 through 2400+) over the first 10 years of serious chess playing.

Source: Derived from Charness et al. (2005).

those in the 2200–2399 group. The latter finding is a bit of a puzzle and warrants replication. It suggests that there is something different about future experts (2000–2199) and masters (2200–2399) in terms of the type of deliberate practice that they engage in, or that those who eventually become master level players are somehow benefiting more from their chess experience. Recall, though, that we asked players about hours of practice, not the specific contents of practice. But, the overwhelming message is that the road to mastery is a long and difficult one in terms of the time investment associated with increasing levels of skill.

The likely reason why cumulative serious study alone is a more powerful predictor of skill level than cumulative tournament play is that study alone is more favorable to learning than what can be gleaned during real-time performance over the board, at least for experienced players. A tournament environment is probably not that conducive to knowledge acquisition given the stress associated with this performance venue. However, the finding that younger but not older players show a significant association with accumulated hours of tournament play suggests that coping with tournament pressure is a necessary precursor to high level skill. Skills such as time management (use of the chess clock), endurance (players typically spend about 4 hours on a game), and coping with the emotions that arise during a game are best honed under tournament conditions.

In summary, questionnaire studies are a valuable adjunct to archival analysis of performance. They provide more detail about the factors that underlie expertise. Here they identified deliberate practice as a potentially critical determinant of skill acquisition. Such investigations can rule out other factors (such as initial age when learning to play, at least in these two samples) that might be construed as indicators of innate abilities, much as the original Chase and Simon (1973a, 1973b) work ruled out innate memory factors using the 5-second perception and recall tasks with structured and random boards. It should be mentioned that there are studies suggesting that general abilities of the sort measured on psychometric tests can differentiate between chess and non-chess samples as well as account for skill within a chess sample (e.g., Grabner, Stern, & Neubauer, 2007). However, such ability factors account for very little of the variance in chess ratings, at least in comparison to a predictor such as deliberate practice. Whereas survey studies can both rule out and rule in factors associated with skill, they cannot provide causal inferences about expertise because they measure associations only. So, I next turn to a sample experimental study that can provide more information about cognitive mechanisms supporting high level performance across the life span.

EXPERIMENTAL STUDIES

Cause and effect relations are best inferred from experiments. However, research on individual difference factors such as skill and age is not truly experimental, but rather quasi-experimental. Neither age nor skill are manipulated in studies, the former because we do not (yet) have access to a time machine, and the latter because it is very expensive to try to train people to high levels of skill in longitudinal studies, given the observations from survey research that the time course might be in the thousands of hours for a knowledge-rich domain such as chess. Of course, some of the most famous work on acquisition of memory skill and mental calculation skill did follow a few individuals over an extended time frame of tens–hundreds of hours (e.g., Ericsson, Chase, & Faloon, 1980; Staszewski, 1988). Nonetheless, even with longitudinal research, causal inferences are risky, given problems with attrition of participants.

What experimental studies can do is to clarify the mechanisms underlying individual differences in skill and in age (the right side of Figure 4.1). For instance, Jastrzembski, Charness and Vasyukova (2006) examined how age and skill jointly contributed to a relatively simple perceptual judgment: whether a King was in check by a piece on a quarter chessboard, or whether a King could be placed in check by a piece. An example of the task can be seen in Figure 4.5.

In the partial chessboard diagram in Figure 4.5, the Rook and the King are not in a check relationship (the Rook cannot capture the King if White is on move). However the two pieces share a more distant relationship, namely that the Rook could threaten to capture the King if it were to make a move to the end square of

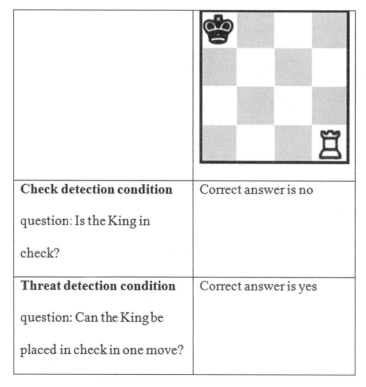

Check detection condition question: Is the King in check?	Correct answer is no
Threat detection condition question: Can the King be placed in check in one move?	Correct answer is yes

Figure 4.5   Chess diagram illustrating a negative (non-)check relationship that is also a positive threat relationship.

either the row or the column on which it sits. Hence, the same diagram would yield two different responses (no/yes) depending on the question posed. The first condition, check detection, queries for a relatively straightforward perceptual judgment that depends on knowing the rules of chess with respect to chess piece movement. The second condition, threat detection, might require a less skilled player to imagine potential movements of the Rook that might put the King in check, through a movement in the mind's eye (Chase & Simon, 1973a; Church & Church, 1983). This judgment task assesses the player's ability to anticipate threats one move in the future from the current board position. A highly skilled player might have stored templates (e.g., Gobet & Simon, 1996) that code potential threats as direct perceptual judgments in the same way that check detection is directly perceived. The evidence for this would be that, for skilled players, threat detection judgments might be about as rapid as check detection judgments.

This predicted finding was basically what was observed in the study, as seen in the top half of Figure 4.6. In this experiment three groups of players, novices (M rating < 1200), intermediates (M rating = 1816), and experts (M rating = 2377), were asked to make yes/no judgments as rapidly as possible for a variety of different potential checking pieces where the King's position varied between the top left and right corners of the quarter chessboard. The significant interaction between skill and experimental condition, Figure 4.6 bottom, revealed that experts showed a non-significant 66 ms difference between check and threat detection speed. The intermediates showed a significant 240 ms difference and the novices showed a large 560 ms difference in response time. Because of the relatively low power to detect check–threat differences in the expert group, it is possible that the difference is a significant one in the population. Nonetheless, it is very obvious that the size of the difference between threat and check decisions diminishes strikingly as skill level increases.

This study also examined age differences with half of the players in each skill group being selected to be younger (M = 33 yr) and half selected to be older (M = 61 yr). Of interest was the skill by age interaction as seen in Figure 4.6 bottom. The results speak to the issue of how the aging process degrades chess performance as seen in the longitudinal declines for chess ratings past the age of 43. Aside from the expected finding of slowing in information process rate with increased age (e.g., Salthouse, 1996; Jastrzembski & Charness, 2007), there is differential slowing by condition. On average, across skill levels (the triple interaction was not significant), players are slower to make a threat judgment than a check judgment, but this difference widens with increasing age. That is, the aging process widens the response time gap for this basic perceptual judgment. Search processes for choosing a move in chess are thought to depend in part on detecting chess chunks and templates (e.g., Gobet & Simon, 1996) that are at least partly bound by inter-piece relationships such as attack (e.g., Chase & Simon, 1973a). Hence, aging can be expected to interfere with chunking and search processes by slowing them down and limiting the ability of older players to fully activate knowledge that they have available, but perhaps render it inaccessible in time pressure.

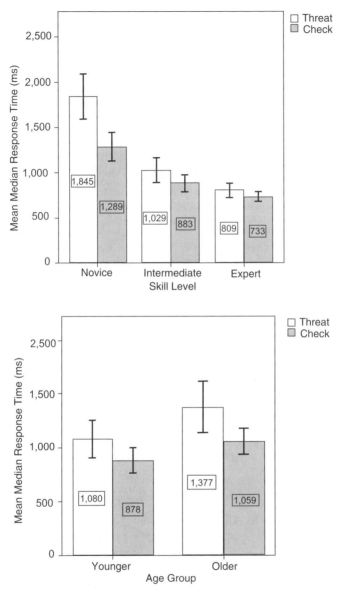

Figure 4.6 Top half shows a significant interaction between skill level and threat versus check condition. Bottom half shows a significant interaction of threat versus check by age group. Error bars show the 95% confidence intervals for the means.

One of my graduate students, Roy Roring found exactly that result when he re-analyzed rapid problem solving performance in the van der Maas and Wagenmakers (2005) psychometric test for chess skill, the Amsterdam Chess

Test (ACT). One component was speeded choice of move, when players were shown unfamiliar chess positions and were given up to 30 seconds to solve the problem. By comparison, in tournament play, players have, on average, about 3 minutes to choose a move. Roring re-analyzed the data to look at age effects, finding that the correlation between age and quality of move selection was r (255) = $-.33$, $p <.001$ in the data set. When he restricted analysis to those players age 30+, he found a stronger relationship: r (103) = $-.37$, $p <.001$. Further, a regression of age and rating on move selection for the age 30+ sample shows that although rating accounts for a large portion of move selection variance on its own, adjusted R^2 = .59, F (1, 95) = 139.973, $p < .001$, age accounts for additional variance above and beyond rating: R^2 change = .041, F (1, 94) = 10.668, $p < .01$. That is, age is making an independent negative contribution to solution accuracy, beyond the expected positive relationship between skill and accuracy.

In summary, experimental studies can advance our understanding of the cognitive mechanisms that support skilled chess problem solving. The threat detection task reviewed here showed that part of a player's skill can be attributed to being able to rapidly perceive critical chess relationships, such as threats, much more quickly than their less skilled opponent. This finding fits with the early work by Chase and Simon (1973a, 1973b) which identified the critical role that chess chunks play. However, the age-related loss in information processing speed that was identified also suggests a mechanism underlying the peak seen in the decade of the forties and subsequent decline. Although it apparently takes decades for players to build up the large knowledge base (chunks, templates) that is required to play at a high level, at some point players can no longer access this knowledge efficiently. They may become one step slower than their younger opponents and when rushed, may not be able to come up with good moves that they could find, if given a longer deadline.

Other work using eye tracking techniques has shown that within the first few fixations strong players are scanning the chess board differently and extracting relevant relationships much more quickly, with some relations extracted in parallel, compared to serially, for weaker players (Charness, Reingold, Pomplun, & Stampe, 2001; Reingold, Charness, Pomplun, & Stampe, 2001; Reingold, Charness, Schultetus, & Stampe, 2001). Thus, experimental studies have gone a good distance toward identifying plausible mechanisms that support chess skill across the life span. I next turn to simulation studies as another important link in the chain of evidence that provides theoretical accounts of expertise.

SIMULATION STUDIES

Formal models, whether implemented in mathematics, or as computer programs, have played a very important role in theory development in many sciences, but are relatively new to psychology. Newell and Simon (1972) argued effectively for the value of computer simulation as a means of understanding cognition pointing to simulation programs such as logic theorist for theorem proving, the General Problem Solver, and EPAM (e.g., for simulating serial position effects in memory: Feigenbaum & Simon, 1962). Other larger-scale cognitive architecture simulations soon followed, such as ACT (Anderson, 1983), Parallel Distributed Processing (neural net) modeling (McClelland & Rumelhart, 1988), and Soar (Newell, 1990). The main advantage to such modeling is that it forces the theorist to be explicit in specifying mechanisms for cognition in comparison to the less explicit way that general verbal models operate. It also affords a firm test of the sufficiency of the assumptions. A simulation model should generate results by doing the same task that the human performs and can be tested against human data to determine adequacy of fit. In an important sense, simulation is also experimental work and it is probably one of the most fruitful approaches for filling in the values for factors listed on the right side of Figure 4.1.

However, relatively few of the models mentioned above have been directed toward understanding individual differences such as those attributable to skill or age. In the field of cognitive aging, one of the initial calls to make use of simulation modeling to develop more rigorous theories was via a neural net model (Salthouse, 1988). Mireles and Charness (2002) aimed to examine potential trade-offs between knowledge, which improves performance, and aging, which tends to degrade performance (e.g., Verhaeghen & Salthouse, 1997), particularly on tasks with onerous working memory requirements such as serial recall of a long list of items.

We chose to explore age-skill trade-offs using a chess opening recall task. The aim was to examine then current theories about mechanisms involved in cognitive aging and at the same time, to model the protective effects of knowledge. We used neural net models, in particular, a recurrent neural net (using 72 input units, 32 hidden units, 32 context units, and 72 output units) because the task involved serial recall of opening moves. There are other important tools for simulating chess recall at the symbolic level of information processing, particularly Gobet's CHREST model (Gobet, 1993; see also Chapter 6 in this volume). However, the neural net model was better suited to testing phenomena that we expected to be at the "sub-symbolic" level of description (Newell, 1990).

We developed two types of nets, one with "low" and one with "high" knowledge of chess openings. An opening sequence consisted of 40 ply: 20 moves for each side (White/Black) taken from standard published chess openings. The high knowledge base (HKB) networks were trained on 13 variants of opening sequences, with 10 of each of the variants, for a total of 130 opening sequences, each trained 600 times. Thus the HKB network experienced 130 x 600 x 40 = 3,120,000 moves. The low knowledge base (LKB) networks were trained on only one of the 13 variants of the opening sequences used for the HKB networks, 10 sequences, each trained 300 times. Thus the LKB network experienced 10 x 300 x 40 = 120,000 moves. By comparison, in a single tournament game, an intermediate-skilled human player might generate and consider as few as 500 moves in total (Charness, 1981b). Following training, the nets were tested on new opening sequences after being "aged" in a variety of ways intended to simulate both normal and pathological processes.

To simulate age effects we tested a large number of mechanisms proposed to account for cognitive aging such as general slowing, inhibition failure, faster forgetting rates, reduced signal to noise theory, etc. One prior simulation model of aging by Li and colleagues (e.g., Li, Lindenberger, & Frensch, 2000) modeled aging by reducing the gain parameter in the model. Reducing gain reduces the responsiveness of a unit to incoming signals, basically slowing down the rate of processing in the network. Perceptual, cognitive, and psychomotor slowing are some of the ubiquitous characteristics of cognitive aging (e.g., Jastrzembski & Charness, 2007) and general slowing has been shown to account for much of the age-related variance in higher-level tasks such as reasoning (Salthouse, 1996). As Figure 4.7 illustrates, we observed the expected reduction in recall accuracy as gain was reduced during the testing phase for both high and low knowledge networks, and observed a significant interaction with low knowledge networks less able to cope with gain reduction than high knowledge ones. Knowledge protected performance against the loss in transmission efficiency represented by reducing gain.

Such results are consonant with current views about "reserve capacity" in the brain (e.g., Stern, 2006). There is evidence that being engaged in challenging work and leisure activities can be protective for cognitive functioning in the latter half of the life span. The hypothesis is that brains that have built up richly connected knowledge networks can better withstand biological processes that degrade those

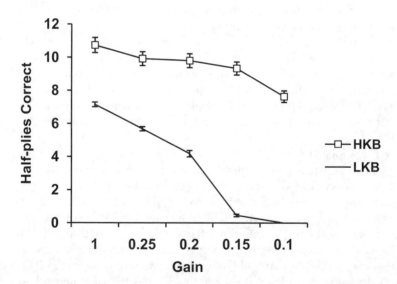

Figure 4.7   Degree of slowing (gain parameter) by knowledge (HKB, LKB) interaction for serial recall of chess opening moves in recurrent neural nets. HKB represents the high knowledge base network and LKB represents the low knowledge base network. Bars represent plus and minus one standard error.

Source: Generated from data in Mireles and Charness (2002).

connections, whether through normal aging or through disease processes such as Alzheimer's disease. The argument is that a disease process like Alzheimer's must degrade the brain to a greater extent for a protected individual to fall below the threshold for a diagnosis. The unfortunate flip side of this prediction is that cognitive decline will then move more swiftly for those with initially richer cognitive networks who are diagnosed with the disease, and this is generally observed.

Simulating normal aging processes by degrading the weights for connections (simulating other normative neural degradation processes) also yielded the same form of interaction, with high knowledge networks more resistant to such interference. So too did manipulations meant to simulate degrading the signal to noise ratio in the network, either by decreasing signal strength (external noise) by adding noise to the presented patterns (sequences of chess moves), or by adding noise to existing connection weights in the network (internal noise). We found a similar interaction when we added noise to the network after a new sequence of moves was initially presented (trained) but before it was tested, simulating either faster decay in a memory trace or greater interference from a retention interval between presentation and test.

Next, we simulated pathological damage by lesioning the network in two ways: directly lesioning hidden units, similar to an ischemic incident such as a stroke, or by severing connections in the hidden layer probabilistically, more like the type of damage that Alzheimer's disease might make to the cortex through formation of neural plaques and neuro-fibrillary tangles. Here we obtained a somewhat unexpected result, seen in Figure 4.8, namely that the high knowledge networks were more severely impaired than the low knowledge ones.

Given that most human adult brains would not survive lesioning on the scale that we attempted (killing off up to a third of all units or connections between units), it is somewhat risky to interpret the findings. Nonetheless, the findings do fit with one of the reserve capacity notions that brains with more enriched connections show faster decline once some degradation threshold is reached. Another way to conceptualize this finding is with the homily: "the bigger they are, the harder they fall". People performing at very high levels show decline in performance sooner for minor brain changes than do those who are less skilled to begin with. Think of the case of aging major league players versus aging recreational athletes and how soon declining performance would become obvious.

In summary, simulation studies provided evidence (interactions) consistent with many of the mechanisms proposed to account for cognitive aging as well as for the protective effects of knowledge in the face of age-related degradation in the brain. Simulation also generated the non-intuitive result that those with higher knowledge levels to begin with became more impaired than those with lower knowledge when pathological processes degraded neural networks. A main weakness of this particular simulation approach using neural nets is how to constrain the parameters that are allowed to change, given that there are quite a few that can be tweaked to produce almost any desired effect. The symbolic level simulation models, such as ACT-R or CHREST try to fix parameter values from study to study so that there are very few free parameters to tweak

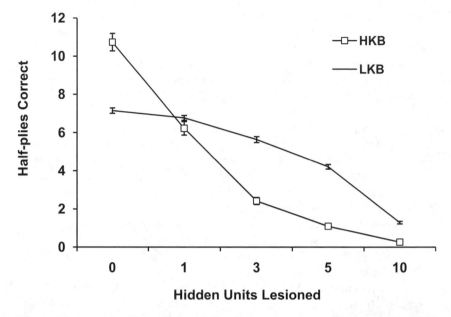

Figure 4.8   Degree of lesion by knowledge (HKB, LKB) interaction for serial recall of chess opening moves in recurrent neural nets. HKB represents the high knowledge base network and LKB represents the low knowledge base network. Bars represent plus and minus one standard error.

Source: Generated from data in Mireles and Charness (2002).

and realistic values for processes such as working memory capacity or speed of a perceptual comparison are maintained across studies. However, it is pretty clear that to simulate individual differences such as those associated with age or skill, some of those values will have to be tuned. The key is to tune them in ways that fit with experimental data, particularly parameters derived in meta-analytic studies (e.g., Jastrzembski & Charness, 2007).

CONCLUSION

I have provided some evidence that these four routes to knowledge about life-span expertise can yield useful data for theory building. Each approach has strengths and weaknesses. Archival analysis relies on the soundness of the data that have been preserved by institutions responsible for its collection. These institutions may not be as concerned with data integrity as are scientists. A strength of archival data analysis is that it can provide macro-level information about societal trends, such as changes in achievement levels by individuals over time. Further, as advances are made in methodology and technology, data can be mined anew to uncover new features. A good example is the multi-level modeling by Roring and Charness (2007) that took advantage of computer programs that run that form of statistical analysis as well as their use of a database assembled from publicly available records that were finally fully computerized by Howard (2006). Similarly, advances in computer technology have produced chess programs that are better than the best humans at discovering tactical errors. Roring (2008) used one of those programs to re-analyze the games played a century ago to find the blunders that world champion competitors made.

Questionnaire studies are relatively easy to assemble and administer to large groups and can identify individual difference variables that may correlate with skill. However, unless conducted with representative samples, the data they provide may be skewed by factors involved in self-selecting into the study. For instance, those who practice and do not advance in skill may not appear in the data set for cross-sectional investigations and there may be selective attrition related to the variable of interest in longitudinal survey studies. Still, survey studies can help rule in and rule out factors for theory construction. However, both survey studies and analysis of archival data sets provide evidence only about relationships among key variables.

Experimental studies have the virtue of providing causal inferences about the roles of the manipulated variables, assuming that confounding variables can be ruled out over a series of studies. Unfortunately for those interested in individual difference variables such as skill or age, these factors cannot be manipulated so most studies are quasi-experimental with respect to these variables. One is forced to weave a compelling story to account for the data, and the biases we bring to that process (e.g., confirmation bias) may lead us astray.

Finally, simulation studies allow experiments to be conducted that would be impossible to perform in human populations, such as lesioning neural circuitry to discover the effects on low and high knowledge individuals. In a sense, they allow for experimental manipulation of skill and age. Simulations also have the virtue that they provide explicit tests of assumptions embedded in the simulation architecture, allowing strong inference about the sufficiency of the simulation mechanisms. They are prone to some weaknesses, such as the difficulty in constraining parameters in the models so that they do not over fit data.

The outlines for a successful information processing theory about skill in chess were established about 35 years ago by Chase and Simon (1973a, 1973b) with their pioneering experimental (and simulation: Simon & Gilmartin, 1973) work using a small sample of chess players.[4] Their focus was on the normative performance of adults. Since that time researchers have attempted to extend the theory to cover skill development across the life span. To reach that goal of understanding the life course for chess expertise, we will undoubtedly need at least these four methodological approaches.

---

4 Ironically, the three players in some of the classic studies varied in age in a manner that was confounded with their skill level, with the novice being the youngest, the Class A player being next oldest, and the Master being the oldest.

REFERENCES

Anderson, J. R. (1983). *The architecture of cognition*. Cambridge, MA: Harvard University Press.

Chabris, C. vF., & Glickman, M. E. (2006). Sex differences in intellectual performance. *Psychological Science, 17*(12), 1040–1046.

Chabris, C. vF. & Hearst, E. S. (2003). Visualization, pattern recognition, and forward search: Effects of playing speed and sight of the position on grandmaster chess errors. *Cognitive Science, 27*, 637–648.

Charness, N. (1979). Components of skill in bridge. *Canadian Journal of Psychology, 33*, 1–16.

Charness, N. (1981a). Aging and skilled problem solving. *Journal of Experimental Psychology: General, 110*, 21–38.

Charness, N. (1981b). Search in chess: Age and skill differences. *Journal of Experimental Psychology: Human Perception and Performance, 7*, 467–476.

Charness, N., & Gerchak, Y. (1996). Participation rates and maximal performance: A log-linear explanation for group differences, such as Russian and male dominance in chess. *Psychological Science, 7*, 46–51.

Charness, N., & Krampe, R. T. (2008). Expertise and knowledge. In D. F. Alwin, & S. M. Hofer (Eds.), *Handbook on cognitive aging: Interdisciplinary perspectives* (pp. 244–258). Thousand Oaks, CA: Sage.

Charness, N., Krampe, R., & Mayr, U. (1996). The role of practice and coaching in entrepreneurial skill domains: An international comparison of life-span chess skill acquisition. In K. A. Ericsson (Ed.), *The road to excellence: The acquisition of expert performance in the arts and sciences, sports and games* (pp. 51–80). Mahwah, NJ: Lawrence Erlbaum.

Charness, N., Reingold, E. M., Pomplun, M., & Stampe, D. M. (2001). The perceptual aspect of skilled performance in chess: Evidence from eye movements. *Memory and Cognition, 29*, 1146–1152.

Charness, N., Tuffiash, M., Krampe, R., Reingold, E. M., & Vasyukova, E. (2005). The role of deliberate practice in chess expertise. *Applied Cognitive Psychology, 19*, 151–165.

Chase, W. G. (1978). Elementary information processes. In W. K. Estes (Ed.), *Handbook of learning and cognitive processes* (vol. 5, pp. 19–90). Hillsdale, NJ: Lawrence Erlbaum Associates.

Chase, W. G., & Simon, H. A. (1973a). The mind's eye in chess. In W. G. Chase (Ed.), *Visual information processing* (pp. 215–281). New York: Academic Press.

Chase, W. G., & Simon, H. A. (1973b). Perception in chess. *Cognitive Psychology, 4*, 55–81.

Chi, M. T. H. (1978). Knowledge structures and memory development. In R. S. Siegler (Ed.), *Children's thinking: What develops?* (pp. 73–96). Hillsdale, NJ: Lawrence Erlbaum Associates.

Church, R. M., & Church, K. W. (1983). Plans, goals, and search strategies for the selection of a move in chess. In P. W. Frey (Ed.), *Chess skill in man and machine* (2nd ed., pp. 131–156). New York: Springer-Verlag.

De Bruin, A. B. H., Smit, N., Rikers, R. M. J. P., & Schmidt, H. G. (2008). Deliberate practice predicts performance over time in adolescent chess players and drop-outs: A linear mixed models analysis. *British Journal of Psychology, 99*, 473–497.

Elo, A. E. (1965). Age changes in master chess performances. *Journal of Gerontology, 20*, 289–299.

Elo, A. E. (1978). *The rating of chessplayers, past and present*. New York: Arco.

Elo, A. E. (1986). *The rating of chessplayers, past and present* (2nd ed.). New York: Arco.

Ericsson, K. A. (2006). The influence of experience and deliberate practice on the development of superior expert performance. In K. A. Ericsson, N. Charness, P. Feltovich, & R. Hoffman (Eds.), *Cambridge handbook of expertise and expert performance* (pp. 683–704). Cambridge: Cambridge University Press.

Ericsson, K. A., Charness, N., Feltovich, P., & Hoffman, R. (Eds.). (2006). *Cambridge handbook of expertise and expert performance*. Cambridge: Cambridge University Press.

Ericsson, K. A., Chase, W. G., & Faloon, S. (1980). Acquisition of a memory skill. *Science, 208*, 1181–1182.

Ericsson, K. A., Krampe, R. T., & Tesch-Römer, C. (1993). The role of deliberate practice in the acquisition of expert performance. *Psychological Review, 100*, 363–406.

Feigenbaum, E. A., & Simon, H. A. (1962). A theory of the serial position effect. *British Journal of Psychology, 53*, 307–320.

Flynn, J. R. (1987). Massive gains in 14 nations: What IQ tests really measure. *Psychological Bulletin, 101*, 171–191.

Gobet, F. (1993). *Les mémoires d'un joueur d'échecs*. Saint-Paul Fribourg, Suisse: Editions Universitaires Fribourg Suisse.

Gobet, F., & Campitelli, G. (2007). The role of domain-specific practice, handedness, and starting age in chess. *Developmental Psychology, 43*, 159–172.

Gobet, F., & Charness, N. (2006). Expertise in chess. In K. A. Ericsson, N. Charness, P. Feltovich, & R. Hoffman (Eds.), *Cambridge handbook of expertise and expert performance* (pp. 523–538). Cambridge: Cambridge University Press.

Gobet, F., & Simon, H. A. (1996). Templates in chess memory: A mechanism for recalling several boards. *Cognitive Psychology, 31*, 1–40.

Grabner, R. H., Stern, E., & Neubauer, A. C. (2007). Individual differences in chess expertise: A psychometric investigation. *Acta Psychologica, 124*, 398–420.

Howard, R. W. (2006). A complete database of international chess players and chess performance ratings for varied longitudinal studies. *Behavior Research Methods, 38*, 698–703.

Howard, R. W. (2009). Individual differences in expertise development over decades in a complex intellectual domain. *Memory & Cognition, 37*, 194–209.

Jastrzembski, T. S., & Charness, N. (2007). The Model Human Processor and the older adult: Parameter estimation and validation within a mobile phone task. *Journal of Experimental Psychology: Applied, 13*, 224–248.

Jastrzembski, T. S., Charness, N., & Vasyukova, C. (2006). Expertise and age effects on knowledge activation in chess. *Psychology and Aging, 21*, 401–405.

Krampe, R. T., & Ericsson, K. A. (1996). Maintaining excellence: Deliberate practice and elite performance in young and older pianists. *Journal of Experimental Psychology: General, 125*, 331–359.

Lehman, H. C. (1953). *Age and achievement*. Princeton, NJ: Princeton University Press.

Li, S., Lindenberger, U., & Frensch, P. (2000). Unifying cognitive aging: From neuromodulation to representation to cognition. *Neurocomputing: An International Journal, 32–33*, 879–890.

McClelland, J. L., & Rumelhart, D. E. (1988). *Explorations in parallel distributed processing: A handbook of models, programs, and exercises*. Cambridge, MA: MIT Press.

Mireles, D. E., & Charness, N. (2002). Computational explorations of the influence of structured knowledge on age-related cognitive decline. *Psychology and Aging, 17*, 245–259.

Newell, A. (1990). *Unified theories of cognition.* Cambridge, MA: Harvard University Press.

Newell, A., & Simon, H. A. (1972). *Human problem solving.* Englewood Cliffs, NJ: Prentice-Hall.

Quetelet, L. A. J. ([1842] 1969). *A treatise on man and the development of his faculties.* Gainesville, FL: Scholars' Facsimiles and Reprints.

Reingold, E. M., Charness, N., Pomplun, M., & Stampe, D. M. (2001). Visual span in expert chess players: Evidence from eye movements. *Psychological Science,12,* 48–55.

Reingold, E. M., Charness, N., Schultetus, R. S., & Stampe, D. M. (2001). Perceptual automaticity in expert chess players: Parallel encoding of chess relations. *Psychonomic Bulletin and Review, 8,* 504–510.

Roring, R. W. (2008). Reviewing expert chess performance: A production based theory of chess skill. Unpublished doctoral dissertation. Florida State University, Tallahassee, FL.

Roring, R. W., & Charness, N. (2007). A multilevel model analysis of expertise in chess across the lifespan. *Psychology and Aging, 22,* 291–299.

Salthouse, T. A. (1988). Initiating the formalization of theories of cognitive aging. *Psychology and Aging, 3,* 3–16.

Salthouse, T. A. (1996). The processing-speed theory of adult age differences in cognition. *Psychological Review, 103,* 403–428.

Simon, H. A. (1974). How big is a chunk? *Science, 183,* 482–488.

Simon, H. A., & Chase, W. G. (1973). Skill in chess. *American Scientist, 61*(4), 394–403.

Simon, H. A., & Gilmartin, K. (1973). A simulation of memory for chess positions. *Cognitive Psychology, 5,* 29–46.

Simonton, D. K. (1988). Age and outstanding achievement: What do we know after a century of research? *Psychological Bulletin, 104,* 251–267.

Simonton, D. K. (2006). Historiometric methods. In K. A. Ericsson, N. Charness, P. Feltovich, & R. Hoffman (Eds.), *Cambridge handbook of expertise and expert performance* (pp. 319–335). Cambridge: Cambridge University Press.

Staszewski, J. J. (1988). Skilled memory and expert mental calculation. In M. T. H. Chi, R. Glaser, & M. J. Farr (Eds.), *The nature of expertise* (pp. 71–128). Hillsdale, NJ: Lawrence Erlbaum Associates.

Stern, Y. (2006). Cognitive reserve and Alzheimer's disease. *Alzheimer's Disease and Associated Disorders, 20,* S69–S74.

Tuffiash, M., Roring, R. W., & Ericsson, K. A. (2007). Expert performance in SCRABBLE: Implications for the study of the structure and acquisition of complex skills. *Journal of Experimental Psychology: Applied, 13,* 124–134.

van der Maas, H. L. J., & Wagenmakers, E-J. (2005). A psychometric analysis of chess expertise. *American Journal of Psychology, 118,* 29–60.

Verhaeghen, P., & Salthouse, T. A. (1997). Meta-analyses of age-cognition relations in adulthood: Estimates of linear and non-linear age effects and structural models. *Psychological Bulletin, 122,* 231–249.

5

Commentary
How Do People Become Experts?[1]

ROBERT S. SIEGLER

Carnegie Mellon University, USA

INTRODUCTION

*B*ill Chase played a large role in my decision to join the Carnegie Mellon faculty. When I interviewed at Carnegie Mellon in 1974, the Carnegie Cognition Symposium volume, *Visual Information Processing* (Chase, 1973) had just been published. To help me choose between Carnegie Mellon and two other universities that were located in areas with noticeably better weather, I asked the department chairs from the three universities to recommend a few publications that reflected the kind of work valued in their departments. Lee Gregg, CMU's department chair at the time, sent me a copy of Bill's book, along with a number of other publications by CMU faculty.

The book was a revelation. At a time when the information processing approach was just emerging as a major force, *Visual Information Processing* presented the thinking and research programs of the best of the best: Al Newell, Herb Simon, Mike Posner, Roger Shepard, David Klahr, Marcel Just, Patricia Carpenter, John Bransford, Marcia Johnson, Tom Trabasso, and Bill Chase. Most of these research programs were new to me; all included theories and methods that were to shape my subsequent research. The Chase and Simon chapter had an especially large and immediate impact on my thinking; their use of reproduction tasks to measure encoding was an approach that I soon emulated in my own studies of children's thinking and learning about

1 The research described in this chapter was funded in part by grants R305A080013 and R305H050035 from the Institute of Education Sciences, in addition by support from the Teresa Heinz Chair at Carnegie Mellon University.

balance scales, shadows projection, time, and a variety of other concepts (e.g., Siegler, 1976). The reproduction tasks yielded strong evidence that developmental differences in thinking and learning are often due to differences in encoding of relevant information. For example, results of the encoding task indicated that young children encoded weight but not distance from the fulcrum on the balance scale task, size of objects but not distance of the objects from the light source and screen on the shadows projection task, and so on. These findings seemed counterintuitive at the time but similar findings have since been obtained on a variety of other tasks (e.g., Alibali, 1999; Calin-Jageman & Ratner, 2005; McNeill & Alibali, 2004).

More generally, Bill Chase's research set the standard for using whatever methods made sense for pursuing a problem, even when those methods were unprecedented. Whether the method involved reproducing organized and disorganized configurations of chess pieces, interviewing expert taxi cab drivers to determine the spatial maps that guided them through the convoluted street system that is among the true mysteries of Pittsburgh, or training a randomly chosen undergraduate for more than 100 sessions in acquiring expertise in recall of long chains of arbitrary digits, Bill pursued issues wherever they took him.

One area where the issues took Bill was learning. Although most of his work focused on people who were already experts, his later work, most notably Ericsson, Chase, and Faloon (1980) and Chase and Ericsson (1982), focused on the learning processes through which people become experts. These investigations, together with the studies of developmental differences in expertise that his wife, Micki Chi, conducted, provided a strong foundation for the work presented in this session, as well as for the broader area of expertise.

Bill's research set a precedent for an outstanding characteristic of research on acquisition of expertise—the use of innovative methods in natural contexts. That approach has taken the investigators who presented papers in this session to such atypical contexts as proving grounds on army bases, chess clubs, and video games in which students try to improve the brains of teachable agents. In the remainder of this commentary, I'll describe how willingness to pursue the research question wherever it took them, both physically and intellectually, has allowed these researchers to advance understanding of how people become experts.

Neil Charness provided a useful organizational framework for illustrating classes of issues likely to affect acquisition of expertise. This organizational framework is useful not only for illustrating the organization of different aspects of Charness' research but for thinking about issues regarding expertise more generally. As shown in Figure 5.1, one or more papers in the present session of this symposium addressed each class of issues identified within Charness' taxonomy. The distribution reflects a nice balance in research in this area between analyses of the roles of internal information processing and external environmental factors, between analyses of the influence of hardware and software characteristics of the information processing system, and between social and technological aspects of the environments in which expertise is acquired.

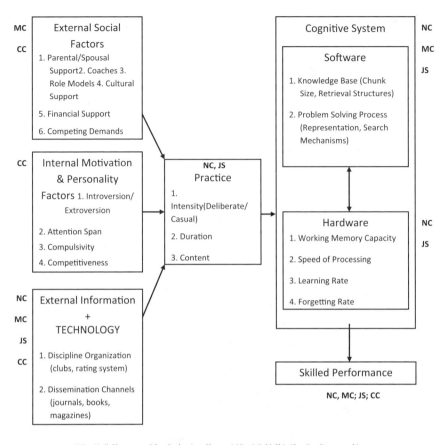

NC = Neil Charness; CC = Catherine Chase; MC = Micki Chi; JS = Jim Staszewski

Figure 5.1   Charness' organizational framework of factors influencing the acquisition of expertise.

ACQUIRING CHESS EXPERTISE

As Figure 5.1 indicates, Charness' research focuses on the roles of external information and technology, practice, and knowledge and processing constraints in chess expertise. As with investigations of expertise in general, this research required deep understanding of the particulars of the domain, both the task and the social milieu in which experts are immersed. A special advantage of research on chess expertise is the existence of a rating system that provides a generally accepted, quantitative measure of individual players' proficiency. Another advantage of studying expertise in this domain is the existence of clubs that bring together experts in sufficient number to study. A third advantage of this domain is the existence of dissemination channels such as chess magazines that allow access to other experts through advertisements. Of course, these potential advantages would only become actual advantages for a researcher who was immersed in the domain sufficiently to utilize them. Fortunately, Charness is such a researcher.

In addition to utilizing this domain-specific information about chess to obtain access to experts and to design revealing measures of chess expertise, Charness applied lessons of research on problem solving, learning, and life-span development that transcend any particular domain. These domain-general lessons concern qualitative and quantitative variables that influence the benefits of practice; effects of the knowledge base on learning; roles of chunking, retrieval structures, and memory search on speed and capacity of processing; and how all of these factors change over the lifespan. Bringing together these varied factors has helped Charness and other researchers such as Gobet move beyond Chase and Simon's pioneering research to make chess the flagship task for research on the acquisition of expertise.

Charness' research has yielded a number of striking findings. Among the ones that I found particularly interesting were that cumulative hours of solitary study is the best predictor of skill level; that high levels of initial knowledge provide some protection from the declines in performance that begin around age 45; and that with age, the speed of detecting threats declines. Hours of solitary study seem to be a proxy for the intensity of engagement in using practice to enhance performance; the goals people pursue during practice, and the intensity of their focus on those goals, appear to be at least as important as the sheer amount of practice in determining who becomes an expert and at what level. Charness' use of computer simulations to illustrate plausible mechanistic bases of protective, adverse, and neutral effects of knowledge on the rate of decline in performance with age is especially illuminating.

One question raised by this research program is whether these findings are unique to chess, general across all areas of expertise, or common to some but not all areas. Consider the protective effects of expertise in reducing rates of decline with age. The same effects were evident in Schulz, Musa, Staszewski, and Siegler's (1994) analysis of major league baseball players. The athletes examined in that study were all of exceptional skill, relative to the general population and even to major league baseball players in general. Only players whose career in the major leagues lasted for at least 10 years were included.

Even within this elite sample, however, the performance of those at the top of the distribution deteriorated from peak performance more slowly with age than the performance of those at lower levels. In particular, baseball players in the top third of the sample, many of whom were Hall of Fame players, remained close to their peak for more years than those in the bottom third. This parallel in protective effects of expertise is particularly interesting, because the factors needed to become a great baseball player so clearly differ from those needed to become a great chess player. The type of life-span developmental work on expertise that Charness has pioneered needs to be extended to a greater range of domains to determine the generality of the negative relation between peak performance and rate of deterioration from that performance, as well as the mechanisms that underlie such protective effects. My personal guess is that the outsized benefits that often accompany the benefits lead elite experts to continue the intense, focused practice needed to gain (and maintain) expertise for a longer period, but that's just a hypothesis at this point.

ACQUIRING LANDMINE DETECTION EXPERTISE

Jim Staszewski's analysis of landmine detection expertise give new meaning to the phrase "high stakes testing." His paradigm of identifying experts, obtaining detailed protocols of their behavior while engaging in the target activity, discussing analyses with the experts to revise and improve the initial analyses, generating computer simulations of the experts' strategies, and using the computer simulations to train novices in the expert strategies is exemplary. It has become the official approach of the U.S. Army to training landmine detection skills and provides a model of how theoretical research can lead to highly successful applications that would never have occurred without the prior theory.

Like Charness' studies, Staszewski's research focuses on external information and technology, notably the landmine detection devices used by the army; the role of focused practice in determining the amount of learning; the software of expert strategies that novices are taught; and the hardware characteristics of spatial pattern recognition. The research differs in that Staszewski constructs a detailed model of how expert performance is generated and uses it in instruction. The relative complexity of the two domains is likely relevant to this difference. Landmine detection is a more circumscribed skill, and one that's easier to learn to a fairly high rate of expertise; it is hard to imagine anyone acquiring high levels of chess skill after five days of training, no matter how inspired the training.

Staszewski's investigations illustrate a pervasive characteristic of research in applied settings that is not widely recognized—the continuous changes in the domain being studied. One large change that occurred during the course of the landmine detection research was substitution of the PSS-14 device for the previously used PSS-12. This change required identification of a new expert and assessment of the cognitive processes that underlie expertise with that device. It turned out that the model of expertise with the earlier technology transferred quite well to the updated technology, but this could easily have been different. Another type of change came when training of the recruits on the PSS-14 needed to be truncated, due to bad weather and changes in the soldiers' deployment. This is very different than research in laboratory settings, where researchers control the experimental situation and can use the same paradigm as long as they want.

Changing conditions are inherent to research in applied settings. Research in educational areas such as math and reading is influenced by the textbooks that students use. Schools frequently change from one textbook series to another, and even if they keep the same series, new editions of the same textbook series sometimes include substantial changes. In addition, teaching approaches change over time, as do the conditions under which teaching occurs, for example, class size. Similarly, research in behavioral medicine is influenced by changes in medications, surgical techniques, diagnostic procedures, and training of medical personnel, and research on financial decision-making is influenced by changes over historical time in experiences with stock and housing markets, the balance between fear and greed among investors, and the political climate. Assessing such moving targets takes cognitive psychologists outside of our comfort zone, namely studies under tightly controlled conditions. However, much, probably most, of what people do is far removed from traditional laboratory tasks. Staszewski's research illustrates that laboratory research on processes such as spatial pattern recognition and prototype formation is useful for understanding real-world tasks, such as landmine detection, but his research, like Charness', also demonstrates that detailed analyses of the particulars of the real-world task are essential for understanding and improving performance in them.

Staszewski's studies demonstrate that directly teaching expert techniques to novices can yield dramatic results. However, it seems unlikely that expert techniques can be taught directly to novices in all domains. For example, directly teaching the slaloming techniques of expert skiers to beginners seems unlikely to produce anything other than bumps, bruises, dislocations, and fractures. This is the reason why intermediate goals are often pursued, for example, teaching snow plowing as a means of stopping on a slope. Establishing principles of when expert techniques can be directly taught to novices and when intermediate goals should first be pursued seems an important direction for future research.

LEARNING FROM OBSERVING EXPERTS

If research on expertise is to have a broad educational impact, we must find ways to extend the benefits to people who neither can interact with the experts directly nor have the benefits of detailed computer simulations that have been translated into instructional programs. Experts are too rare, and their time too precious, for large numbers of people to interact directly with them, and many domains are too varied and complex for the type of detailed analysis that underlay Stazsewski's model of landmine expertise.

Micki Chi's research reported in this volume examines a promising solution to these limits: Record interactions of an expert and a novice who is trying to acquire expertise, and use the tutorial DVDs to provide instruction. Her research demonstrates that observing expert–novice tutoring sessions can produce as great learning as being tutored directly.

Chi reports considerable progress toward the challenging but essential goal of specifying the conditions under which observing such interactions produces substantial learning. The engagement of the observer matters; substantial learning only occurs when learners are intent on learning. Collaborations and discussions of the DVDs' content between pairs of students produce greater learning than that which occurs when individuals watch the DVDs alone. The quality of the tutee in the DVD also matters; greater learning occurs when tutees ask good questions than when their questions are less apt. Interestingly, when watching the DVDs, learners appear to attend primarily to the tutee rather than to the tutor and to discuss the tutee's comments more than those of the tutor. As Chi suggests, this might be due to the tutee's comments fitting within the zone of proximal development of the observers, so that there is more overlap between the tutee's and observers' representations of the domain and therefore greater understanding of the beliefs that underlie the tutee's questions and comments. This seems a very plausible hypothesis.

Chi also notes that observers learn a great deal from watching and discussing the tutee's errors. This finding is consistent with previous results on how analyzing errors can promote learning. For example, asking students to explain why errors that have been labeled as errors are incorrect, as well as asking the students to explain why correct answers are correct, lead to greater learning than just requesting explanations of the correct answers. This effect has been shown in both mathematical and scientific domains (Siegler, 2002; Siegler & Chen, 2008). A likely reason is that telling students that a wrong answer is wrong, and even explaining or having the student explain why a correct answer is correct, does not necessarily undercut the logic that led to the incorrect answer. As long as that logic remains unchallenged, it can lead to the incorrect answer winning competitions with the correct answer, much as planting grass seed or pulling crabgrass will not extirpate the crabgrass unless the roots are extirpated. Encouraging collaborating students who are observing expert tutorials to discuss why wrong answers are wrong, as well as why right answers are right, may lead to even greater learning than already produced by Chi's procedures.

ACQUIRING EXPERT MOTIVATION

Despite Thomas Edison's famous observation that "Genius is 1% inspiration and 99% perspiration," despite well-known findings that acquiring expertise in a domain demands roughly 10,000 hours of practice (Chase & Simon, 1973), and despite findings that above and beyond the sheer amount of practice, becoming an expert requires intense, focused practice (Ericsson, 2002), we know very little about the experiences and processes that lead to such extraordinary dedication. As Cathy Chase notes in her highly original and important chapter, no one becomes an expert without failing. However, such failures can either be debilitating or invigorating. The two basic questions addressed in this chapter are how experts are able to maintain high levels of motivation in the face of failure, and whether placing novices in the position of experts can lead to greater perseverance among them as well.

Chase proposes that a suite of motivational tools —an ego-protective buffer, acceptance of responsibility, and a path to success—helps experts persevere in the face of failure. The ego-protective buffer allows learners to partially blame external factors, such as problem difficulty, luck, or unreasonable evaluators for failures. At the same time, acceptance of responsibility leads learners to focus on what they can do to avoid future failures, regardless of the influence of external factors. Finally, avoiding future failures requires more than the desire to do so; it also requires planning actionable paths toward improvement and implementation of the plans. Experts have been found to use all three of these techniques in ways that increase their likelihood of success in the future.

In addition to identifying these three motivational techniques of experts, Chase demonstrates that application of the motivational tools is specific to the domain in which experts are experts. As would be expected, experts persevere for a longer time in their domain of expertise, and are more likely to revisit unsolved tasks in it, than in domains in which they are not expert. Less intuitively, experts are more likely to blame task difficulty for their failure to solve problems in their area of expertise. Chase advances the explanation that experts know that they have high ability in their area of expertise, so they are less likely to blame failures on their own lack of ability. This explanation seems reasonable, though it probably depends on the framing of the problem and on the comparison group. If the graduate students in math and English studied by Chase were informed that 80% of other graduate students in their discipline had solved the problem, many might blame their failures on their own relative lack of ability.

As the tendency of experts to return to unsolved problems in their area of expertise demonstrates, people do not become experts without high intrinsic motivation in that domain. Chase's ideas about this phenomenon are reminiscent of ideas proposed in Gordon Allport's (1937) classic article on the functional autonomy of motives. Allport suggested that the reasons why people begin to participate in an area are often not the same ones that lead them to persevere in it. Parental hopes and dreams, and social and economic rewards, might lead a student to attend medical school, but fascination with the workings of the circulatory system would likely be needed for the person to become a great cardiologist. Similarly, many children initially read to please their parents and teachers and to act like older children, but lifelong love of reading depends on reading becoming its own reward. As these examples suggest, initial engagement in an area often reflects external incentives, but the long-term commitment required to become an expert generally requires intrinsic motivation. Dedicating the 10,000 or more hours needed to become an expert, and engaging in focused practice that requires repeatedly facing and surmounting one's limits, seem extraordinarily unlikely without love of the activity.

This analysis raises the question of how we can help children gain the motivation to engage in desirable activities sufficiently for the activities to become their own reward. Chase uses research on expert motivation to construct conditions that achieve this goal, in particular, software involving a teachable agent known as "Betty's Brain." The fact that the teachable agent, rather than the student, is being asked to solve a problem provides an ego-protective buffer to mitigate the impact of failing to solve problems. At the same time, the teachable agent leads students to have a sense of responsibility for failures as well as successes, because the student creates the agent's knowledge base, and thus in large part is responsible for its success or failure. Chase's qualitative observations of students' emotional connection to their teachable agents and their guilt when the agent fails, indicate that the students do develop a sense of responsibility for the agent. Balancing this sense of responsibility is the agent's inferential reasoning engine, which utilizes the information that the students provide, and thus can shoulder some of the blame for failures. Finally, when the agent fails to solve a problem, the software provides hints concerning how to do so, thus helping students generate actionable paths for generating correct problem solving. Previous research shows that Betty's Brain produces superior learning outcomes relative to other concept mapping software packages that can teach the same content (Schwartz et al., 2009).

Chase's focus in this chapter is on motivational aspects of learning through Teachable Agents. Students who helped the Teachable Agent learn were more likely than students who learned for themselves to acknowledge failure explicitly. In particular, students who used the Betty's Brain software distributed responsibility for failures roughly equally to themselves and to the teachable agent, whereas students who learned on their own had no one to blame other than themselves. Students who worked with the Teachable Agent also were considerably more likely to review the passage and the feedback they received than were students learning for themselves, and when given the chance to engage in irrelevant activities, spent less time doing so than students who were learning for themselves. Even when the control group also produced concept maps, students working with the Teachable Agents learned more than students who were learning for themselves. The difference was especially great for low-achieving students.

Chase closes her chapter with an anecdote about her father's expertise in psychological experimentation. Another anecdote that she told at the symposium conveys additional information of interest. She noted that her father was an expert runner. However, his expertise lay not in generating superior running times—he was a respectable but not great runner—but in getting the most out of himself. He utilized many strategies for becoming the best runner that he could be—setting difficult but attainable goals for the number of miles to run each year, exceeding previous personal bests, mixing in sprints with his usual jogging pace, and so on. In this sense, Bill's love of running, as well as his love of research, allowed him to become an expert in both areas. How fitting that his daughter is advancing understanding of expert motivation and the conditions that promote it!

REFERENCES

Alibali, M. W. (1999). How children change their minds: Strategy change can be gradual or abrupt. *Developmental Psychology, 35*, 127–145.

Allport, G. W. (1937). The functional autonomy of motives. *The American Journal of Psychology, 50*, 141–156.

Calin-Jageman, R. J., & Ratner, H. H. (2005). The role of encoding the self-explanation effect. *Cognition and Instruction, 23*, 523–543.

Chase, W. G. (1973). *Visual information processing*. New York: Academic Press.

Chase, W. G., & Ericsson, K. A. (1982). Skill and working memory. *The Psychology of Learning and Motivation, 16*, 1–58.

Chase, W. G., & Simon, H. A. (1973). Perception in chess. *Cognitive Psychology, 4*, 55–81.

Ericsson, K. A. (2002). Attaining excellence through deliberate practice: Insights from the study of expert performance. In M. Ferrari (Ed.), *The pursuit of excellence in education* (pp. 21–55). Hillsdale, NJ: Erlbaum.

Ericsson, K. A., Chase, W. G., & Faloon, S. (1980). Acquisition of a memory skill. *Science, 208*, 1181–1182.

McNeill, N. M., & Alibali, M. W. (2004). You'll see what you mean: Students encode equations based on their knowledge of arithmetic. *Cognitive Science, 28*, 451–466.

Schulz, R., Musa, D., Staszewski, J., & Siegler, R. S. (1994). The relation between age and baseball performance: Implications for development. *Psychology and Aging, 9*, 274–286.

Schwartz, D. L., Sears, D., & Bransford, J. D. (2009). Efficiency and innovation in transfer. In J. Mestre (Ed.), *Transfer of learning from a modern multidisciplinary perspective* (pp. 1–51). Greenwood, CT: Information Age Publishing.

Siegler, R. S. (1976). Three aspects of cognitive development. *Cognitive Psychology, 8*, 481–520.

Siegler, R. S. (2002). Microgenetic studies of self-explanations. In N. Granott, & J. Parziale (Eds.), *Microdevelopment: Transition processes in development and learning* (pp. 31–58). New York: Cambridge University Press.

Siegler, R. S., & Chen, Z. (2008). Differentiation and integration: Guiding principles for analyzing cognitive change. *Developmental Science, 11*, 433–448.

6

Chunks and Templates in Semantic Long-Term Memory

The Importance of Specialization

FERNAND GOBET

Brunel University, Uxbridge, UK

INTRODUCTION

*T*his chapter will weave together several themes, focusing on two main questions. The first question relates to the use of single-subject designs in psychology. The second question pertains to the role of specialization of knowledge in experts. Specifically, it assesses the relative contributions of perceptual knowledge (e.g., chunks) and general knowledge (heuristics and strategies) to expertise. These two questions are interrelated because probing experts' knowledge is a complex and intensive task, and single-subject designs are one possible avenue to address this issue.

My views on the two questions are deeply influenced by Bill Chase: he carried out highly influential studies investigating experts' knowledge with the use of single-subject designs, and the main theoretical tools used in this chapter directly derive from the research he carried out on chess with Herb Simon.

The chapter starts with a discussion of multiple-subject designs, which clearly dominate research in psychology. After having discussed some limits of such designs, I will consider single-subject designs and highlight their advantages. Strengths and weaknesses of experimental designs resonate with many important questions in the field of cognitive modeling, which can be summarized as "What are the best experimental designs for developing cognitive models?" I will build on a proposal offered by Gobet and Ritter (2000), arguing that single-subject design can provide a powerful tool for developing and testing computational models in psychology. This will be illustrated by an experiment on chess memory, in which a single participant was trained to memorize as many briefly presented chess positions as possible. The analysis will focus on the effect of specialization in this master's performance, and computer simulations will show that the CHREST architecture captures important aspects of the empirical results. I will then show that these results generalize well, by discussing an experiment in which the question of specialization in chess was studied with a larger sample, with respect to both memory and problem solving. The final section of this chapter will draw implications of this research for the question of specialization in science, taking as an example the recent Research Assessment Exercise (RAE) in England. The general conclusion is that experts' ability to successfully transfer their skills beyond their domain of specialization is more limited than generally thought.

MULTIPLE-SUBJECT AND SINGLE-SUBJECT DESIGNS

Research in cognitive psychology (and psychology in general) is predominantly done with groups of participants. This is also the case in expertise research, where it is difficult to publish results if the study does not contain several participants for each skill level. There is no doubt that this methodology is powerful, in particular due to the increased availability of sophisticated statistical techniques to make sense of the data. However, this methodology does have its undeniable limitations, as was noted by Newell and Simon (1972) and Siegler (1987), among others. For example, data averaged across people may not accurately reflect the behavior of any one person; participants may use different strategies and have different knowledge bases; and, with respect to the study of expertise, experts specialize in different sub-fields.

Single-subject designs are an obvious way to get around these limitations. Such a methodology has long history in psychology. Ebbinghaus ([1885] 1964) single-handedly created the field of memory research by using himself as his only subject. In their seminal study on telegraphers learning Morse, Bryan and Harter (1899) studied only two participants—but in great detail. Although De Groot's (1965) classic work on chess included a number of players as participants, his analyses were in large part qualitative and non-statistical—essentially a sequence of single-subject studies. And, of course, some of Bill Chase's most influential studies were carried out with very few participants. His study on chess skill (Chase & Simon, 1973a, 1973b; Simon & Chase, 1973) had only three participants (and only one per skill level). Similarly, his research on the digit span task focused on the study of a single participant, SF (Chase & Ericsson, 1981, 1982; Ericsson, Chase, & Faloon, 1980).

Indeed, Chase and Ericsson's work on the digit-span task offers a beautiful example of the power of single-subject designs. During the 25 months that the study lasted, they carried out a number of experiments aimed at testing the theory they had developed based on verbal protocols. One experiment tested the hypothesis that digit sequences difficult to encode as running times should lead to a poor performance. Another tested the converse hypothesis that digit sequences that fit SF's coding strategy should lead to an increase in performance. A third experiment tested the reliability of SF's encoding rules; this was done by presenting again a sequence that had been used one month earlier. Further experiments investigated the role of short-term memory in SF's behavior, by using several rehearsal-suppression techniques. Other experiments measured SF's short-term memory capacity and the possibility of transfer of his digit memory skills to other material. Together with the practice experiment itself and the associated verbal protocols, these experiments produced a uniquely rich set of data.

As illustrated by the research on digit span, single-subject designs offer a number of advantages and nice features (Campitelli, Gobet, Williams, & Parker, 2007; Gobet & Ritter, 2000). There is a rapid interplay between data collection and theory building, and, depending on the research design, new hypotheses can be tested quickly. Specifically, the results of one session lead to a new hypothesis, which can be tested in the next session. These features make single-subject designs particularly suitable for expertise research, as experimental effects tend to be large in this field of research and can be detected with a very small sample size—including one subject. However, in spite of these features, single-subject designs have a bad reputation in psychology. They have been criticized for lack of generalizability, lack of a control group, carry-over and order effects across tasks, and development of idiosyncratic strategies by the participant, who becomes an expert in participating in an experiment.

What Kind of Data to Use for Developing Cognitive Models?

Most models in cognitive psychology are tested with averaged data. This of course raises the same type of issues as those just discussed: average data may not reflect the behavior of any specific participant, and the fact that participants can have different strategies and knowledge bases is ignored. Most models in cognitive psychology also have multiple free parameters, an obvious weakness as it is often not clear whether the success of a model in simulating the data is due to its mechanisms or rather to its free parameters. One way around this problem, proposed by Newell (1990), is to develop Unified Theories of Cognition (UTCs). Here, a single architecture is to be used to account for as much empirical data as possible. According to Newell (and I agree with him), this allows one to limit the number of free parameters. However, this only addresses part of the problem: if the data to simulate are data averaged over, say, 50 participants, we still do not know whether they represent the actual behavior of any participant, and we still do not know the role played by differential strategy use and different levels of experience and knowledge.

Combining Single-Subject Designs and Cognitive Modeling

Gobet and Ritter (2000) have argued that combining single-subject designs with cognitive modeling combines the best of the two approaches. The idea is to gather a large number of empirical/experimental observations on a single participant (or a few participants analyzed individually), and then to develop a detailed computational model of each participant. The data should be detailed and varied enough—Chase and Ericsson's research on the digit span offers a good example of this—and, ideally, various task domains should be used.

Gobet and Ritter's (2000) methodology is not antagonistic to using group summaries. However, rather than using the observed data (e.g., percentage correct, reaction times, etc.) to compute aggregate statistical parameters such as the mean, they suggest first estimating UTC parameters for each subject individually, and then calculating aggregate values over these parameters. This methodology for estimating aggregate values, which they call "between-subject analysis of parameters," is summarized in Table 6.1. According to Gobet and Ritter, this methodology can provide more robust and theoretically more meaningful estimates than the standard method for aggregating data.

It is important to emphasize that UTC parameters are not limited to numeric values. For example, they can correspond to strategies. Possible strategies can be represented with a probability distribution, and, if one wants a single value, one could select the most common strategy (modal strategy). Siegler's (1987) work on children's addition strategies offers a good example of this approach. Incidentally, this highlights the dangers of averaging across participants, as done traditionally. For example, participants in a given task may use strategies that do not overlap, which makes averaging strategies meaningless. Across different trials with a same task and across several different tasks, participants are likely to show a pattern that clearly identifies their most common strategies.

Among other things, the benefit of this approach is that systematic sources of between-subject variability are illuminated rather than obscured: strategies and knowledge can be systematically studied rather than being ignored as

TABLE 6.1   Two Complementary Ways of Summarizing Data. In the traditional approach (second column), observables are summarized across subjects. In the Individual Data Modeling (IDM) approach (fourth column), theoretical parameters are first estimated for each subject using observables, and only then summarized across subjects

Subjects	Subjects' observables (over tasks)			Estimated UTC parameters
S_1	$o_{11}, o_{12}, o_{13}...o_{1t}$	$\Rightarrow$ IDM	$\Rightarrow$	$p_{11}, p_{12}, p_{13} \cdots p_{1n}$
S_2	$o_{21}, o_{22}, o_{23},....o_{2t}$	$\Rightarrow$ IDM	$\Rightarrow$	$p_{21}, p_{22}, p_{23} \cdots p_{2n}$
–				
–				
–				
S_m	$o_{m1}, o_{m2}, o_{m3},... o_{mt}$	$\Rightarrow$ IDM	$\Rightarrow$	$p_{m1}, p_{m2}, p_{m3} \cdots p_{mn}$
Summary values	$O_1, O_2, O_3... O_t$			$P_1, P_2, P_3, ... P_n$

Source: After Gobet & Ritter (2000).

random variation; learning is not noise but something to model and explain; and, if one is interested in expertise, the effects of specialization of knowledge can be studied. Thus, the "between-subject analysis of parameters" offers a powerful complement to group data analysis.

SPECIALIZATION IN CHESS: A SINGLE-SUBJECT TRAINING EXPERIMENT ON MEMORIZING MULTIPLE CHESS POSITIONS

Theoretical Motivation

The main aim of this experiment was to collect data to help revise Chase and Simon's (1973a) chunking theory. This theory was developed to explain the two key findings of De Groot's (1965) seminal research. First, chess masters can identify potentially good moves rapidly, often after only a few seconds. Second, they have an excellent memory for chess positions, even after a presentation as brief as 5 seconds. Chase and Simon replicated and extended De Groot's memory experiment. Based on an analysis of the latencies between the placements of pieces in a copy and a recall task, they proposed that masters encode information using *chunks*. Chunking had of course been well known in cognitive psychology since Miller's (1956) paper, but while Miller emphasized chunking as a strategic device to recode information in short-term memory (STM), Chase and Simon were interested in how chunks encode information in long-term memory (LTM). In this respect, chunks shared some resemblance to the "knowledge complexes" that De Groot had proposed, although he regarded the latter are more dynamic than the former. Chase and Simon argued that, compared to weaker players, chess masters have both more chunks and larger chunks in LTM. These chunks, whose maximum size was estimated at five or six pieces, encode information such as typical castle formations, pawn chains, common configurations on the first or eighth rank, and typical attacking patterns. Their data suggested that more than half of these chunks were pawn structures, which tend to remain relatively stable during a game.

To explain the roles of imagery and problem-solving in chess, Chase and Simon (1973b) proposed that LTM chunks are associated with processes that make it possible for the patterns to be reconstructed and manipulated as an image in the mind's eye. In addition, the chunks automatically activated by the patterns on the external chessboard trigger potential moves, which will be then further investigated by look-ahead search. What we have here is in effect a production system (Newell & Simon, 1972). It is important to stress that, in this theory, selecting a move involves not only pattern recognition, but also selective search.

This theory did a good job at explaining how the perceptual patterns that players acquire not only help them to memorize positions rapidly but also to find good moves in novel positions. It also provided a plausible explanation as to why it takes a long time—Chase and Simon proposed 10 years—to become a top-level player. With about 8 seconds to create a chunk (Simon, 1969), time is needed to acquire the 50,000 chunks that are necessary to attain expert level. In addition to this, time is also necessary to learn the actions to carry out, given a specific chunk, and to learn to pair chunks with these actions. As noted by Richman, Gobet, Staszewski, and Simon (1996), provision must also be made for relearning and over-learning information in order to compensate for the negative effects of forgetting, and for the fact that opportunity for learning novel information decreases as expert levels increase.

However, the chunking theory had two main weaknesses. First, as was shown shortly after its publication, the theory overestimates the time of encoding information in long-term memory (Charness, 1976; Frey & Adesman, 1976). Second, the theory underestimates the role of high-level knowledge: chunks are supposed to be fairly small (5–6 pieces at most), but evidence from verbal protocols clearly indicates that players use structures that are much larger. In fact, in some cases, the structures they use refer to the entire position (Cooke, Atlas, Lane, & Berger, 1993; De Groot, 1965; De Groot & Gobet, 1996). Although it is not strictly speaking a theoretical weakness, another issue should be mentioned here. Simon and Gilmartin's (1973) computer program, which simulated aspects of the Chase and Simon chunking theory, did not learn chunks autonomously but used chunks pre-selected by the modelers, and was not able to reach the recall performance of master level.

To correct these weaknesses, while still keeping the strengths of chunking theory, together with Herb Simon I proposed what we called the template theory (Gobet & Simon, 1996d). Chunks are still important in the theory, but are also complemented by more powerful memory structures—templates. Templates are schemas, with a core that encodes stable information and slots that encode variable information. They are created with chunks that are recognized often in a given domain. The originality of our proposal was that it assumed that information can be encoded rapidly (250 ms) in the template slots. Templates are also assumed to be linked to useful information, such as possible moves, evaluations, likely plans, and so on.

Another important aspect of templates is that they can be linked to other templates, either as a function of their similarity or a function of the temporal order they would normally occur in a game. For example, a template coding for a class of positions in the Scheveningen variation of the Sicilian defense (a common chess opening)[1] might be linked to typical middle game positions, which in turn can be linked to likely endgame positions. This makes it possible for chess experts to carry out a search at an abstract level, and not only at the move level. Thus, the search would incorporate key positions and the focus would be on broad plans that could take the player from one favorable key position to another. The detail of the exact sequence of moves is left for later analysis.

---

1 In chess, the term "opening" refers to the first moves of the game. Over the years, an extensive body of knowledge—called "opening theory"—has developed about openings, and tens of thousands of books have been devoted to them. The length of theoretical variations varies from just a few ply to 40 or even 50 ply for popular variations that have been extensively analyzed.

Observation of discussions between chess players and perusing of commented games in chess books and magazines offer clear, albeit anecdotal, evidence that chess players carry out this kind of macro-level search. Templates can be seen as a type of retrieval structure, although they differ from the kinds of retrieval structures proposed by Chase and Ericsson (1982) and Ericsson and Kintsch (1995); see Ericsson and Kintsch (2000), Gobet (2000), and Gobet and Simon (1996d) for a discussion. I will have more to say about templates below, when presenting the computer model used for the simulations.

Thus, template theory combines low-level, perceptual memory structures with high-level and more abstract memory structures. The presence of templates explains why chess masters use larger chunks that those proposed by the chunking theory.[2] It also explains why information is stored in LTM more rapidly than proposed by Chase and Simon. An important piece of information supporting both assertions was provided by experiments where players had to memorize not only one position at a time, as in the classic experiments by De Groot (1965) and Chase and Simon (1973a), but several positions presented in rapid sequence. The results obtained by Cooke, Atlas, Lane and Berger (1993) and Gobet and Simon (1996d) clearly established that chess players could encode much more information than what could be stored in seven STM chunks, assuming a maximal size of 5–6 pieces, as Chase and Simon did. This result is reminiscent of the semantic chunks for digit groups that SF and DD were able to encode and recall in the digit-span task (Chase & Ericsson, 1982; Staszewski, 1990).

The aim of the experiment, then, was to probe the limits of expert memory further, using the technique of presenting several chessboards. The methodology of this experiment was inspired by Ericsson and Chase's (1981), but uses chess as a task domain rather than the digit-span task. The task consisted of remembering as many positions as possible, with each position being presented for 8 seconds. (A preliminary report of this experiment was provided in Gobet and Simon, 1996d.)

Method

A single participant P (the author of this chapter) took part in this experiment, which lasted about two years (213 sessions), with some interruptions due to holiday or work commitments. A former chess professional who then trained as a researcher in psychology, P was an International Master. At the time of the experiment, he had an USCF rating of 2396 Elo, which put him among the best

---

2 The reader might wonder why evidence for templates did not show up in the Chase and Simon's experiment. As established by further research using a computer program to present the positions and record the players' placements (Gobet & Simon, 1998), the limited capacity of the hand to hold chess pieces has led to an underestimation of the units encoded. Of particular interest in this respect is Gobet and Clarkson's (2004) experiment, in which the same participants carried out the experiment both with a computer display and physical pieces. The size of the chunks was much larger in the former case.

250 players in the United States.[3] However, he had barely played any competitive game for the four years before the experiment, and totally stopped practicing. During the experiment, P played little chess.

P was exposed to a number of positions and then afterwards attempted to reconstruct them on empty chessboards. The positions were randomly selected from a large database of games, and were taken after Black's 20th move. They were displayed and reconstructed using a computer program (see Gobet & Simon, 1996d; 1998 for details). Each position was displayed for 8 seconds, and the inter-position latency was 2 seconds, during which the screen was blank.

The random selection of the positions meant that some positions were taken in the middle of an exchange or of some other tactical complications. Such positions are normally not used in chess research, because players find them distracting. Therefore, the positions that P received were on average less typical that the positions normally used in chess research, which made them somewhat harder to memorize. P increasingly got used to the presence of these atypical positions.

The experimental sessions took normally place from Monday through Friday, between 9 a.m. and 10 a.m., in a quiet room. Each session had two parts. First, there was the presentation of two warm-up positions. Then, after a short break, there was the multiple-position task proper. The progression rules for this second task were as follows: (1) the minimum number of positions was four; (2) if more than one position in the previous session fell below 60% correct recall, then the number of positions was decreased by one; otherwise, this number was increased by one.

P had the freedom to pace the two parts of a session as he wished. The typical behavior was as follows. At the very beginning of the experiment, P would select the cue list (see below) matching the current number of positions that he would receive on that day, and concentrate on it, going through the names subvocally. He would then do the two-position warm-up (the cue list was not used for these two positions), then concentrate again on the cue list, and finally perform the multiple-board task.

Overall Results

Inspired by Chase and Ericsson's (1981) research on the digit-span, P created a mnemonic system aimed at facilitating LTM encoding of chess positions. For sequences of four positions and more, he attempted to associate each position with the corresponding element in a pre-learned list containing the chess world champions in historical order (see Table 6.2 and Figure 6.1). The list of world champions was used so that P could fairly easily create meaningful associations between the position currently being displayed and the corresponding name in

---

3 The skill level of competitive chess players is measured using the international Elo rating scale, which has a theoretical mean of 1500 points and standard deviation of 200 points.

TABLE 6.2   List of the Chess World Champions Used by P as
a Cue List (Retrieval Structure)

Name	Abbreviation
Steinitz	Stein
Lasker	Las
Capablanca	Cap
Alekhine	Al
Euwe	Euw
Botvinnik	Bot
Smyslov	Smys
Tal	Tal
Petrossian	Pet
Spasski	Spass
Fischer	Fish
Karpov	Kar
Kasparov	Kas

Source: After Gobet and Simon (1996d).

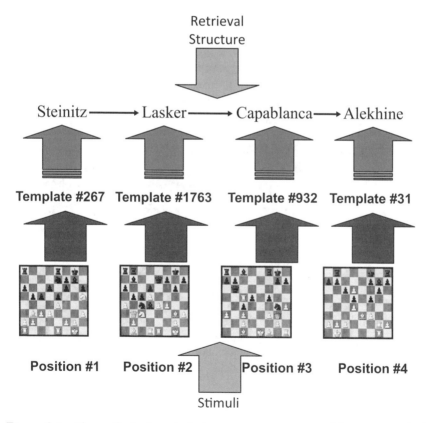

Figure 6.1   The method of magistri: the mnemonic system used by P consisted of
combining a retrieval structure with templates.

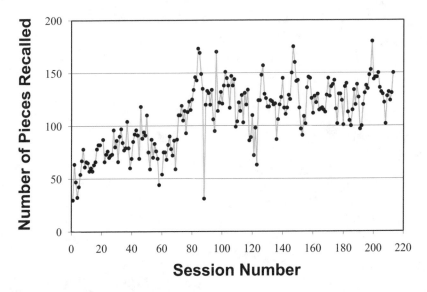

Figure 6.2 Multiple-board experiment: number of pieces correctly recalled as a function of session number.

the list. Associations were mediated by verbal labels. When attempting to recall the positions, each name in the list would serve as a retrieval cue. After about 10 weeks, the names were abbreviated to their first syllables so that they could be pronounced more rapidly sub-vocally.

The following examples, taken from Gobet and Simon (1996d), illustrate how the cue list was used. The examples go from rich associations (cases 1 and 2, where the type of position is recognized and an association made with the name in the cue list) to poor associations (in case 3, a verbal label coding only two pieces is associated, and, in case 4, there is failure to associate an otherwise useful label with the current name in the cue list).

(1) Position #5. Name on the list: Euwe.
   "A Panov attack. Black has a strong Knight on d5, typical for Euwe's play."
(2) Position #6. Name on the list: Botvinnik.
   "A Grünfeld defence, as in the match Karpov–Kasparov, Seville. Botvinnik used to play the Grünfeld."
(3) Position #1. Name on the list: Steinitz.
   "White has the Bishop pair. Steinitz liked the Bishop pair."
(4) Position #2. Name on the list: Lasker.
   "A Maroczy without g6."

Figure 6.2 shows the number of pieces recalled as a function of session number, and Figure 6.3 shows the number of positions attempted also as a function of session number. Both figures suggest that there is first a period of slow improvement, roughly until session 80, followed by a long plateau with

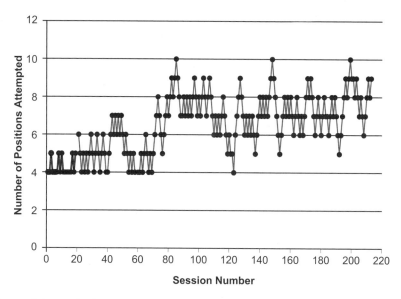

Figure 6.3   Multiple-board experiment: number of positions attempted as a function of session number.

little, if any, improvement. This impression is confirmed by statistical analysis. A linear regression analysis shows that, until session 80, session number is a statistically significant predictor of the number of pieces correct (pieces = 57.4 + 0.54 × session_number; r^2 = .38, $p < .001$) and boards attempted (board_attempted = 4.1 + 0.024 × session_number, r^2 = .26, $p < .001$). Thus, P gains about half a piece per session and it takes about 40 sessions to increase the number of attempted boards by one. From session 81 to 213, there is no linear relationship (pieces correct by session: r^2 = .005, ns; boards attempted by session: r^2 = .001, ns). Note also that P managed to recall 150 pieces or more in 12 cases only, and attempted 10 positions in 3 cases only.

Specialization Effects in Expertise: The Question

If, as argued by De Groot (1965), Chase and Simon (1973b), and others, expertise relies primarily on perceptual information encoded either as knowledge complexes or chunks, then it follows rather directly that it should be difficult to transfer one's expertise in a given domain to another one. The perceptual chunks acquired over years of practice and study, which enable fluid behavior in the first domain with rapid recognition of the key features, simply will not be useful in other domains. We know at least since Thorndike and Woodworth (1901) that transfer between domains is difficult, and a recent meta-analysis shows that chess, the domain addressed in this chapter, is no exception (Gobet & Campitelli, 2006). But what about transfer between several within-domain specializations, for example, neurology and pediatrics, or expertise in Chinese foreign policy and expertise in India's parliamentary system?

Theories emphasizing specific perceptual knowledge, including chunk-based theories, still make the prediction for domain-specificity, that is, that experts with one specialization should be better in that domain than experts with other specializations. However, this view is not shared by some theorists. For example, in his discussion of chess expertise, Holding (1985) claimed that the main components of skill is not pattern recognition, but forward search and general analytical reasoning abilities. So, Holding (1985, pp. 249–250) argued that "there is no doubt that experienced players possess extremely rich and highly organized chess memories, but the most useful attributes of these memories seem to be more general than specific and, if specific, not necessarily concerned with chunked patterns." More recently, Linhares (2005) has criticized the emphasis on chunks and templates in problem solving and argued that experts used "abstract roles" derived not on surface, perceptual information, but on the deep meaning of chess positions. (How this deep meaning is accessed, however, is not spelled out in detail.)

Another criticism of the theoretical role of specialized chunks has been put forward by Ericsson and colleagues, who argued that superior performance can be achieved with relatively small amounts of practice. SF and DD practiced just several hours a week for about two and three years, respectively, but had a better memory for digits than professional memory experts who had practiced for more than 20 years of experience (Chase & Ericsson, 1982). Similarly, a novice trained by Ericsson and Harris (1990) was able, after about 50 hours of practice, to recall unfamiliar chess positions to the level of experienced chess players who had spent thousands of hours practicing and studying chess. Based on these studies, Ericsson and Kintsch (2000) concluded that:

> If expert memory performance can be attained in a fraction of the number of years necessary to acquire expert chess-playing skill, then this raises doubts about the necessity of a tight connection between expert performance and experts' superior memory for representative stimuli.
>
> (p. 578)

However, their argument fails to consider that SF and DD used a powerful coding strategy and brought to the digit span task extensive knowledge of numbers and dates, and the novice trained by Ericsson and Harris acquired only one component of the knowledge necessary for chess expertise, namely perceptual chunks. That this last result is consistent with chunking and template theories has been shown by Gobet and Jackson (2002), who replicated Ericsson and Harris's study and showed that simulations with CHREST (see below) could account for the results very well.

Specialization Effects: Method of Analysis and Results

Chess players specialize in the type of openings they use—it is simply impossible to know enough about all openings to be able to play them at a competitive level. In addition, it is important to find openings that match one's style of play, and an important role of coaches is to help players select such openings. Each player thus develops an "opening repertoire," for both White and Black. To avoid being too predictable, and also to anticipate the possibility that an opening would be in crisis because of the discovery of some new way to handle it, chess masters typically build some variability in their repertoire. For example, they could have two different replies against White's 1.e2–e4.

P was no exception to this, and had chosen a subset of openings that he studied in great detail and that he regularly used in competitive games, although there were a few changes over the years. He was able to identify apparently minute variations in the positions arising from the openings in which he specialized, and these could make the difference between a win and a loss. With the openings that did not belong to his repertoire, he knew the general ideas and plans, but would not be able to discriminate positions in the same way. It is then possible to use the data of the training experiment presented above to directly test the hypothesis that experts encode specific perceptual patterns. If this hypothesis is correct, P should on average obtain better recall performance with positions coming from his pet openings, or with positions resembling those positions.

In order to carry out the analysis, the stimulus positions were coded as: (1) belonging to the type of openings P used to play; (2) belonging to openings P never played; and (3) positions that could not be classified (e.g., because too few pieces were left on the chessboard). Note that all stimulus positions were taken after White's twentieth move. This coding was carried out by P himself, being the best expert of the kind of openings he had used during his chess career. The following analyses will be on the first 600 positions used in the training experiment.

As Figure 6.4 shows, P better remembered the type of positions he used to play than the other types of positions, with the exception of the cases where he attempted 9 and 10 boards. The differences are statistically significant both in the played vs. non-played comparison, $t(7) = 6.52$, $p < .001$ (one-tailed), and in the played vs. unclear comparison, $t(7) = 3.26$, $p < .01$ (one-tailed). In general, the positions coming from openings he did not play had the lowest recall. These data thus add support to the hypothesis that the encoding of specific perceptual information plays an important role in chess expertise and that restricting task practice to a particular subset of the task environment constrains transfer of skill, hence performance, outside of the selected practice environment. At the same time, it is important to note that P did not do that badly (62% correct) with positions that did not belong to his repertoire, as compared to 75% correct with positions that did. It is reasonable to suspect that knowledge—either perceptual chunks or general knowledge—he had acquired during his training and practice (for example, by replaying games of famous players) allowed him to encode at least part of most unfamiliar positions and thus achieve this level of recall.

Of course, the chunking and template theories, which account for participants' performance in other studies, predicted this result. It is thus important to check whether computational models based on these theories can simulate it. In the next section, I address this question by reporting computer simulations with CHREST.

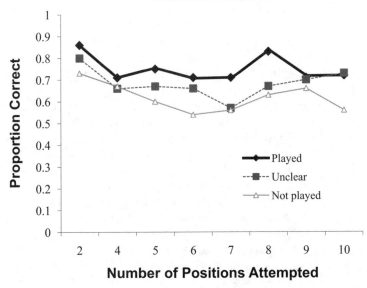

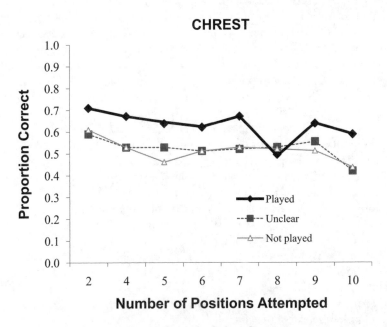

Figure 6.4 Specialization effect in the multiple-board experiment: proportion correct as a function of number of positions attempted and type of positions. Top panel: human data. Bottom panel: computer simulations with CHREST.

SPECIALIZATION IN CHESS: COMPUTER SIMULATIONS

The CHREST Model

Converging evidence for current claims about chess specialization come from computer simulations that used CHREST (Chunk Hierarchy and REtrieval STructures), a model implementing important aspects of the template theory (Gobet & Lane, 2005; Gobet et al., 2001; Gobet & Simon, 2000). The first version of CHREST was developed in the early 1990s to provide a unified model of perception and memory in chess. In particular, the aim was to put together the key insights of chunking theory and previous models of chess perception (Simon & Barenfeld, 1969) and memory (Simon & Gilmartin, 1973). The development of the model was also informed by the collection of new experimental data (Gobet & Simon, 1996a, 1996b, 1996c, 1996d) and theoretical reflections that led to the template theory. The later versions of CHREST were more ambitious with respect to their scope, first, covering other domains of expertise and later addressing cognition more generally. To date, the CHREST architecture has been used to simulate phenomena in a number of domains including concept formation (Lane & Gobet, 2007), problem solving in physics (Lane, Cheng, & Gobet, 2000) and awele (an African game; Gobet, 2009), children's acquisition of vocabulary (Jones, Gobet, & Pine, 2007), and children's acquisition of syntax (Freudenthal, Pine, Aguado-Orea, & Gobet, 2007). CHREST's ability to simulate these phenomena illustrates the explanatory power of the chunking hypothesis, something Bill Chase was undoubtedly aware of. The following paragraphs provide a rather basic introduction to CHREST. A fuller description is provided in Gobet and Chassy (2009) and the computer code can be found at www.CHREST.info.

As the simulations will focus on chess, a domain where the processing of verbal information plays only a limited role (see Gobet, de Voogt, & Retschitzki, 2004, for details), description of CHREST will focus on the visual aspects of the model. CHREST comprises four main components: (1) an LTM where chunks are stored; (2) a visual STM; (3) a simulated eye; and (4) a mind's eye, where visuo-spatial information can be manipulated. Figure 6.5 illustrates these four components. The simulated eye moves around the chessboard, fixating squares, and the information within the visual field is sent to a discrimination network in LTM which mediates recognition of a chunk. A pointer to this chunk is then placed in STM, and the information is also unpacked in the "pictorial short-term memory," another name for the mind's eye. This sequence of operations is then repeated.

With respect to LTM, the interest focuses on the creation and use of chunks. Chunks, together with the links that connect them, form a discrimination net. The links have tests, which are applied to check features of the external stimuli. This component of the model borrows several mechanisms from Feigenbaum and Simon's (1984) EPAM model. As noted above, chunks

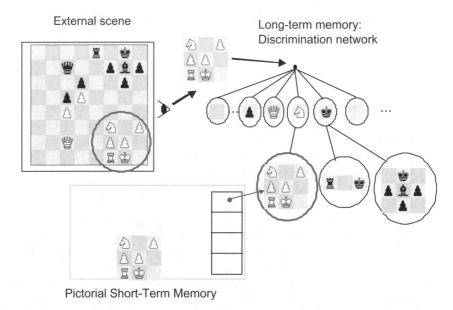

Figure 6.5   Application of CHREST to the chess domain.

that are recognized often evolve into more complex data structures. The core of templates is similar to the information stored in chunks, and this information is stable. Templates also have slots, which make it possible for the value of variables to be encoded rapidly. Based on computer simulations, it is assumed that it takes 250 ms to instantiate a template slot. In the current simulations, slots can encode information about piece location, piece type, or chunks. Slots are automatically created where the links irradiating from a given chunk show enough variation on a given type of information (e.g., information about squares, type of pieces, or groups of pieces; see Figure 6.6). Template slots are created when the number of nodes that are linked to a given node and share identical information is greater than a parameter, arbitrarily set to 3 in the simulations. A further constraint is that a chunk should contain at least five elements. Chunks and templates can be linked to other chunks and templates, as well as other information stored in LTM, most notably moves and sequences of moves.

Visual STM has a capacity of three chunk pointers. When STM is already full and a new chunk is recognized, the oldest pointer leaves STM. There is an exception to this rule with the largest chunk: its pointer leaves STM only when a larger chunk is recognized. This idea of pointers has often been criticized on the grounds that it is too close to computer programming and lacks biological plausibility, but this criticism is misguided. A neurally plausible implementation for such pointers has been proposed by Ruchkin, Grafman, Cameron, and Berndt (2003). These authors suggest that STM neurons in the prefrontal cortex fire in synchrony with neurons located in the posterior areas of the cortex. This mechanism has the advantage of explaining why STM has a limited

**Template
formation**

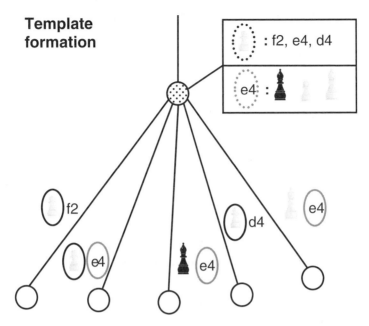

Figure 6.6   An example of template formation.

capacity; it is due to the limited number of distinct frequencies available for synchrony, which limits the number of pointers available.

Eye movements that serially scan a position are directed from a combination of heuristics (e.g., heeding a square on a part of the board that has not been visited by the eye yet) and acquired knowledge, which is mediated by the structure of the discrimination net. Specifically, the model uses the largest chunk recognized so far to direct eye movements (see De Groot & Gobet, 1996, for details).

The final component of CHREST, the mind's eye, clearly shows the influence of Chase and Simon's (1973a) paper "The mind's eye in chess on the model." The mind's eye is similar to Kosslyn's (1994) visual buffer and Baddeley's (1986) visuo-spatial sketchpad, and stores perceptual structures, both from memory stores and external inputs, for a short amount of time. Its content is encoded as a network of nodes and links that can be manipulated by visuo-spatial mental operations. It is worth pointing out that the information encoded in the mind's eye is much more abstract than the information impinging the retina. Unless it is refreshed, information in the mind's eye suffers from rapid decay, within around 250 ms (Kosslyn, 1994). The processes taking place in the mind's eye (e.g., the time to move a piece mentally) are assumed to be carried out serially; Kosslyn, Cave, Provost, and Von Gierke (1988) provide data supporting this assumption. Finally, CHREST includes mechanisms linking LTM, STM, and the mind's eye. When a chunk is elicited, either by external or internal information, a pointer to it is placed in STM. Concurrently, the visuo-spatial information referred to in LTM by this pointer is unpacked in the mind's eye. As information in the mind's eye fades rapidly, it needs to be refreshed regularly. Waters and Gobet (2008) provide more details on how CHREST's mind's eye works, and present an experiment testing some of the assumptions discussed in this paragraph.

Four characteristic features of CHREST might be highlighted. First, there is an emphasis on cognitive limitations, for example, limitations in memory capacity (visual STM can hold only three items) and learning rates (it takes about 8 seconds to create a new chunk). This emphasis can be traced back to Simon's work on bounded rationality (e.g., Simon, 1969). Second, CHREST is a self-organizing, dynamic system. The structure of its discrimination net cannot be predicted on general considerations alone, and depends both on internal mechanisms and on the statistical structure of the environment. Third, and closely related to the previous point, learning and thus the quality of the simulations depend on realistic input capturing the detail of the structure of the environment. Finally, time parameters are used for each cognitive process (e.g., 8 seconds to create a new chunk, or 50 ms to encode a chunk in STM), which makes it possible to derive detailed quantitative predictions.

Simulation Methods

The simulations aim to establish whether CHREST's structures and mechanisms are sufficient to reproduce the specialization effect found in P's training experiment. This investigation uses the same model as that used in previous simulations (Gobet & Simon, 2000; Gobet & Waters, 2003; Waters & Gobet, 2008), including the same mechanisms for template creation and use. The only novel addition is that the model also uses a retrieval structure, which is similar to the list of world champions used by P for the recall of four and more positions (see Table 6.2 and Figure 6.1). For the recall of two positions (warming-up), a retrieval structure with two items (encoding the positions as "first" and "second") is postulated. The probability of storing a chunk or template into the retrieval structure was set at 1 with 2 positions and .84 with 4 and more positions.

During the learning phase, the program incrementally acquired chunks and templates by scanning a large database of positions (about 50,000) taken from master-level games. With CHREST, skill differences are simulated by growing nets of various sizes. For the purpose of these simulations, the learning set consisted of a mixture of positions related to P's opening repertoire (about 90%), positions taken from P's games (about 200, shown 10 times, 5%), and positions randomly selected from databases (5%). These numbers were supposed to reflect the kind of positions P was familiar with: the most familiar were the positions from games he had played, followed by positions he was likely to have studied, and then finally positions from openings he did not play. The network used in the simulations had ~300,000 chunks and ~20,000 templates.

Results

As shown in the lower panel of Figure 6.4, the model does a good job at capturing the difference between positions belonging to P's repertoire and other positions. Like P, the model recalls the openings from his repertoire better than openings he did not play, $t(7) = 5.46$, $p < .001$ (one-tailed), and better than openings difficult to classify, $t(7) = 4.97$, $p < .002$ (one-tailed). The model replicates the specialization effect because it can find more chunks and in particular more templates in the positions that were predominantly used for training (i.e. positions belonging to P's repertoire). However, it should be pointed out that the model performs rather consistently about 10% below the level reached by the player. This probably could be corrected by using a network with more chunks and templates for the simulations.

In summary, the simulations showed that CHREST's mechanisms for creating and using chunks and templates lead to knowledge that is consistent with the specialization effect observed in the single-case experiment. They also show that part of this knowledge can be recruited to recall positions that do not belong to the domain of specialization of the model, albeit with weaker recall performance.

SPECIALIZATION IN CHESS: FRENCH CONNECTION AND SICILIAN MOVES

The case study presented earlier offered relatively clear results, and the computer simulations provided a mechanism for them. But do the results generalize to a larger sample? Do they apply to other tasks such as problem solving, where one has to find the best move in a position? A recent study (Bilalić, McLeod, & Gobet, 2009) addressed these very questions.

In this study, we combined two research paradigms typical of expertise research. The first paradigm, the most common and that used for example in Chase and Simon's study, consists of comparing individuals of different skill levels. The second paradigm consists of comparing groups of individuals with the same skill level, but with different fields of specialization. This second paradigm has the advantage that factors such as amount of experience and general skill level are controlled for; what differs between the two groups is the subset of domain knowledge individuals specialized in. Researchers have used the specialization paradigm for studying expertise in medicine (Rikers et al., 2002), political science (Chiesi, Spilich, & Voss, 1979), and the design of experiments (Schunn & Anderson, 1999). In general, the results indicate that, when specific domain knowledge is not available, experts fall back on weaker methods. These results have sometimes been taken as contradicting theories of expertise such as the chunking theory, which emphasize the role of domain-specific patterns and methods (e.g., Schunn & Anderson, 1999). There is no doubt that experts use general problem-solving methods in addition to domain-specific methods. The interesting question, however, is how expert performance changes when only domain-general methods are used.

The study presented in Bilalić et al. (2009) is based on one of the experiments that Merim Bilalić carried out for his PhD thesis. Bilalić's elegant design addressed some of the weaknesses of previous studies using the specialization paradigm. For example, many studies used one type of problem, which has the disadvantage that it is from the field of one group of experts but not of the other. Bilalić et al. (2009) presented two kinds of problems, which mapped onto the specialization of each group. Also, few studies used neutral problems (i.e., problems unfamiliar to both groups), which seem necessary to tease apart the effect of knowledge. Finally, in many studies, the participants' level of expertise, and therefore the effect of expert specialization, were difficult to quantify.

Chess offered a great domain for addressing these issues. The Elo rating makes it possible to measure skill precisely; chess players love trying to solve chess problems; and the fact that players specialize in different openings, as explained in the case study above, makes it easy to find players of the same skill level (as measured by the Elo rating) but with different knowledge for a specific opening.

Method

Thus, Bilalić's idea was to compare performance of players within and outside their domain of specialization. He used three types of middle game positions: positions from the Winawer variation of the French defense (see Figure 6.7, left), positions from the Najdorf variation of the Sicilian defense (see Figure 6.7, right), and neutral positions. The neutral problems came from middle game positions difficult to classify with respect to the opening they came from, and were used to measure more general memory and problem-solving abilities. There were two tasks. In the memory recall task, positions were presented for 5 seconds. The stimuli consisted of 12 positions (four positions for each of the French, Sicilian, and neutral conditions) that were presented in random order. In the problem-solving task, players were required to think aloud while trying to find the best move. They were not allowed to move the pieces,

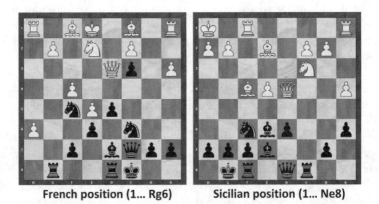

French position (1... Rg6)   Sicilian position (1... Ne8)

Figure 6.7   An example of a position coming from the French defense, Winawer variation (left) and from the Sicilian defense, Najdorf variation (right). In parentheses, the best move.

and there was no time limit. There were two problems for each of the three kinds of positions, and positions were presented in a random order. It took on average one hour for the participants to go through all six problems.

The participants were eight candidate masters (with an average of 2140 Elo), eight masters (2300 Elo), and eight international masters/grandmasters (2490 Elo). Half the players specialized in the Winawer variation of the French defense, and the other half in the Najdorf variation of the Sicilian defense.

Results

Figure 6.8 shows the results for the memory task. In line with previous experiments, there was a reliable skill effect, with better players obtaining better scores than less skilled players, $F(2, 18) = 19.88$, $p < .01$, $\eta_p^2 = .69$. The key

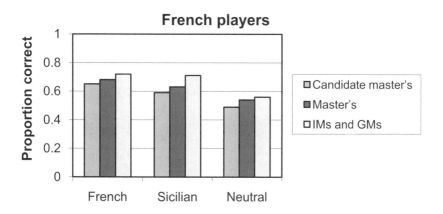

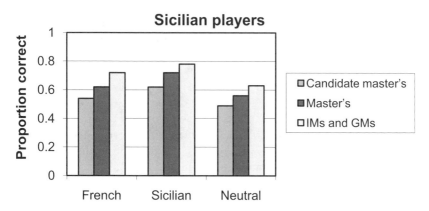

Figure 6.8   Specialization in a memory task: proportion correct as a function of the type of players, type of positions, and skill level.

Source: Bilalić, McLeod, & Gobet (2009).

result was that players were better at recalling positions from their opening repertoire than positions they did not play. Thus, French players recalled French positions better, and Sicilian players recalled Sicilian positions better, yielding a significant interaction player type × position type: $F(1, 156) = 46.96$, $p < .01$, $\eta_p^2 = .23$. The effect of familiarity is strong enough to take precedence over skill. With the Sicilian positions, the performance of Sicilian candidate masters was close to the performance of French masters, and the performance of Sicilian masters was close to that of French grandmasters/international masters. The same pattern of results was observed with French positions, where French candidate masters and masters obtained comparable results to those obtained by Sicilian masters and grandmasters/international masters, respectively. Thus, the magnitude of the specialization effect on chess memory is about one standard deviation in skill (see footnote 3). As both groups memorized the neutral middle-game positions equally well, one can be confident that the two groups were of similar strength.

Move quality in the problem-solving task was computed as the difference between the assessment of the best move in the position, as estimated by Fritz 8 (a very strong computer chess program) and the chosen move. Note that Fritz 8 evaluates moves using pawn units. Thus, to give an example, a score of 0.5 means that the selected move was inferior by half a pawn to the best move in the position.

The problem-solving task yielded very similar results to the memory task (see Figure 6.9). There was a reliable skill effect, better players choosing better moves, $F(2, 18) = 7.35$, $p < .01$, $\eta_p^2 = .45$. Crucially, the interaction player type × position type was statistically significant. Players faced with positions from within their opening specialization found better moves than those faced with positions outside it, $F(1, 64) = 13.87$, $p < .01$, $\eta_p^2 = .18$. Moreover, the magnitude of the specialization effect—about one standard deviation in skill level—was comparable to that found in the memory task. With the French positions, the French candidate masters and masters found slightly better moves than the Sicilian masters and grandmasters/international masters, respectively. (It is not known why the Sicilian masters performed so poorly in the French positions.) The effect was even stronger with the Sicilian positions.

In summary, players outside their domain of specialization perform about 200 Elo points (one standard deviation in skill) below their level with familiar positions, both with a memory and problem-solving task. Thus, a grandmaster (≈ 2600 points) performs at the level of an international master (≈ 2400 points). Or, to put it another way, a player ranked #186 in the world would perform roughly like a player ranked #2837 in the world.

SPECIALIZATION IN SCIENCE

Rather unexpectedly, the results I have presented here have implications for policy, more precisely for science policy in the context of peer review. The quality of the research undertaken by all UK universities is evaluated about every

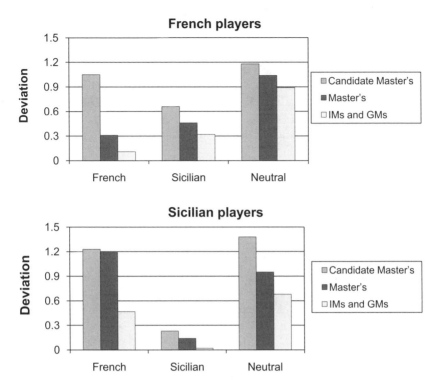

Figure 6.9   Specialization in a problem-solving task: deviation from the optimal move as a function of the type of players, type of positions, and skill level. Lower values indicate better moves.

Source: Bilalić, McLeod, & Gobet (2009).

five years, in a mammoth data collection exercise previously called the Research Assessment Exercise (RAE; www.rae.ac.uk), and renamed in 2007 as the Research Excellence Framework (REF; www.hefce.ac.uk/research/ref). The rankings obtained are used to allocate a subset of research funding (the equivalent of about $2.5 billion a year). The RAE is thus no laughing matter, and universities spend a considerable amount of time and money to optimize the information they return.

The key evaluation criterion is the quality of research papers produced by a department. Each academic discipline is judged by a panel of experts (13 for psychology) coming from the same discipline. The panel members read the best four papers of each academic, and rate them.[4] The scale used has changed

---

4 This of course imposes a considerable burden on the panel members—the time spent evaluating papers is not spent on their own research. For an interesting and early discussion of the cost of reviewing, as well as other related questions such as the efficiency of the peer-review system at the NSF, see Klahr (1985).

over the years, and included five levels in the last RAE, conducted in 2008. And this is here that the specialization effect crops up, I believe.

Panels have to evaluate a wide range of papers. For example, in psychology, papers would cover subfields as varied as clinical psychology, social psychology, cognitive neuroscience, and cross-cultural psychology, to mention just a few. And, of course, each sub-discipline will carry out research that has little in common with other sub-disciplines. Think, for example, within cognitive psychology, of the research carried out in perception with fMRI and in problem solving with protocol analysis.

In these circumstances, is the judgment of the panel experts reliable? We simply do not know, as only the aggregated results are published, and the evaluation of individual papers is destroyed. However, Bilalić et al.'s (2009) data clearly suggest that the RAE approach is not reliable: Top experts are likely to behave like average experts when outside their domain of specialization. They still will be experts, but their level will be far from the level of expertise for which they have been selected in the first place.

One could object that it is inappropriate to generalize from chess to the evaluation of scientific papers. I would argue that, if anything, the situation is probably worse with the RAE than with chess. Evaluating the quality of scientific papers is a subjective process, prone to noise. In chess, a checkmate in three moves does not leave much space for discussion. In science, whether an idea is good or bad, or an experimental result important or not, can lead to endless deliberations—just think how even experts in the same subfield disagree when it comes to review manuscripts or grant applications. Finally, the distance between specializations in science seems larger than between specializations in chess. Chess openings might differ, but the strategies and tactics for handling the middle game and the endgame tend to converge, irrespectively of the first moves. In science, such convergence is less likely, in great part due to differences in methods—evaluating research using brain imaging is miles apart from evaluating research on Freudian psychotherapy.

If the results of Bilalić et al.'s (2009) experiments generalize to the type of evaluation done in the RAE, then there is room for doubt that the assessors are properly qualified for their task. In other experiments carried out within the framework of Bilalić's PhD research, it was found that, as expertise diminishes, the likelihood of being victim to biases in thinking increases (Bilalić, McLeod, & Gobet, 2008a, 2008b). Having papers evaluated by two experts, as was usually done in the RAE, might reduce this effect, but it is not clear that two experts outside their domain of special expertise can reach the level of an expert from within the domain.

ADAPTABILITY AND TRANSFER

In order to survive, organisms must adapt to their environment. As noted by Simon (1969), among others, one of the means to do so is to learn. Thus, the chunking and template mechanisms I have discussed in this chapter contribute in important ways to humans' adaptation. Their strengths are that they capture the statistical regularities of the environment while providing at the same time enough flexibility to insure adaptability to unexpected events. But what happens when the environment changes? What happens when experts face a new domain?

One must distinguish between two types of changes. In the first case, the new environment still overlaps to a large extent with the old one. This is the case that was considered in this chapter. Within the same domain, experts in one sub-domain (e.g., chess players specializing in the Sicilian defense) faced problems from a different sub-domain (e.g., positions from the French defense). A decrease in performance was found, but not a drastic one. Obviously, players could use general heuristics or other types of abstract knowledge to cope with the less familiar situations. They could also use knowledge coded as chunks and templates, as suggested by the CHREST simulations. While optimized for a specific environment, these knowledge structures are flexible enough that at least some of them can be used in a different, but related environment.

In the second case, the new environment has little to do with the old one. This is of course the classic question of transfer studied in psychology and education for more than one century. Here, researchers, starting with Thorndike and Woodworth (1901), have been more pessimistic about the possibility of using knowledge structures in the new domain. For example, while DD was able to memorize more than one hundred digits, this skill did not transfer to the memory for words (Chase & Ericsson, 1982). Similarly, contrary to a widely held opinion in the chess community, skill in chess does not transfer to other domains such as English and mathematics (Gobet & Campitelli, 2006). Rare exceptions to this pattern of results are offered with transfer from violent action video games (Green, Li, & Bavelier, 2009) and by the transfer of highly abstract kinds of knowledge, such as mathematical techniques.

However, contrasting with these rather depressing conclusions, "real-world" experts offer some spectacular counter-examples. Eric Heiden is widely considered as the best speed skater of all times. Among other feats, he won all five races in the 1980 Olympics Games at Lake Placid, both in sprint and endurance, establishing four Olympic records and one world record. In his second career, he was a professional road racing cyclist, winning the USA championship in 1985. In his third career, he specialized in orthopedic surgery after obtaining an MD. Simen Agdestein carried out two international careers in parallel: the first as a chess grandmaster (he was seven times Norwegian champion) and the second as a football player (he played eight times for the Norwegian national team). Later, he became a successful chess coach, having notably advised current chess number 1, Magnus Carlsen. And, of course, there is Arnold Schwarzenegger. First, one of the most successful body builders ever (five Mr. Universe titles and seven Mr. Olympia titles); then a successful businessman in the bricklaying business and real-estate investing; then one of the most famous actors in the world; and finally a successful politician (Governor of California).

How can we explain this discrepancy between academic research and actual expertise? Do these individuals use better heuristics? Do they somehow acquire chunks and templates that are more generalizable? Have they developed a particular efficacious type of opportunism, optimizing the reuse of assets acquired in a previous career? Is it "only" a question of talent, for example, better motivation, will power and stamina? Surprisingly, little research has addressed these issues.

CONCLUSION

As this chapter has made it clear, my research has been greatly influenced by Bill Chase, although I never had the pleasure to meet him. His influence includes the study of specialized knowledge in expertise, the general idea of chunking as a key theoretical mechanism of human cognition, and the use of single-subject designs. The overall message of this chapter is that specialization plays a powerful role in determining expert performance. This was first shown in a memory task with a single expert. Computer simulations with CHREST replicating the specialization effect contributed converging evidence. An additional study with a larger sample showed that the result could be generalized beyond memory tasks to problem solving. In general, the results support the link between memory of specific experiences and problem-solving ability; thus, problem-solving strategies that are context-independent and general-purpose are not sufficient to make somebody an expert. This is consistent with what Bill Chase claimed about domain-specificity in the skilled memory effect (Chase, 1986).

REFERENCES

Baddeley, A. (1986). *Working memory*. Oxford: Clarendon Press.

Bilalić, M., McLeod, P., & Gobet, F. (2008a). Inflexibility of experts: Reality or myth? Quantifying the Einstellung effect in chess masters. *Cognitive Psychology, 56*, 73–102.

Bilalić, M., McLeod, P., & Gobet, F. (2008b). Why good thoughts block better ones: The mechanism of the pernicious Einstellung (set) effect. *Cognition, 108*, 652–661.

Bilalić, M., McLeod, P., & Gobet, F. (2009). Specialization effect and its influence on memory and problem solving in expert chess players. *Cognitive Science, 33*, 1117–1143.

Bryan, W. L., & Harter, N. (1899). Studies on the telegraphic language: The acquisition of a hierarchy of habits. *Psychological Review, 6*, 345–375.

Campitelli, G., Gobet, F., Williams, G., & Parker, A. (2007). Integration of perceptual input and visual imagery in chess players: Evidence from eye movements. *Swiss Journal of Psychology, 66*, 201–213.

Charness, N. (1976). Memory for chess positions: Resistance to interference. *Journal of Experimental Psychology: Human Learning and Memory, 2*, 641–653.

Chase, W. G. (1986). Visual information processing. In K. R. Boff, L. Kaufman, & J. P. Thomas (Eds.), *Handbook of perception and human performance (Vol. III, Cognitive processes and performance)* (pp. 1–73). New York: Wiley.

Chase, W. G., & Ericsson, K. A. (1981). Skilled memory. In J. R. Anderson (Ed.), *Cognitive skills and their acquisition* (pp. 141–189). Hillsdale, NJ: Erlbaum.

Chase, W. G., & Ericsson, K. A. (1982). Skill and working memory. *The Psychology of Learning and Motivation, 16*, 1–58.

Chase, W. G., & Simon, H. A. (1973a). The mind's eye in chess. In W. G. Chase (Ed.), *Visual information processing* (pp. 215–281). New York: Academic Press.

Chase, W. G., & Simon, H. A. (1973b). Perception in chess. *Cognitive Psychology, 4*, 55–81.

Chiesi, H. L., Spilich, G. J., & Voss, J. F. (1979). Acquisition of domain-related information in relation to high and low domain knowledge. *Journal of Verbal Learning and Verbal Behavior, 18*, 257–273.

Cooke, N. J., Atlas, R. S., Lane, D. M., & Berger, R. C. (1993). Role of high-level knowledge in memory for chess positions. *American Journal of Psychology, 106*, 321–351.

De Groot, A. D. (1965). *Thought and choice in chess*. The Hague: Mouton Publishers.

De Groot, A. D., & Gobet, F. (1996). *Perception and memory in chess: Heuristics of the professional eye*. Assen: Van Gorcum.

Ebbinghaus, H. ([1885] 1964). *Memory: A contribution to experimental psychology*. New York: Dover.

Ericsson, K. A., Chase, W. G., & Faloon, S. (1980). Acquisition of a memory skill. *Science, 208*, 1181–1182.

Ericsson, K. A., & Harris, M. S. (1990, November). Expert chess memory without chess knowledge: A training study. Paper presented at the 31st Annual Meeting of the Psychonomics Society, New Orleans.

Ericsson, K. A., & Kintsch, W. (1995). Long-term working memory. *Psychological Review, 102*, 211–245.

Ericsson, K. A., & Kintsch, W. (2000). Shortcomings of generic retrieval structures with slots of the type that Gobet (1993) proposed and modelled. *British Journal of Psychology, 91*, 571–590.

Feigenbaum, E. A., & Simon, H. A. (1984). EPAM-like models of recognition and learning. *Cognitive Science, 8*, 305–336.

Freudenthal, D., Pine, J. M., Aguado-Orea, J., & Gobet, F. (2007). Modelling the developmental patterning of finiteness marking in English, Dutch, German and Spanish using MOSAIC. *Cognitive Science, 31*, 311–341.

Frey, P. W., & Adesman, P. (1976). Recall memory for visually presented chess positions. *Memory and Cognition, 4*, 541–547.

Gobet, F. (2000). Some shortcomings of long-term working memory. *British Journal of Psychology, 91*, 551–570.

Gobet, F. (2009). Using a cognitive architecture for addressing the question of cognitive universals in cross-cultural psychology: The example of awalé. *Journal of Cross-Cultural Psychology, 40*, 627–648.

Gobet, F., & Campitelli, G. (2006). Education and chess: A critical review. In T. Redman (Ed.), *Chess and education: Selected essays from the Koltanowski conference* (pp. 124–143). Dallas, TX: Chess Program at the University of Texas at Dallas.

Gobet, F., & Chassy, P. (2009). Expertise and intuition: A tale of three theories. *Minds & Machines, 19*, 151–180.

Gobet, F., & Clarkson, G. (2004). Chunks in expert memory: Evidence for the magical number four . . . or is it two? *Memory, 12*, 732–747.

Gobet, F., de Voogt, A. J., & Retschitzki, J. (2004). *Moves in mind: The psychology of board games*. Hove, UK: Psychology Press.

Gobet, F., & Jackson, S. (2002). In search of templates. *Cognitive Systems Research, 3*, 35–44.

Gobet, F., & Lane, P. C. R. (2005). The CHREST architecture of cognition: Listening to empirical data. In D. Davis (Ed.), *Visions of mind: Architectures for cognition and affect* (pp. 204–224). Hershey, PA: IPS.

Gobet, F., Lane, P. C. R., Croker, S., Cheng, P. C. H., Jones, G., Oliver, I., et al. (2001). Chunking mechanisms in human learning. *Trends in Cognitive Sciences, 5*, 236–243.

Gobet, F., & Ritter, F. E. (2000). Individual data analysis and Unified Theories of Cognition: A methodological proposal. In N. Taatgen, & J. Aasman (Eds.), *Proceedings of the Third International Conference on Cognitive Modelling* (pp. 150–157). Veenendaal, The Netherlands: Universal Press.

Gobet, F., & Simon, H. A. (1996a). Recall of random and distorted positions: Implications for the theory of expertise. *Memory & Cognition, 24*, 493–503.

Gobet, F., & Simon, H. A. (1996b). Recall of rapidly presented random chess positions is a function of skill. *Psychonomic Bulletin & Review, 3*, 159–163.

Gobet, F., & Simon, H. A. (1996c). The roles of recognition processes and look-ahead search in time-constrained expert problem solving: Evidence from grandmaster level chess. *Psychological Science, 7*, 52–55.

Gobet, F., & Simon, H. A. (1996d). Templates in chess memory: A mechanism for recalling several boards. *Cognitive Psychology, 31*, 1–40.

Gobet, F., & Simon, H. A. (1998). Expert chess memory: Revisiting the chunking hypothesis. *Memory, 6*, 225–255.

Gobet, F., & Simon, H. A. (2000). Five seconds or sixty? Presentation time in expert memory. *Cognitive Science, 24*, 651–682.

Gobet, F., & Waters, A. J. (2003). The role of constraints in expert memory. *Journal of Experimental Psychology: Learning, Memory & Cognition, 29*, 1082–1094.

Green, C. S., Li, R. J., & Bavelier, D. (2009). Perceptual learning during action video game playing. *Topics in Cognitive Science, 2*, 202–216.

Holding, D. H. (1985). *The psychology of chess skill*. Hillsdale, NJ: Erlbaum.

Jones, G., Gobet, F., & Pine, J. M. (2007). Linking working memory and long-term memory: A computational model of the learning of new words. *Developmental Science, 10*, 853–873.

Klahr, D. (1985). Insiders, outsiders and efficiency in an NSF Panel. *American Psychologist, 40*, 148–154.

Kosslyn, S. M. (1994). *Images and brain: The resolution of the imagery debate*. Cambridge, MA: Bradford.

Kosslyn, S. M., Cave, C. B., Provost, D. A., & Von Gierke, S. M. (1988). Sequential processes in image generation. *Cognitive Psychology, 20*, 319–343.

Lane, P. C. R., Cheng, P. C. H., & Gobet, F. (2000). CHREST+: Investigating how humans learn to solve problems using diagrams. *AISB Quarterly, 103*, 24–30.

Lane, P. C. R., & Gobet, F. (2007). Developing and evaluating cognitive architectures using behavioural tests. In *AAAI Workshop on Evaluating Architectures for Intelligence* (pp. 109–114). Hove, UK: Psychology Press.

Linhares, A. (2005). An active symbols theory of chess intuition. *Minds and Machines, 15*, 131–181.

Miller, G. A. (1956). The magical number seven, plus or minus two: Some limits on our capacity for processing information. *Psychological Review, 63,* 81–97.

Newell, A. (1990). *Unified theories of cognition.* Cambridge, MA: Harvard University Press.

Newell, A., & Simon, H. A. (1972). *Human problem solving.* Englewood Cliffs, NJ: Prentice-Hall.

Richman, H. B., Gobet, F., Staszewski, J. J., & Simon, H. A. (1996). Perceptual and memory processes in the acquisition of expert performance: The EPAM model. In K. A. Ericsson (Ed.), *The road to excellence* (pp. 167–187). Mahwah, NJ: Lawrence Erlbaum.

Rikers, R. M. J. P., Schmidt, H. G., Boshuizen, H. P. A., Linssen, G. C. M., Wesseling, G., & Paas, F. G. W. C. (2002). The robustness of medical expertise: Clinical case processing by medical experts and subexperts. *American Journal of Psychology, 115,* 609–629.

Ruchkin, D. S., Grafman, J., Cameron, K., & Berndt, R. S. (2003). Working memory retention systems: A state of activated long-term memory. *Behavioral and Brain Sciences, 26,* 709.

Schunn, C. D., & Anderson, J. R. (1999). The generality/specificity of expertise in scientific reasoning. *Cognitive Science, 23,* 337–370.

Siegler, R. S. (1987). The perils of averaging data over strategies: An example from children's addition. *Journal of Experimental Psychology: General, 116,* 250–264.

Simon, H. A. (1969). *The sciences of the artificial.* Cambridge, MA: MIT Press.

Simon, H. A., & Barenfeld, M. (1969). Information processing analysis of perceptual processes in problem solving. *Psychological Review, 7,* 473–483.

Simon, H. A., & Chase, W. G. (1973). Skill in chess. *American Scientist, 61,* 393–403.

Simon, H. A., & Gilmartin, K. J. (1973). A simulation of memory for chess positions. *Cognitive Psychology, 5,* 29–46.

Staszewski, J. J. (1990). Exceptional memory: The influence of practice and knowledge on the development of elaborative encoding strategies. In F. E. Weinert, & W. Schneider (Eds.), *Interactions among aptitudes, strategies, and knowledge in cognitive performance* (pp. 252–285). New York: Springer.

Thorndike, E. L., & Woodworth, R. S. (1901). The influence of improvement in one mental function upon the efficiency of other functions. *Psychological Review, 9,* 374–382.

Waters, A. J., & Gobet, F. (2008). Mental imagery and chunks: Empirical and computational findings. *Memory & Cognition, 36,* 505–517.

7

Paths to Discovery

ROGER W. SCHVANEVELDT

Arizona State University, USA

TREVOR A. COHEN

University of Texas at Houston, USA

G. KERR WHITFIELD

University of Arizona, USA

INTRODUCTION

*I*t is a great honor to participate in this symposium honoring the scientific work of Bill Chase. Author Roger Schvaneveldt was fortunate to work with Bill as a fellow graduate student at Wisconsin in the 1960s, a time of great ferment in cognitive psychology. Roger learned many things from Bill—among them were rigor, not to beg the question (in the proper sense of the expression), to enjoy doing research, and the fruits of collaboration (Schvaneveldt & Chase, 1969). Much of Roger's work was also inspired by Bill's later work in expertise (Chase & Simon, 1973), and while the material we present for this symposium is not directly on expertise, it is inspired by the recognition that expertise involves acquiring extensive knowledge. The work is also intimately concerned with search, a theme central to much of Bill's work. Search is an essential aspect of discovery. One goal of our work is to provide some tools to aid the development of expertise by identifying new connections among ideas. Such new connections are central to building chunks, another of Bill's key ideas about expertise. Some of the new connections we identify may just be new for a particular investigator, but we are also interested in assisting in the discovery of new connections that have not been made in a scientific community. In short, we are tackling one aspect of scientific discovery.

There are many strands of investigation in the study of scientific discovery. Carnegie Mellon University has been the source of many contributions to this area of research. The seminal work developing a means-ends analysis of problem solving by Newell and Simon and colleagues on the General Problem Solver (Newell, Shaw, & Simon, 1958; Newell & Simon, 1972) provided early impetus to the newly developing fields of cognitive psychology and artificial intelligence. This pioneering work led to subsequent efforts directed specifically at scientific discovery (Langley, Simon, Bradshaw, & Zytkow, 1987; Shrager & Langley, 1990). The Bacon program for discovering scientific laws from scientific data was among the important accomplishments of that work. Pat Langley has continued work on scientific discovery with numerous colleagues. The major goal of much of this work is to develop computational models capable of making scientific discoveries without direct human intervention, aside from the design and implementation of the software, of course. Our goal is, in some ways, more modest. We aim to develop computational tools to aid human experts expand their expertise, or perhaps, to make some new discoveries.

We have been pursuing an approach to scientific discovery stemming from abductive reasoning as proposed by C. S. Peirce in the late 19th Century (see Peirce, 1940, for a summary). Peirce held that a complete logical analysis of scientific reasoning should include an analysis of the discovery of hypotheses in addition to the logic involved in testing, confirming, revising, and rejecting hypotheses. The introduction of new hypotheses involves abductive reasoning in contrast to the deductive and inductive reasoning apparent in other aspects of hypothesis testing. Abductive reasoning goes from observations to hypothesis. Despite Sherlock Holmes' claim to using deduction, he was actually using abductive reasoning in his detective work, and he recognized an essential quality: "I have no data yet. It is a capital mistake to theorize before one has data. Insensibly one begins to twist facts to suit theories, instead of theories to suit facts" (Sir Arthur Conan Doyle, *The Adventures of Sherlock Holmes*, [1891] 2009, p. 4).

Harman (1965) provides persuasive arguments for abductive reasoning (reasoning to the best explanation) as a better account of the development of scientific theory than is inductive inference which is often given that role in logical accounts of scientific practice. For a compelling example, Hanson (1958) traces the abductive reasoning at work in the 30-year effort by Kepler to arrive at his laws of planetary motion. Peirce proposed that abductive reasoning operated according to logic just as deductive and inductive reasoning do. Simon (1973) agrees with Peirce, Harman, and Hanson that there is a logic to discovery. He points out that we call a process "logical" when it satisfies norms we have established for it. The study of the logic of discovery involves identifying such norms. In a previous paper, we examined abductive reasoning in some detail, drawing out some of the many factors that influence the proposing of new hypotheses (Schvaneveldt & Cohen, 2010). As we studied the various factors, it seemed useful to distinguish between influences on the *generation* of hypotheses as opposed to influences on the *evaluation* of hypotheses. Although the generation and evaluation of hypotheses appear to be closely intertwined in practice, some factors seem to be more involved in generation and others more in evaluation. Generating new ideas is an essential step in abductive inference. Some of our computational tools are more focused on the generation of potential hypotheses while other tools are designed to evaluate the generated hypotheses in the interest of focusing on the most promising candidates first. In either case, we conceive of our effort as providing tools to assist experts who are the final arbiters of the value of the candidates identified by our EpiphaNet software.

Generation often involves identifying new connections among ideas. Koestler (1990) argued that creativity usually entails bringing previously unconnected ideas together, and he proposed the term, *bisociation* to refer to this joining of ideas. We can see the operation of bisociation in the formation of analogies (Gentner, 1983; Gentner, Holyoak, & Kokinov, 2001). Falkenhainer (1990) argued that similarity was at the heart of all scientific discovery whether it be seen as deduction, abduction, or analogy because proposing explanations of phenomena are driven by their similarity to understood phenomena. Perhaps such processes can be usefully seen as extensions of the basic operation of association at work in the basic learning processes long studied in psychological laboratories. However, more than regular co-occurrence is involved in discovery. Similar patterns of occurrence can signal interesting relationships regardless of co-occurrence. So while connecting ideas is an important step in discovery, there still remains the question of just which ideas to connect. Random connections seem too remote to be useful,[1] so some constraints to guide the search for plausible ideas are necessary. In the generation of possibilities, some basis for connecting ideas could improve the likelihood of finding a fruitful line of investigation. Of course, strong or direct connections are found among already known relationships so weaker or indirect connections are where new discoveries are to be found. Our approach has been to employ measures of similarity that go beyond direct association which can be used to identify potential hypotheses. In this chapter, we summarize some of our work on this problem in the context of literature-based discovery, finding new connections among ideas expressed in different literatures.

The overall objective of our project is to develop scalable computational tools to assist discovery from text corpora. Our approach involves developing abductive reasoning theory to analyze the process of discovery (Schvaneveldt & Cohen, 2010) and develop models of high-dimensional distributional semantics (see Widdows, 2004, for an overview) for measuring semantic similarity in text. We broaden the notion of semantic similarity to include various kinds of semantic relationships, all contributing to the semantic similarity among terms found in text. Our approach also employs Pathfinder networks (McDonald, Plate, & Schvaneveldt, 1990; Schvaneveldt, 1990; Schvaneveldt, Durso, & Dearholt,

---

1 However, random processes in a mix with other factors do constitute one method of adding new information as in genetic algorithms (Holland, 1992).

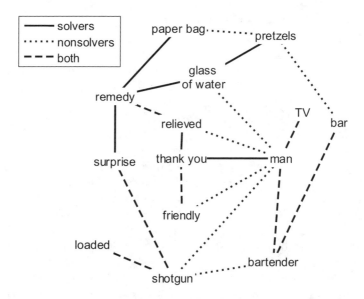

Figure 7.1   PFNets from ratings of relatedness for concepts related to the puzzle.

1989) to aid visualization of relationships and to reveal significant connections among terms. The Pathfinder algorithm identifies links between terms by retaining those links on minimum distance paths between terms where distances are derived from representations of terms in high-dimensional space such that semantically related terms are closer together than less related terms.

A puzzle might help illustrate the role of connections in providing explanations. How might the following events be explained?

> A man walks into a bar and asks the bartender for a glass of water. The bartender pulls a shotgun from under the bar and points it at the man. The man says, "Thank you," and leaves.

Frank Durso and his colleagues (Dayton, Durso, & Shepard, 1990; Durso, Rea, & Dayton, 1994) presented this puzzle to people and asked them to rate the relatedness among a collection of concepts during the period of time they were working on the problem. They showed that people who provided the key answer to the puzzle (solvers) tended to emphasize certain key relations more than those who could not see the key answer (non-solvers). Figure 7.1 shows Pathfinder networks (PFNets) that link strongly related concepts in the ratings for solvers and non-solvers. People are often able to identify the key answer after seeing the solver connections. Interestingly, the studies showed that the solvers often began to notice the critical connections *before* coming up with the key answer.[2] This

---

2 Would hiccups explain the puzzle and the connections in the network?

example illustrates the value of making critical connections in the discovery process. In this case, the connections of "remedy" to "shotgun" through "surprise" and the connection of "remedy" to "glass of water" is the key to seeing the connection of "shotgun" and "glass of water," both provide remedies.

Our approach to discovering interesting new connections from textual sources grows out of work on high-dimensional wordspace models. In such models, vectors represent various texts ranging from words to whole documents, and similarity or relatedness between text units can be assessed by computing relations between vectors such as the distances between the points represented by the vectors or the cosine of the angle between vectors.

The use of geometric models of meaning is familiar in cognitive science. The semantic differential scale of connotative meaning proposed by Osgood, Suci, and Tannenbaum (1957) is an early example of a model that provides measures of concepts on a variety of different dimensions. Multidimensional Scaling (Kruskal, 1964a, 1964b; Shepard, 1962a, 1962b) has provided spatial models of proximity data in a wide variety of situations. Gärdenfors (2000) argues that human judgments of similarity relations call for a spatial mode of representation that can provide the basis of the ability to see such similarity. Widdows (2004) provides a very readable overview of the use of geometry to model meaning, and Van Rijsbergen (2004) provides a rigorous account of the way geometry figures into information retrieval.

WORDSPACE MODELS

Several variations on wordspace models have been developed following the work of Salton and his colleagues in which they proposed representing each document in a database with a vector containing weighted occurrences of each term in the database (Salton, 1989; Salton & McGill, 1983). The original model placed documents in a space with dimensionality equal to the number of terms in the database. Similarity of documents is represented by the proximity of documents in the space, and proximity is determined by the degree of correspondence of terms in documents. More recently several other variations have been developed including Hyperspace Analog to Language (HAL),[3] Latent Semantic Analysis (LSA),[4] and Random Indexing (RI).[5] Evaluations of these models tend to focus on the extent to which the associations derived between

---

3 For papers on HAL, see Burgess, Livesay, and Lund (1998); Lund and Burgess (1996).
4 LSA is an outgrowth of an earlier model, Latent Semantic Indexing (LSI), designed specifically for information retrieval. LSA now represents a more general model of semantic similarity which is used in many different ways. Some relevant publications include: Deerwester, Dumais, Furnas, Landauer, and Harshman (1990); Landauer and Dumais (1997); Landauer, Foltz, and Laham (1998); Landauer, McNamara, Dennis, and Kintsch (2007).
5 RI derives from work on sparse distributed memory by Kanerva (1988). For additional papers, see Cohen (2008); Cohen, Schvaneveldt, & Rindflesch (2009); Cohen, Schvaneveldt, & Widdows (2010); Kanerva (2000); Kanerva, Kristofersson, & Holst (2000); Sahlgren (2006); Widdows (2004); Widdows & Ferraro (2008); Widdows & Peters (2003).

terms are consistent with human judgment, although their utility for information retrieval has also been investigated. While distributional models all derive quantitative estimates of the semantic relatedness of terms from contextual co-occurrence, the models differ in the way in which a context is defined.

HAL vectors come from a matrix of co-occurrences of the unique terms in a text database where co-occurrence corresponds to terms appearing together in a sliding window of k terms moved through the text. The data can reflect both distances between the terms in the text as well as the order of the terms in the text when a distinction is made between terms occurring before and after a particular term. In any case, each term is then represented by the vector of its co-occurrences across all of the terms in the text. The dimensionality of the space is the number of terms in the database. Optionally, the dimensionality can be reduced using the method employed by LSA. An important characteristic of this method is the compilation of the frequencies of co-occurrence of terms in the database. The matrix constructed is a *term-by-term matrix*. Vectors for terms come from the rows (or columns) of this matrix. Similarity of terms can be determined by taking the cosine of the angle between the two vectors corresponding to the terms. Because the cosine is basically a correlation of the vectors, it reflects both the degree to which terms co-occur and the similarity of their patterns of occurrence with other terms in the database. As we develop in more detail later, we would like to distinguish between *direct* similarity (stemming from co-occurrence of terms) and *indirect* similarity (stemming from the correlation due to patterns of co-occurrence across other terms in the database). Indirect similarity is referred to as indirect inference in the LSA literature, and is considered to make an important contribution to the model's human-like performance.

LSA vectors are derived from applying singular value decomposition (SVD) to a *term-by-document matrix* containing the frequency of occurrence of each term in the database in each document in the database. Documents are often full documents such as scientific articles or other units such as abstracts or titles or even phrases, sentences, paragraphs, or chapters. The matrix is usually modified to dampen the effects of term frequency and to give greater weight to terms that occur more selectively in documents. In any case, performing SVD on the matrix allows one to identify the factors that account for the most variance in the documents analogous to the method of factor analysis. The goal is to retain a subset of the factors which reflect the essential semantic relations. Typically between 100 and 300 dimensions are retained. Subsequently, each term and each document in the database are represented by a vector of this reduced dimensionality, a rather remarkable reduction. Focusing on terms, the original term by document matrix yields vectors for terms of dimensionality corresponding to the number of documents where each vector represents the frequency of occurrence of each term across all the documents. With such vectors, the similarity between terms would simply reflect the degree to which terms co-occur in documents. The cosine for terms that never occur in the same document is zero because the representation for documents makes them orthogonal. However, the dimension reduction accomplished by LSA not only results in a more compact representation, but it also reveals the semantic similarity of terms that do not occur together, but are nonetheless related. Synonyms are one example of such terms. Synonyms tend not to occur together, but they do tend to co-occur with similar other terms. LSA systems recognize such similarity which is important to our project.

Originally, random indexing (RI) derived its vectors by assigning sparse randomly constructed vectors to documents in a database. The vectors are of fixed length (typically 1,000 to 4,000 elements long consisting mostly of 0s with non-zero values in a small number (usually about 20) of randomly chosen elements, usually consisting of an equal number of 1s and -1s (Kanerva et al., 2000). In any case, the random vectors are nearly orthogonal because the occurrence of non-zero elements in the same position in two vectors is rare. In fact, most pairs of such vectors are orthogonal (cosine is zero). The non-zero cosines that occur by chance induce a small degree of random similarity between the documents associated with such vectors. Vectors for the terms in the documents are constructed by adding together all the document vectors for each time a term occurs in a document. Importantly, this procedure for creating a wordspace can be done incrementally. A new document can be incorporated by simply updating all the terms in the new document. Constructed in this way, the cosine similarity of term vectors primarily reflects the co-occurrence of terms in documents. Two terms will have higher cosines to the extent that they tend to occur in the same documents. Nevertheless, RI models constructed in this way do capture some of the semantics of terms. Kanerva et al. (2000) reported comparable performance of RI and LSA on the TOEFL test where the models must select an appropriate synonym from a set of alternatives. The RI method performs well across a range of vector lengths. Kanerva et al. (2000) showed that performance on the TOEFL test increased as vector length increased from 1,000 to 10,000, but the increase was small with vector lengths greater than 4,000. Obviously sparsity also increases with vector length. The random vectors have non-zero values in 20/length entries (for vectors with 20 non-zero elements); 2% for vectors of length 1,000. Table 7.1 shows the results of a Monte Carlo simulation of the cosine similarity of collections of random vectors. In the simulation, 1,000 random vectors of each length were generated and the cosine similarities for all pairs of vectors were computed. The mean cosines are all very close to zero. Table 7.1 shows the probability of obtaining a cosine not equal to zero, the standard deviation of the cosines, the minimum cosine observed and

TABLE 7.1   Monte Carlo Simulation of Random Vector Similarity

Vector length	$p(\cos \neq 0)$	stddev cos	min cos	max cos
500	0.490	0.045	− 0.250	0.250
1000	0.309	0.032	− 0.200	0.200
2000	0.175	0.022	− 0.200	0.200
4000	0.094	0.016	− 0.150	0.150

the maximum cosine observed. Clearly, the vectors show an increasing degree of orthogonality as the vector length increases, so with shorter vectors more incidental (random) similarity of the vectors is introduced. In our applications, we use thresholds for cosine values to avoid including relations introduced by noise. In one study, we found that higher thresholds were required for the shorter vectors to eliminate noise which is what would be expected from the greater degree of random overlap with shorter vectors.

Cohen, Schvaneveldt, and Widdows (2010) proposed a variation on RI to improve its ability to find meaningful indirect connections. Reflective Random Indexing (RRI) begins in the same way as RI, but an additional iteration of vector creation is introduced. Specifically, new document vectors are created for all the documents as described previously, then new term vectors are created by adding together the new document vectors each time a term occurs in the documents. These new term vectors reflect both direct and indirect similarity as we document in subsequent sections.

This cyclic process of creating document and term vectors, if carried on, converges to a single vector,[6] and all terms will have identical vectors. Our tests have shown that one or two iterations is sufficient to capture indirect similarity. Going beyond that yields poorer performance because of the convergence of the vectors. Interestingly, computing only an iteration or two appears to be sufficient to accomplish the objective of creating the indirect similarity lacking from RI. The iteration can be performed starting with random vectors for terms as opposed to documents. Thus, we can distinguish between DRRI (which starts with random vectors for documents) and TRRI (which starts with random vectors for terms). Figure 7.2 shows the steps involved in creating wordspaces using random vectors.

There are several advantages to the random vector approach. The use of sparse vectors can improve both the time and space requirements of algorithms for creating and updating wordspace models. As we discuss later, we have been able to build wordspace models for all of the abstracts in the MEDLINE database of abstracts (over 9 million documents and about 4 million unique terms). We do not have the computational resources to accomplish the SVD required of LSA for a database of this size. Models based on random indexing can also be created and updated incrementally because adding a new document to the model simply involves updating the existing vectors. Vectors for documents or, more generally, combinations of words, can be created at any time by just adding together all the term vectors for terms in the documents with provision for weighting the terms and normalizing the vectors.

NEAREST NEIGHBORS IN WORDSPACES

We find that displaying the nearest neighbors of terms in the form of a network aids in seeing what terms are present as well as identifying some of the strongest

---

6 Such iteration is the technique employed in the power method of computing the matrix eigenvector of greatest magnitude.

Step

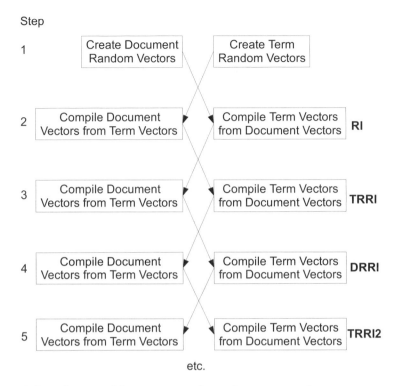

Figure 7.2   Schematic of the steps in creating random vector wordspaces.

relations among the terms. Pathfinder networks (PFnets, Schvaneveldt, 1990; Schvaneveldt, Durso, & Dearholt, 1989) produce a pruned set of connections by preserving shortest paths between nodes.[7] We present a number of such networks to illustrate the kind of neighbors retrieved by different wordspace models. The networks are created by identifying the 20 nearest neighbors to a key term by finding the terms with the greatest cosine similarities to the key term in the wordspace. Of course, a term is always a nearest neighbor to itself by this method. Once the nearest neighbors are retrieved, a half matrix of cosine similarities is computed representing all the pairs of terms in the set of neighbors. Pathfinder is then used to identify the paths of greatest similarity between terms, and the links on these paths are preserved. The network is displayed using a force-directed layout algorithm (see e.g., Kamada & Kawai, 1989).

---

7 Using all known proximities between nodes, Pathfinder computes the minimum distance between nodes and eliminates links that have a distance greater than the minimum distance. Two parameters are used to compute distance, q, which is the maximum number of links permitted in paths, and r, which is the norm for the Minkowski r-metric. With $r = \infty$, only ordinal properties of the proximity data determine which links are included in the PFnet.

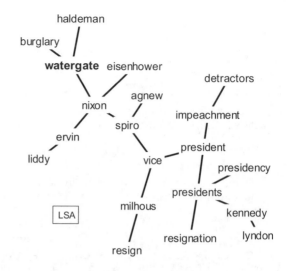

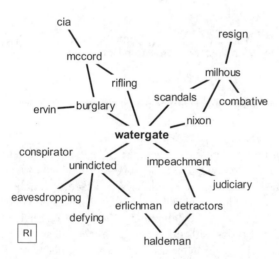

Figure 7.3   PFnets for nearest neighbors of *Watergate* in LSA and RI wordspaces.

To focus on indirect relations, we can optionally screen out any nearest neighbors that co-occur with a particular term, so we create a set of indirect neighbors when we find the nearest neighbors of a term and screen out neighbors that co-occur with the term. Then we can compute a Pathfinder network (PFnet) in the same way.[8] Figure 7.3 shows the nearest neighbors of *Watergate* in the Touchstone Applied Sciences (TASA) Corpus for two wordspace models,

8 The networks we present in this section were computed with PFnet parameters $r = \infty$ and $q = 2$.

LSA and RI. The General Text Parser (Giles, Wo, & Berry, 2001) was used to create the LSA wordspace, and the Semantic Vectors package (Widdows & Ferraro, 2008) was use to create the RI wordspace.

The LSA model consists of 150 dimensions, and the RI model used 500 dimensions with 20 non-zero elements in the document random vectors. Both models produce sets of terms that are clearly related to *Watergate* with some overlap of terms but several distinct terms as well. Essentially both models produce a reasonable set of nearest neighbors.

Figure 7.4 shows Pathfinder networks for the indirect neighbors of Watergate in both LSA and RI wordspaces. The solid links indicate terms that co-occur (direct links), and the dashed links indicate terms that do not co-occur in any document (indirect links). Because the terms are all indirect neighbors of *Watergate*, links to *Watergate* will all be indirect. LSA reflects both direct and indirect similarity among terms so it produces indirect neighbors that are semantically related to *Watergate*. However, the same cannot be said for the nearest indirect neighbors obtained in the RI wordspace. With effort one can find some meaningful connections, but, in general, the terms in the RI indirect network are not particularly related to *Watergate*. Here we clearly see the consequences of the near orthogonality of the random vectors used to establish the RI wordspace; the vectors for a pair of terms that do not co-occur have a high probability of being near-orthogonal. The similarity of term vectors in that wordspace only reflects the co-occurrence of terms in the documents plus some incidental similarity produced by random overlap in the random vectors created for documents. Sometimes this random overlap leads to groups of related terms occurring as neighbors of the source term as with *Swaziland* and *Lesotho*, both landlocked countries in Southern Africa and with *Nerva, Domitian, Comitia, Curiata, Centuriata*, and *imperium*, all referring to political entities in Ancient Rome. These groups of interrelated terms are presumably only related to *Watergate* by virtue of incidental overlap in random vectors; these related terms probably co-occur in a particular document that by chance has a similar elemental vector to a document containing *Watergate*. As indirect neighbors, we know that none of the terms occurred with *Watergate* in any document. Such similarity would not be expected to be present in another RI model created with new random vectors.

Figure 7.5 illustrates the nearest neighbors and the nearest indirect neighbors of *Watergate* in the TRRI wordspace created by starting with random term vectors, creating document vectors by adding the random term vectors in the documents, and then creating new term vectors by adding document vectors for each time a term occurs in a document.

All of the terms seem somewhat related to *Watergate*. The nearest indirect neighbors in the TRRI wordspace are reasonably related to *Watergate* just as they are in the LSA wordspace. However, the indirect neighbors in LSA and TRRI wordspaces show only minor overlap (*appointees* and *impounded*). An inspection of the non-overlapping terms reveals a few in each set that have a close relation to the Watergate affair (*attempted, resigns,* and *tempore* for LSA;

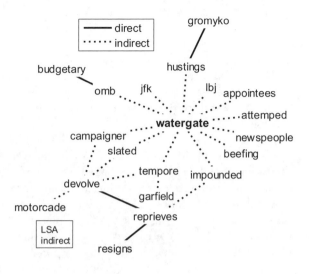

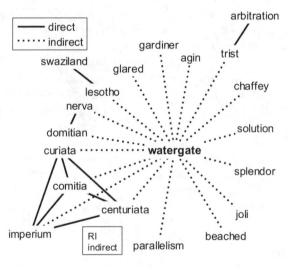

Figure 7.4 PFnets for nearest indirect neighbors of *Watergate* in LSA and RI wordspaces.

impeach, inaugurated, and *withdrew* for TRRI). Other terms are related to *Watergate* in a more general way.

Figure 7.6 shows a comparison of the nearest neighbors of *Watergate* in each of the three wordspaces (LSA, RI, and TRRI). The intersection of all three sets contains terms centrally involved in the Watergate affair. Others are clearly connected to *Watergate* (*Liddy, resignation, scandal, senate, McCord, rifling, Erlichman, scandals,* to list a few), but some are related more generally to Nixon or government.

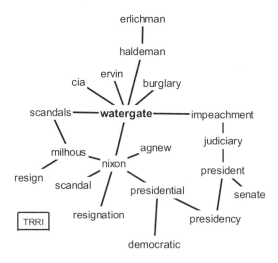

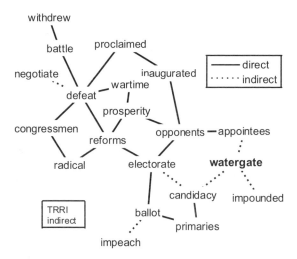

Figure 7.5   PFnets for nearest neighbors and nearest indirect neighbors of *Watergate* in the TRRI wordspace.

LITERATURE-BASED DISCOVERY

Don Swanson (1986, 1987) spawned a line of research known as literature-based discovery with his proposal that fish oil is a potential treatment for Raynaud's syndrome, intermittent blood flow in the extremities. This discovery came about as a result of linking two distinct literatures through the realization that blood flow can be affected by blood viscosity which means that factors that reduce blood viscosity may offer a treatment for Raynaud's syndrome.

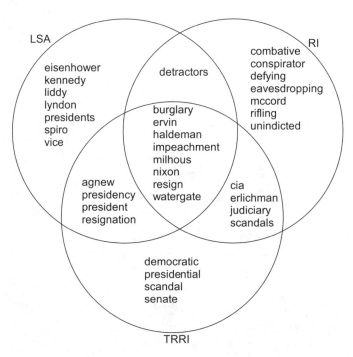

Figure 7.6   Overlap in the nearest neighbors of *Watergate* in the LSA, RI, and TRRI wordspaces.

Searching for such factors leads to fish oil, among other possibilities. Swanson developed these ideas into a method for discovery that has become known as "Swanson linking." Swanson (1991) subsequently used the method to find other interesting connections, including linking migraine and magnesium.

Other researchers (Bruza, Cole, Song, & Bari, 2006; Cohen, Schvaneveldt, & Widdows, 2010; Gordon & Dumais, 1998) have attempted to reproduce Swanson's discovery using automated systems with varying degrees of success. Bruza et al., using a HAL model, were able to find a wordspace that produced *fish* and *oil* in the top 10 ranked results by weighting the dimensions of the vector for *Raynaud* that correspond to a manually created set of intermediate terms (such as *viscosity*). However, this result was only found for particular metrics and weighting and not for others, limiting the generality of the finding. Cohen et al. (2010) also met with mixed success in attempting to reproduce Swanson's discoveries. Using a small corpus of titles of MEDLINE articles from 1980 to 1985 (the period Swanson used in his original work), two wordspaces including TRRI consistently produce reasonably good rankings for the *Raynaud's* and *migraine* discoveries. A term–term wordspace consistently produced a ranking in the top 5 for *eicosapentaenoic* (the acid that is the active ingredient in fish oil) among the nearest indirect neighbors of *Raynaud* in over 100 simulations with changing random vectors. By looking for indirect

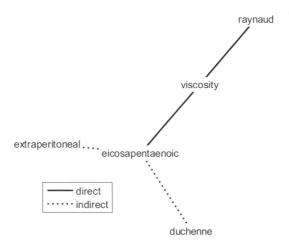

Figure 7.7   PFnet for the five nearest neighbors of *Raynaud + eicosapentaenoic (acid)*.

(non-co-occurring) neighbors, it is not necessary to explicitly identify a linking term. This is appealing for both theoretical and practical reasons, because an exhaustive search through the space of potential middle terms for new hypotheses is not feasible given the constraints on both human cognition and the computational resources available to many researchers. This result confirms the potential value of exploring indirect similarities with a term of interest. Once a new term of interest is found, it can be conjoined with the original term to find linking terms. The PFnet in Figure 7.7 illustrates this effect. As noted by Swanson and Smalheiser (1997), dietary eicosapentaenoic acid can decrease *blood viscosity*, and abnormally high blood viscosity has been reported in patients with Raynaud's disease. Not only does the linking term *viscosity* occur as a nearest neighbor, it also is appropriately linked to the two search terms.

EPIPHANET

Our research has led Trevor Cohen to develop a software suite, EpiphaNet.[9] The software embodies our developing thinking about abductive reasoning, and it allows some testing of the ideas in real research endeavors. As mentioned earlier, we recognize that abductive reasoning involves both generation of potential new ideas as well as evaluation of the new ideas to determine their value for further consideration. The tools in EpiphaNet are designed to aid abductive discovery by a researcher in both the generation of potentially interesting new connections among ideas and in the evaluation of the new connections to learn more about them.

9 Cohen (2010) provides links to a website with an implementation of EpiphaNet.

Generation of ideas is aided by displaying PFnets of neighbors to a term (or terms) of interest. Indirect neighbors can be generated if the interest is in examining possible connections that have not already occurred in the database. Optionally, the user can choose to see PFnets depicting general associations or predications involving the terms of interest. We explain more about the predication option in the following section.

Evaluation of ideas is aided by additional PFnets which include newly discovered terms or sets of terms, often looking for terms that may link other terms of interest. Direct access to PubMed[10] searches is also provided by EpiphaNet allowing the user to refer to specific MEDLINE citations for more information. Consequently EpiphaNet allows the user to evaluate novel connections generated by the system, which may in turn lead to new directions for exploration.

The primary testbed for EpiphaNet has been the MEDLINE database of titles and abstracts of articles in the biomedical literature. In 2008, the full MEDLINE index of abstracts contains 9,003,811 documents and 1,125,311,210 terms of which 3,948,887 terms are unique. Our complete wordspaces consist of 453,646 unique terms which excludes terms occurring less than 10 times and terms that contain more than three non-alphabetic characters.

In EpiphaNet, rather than use associations between terms as the basis for retrieval, the fundamental units of analysis are unique concepts as defined in the Unified Medical Language System (UMLS, Browne, Divita, Aronson, & McCray, 2003). The UMLS represents an ambitious effort by the US National Library of Medicine to provide unique names of biomedical concepts to accelerate the development of computational systems to support natural language understanding in this domain. The primary knowledge resource in the UMLS is the Metathesaurus which provides unique identifiers for known biomedical concepts, as well as mappings between these unique concepts and the different ways in which they are known to be expressed in free text. Using defined UMLS concepts rather than individual terms as a basis for knowledge discovery allows the normalization of synonymous terms and the ability to address concepts that are characteristically expressed with more than one term (such as *Raynaud's disease* or *fish oil*). Because the preferred way of expressing a particular concept in the UMLS may not match the way a user expresses this concept, EpiphaNet includes a statistically based translation service to map between terms and UMLS concepts.

Translation is accomplished using a variant of the Reflective Random Indexing (Cohen et al., 2010) method, based on the term-by-document and UMLS concept-by-document statistics from the titles and abstracts added to MEDLINE over the past 10 years. UMLS concepts are identified in text by the

---

10 PubMed is a free search engine for accessing the MEDLINE database of citations, abstracts and some full text articles on life sciences and biomedical topics.

TABLE 7.2   Cosine Similarity and Terms Retrieved from Translating the Terms "GORD" and "AIDS"

GORD	AIDS
0.53: gastroesophageal_reflux_disease	0.953: aids_patient
0.53: acid_reflux_(esophageal)	0.939: acquired_immunodeficiency_syndrome
0.53: intra-oesophageal	0.840: aids_diagnosis
0.52: reflux	0.829: aids_population
0.47: retrosternal_burning	0.828: anti-hiv_agents

Note: The term "GERD" is used to refer to "GORD" in the United States. "GORD" is preferred in much of the English-speaking world. Both terms appear in the unique concepts.

Metamap system (Aronson, 2001) (which also identifies UMLS concepts in the SemRep system). A common set of document vectors is generated based on the distribution of terms in each document in this corpus, and both term and UMLS vectors are generated based on the frequency with which they occur in each document using vector addition. Log-entropy weighting and the stopword list distributed with Swanson's Arrowsmith system (Swanson & Smalheiser, 1997) are used to emphasize content-bearing words and eliminate frequently occurring and uninformative terms. Examples of mappings between terms and concepts are shown in Table 7.2. Because these searches are based on similarity between vectors, related concepts (such as retrosternal_burning) as well as matching concepts are retrieved.

EpiphaNet supports both general associations and predications to determine the nearest neighbors that are retrieved when a particular concept (or set of concepts) occurs as a cue.

General Associations

In the case of general associations, EpiphaNet employs Reflective Random Indexing (Cohen et al., 2010) to derive a general measure of semantic relatedness between terms. As described previously, this reflective approach allows for the derivation of meaningful associations between terms that do not co-occur directly. In EpiphaNet, general associations between concepts are derived based on document vectors produced by TRRI. This wordspace provides meaningful estimates of the similarity between documents according to the distribution of terms in documents. Vectors for UMLS concepts are generated as the linear sum of the vectors for the documents they occur in, in a similar manner to the generation of term vectors in TRRI. Consequently, it is possible to map between general terms and UMLS concepts based on the distance between them in this shared wordspace. At the time of this writing, the distributional statistics for UMLS concepts include all occurrences recognized by the MetaMap sub-component of the SemRep system (see below) in abstracts or titles added to MEDLINE over the past decade.

Predications

Research on empirical distributional semantics tends to focus on general associations between terms. However, it has been argued that the atomic unit of meaning in text comprehension is not an individual concept but an object–relation–object triplet, or proposition. This unit of meaning is also termed a predication in the computational linguistics literature. These propositions are considered to be the atomic units of meaning in memory, or the "semantic processing units of the mind" (Kintsch, 1998). Empirical evidence to support the psychological reality of the propositional level of representation has been provided by experiments assessing memory and reading times (e.g., Goetz, Anderson, & Schallert, 1981; Kintsch & Keenan, 1973). In essence these studies suggest that terms in a propositional relationship to one another cue one another for recall and tend to be recalled together, and that both the accurate recall and the time taken to read text are affected more by the number of propositions in a passage than by the number of terms. While not primarily motivated by cognitive phenomena, the desire to derive empirically a more constrained measure of semantic relatedness than co-occurrence-based general association has led to the development of wordspace models derived from grammatical relations produced by a parser (see Pado & Lapata, 2007, for an example and review). However, these models do not encode the type of relationship that exists between terms in a retrievable manner. For the purpose of abductive reasoning, the encoding and retrieval of the type of relationship between concepts are desirable because it provides one way of constraining search, and it raises the possibility of simulating cognitive processes involving specific relations within a vector space.

In our research we address this issue by encoding predications produced by the SemRep system (Rindflesch & Fiszman, 2003) into a vector space. SemRep combines shallow grammatical parsing with semantic knowledge provided by specialized biomedical knowledge resources such as the UMLS to extract object–relation–object triplets (e.g., *aspirin* DISRUPTS *sunscreen effect*) from the biomedical literature. SemRep builds on a suite of natural language tools and knowledge resources developed at the US National Library of Medicine including software to map free text to UMLS concepts (Aronson, 2001), a semantic network describing permitted relations between UMLS concepts (for example, TREATS is permitted between drugs and diseases), and further natural language processing software and knowledge resources that have been customized for the biomedical domain (Browne et al., 2003). SemRep ignores much of English grammar for identifying propositions because knowledge-rich domains provide the information needed from the semantics of the domain. The approximately 80% precision SemRep has shown in several evaluations (Fiszman, Demner-Fushman, Kilicoglu, & Rindflesch, 2009; Fiszman, Rindflesch, & Kilicoglu, 2004; Rindflesch & Fiszman, 2003; Rindflesch, Libbus, Hristovski, Aronson, & Kilicoglu, 2003) is impressive in light of the difficulty of extracting predicates from text. The proportion of propositions available in the text that is extracted by

TABLE 7.3   The Forty Predicates Encoded for the MEDLINE Database

Administered_to	Contains	Interconnects	Predisposes
Affects	Converts_to	ISA	Prevents
Associated_with	Degree_of	Issue_in	Process_of
Augments	Diagnoses	Location_of	Produces
Branch_of	Disrupts	Manifestation_of	Property_of
Carries_out	Evaluation_of	Measurement_of	Result_of
Causes	Exhibits	Measures	Stimulates
Coexists_with	Indicates	Method_of	Surrounds
Complicates	Inhibits	Part_of	Treats
Conceptual_part_of	Interacts_with	Precedes	Uses

SemRep is more difficult to evaluate, and is not known. Nonetheless, the predications extracted by SemRep represent a significant quantity of biomedical knowledge, and EpiphaNet currently encodes such information from more than 20 million predications extracted by SemRep from titles and abstracts added to the MEDLINE database over the past decade.

Predication-based Semantic Indexing (PSI), the model we employ to encode these predications within a vector space, is based on recent distributional models that are able to encode information concerning word order into wordspace models (Jones & Mewhort, 2007; Plate, 2003; Sahlgren, Holst, & Kanerva, 2008; Widdows & Cohen, 2009).

PSI codes predication by transforming random elemental vectors for UMLS concepts and then combining these to generate semantic vectors for the same UMLS concepts. The sparse-random elemental vectors are transformed using position shifts according to the type of predication relationship that connects two terms. Each of 40 predication types (shown in Table 7.3) is assigned a numerical value such that the number of positions shifted encodes the type of relationship between terms. To encode "*smoking* CAUSES *cancer*," we shift the sparse elemental vector for *cancer* seven positions to the right (the shift code for CAUSES) and add it to the semantic vector for *smoking*. A similar process will occur each time *smoking* occurs in a predication. Consequently, the semantic vector for *smoking* will be the linear sum of the shifted sparse elemental vectors representing the other concept and type of predicate for every predication involving *smoking*. Also the semantic vector for *cancer* is updated by adding to it the elemental vector for *smoking* shifted seven positions to the left. These directional shifts code for the subject, the object and the predication. Each concept is thus represented by both a semantic vector and the original elemental vector. Both of these representations are used for search and retrieval in the PSI space.

To retrieve predications involving *smoking*, the elemental vector for *smoking* is shifted and the similarity of the shifted vector to all semantic vectors is assessed. In addition, the semantic vector for *smoking* is shifted, and the similarity of the shifted vector to all the elemental vectors is assessed. We perform this search in both directions (elemental vector as cue for semantic vectors and vice versa) because both directions retrieve more predications than either taken alone. Consequently, we take the strongest associations across both directions. This ensures that the predication search is reflexive (if " $\underline{?}$ CAUSES *cancer*" retrieves *smoking*, "*smoking* CAUSES $\underline{?}$" will retrieve *cancer*).

For searches across all predications, the search in both directions is done for each possible shift to the right (retrieving predications with *smoking* as the subject term) and each possible shift to the left (retrieving predications with *smoking* as the object term) across the 40 predications. For example, shifting the *smoking* elemental vector by 22 positions to the right would retrieve the ISA predications with *smoking* as the subject so the predication "*smoking* ISA *habit*" could result from searching for predications involving *smoking*.[11]

An actual retrieval using the PSI model for the concepts that best fit a TREATS predication relationship with the concept *depressive disorders* finds *lexapro* (cosine = 0.98), a commonly used antidepressant. In contrast, a query for the concepts that best fit a DIAGNOSES relationship with *depressive disorders* produces *psychiatric interview* and *evaluation* (cosine = 0.53). An evaluation of the accuracy with which predications are encoded into the PSI space is presented in Cohen, Schvaneveldt and Rindflesch (2009), in which precision on average was found to be greater than 95% for the most strongly associated predication relationships (across all predications) for 1000 randomly selected concepts.

Encoding predications into semantic type opens new possibilities for computer-aided knowledge discovery. One possibility involves the identification of pathways to explain an observed indirect association. This can be achieved by searching with two cue concepts through a space that includes only those concepts that occur in documents with both of these cues. It should be noted that the measure of semantic distance utilized in PSI is of a different nature than that employed by previous distributional models. Rather than conflating many types of association into a single metric, PSI selects nearest neighbors on the basis of their strongest typed relationship across all permitted predication types. This allows for the generation of networks of concepts with links that are weighted according to the strength of the best possible predication relationship between them. Consequently, when Pathfinder is applied to this network, it preserves the strongest paths across predicates revealing a logical explanation for the connection between terms.

Figure 7.8 illustrates the use of this procedure to link the terms *viagra* and *tadalafil*. Pathfinder was configured to preserve only the strongest associative links, revealing a logical explanatory pathway connecting these two high-profile pharmaceutical agents. The pathway also includes the predication *viagra ISA sildenafil* revealing the generic name of this drug.

Predications can also be used to model simple analogies. Analogy and metaphor are powerful and, some would argue, pervasive modes of human thinking

---

11 Despite the positional shifts involved, the computation is efficient, because a comparison with an elemental vector involves S floating point comparisons, where S is the seed length, or number of non-zero values in the sparse vector (in our case, 20).

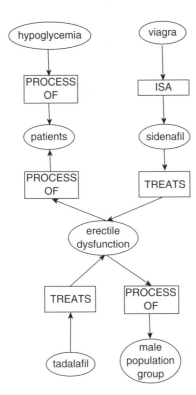

Figure 7.8   Predication EpiphaNet linking *Tadalafil* and *Viagra*.

both in ordinary and creative contexts (Fauconnier & Turner, 2002; Gentner & Markman, 1997; Holyoak & Thagard, 1995; Lakoff & Johnson, 1980). In EpiphaNet, the strongest predication linking two concepts can be identified by finding the largest cosine between their vectors across all possible predicate shifts, so it is possible to model analogy, as illustrated in Table 7.4 where the term with "?" is retrieved by finding the positional shift corresponding to the strongest predication between the known pair of terms and then finding a term with the same predication relationship with the one remaining known term.

Although these are admittedly simple analogical processes, the association strengths produced by PSI could be used to model more complex analogical mappings.

PREDICTING FUTURE CO-OCCURRENCE

By our definition, indirect similarity between terms indicates a relationship in the absence of co-occurrence of the terms in the database in question. Some terms exhibiting indirect similarity may point to an unfamiliar relationship between the concepts corresponding to the terms, a potential discovery. For such terms, we might expect that indirect neighbors would tend to become

TABLE 7.4 Modeling Analogy in PSI Space (The Model Supplied the Term with ?)

A	is to	B	as	C	is to	D	Cosine	Relation / Predicate	Comment
Viagra	is to	*Erectile Dysfunction*	as	*Lexapro*	is to	? *Depressive Disorder*	0.98	TREATS	Lexapro is used to treat depression
Viagra	is to	*Sildenafil*	as	? *Sintamil*	is to	*Anti-depressive Agents*	1	ISA	Sintamil is one example of an antidepressant
Psychogenic Factor	is to	*Erectile Dysfunction*	as	? *Abnormal Cortisol*	is to	*Depressive Disorder*	1	PREDISPOSES	Chronically raised cortisol levels are associated with the development of depression

direct neighbors over time. We investigated such tendencies using the MEDLINE database. In particular, we assessed the proportion of nearest indirect neighbors between 1980 and 1986 that co-occurred in one or more documents after 1986. We examined four different wordspaces all based on random indexing, [RI] the original random indexing method developed by Kanerva et al. (2000), [TTRI] random indexing using a sliding window method to create a term–term matrix of term co-occurrences, and two methods using a new reflective random indexing method adjusted to improve indirect similarity (Cohen et al., 2010), [DRRI] reflective random indexing starting with random vectors for documents, and [TRRI] reflective random indexing starting with term random vectors.

The 50 nearest indirect neighbors (NINs) of each of 2,000 randomly selected target terms were found in the database between 1980 and 1986. Then each of the indirect neighbors was checked to determine whether it co-occurs with its target after 1986. The proportion of the indirect neighbors co-occurring later as a function of the rank of the cosine similarity is shown for each of the wordspaces in Figure 7.9.

The indirect neighbors in the RI wordspace did not co-occur later with their targets very often, a maximum of 4.5%, and the effect of cosine rank on the rate of future co-occurrence was negligible. This result confirms the earlier observation that standard RI does not yield meaningful indirect neighbors. It is reasonable to suppose that about 4.5% of randomly selected pairs of

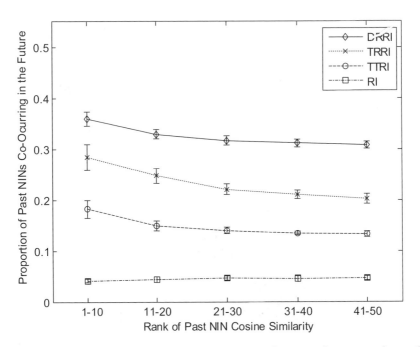

Figure 7.9   Proportion of future co-occurrences as a function of cosine similarity of NINs for various wordspaces.

non-co-occurring terms would later appear as co-occurring. In contrast to RI, all of the other wordspaces show a decline in the proportion of future co-occurrences as cosine similarity decreases, but they do vary considerably in the overall proportions.

To determine whether the various wordspaces tend to produce NINs of different term frequency, we examined the frequencies resulting in the summary statistics shown in Table 7.5 and the distributions of term frequency are shown in Figure 7.10. The TRRI wordspace tended to produce NINs of lower term frequency which may prove to be potentially more interesting as potential discoveries. The higher frequency terms may be more likely to co-occur with the

TABLE 7.5   Summary Statistics on the Term Frequency of NINs

	Wordspace			
	DRRI	**TRRI**	**TTRI**	**RI**
n	41,866	29,281	18,306	7,025
Median	3,622	1,642	2,433	1,700
Mean	11,613	10,626	11,863	11,356
Std Dev	34,435	49,979	39,961	52,090
Minimum	13	13	13	10
Maximum	1,462,238	1,738,132	2,220,191	2,220,191

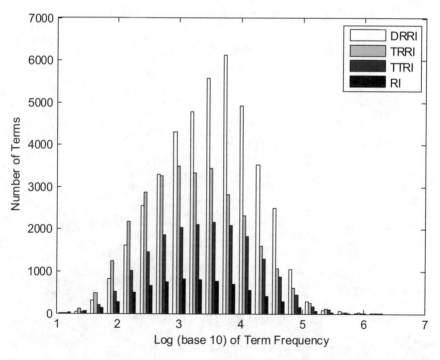

Figure 7.10   Frequency distributions of term frequencies of indirect neighbors.

source term later simply because the term occurs more often.[12] The TRRI wordspace also shows the greatest sensitivity to the cosine similarity of indirect neighbors; there is a greater decrease in rate of future co-occurrences as cosine similarity decreases. The TRRI wordspace is also constructed in three steps compared to four steps for the DRRI wordspace (Figure 7.2). Thus, by the criteria of lower NIN term frequency, greater sensitivity to cosine similarity, and efficiency of computation, the TRRI wordspace may be seen to produce the "best" results, although the DRRI wordspace does produce the highest proportion of NINs with future co-occurrence. Of course, additional methods of evaluating the indirect neighbors should be used to make a final determination about which wordspace to use. A promising line of future investigation involves the effectiveness of frequency-normalized adjustments in selecting promising predictions.

REPORT BY A MOLECULAR BIOLOGIST USING EPIPHANET

Our research team is fortunate to have an active molecular biologist to assist in the development and evaluation of the EpiphaNet software. Dr. Kerr Whitfield has used EpiphaNet to develop further his expertise in the biological roles of vitamin D. After some experience with EpiphaNet, Dr. Whitfield has come to follow-up encounters with novelty to determine whether there is something in the novel information that he should add to his knowledge. The novelty either takes the form of encountering new terms or new relationships among known terms. What follows is a first-hand description of how he uses the tools.

> My experience with EpiphaNet has mainly been a challenge for me to rethink how I search the literature. My accustomed way to search the literature is to search PubMed, using terms I already know to see if new reports have appeared that contain that term. In the case of one of my favorites, namely vitamin D, these searches often return many articles of a nutritional nature; using the term "vitamin D receptor" (which I will abbreviate as VDR, and which actually is "vitamin d3 receptor" in the standardized vocabulary), searches usually return many reports of associations between genetic variants of VDR and various diseases. Neither of these matches my primary interest, which is in the molecular action of VDR as a transcription factor and the role of VDR target genes in normal physiology and disease. This has remained, however, my major way of searching the literature until I encountered EpiphaNet.
>
> [...]

---

12 It would be useful to develop a quantitative method for scoring the retrieval results combining both the number and frequency of the retrieved terms. We plan to pursue this goal along with additional evaluations of the quality of the retrieved items. This line of work will probably require a more controlled method of selecting original terms than the random selection method employed here.

EpiphaNet has challenged me to be open to novel or unexpected associations between VDR and various other terms, concepts or genes as returned by the EpiphaNet program. I must confess that my current understanding of the way EpiphaNet works is somewhat fuzzy, but I am quite excited about the possibilities of this program, which even it its early, experimental, versions, has broadened my horizons in my tiny niche of science, a niche that I thought I already knew a lot about.

[...]

There are two main ways that EpiphaNet has been very useful for me. The first way is in identifying the components of a signaling pathway that is unfamiliar to me, such as the WNT-β-catenin pathway. I should clarify by saying that the canonical WNT-β-catenin has been vaguely familiar to me for some time, but it is known to contain a steadily expanding number of components, most of which I did not learn about until recently. While there are certainly review articles on this pathway, the diagrams are seldom complete or contain all of the known components due to restraints on file size and/or complexity. My typical approach to familiarize myself with a new pathway is to draw my own diagrams. EpiphaNet has aided me in that process by rather reliably identifying names of gene products that are associated with "WNT," "catenin," or combinations of either with or without VDR (VDR in this case did not help much). EpiphaNet does not identify all components in a single diagram either, but I find EpiphaNet to be not only very effective, but also fun and entertaining to use.

[...]

One of the features I particularly like about EpiphaNet is the ability (in later versions) to instantly use interesting terms or combinations of terms in a PubMed search using a built-in link. This allows me to very quickly confirm whether the relationship of a particular term to the pathway is real or spurious by accessing relevant abstracts.

A similar link is provided to the Online Mendelian Inheritance in Man (OMIM), a database of human genes and genetic disorders, and I find this also very useful, but probably not for its intended purpose. Rather, I take advantage of the list of synonyms provided for each OMIM entry to resolve any confusion about nomenclature, a common problem in literature searches for which no ideal solution seems to be available.

[...]

The second way I use EpiphaNet is probably more related to its original purpose. I simply type in my favorite search term (again, vitamin d3 receptor is a good example) and see what relationships are revealed in EpiphaNet (the latest version of which is quite up-to-date, containing references as late as mid-2009). For this, I have a choice of "predications," the list of which is subdivided into "biological", "clinical," or none. My preference is usually biological or none. I also have the option of choosing the number of "nearest neighbors," usually in the range of 10–30. This very simple use of EpiphaNet has provided me with some important new insights, most recently into a complicated set of relationships between the vitamin d3 receptor, the oncogene BRCA2, the bone differentiation gene Runx2 and two related transcriptional repressors Snail1 (a.k.a.

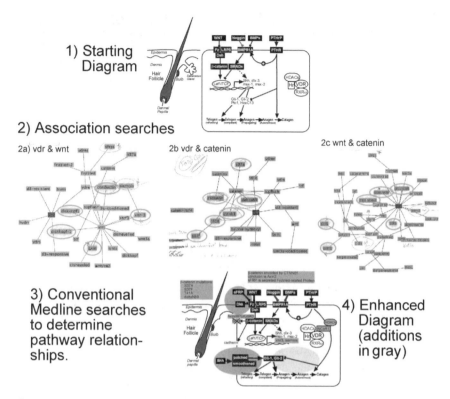

Figure 7.11   An example of the results of some searches with EpiphaNet.

Snail) and Snail2 (a.k.a. snai2 or SLUG). I have yet to fully explore this relationship, but EpiphaNet made me aware of this small facet of vitamin D biology
of which I was previously totally unaware (references from 2005, 2008, and
even June 2009). Other interesting discoveries with EpiphaNet were two vitamin d3 receptor target genes that were new to me, as well as an interesting connection between prolactin and the vitamin d3 receptor in human prostate cells.
Some of these novel connections will find their way into our lab discussions and
possibly into future hypotheses, particularly the connection between the snail
proteins and vitamin d3 receptor, Runx2 and BRCA2.

Figure 7.11 illustrates what Dr. Whitfield learned from some searches involving
vitamin D receptor (vdr), catenin (proteins), and wnt (a signaling pathway involving a complex network of proteins). From the EpiphaNet searches for nearest
neighbors of combinations of terms, he discovered new pathways that he was
able to add to his current knowledge (the starting diagram) to produce a new
schematic (the enhanced diagram with additions shown in gray). The networks
produced by EpiphaNet show his notes and marks that led him to the new
pathways.

Table 7.6 shows a summary of the number of new concepts or associations
between concepts Dr. Whitfield encountered in a series of sessions with

TABLE 7.6   Summary Statistics for Seven Sessions with EpiphaNet

Session	Duration (min:sec)	New concepts or associations	Literature searches
1	20:27	6	4
2	34:57	11	9
3	36:08	5	13
4	35:22	2	9
5	44:58	17	19
6	42:21	7	7
7	31:16	12	10
Total	4.1 hrs	60	70

EpiphaNet.[13] The data seem to clearly indicate that interesting new information is being discovered with the use of the system. Additional tests with more researchers are underway.

CONCLUSION

In our quest to find paths to discovery, we are exploring various applications of the idea of using random projection methods (Vempala, 2004) to create word-space models that support abductive reasoning. EpiphaNet is a software tool under development that provides access to the models and other resources for active researchers. Using these tools, users can find new terms related to terms of interest. Optionally, the new terms may have been directly related to the terms of interest previously in the literature. Various models provide either general associations between terms or propositions involving the terms with control over which predications to consider. Users can also find new pathways linking terms of interest to help expand knowledge and understanding. Testing, to date, has been encouraging, but continuing evaluation is an important part of our project as is the extension of the work into additional domains.

This is an interesting and enjoyable journey for us, and there are still many directions to explore and develop. In future work, we will explore methods for identifying middle terms to help account for the indirect similarity we observe with nearest indirect neighbors. Finding middle terms further expands the linking of concepts which is the goal of our work. We are also interested in exploring still other scalable methods for creating wordspaces.

REFERENCES

Aronson, A. R. (2001). Effective mapping of biomedical text to the UMLS Metathesaurus: The MetaMap program. *Proceedings of the American Medical Informatics Association Symposium, 17*, 17–21.

13 These statistics were compiled by Kavitha Mukund (Mukund, 2009) through her analysis of the protocols generated during Dr. Whitfield's sessions with EpiphaNet.

Browne, A. C., Divita, G., Aronson, A. R., & McCray, A. T. (2003). UMLS language and vocabulary tools. In *Proceedings of the American Medical Informatics Association, 2003*, 798.

Bruza, P., Cole, R., Song, D., & Bari, Z. (2006). Towards operational abduction from a cognitive perspective. *Logic Journal of the IGPL*, pp. 161–177.

Burgess, C., Livesay, K., & Lund, K. (1998). Explorations in context space: Words, sentences, discourse. *Discourse Processes*, 25(2&3), 211–257.

Chase, W. G., & Simon, H. A. (1973). The mind's eye in chess. In W. G. Chase (Ed.), *Visual information processing*. New York: Academic Press.

Cohen, T. (2008). Exploring MEDLINE space with random indexing and Pathfinder networks. In *Proceedings of the American Medical Informatics Association Symposium*. Washington, DC.

Cohen, T. (2010). EpiphaNet. Retrieved from: http://epiphanet.uth.tmc.edu or http://epiphanet.dnsdojo.org (accessed April 27, 2010).

Cohen, T., Schvaneveldt, R. W., & Rindflesch, T. C. (2009). Predication-based semantic indexing: Permutations as a means to encode predications in semantic space. In *Proceedings of the American Medical Informatics Association Symposium*. San Francisco.

Cohen, T., Schvaneveldt, R. W., & Widdows, D. (2010). Reflective random indexing and indirect inference: A scalable method for discovery of implicit connections. *Journal of Biomedical Informatics*, 43, 240–256.

Dayton, T., Durso, F. T., & Shepard, J. D. (1990). A measure of the knowledge organization underlying insight. In R. Schvaneveldt (Ed.), *Pathfinder associative networks: Studies in knowledge organization*. Norwood, NJ: Ablex.

Doyle, A. C. ([1891] 2009). *The Adventures of Sherlock Holmes: A Scandal in Bohemia*. Mineola, NY: Dover Publications.

Durso, F. T., Rea, C. B., & Dayton, T. (1994). Graph-theoretic confirmation of restructuring during insight. *Psychological Science*, 5, 94–98.

Falkenhainer, B. (1990). A unified approach to explanation and theory formation. In J. Shrager, & P. Langley (Eds.), *Computational models of scientific discovery and theory formation*. Palo Alto, CA: Morgan Kaufmann.

Fauconnier, G., & Turner, M. (2002). *The way we think: Conceptual blending and the mind's hidden complexities*. New York: Basic Books.

Fiszman, M., Demner-Fushman, D., Kilicoglu, H., & Rindflesch, T. C. (2009). Automatic summarization of MEDLINE citations for evidence-based medical treatment: A topic-oriented evaluation. *Journal of Biomedical Informatics*, 42(5), 801–813.

Fiszman, M., Rindflesch, T. C., & Kilicoglu, H. (2004). Summarization of an online medical encyclopedia. *Studies in Health Technology and Informatics*, 107(Pt 1), 506–510.

Gärdenfors, P. (2000). *Conceptual spaces: The geometry of thought*. Cambridge, MA: MIT Press.

Gentner, D. (1983). Structure-mapping: A theoretical framework for analogy. *Cognitive Science*, 7, 155–170.

Gentner, D., Holyoak, K. J., & Kokinov, B. N. (Eds.). (2001). *The analogical mind: Perspectives from cognitive science*. Cambridge, MA: MIT Press.

Gentner, D., & Markman, A. B. (1997). Structure mapping in analogy and similarity. *American Psychologist*, 52, 45–56.

Giles, J. T., Wo, L., & Berry, M. W. (2001). GTP (General Text Parser) software for text mining. In H. Bozdogan (Ed.), *Statistical data mining and knowledge discovery* (pp. 455–471). Boca Raton, FL: CRC Press.

Goetz, E. T., Anderson, R. C., & Schallert, D. L. (1981). The representation of sentences in memory. *Journal of Verbal Learning and Verbal Behavior, 20*, 369–385.

Gordon, M. D., & Dumais, S. (1998). Using latent semantic indexing for literature based discovery. *Journal of the American Society for Information Science, 49*(8), 674–685.

Hanson, N. R. (1958). *Patterns of discovery: An inquiry into the conceptual foundations of science.* Cambridge: Cambridge University Press.

Harman, G. H. (1965). The inference to the best explanation. *The Philosophical Review, 74*, 88–95.

Holland, J. H. (1992). *Adaptation in natural and artificial systems: An introductory analysis with applications to biology, control, and artificial intelligence.* Cambridge, MA: MIT Press.

Holyoak, K. J., & Thagard, P. (1995). *Mental leaps: Analogy in creative thought.* Cambridge, MA: MIT Press.

Jones, M. N., & Mewhort, D. J. K. (2007). Representing word meaning and order information in a composite holographic lexicon. *Psychological Review, 114*, 1–37.

Kamada, T., & Kawai, S. (1989). An algorithm for drawing general undirected graphs. *Information Processing Letters, 31*, 7–15.

Kanerva, P. (1988). *Sparse distributed memory.* Cambridge, MA: Bradford.

Kanerva, P. (2000). Hyperdimensional computing: An introduction to computing in distributed representation with high-dimensional random vectors. *Cognitive Computation, 1*(2), 139–159.

Kanerva, P., Kristofersson, J., & Holst, A. (2000). Random indexing of text samples for Latent Semantic Analysis. In L. R. Gleitman, & A. K. Josh (Eds.), *Proceedings of the 22nd Annual Conference of the Cognitive Science Society* (p. 1036). Mahwah, NJ: Lawrence Erlbaum Associates.

Kintsch, W. (1998). *Comprehension: A paradigm for cognition.* Cambridge: Cambridge University Press.

Kintsch, W., & Keenan, J. (1973). Reading rate and retention as a function of the number of propositions in the base structure of sentences. *Cognitive Psychology, 5*, 257–274.

Koestler, A. (1990). *The act of creation.* New York: Penguin.

Kruskal, J. B. (1964a). Multidimensional scaling by optimizing goodness of fit to a nonmetric hypothesis. *Psychometrika, 29*, 1–27.

Kruskal, J. B. (1964b). Nonmetric multidimensional scaling: A numerical method. *Psychometrika, 29*, 115–129.

Lakoff, G., & Johnson, M. (1980). *Metaphors we live by.* Chicago: University of Chicago Press.

Landauer, T. K., & Dumais, S. T. (1997). A solution to Plato's problem: the Latent Semantic Analysis theory of acquisition, induction and representation of knowledge. *Psychological Review, 104*(2), 211–240.

Landauer, T. K, Foltz, P. W., & Laham, D. (1998). An introduction to Latent Semantic Analysis. *Discourse Processes, 25*, 2–3, 259–284.

Landauer, T. K., McNamara, D. C., Dennis, S., & Kintsch, W. (2007). *Handbook of latent semantic analysis.* Mahwah, NJ: Erlbaum.

Langley, P., Simon, H. A., Bradshaw, G. L., & Zytkow, J. M. (1987). *Scientific discovery: Computational explorations of the creative process.* Cambridge, MA: MIT Press.

Lund, K., & Burgess, C. (1996). Producing high-dimensional semantic spaces from lexical co-occurrence. *Behavior Research Methods, Instruments & Computers, 28*(2), 203–208.

McDonald, J. E., Plate, T. A., & Schvaneveldt, R. W. (1990). Using Pathfinder to extract semantic information from text. In R. Schvaneveldt (Ed.), *Pathfinder associative networks: Studies in knowledge organization* (pp. 149–164). Norwood, NJ: Ablex.

Mukund, K. (2009). Augmenting abduction: A cognitive evaluation of EpiphaNet. Unpublished Master's thesis, Department of Biomedical Informatics, Arizona State University.

Newell, A., Shaw, J. C., & Simon, H. A. (1958). Elements of a theory of human problem solving. *Psychological Review, 65*, 151–166.

Newell, A., & Simon, H. A. (1972). *Human problem solving.* Englewood Cliffs, NJ: Prentice-Hall.

Osgood, C. E., Suci, G., & Tannenbaum, P. (1957). *The measurement of meaning.* Urbana: University of Illinois Press.

Pado, S., & Lapata, M. (2007). Dependency-based construction of semantic space models. *Computational Linguistics, 33*, 161–199.

Peirce, C. S. (1940). Abduction and induction. In J. Buchler (Ed.), *Philosophical writings of Peirce.* New York: Routledge.

Plate, T. A. (2003). *Holographic reduced representation: Distributed representation for cognitive structures.* Stanford, CA: CSLI Publications.

Rindflesch, T. C., & Fiszman, M. (2003). The interaction of domain knowledge and linguistic structure in natural language processing: Interpreting hypernymic propositions in biomedical text. *Journal of Biomedical Informatics, 36*, 462–477.

Rindflesch, T. C., Libbus, B., Hristovski, D., Aronson, A. R., & Kilicoglu, H. (2003). Semantic relations asserting the etiology of genetic diseases. *Proceedings of the American Medical Informatics Association, 2003*, 554.

Sahlgren, M. (2006). The word-space model: Using distributional analysis to represent syntagmatic and paradigmatic relations between words in high-dimensional vector spaces. Doctoral thesis. Department of Linguistics, Stockholm University.

Sahlgren, M., Holst, A., & Kanerva, P. (2008). Permutations as a means to encode order in word space. In *Proceedings of the 30th Annual Meeting of the Cognitive Science Society (CogSci'08)*, Washington DC, July 23–26.

Salton, G. (1989). *Automatic text processing: The transformation, analysis, and retrieval of information by computer.* Reading, PA: Addison-Wesley.

Salton, G., & McGill, M. J. (1983). *Introduction to modern information retrieval.* New York: McGraw-Hill.

Schvaneveldt, R. W. (1990). *Pathfinder associative networks: Studies in knowledge organization.* Norwood, NJ: Ablex.

Schvaneveldt, R. W., & Chase, W. G. (1969). Sequential effects in choice reaction time. *Journal of Experimental Psychology, 76*, 642–648.

Schvaneveldt, R. W, & Cohen, T. A. (2010). Abductive reasoning and similarity: Some computational tools. In D. Ifenthaler, P. Pirnay-Dummer, & N. M. Seel (Eds.), *Computer based diagnostics and systematic analysis of knowledge.* New York: Springer.

Schvaneveldt, R. W., Durso, F. T., & Dearholt, D. W. (1989). Network structures in proximity data. In G. Bower (Ed.), *The psychology of learning and motivation: Advances in research and theory* (vol. 24, pp. 249–284). New York: Academic Press.

Shepard, R. N. (1962a). The analysis of proximities: Multidimensional scaling with unknown distance function, Part I. *Psychometrika, 27*, 125–140.

Shepard, R. N. (1962b). The analysis of proximities: Multidimensional scaling with unknown distance function, Part II. *Psychometrika, 27*, 219–246.

Shrager, J., & Langley, P. (Eds.) (1990). *Computational models of scientific discovery and theory formation.* Palo Alto, CA: Morgan Kaufmann.

Simon, H. A. (1973). Does scientific discovery have a logic? *Philosophy of Science, 40,* 471–480.

Swanson, D. R. (1986). Fish oil, Raynaud's Syndrome, and undiscovered public knowledge. *Perspectives in Biology and Medicine, 30*(1), 7–18.

Swanson, D. R. (1987). Two medical literatures that are logically but not bibliographically related. *Journal of the American Society for Information Science, 38,* 228–233.

Swanson, D. R. (1991). Complementary structures in disjoint science literatures. In *Proceedings of the 14th Annual International ACM SIGIR Conference on Research and Development in Information Retrieval,* pp. 280–289.

Swanson, D. R., & Smalheiser, N. R. (1997). An interactive system for finding complementary literatures: A stimulus to scientific discovery. *Artificial Intelligence, 91,* 183–203.

Van Rijsbergen, C. J. (2004). *The geometry of information retrieval.* Cambridge: Cambridge University Press.

Vempala, S. S. (2004). *The random projection method.* Providence, RI: The American Mathematical Society.

Widdows, D. (2004). *Geometry and meaning.* Stanford, CA: CSLI Publications.

Widdows, D., & Cohen, T. (2009). Semantic vector combinations and the synoptic gospels. In P. Bruza, D. Sofge, W. Lawless, C. J. Van Rijsbergen, & M. Klusch (Eds). *Proceedings of the Third Quantum Interaction Symposium* (March 25–27, DFKI, Saarbrücken) (pp. 251–265). New York: Springer.

Widdows, D., & Ferraro, K. (2008). Semantic vectors: A scalable open source package and online technology management application. In *Sixth International Conference on Language Resources and Evaluation (LREC 2008).*

Widdows, D., & Peters, S. (2003). Word vectors and quantum logic: Experiments with negation and disjunction. *Mathematics of Language, 8,* Bloomington, Indiana, June 2003.

8

Development of Expertise and the Control of Physical Action[1]

DAVID A. ROSENBAUM

Pennsylvania State University, USA

INTRODUCTION

Thanks to Bill Chase, we know much more about the development of expertise than we would if this energetic, insightful, and influential researcher had not graced our discipline. Bill Chase, along with Anders Ericsson, showed that people can remember much more than you would think if you subscribed to the view that memory capacity is a fixed feature of the rememberer. Chase and Ericsson (1981) showed that people can remember more incoming information as they get increasingly skilled at using cognitive strategies for relating that information to material already established in their memories. The amount that individuals can remember grows to levels that seem almost super-human if they successfully relate what comes in to what they already know. The benefits to learning are specific to the materials to which the strategy is applied, however, implying that short-term memory does not simply bulk up as a result of experience. What grows is the capacity for relating incoming information to already formed chunks.

1 The research described in this chapter was supported by grants from the National Science Foundation, the National Institutes of Health, and the Penn State Social Science Research Institute. The author is indebted to his colleagues who not only played such an integral role in the research reported here but who also provided very helpful comments on the chapter: Rajal Cohen, Steven Jax, Ruud Meulenbroek, Robrecht van der Wel, Jonathan Vaughan, and Dan Weiss. Jim Staszewski also deserves a word of special thanks for all he did to supply me with helpful feedback on a draft of this chapter and for all he did to make this volume and the conference from which it emerged so successful.

How can we build on this remarkable discovery? One of the remaining challenges is to understand the neural underpinnings of the effect. A second is to help people learn more by helping them use the strategy. A third is to consider the domain for which the discovery was made and ask whether there are other domains to which the discovery could be applied. That last challenge is the one taken up in this chapter. As indicated in the chapter's title, the focus is on the development of expertise and the control of physical action.

A VISIT TO A CHESS TOURNAMENT

Imagine being a fly on a wall at a chess tournament. Chess tournaments fascinated Bill Chase and his colleagues. In fact, chess was the paradigm for much of the research that was done at Carnegie Mellon in its "golden years," when Newell, Simon, Chase, and others demonstrated that chunks were building blocks for problem solving.

Perched on the wall of the chess tournament hall, you watch as people begin to file in and take their seats around the stage where the chess masters will face off. These audience members are a motley crew. An athletic young woman glides effortlessly to her seat. An older gentleman walks with an obvious limp and manages, after some difficulty, to plant himself beside her. A woman wearing a cast on her leg comes in on crutches and succeeds, after some shuffling, to land on her chair. Others move sideways down the narrow aisles between the rows of seats set up for the event. Before they sit down, they remove their backpacks and take off their coats, placing these items on or under the chairs they occupy. Finally, as the audience gets settled, two men carry a table to the middle of the stage and set it down at what they judge to be the optimal position for everyone to watch the game. A woman then appears carrying a large wooden box, which she sets on the table at a location that lets her open the lid and remove its contents on the center of the table. She places the chess pieces on the board in an order that, upon close inspection, seems sensible. She puts the white pieces down first, perhaps because they are farther from her than the black, proceeding from left to right and from outer row to inner row. Then she puts the black pieces down, going from left to right, this time from inner row to outer row. You realize that she may be setting the pieces down in a way that not only reflects a left–right bias but also a clever way of reducing the likelihood she will bump into any pieces that have already been set on the board. A few other items are set up by the people running the match. Finally the two chess masters walk in and the game begins.

Clearly, these pre-game events are not what people came here to watch. It was for the *intellectual* contest that the audience came here. Nonetheless, without the mundane physical acts leading up to the match, it could not go on.

Are these physical events of any interest to cognitive psychologists? One reason they are or at least should be is that a complete account of cognition cannot stop at the placement of information into memory, though that is where most accounts of information processing stop. Cognition includes action, so action cannot be ignored.

A second reason not to ignore the control of physical action is that expertise probably has its roots in action. As Piaget (1952) and others observed, the first domain where expertise needs to be cultivated is in perceptual-motor control—in activities like learning to suck for milk, learning to reach for objects, and learning to crawl, stand, and walk. It would be odd if the mechanisms used for developing expertise in these domains had no connection to the mechanisms used for developing expertise in other, more intellectual, spheres.

Third, the mechanisms underlying learning in the perceptual-motor domain surely have things in common with the mechanisms underlying learning in the intellectual domain. It is not just that both mechanisms rely on neurons or, even more trivially, atoms. There are likely to be more interesting psychological connections (Rosenbaum, Carlson, & Gilmore, 2001; Schmidt & Bjork, 1992).

It turns out that we know far more about intellectual expertise than about perceptual-motor expertise, at least judging from the fact that computers can beat the best chess players in the world, as IBM's Deep Blue computer did in a famous match against Gary Kasparov, the top player in the world at the time. On the other hand, computers, embodied in robots, cannot complete physical tasks that most typically developing 2- or 3-year-olds can (e.g., putting on shirts or scampering over rocks). Given this state of affairs, it may be that some of the insights expressed in computerized systems like IBM's Deep Blue can inform the development of smarter robots (i.e., robots capable of autonomous planning and successful control of physical actions in unpredictable environments). At the same time, it may be that insights gained from attempts to analyze perceptual-motor expertise can inform the development of more intellectually sophisticated computer systems.

GRAPH THEORY

The classic work on chess by Chase, Simon, Newell, and others relied on problem spaces, and these in turn relied on graph theory. Graph theory is a branch of mathematics that relies on points (or nodes) and lines between those points, some of which may be "directed." If two points A and B are connected with a directed line segment that goes from A to B, A is activated before B such that the change in the state of A influences the state of B, but not vice versa (Ore, 1963).

No matter how obvious this is nowadays, one can scarcely imagine the inconvenience of not having such a way of representing problem spaces when it comes to analyzing cognition and control. In the case of chess, for example, each point in the problem space is a (legal) state of the board (i.e., the pieces and their positions). Directed lines from any such state go to each of the other states that can be reached next given the rules of the game. Through this means of representing possible states and transitions for chess, it is possible to evaluate a finite number of alternative next states given any current state, and it is possible to speak of different kinds of searches (e.g., depth-first or breadth-first search) as well as search speed (number of states considered per unit time).

IBM's Deep Blue mainly relied on sheer speed to outwit, and ultimately out-pace, Gary Kasparov.

Why speak of graph theory here? The reason is that when it comes to the analysis of body movements, it seems well nigh impossible to discern discrete states and transitions between them. It is not even clear whether it makes sense to think along these lines considering the grace of physical motions, as in dancing or playing the cello. Such activities are marked by their smoothness and fluidity of motion. Saying that body movements are achieved by moving from one discrete state to another seems almost sacrilegious. Nevertheless, my colleagues have found considerable evidence for this possibility. We argued that, as in chess or checkers, movements of the body can be conceptualized as transitioning from one discrete state to another (Rosenbaum, Loukopoulos, Meulenbroek, Vaughan, & Engelbrecht, 1995; Rosenbaum, Meulenbroek, Vaughan, & Jansen, 2001). In particular, we suggested that body movements consist of transitions between discrete body postures. We proposed that even when movements are smooth, their underlying representations and means of control are discrete. Other authors, mainly in the field of computational neuroscience, have made similar claims (Berthier, 1996; Doeringer & Hogan, 1998; Edelman & Flash, 1987). Our group is the main team of cognitive psychologists who have advocated this point of view.

POSTURE-BASED MOTION PLANNING

If the number of possible moves in chess is astronomical, the number of possible moves of the body is "super-galactic." To touch your nose with your right index finger, for example, you can adopt any of an infinite number of shoulder, elbow, wrist, and finger angles, any one of which maintains contact of your fingertip with the tip of your nose. In general, the number of body postures (vectors of joint angles) that permit a part of the body to occupy a given position in 3-space is infinite. This is because the body has more degrees of freedom than does a position in space. In Cartesian coordinates, a point in 3-space has three degrees of freedom—its x, y, and z values. Yet a posture that allows a given body part to occupy that same spatial position has many more degrees of freedom (dfs). The shoulder has three dfs, the elbow has two dfs, the wrist has two dfs, and the finger joints have still more dfs. Moving to a body position amplifies the indeterminacy even more. For any given final position of the body, there are an infinite number of trajectories (series of body positions) that can get the finger from wherever it started to wherever it ends. Considering the different time profiles for the movement and different forces and torques, the number of possibilities grows still larger.

These issues may be problems for researchers interested in motor control, but they provide *opportunities* for people (and animals) wishing to move. Having a plethora of options can get you out of a jam. If you have an injury or if your arms are filled with packages, it's a good thing that you have many ways of scratching your nose. It does not follow, however, that the motor system finds itself unchallenged by this surplus of options. Finding one movement from infinitely many might be hard, but even if it is not obviously difficult, the research challenge is to understand how particular, adaptive solutions are found.

Separation of Goal Postures and Movements

A useful way to solve the degrees of freedom problem is to target body positions and then, having specified those goal positions, to find ways of moving to them. It turns out that there is considerable evidence for the view that the motor system targets body positions separately from movements to those body positions. Space does not permit a full review of all the sources of evidence for this hypothesis (but see Rosenbaum, 2010), but a few highlights will be presented here.

One source of evidence is indirect but is listed first because it should resonate with cognitive psychologists. This source of evidence is that memory for positions is superior to memory for movements. If people aim for a target and then are asked to move back to that target from a variety of start positions, they can do so very well. However, if those same people aim for a target and then are asked to cover the *distance* they just did, starting once again from different start positions, they do so poorly (Smyth, 1984). The superior memory for the target is not just better memory for external (spatial) as opposed to internal (body) information. Limb positions *per se* are better remembered than movements to those limb positions, though there is also memory for external spatial locations *per se* (Rosenbaum, Meulenbroek, & Vaughan, 1999). Such results bear on the hypothesis that body positions are represented separately from body movements and at a higher functional level. The reason is that information tends to be better remembered the more important it is. To cite a well-known example, the meaning of a sentence is remembered better than the syntax of the sentence, consistent with the idea that, in the long run, sentence meaning is more important than sentence structure (Sachs, 1967).

A more direct source of information for the prominence of body positions over movements to body positions comes from neurophysiological research. In classic work, Polit and Bizzi (1978) showed that monkeys can continue to move their arms to point to targets even after sensory nerve fibers from the monkeys' arms and associated postural-support muscles have been severed. The monkeys could point to series of targets even without visual or auditory feedback about the arm's position. What made this finding all the more remarkable was that the monkeys were able to point to the targets even if the arm was mechanically perturbed on the way to the target. If the arm was briefly poked with a torque motor, the arm still managed to "bounce" to the target, no matter which of several targets was tested. This seemingly impossible result can be explained by saying that the motor system establishes goal positions to which the muscles are driven. The exact mechanism responsible for achieving the effect—setting muscle stiffnesses as Polit and Bizzi (1978) argued, or setting thresholds for muscle stretch reflexes, as others have proposed (Feldman & Latash, 2005)—is a debate whose resolution (reachable or not) is unimportant for present purposes.

In neurologically normal adults there is evidence for a similar goal-setting strategy. You can demonstrate this for yourself by holding a soda can in one hand and then having the can yanked out from between your fingers by a friend (or you can yank the can yourself with your other hand). Your fingers will immediately close in on a new position. This is an equilibrium position to which your fingers were striving while the can stood in the way. If you hold the same soda can with a stronger grip, your fingers will come closer together when the can is released, indicating that the virtual target is adjusted to the grip forces applied. Saying this another way, grip forces are adjusted, at least in part, by specifying different neuro-muscular equilibrium positions "within" the held object. Karate practitioners are familiar with this concept. They are trained to aim for positions *past* the concrete slab or wooden board to be broken when they make their karate strikes.

Other demonstrations of such neuro-muscular equilibrium positions have also been provided, both in behavioral and neurophysiological realms. In neurophysiology, it has been shown that the frog spinal cord can achieve flexibly altered equilibrium positions (Bizzi, Mussa-Ivaldi, & Giszter, 1991), an outcome suggesting that the capacity for such flexible alterations of equilibrium positions is phylogenetically ancient. The monkey motor cortex and pre-motor cortex (Graziano, Taylor, & Moore, 2002) also have this capability, indicating that it is preserved through evolution. Graziano et al. showed that if a monkey's motor cortex or pre-motor cortex is stimulated for about half a second, the monkey adopts different limb and face postures depending on where the stimulation is applied. Which posture is adopted depends less on the posture the animal happens to be in when the stimulation is applied than on where in the brain the stimulation is introduced. This result suggests that there are neural representations for goal postures *per se*, although some neurons stimulated in this way appear to trigger movements rather than goal postures (Graziano, Aflalo, & Cooke, 2005).

A Cognitive Psychological Model of Motor Planning

My colleagues and I have been inspired by results like these to develop a cognitive psychological model of motor planning. The model takes equal inspiration from the view, mentioned earlier, that problem spaces can be profitably analyzed as layouts of states and possible transitions between those states. Arguably, the most important contribution of the model of motor planning that my colleagues and I have developed is its postulation of distinct states for motor planning.

As already mentioned, the distinct states in our model are goal postures of the body (i.e., target vectors of joint angles). According to our model, motor planning has two main stages. The first is selection of a goal posture for the task to be achieved. The second is selection of a movement to the selected goal posture. Normally, or at least canonically, the selection of movement does not impact the selection of a goal posture. However, if the selection of a movement, given the prior selection of a goal posture, is expected to result in an unwieldy movement, the candidate goal posture can be re-evaluated.

The way goal postures are selected in the model reflects two desiderata of movement production. First, many physical tasks need to be repeated. Second, it is necessary on occasion to generate novel actions. These two constraints are addressed in our model as follows.

First, to benefit from consistencies in recent task requirements, we assume that recently adopted goal postures (the last m goal postures) are stored. Any of those stored goal postures can serve as a seed for a search for a new goal posture (see below). Whichever previously stored posture that is picked as the seed for the search is picked on the basis of how well it satisfies the constraints for the current task. Those constraints define the task to be performed and are established in the mind of the participant (even if someone else tells that participant what to do). Constraints that are important have larger weights or occupy higher positions in a constraint hierarchy than do constraints that are less important.

Second, to generate novel behaviors, we assume that once a previously stored goal posture is selected as the most promising candidate goal posture, it can be altered via random "tweaking" to yield a goal state that may be even better for the task to be performed than the previously stored goal posture that is chosen as the most promising candidate. This method is explicitly Darwinian in the sense that it relies on random variation to allow for "more fit" goal postures than were possible given the goal postures that were stored previously. The method used is also Darwinian in that, as mentioned in the preceding paragraph, only the last m goal postures are stored. Any goal postures adopted more than m trials back "die."

Once a goal posture is found, a movement to it is sought. This process also relies, in our model, on prioritized task constraints. The movement that is selected not only achieves the primary aim of bringing the body to the goal posture; it also satisfies, or is supposed to satisfy, other constraints like taking a preferred amount of time for the movement given the inertial properties of the limb segments to be moved (van der Wel, Sternad, & Rosenbaum, 2010) or following a path whose shape ensures obstacle avoidance (Vaughan, Rosenbaum, & Meulenbroek, 2001).

Performance of the Model

How well does the model perform? Within the domain for which it was developed, it has done reasonably well. That domain is reaching in a plane. The creature we have modeled can reach for targets in ways that appear lifelike, using its limb segments in ways that people do when they carry out analogous tasks. Such verisimilitude can be judged not just informally, by eye, but also by comparing the model's limb kinematics to the kinematics of human subjects carrying out analogous tasks (Fischer, Rosenbaum, & Vaughan, 1997; Rosenbaum et al., 1995, 2001; Vaughan Rosenbaum, Harp, Loukopoulos,

& Engelbrecht, 1998; Vaughan et al., 2001). In general, the correspondence of the model's movements to any given subject's movements is as good as the correspondence of any other subject's movements to the movements of the subject in question (Rosenbaum et al., 2001b).

The model can achieve some general abilities that any motor planning model should exhibit. It can bring any desired part of its body to a reachable target. Thus, it can reach with its elbow and can also reach with a hand-held tool. Being able to reach with an arbitrary effector is an important ability to simulate because people (and animals) can likewise improvise when they carry out actions. Someone entering an elevator with his or her arms filled with packages can press the button for a desired floor with the elbow, for example. To cite another example, a neurologically normal, literate, person can write with virtually any part of his or her body—with a pen held with the preferred or non-preferred hand, with a pen held with the preferred or non-preferred foot, or even with the mouth. His or her writing style is preserved no matter which effector is used. This ability has long been offered as a prime example of *motor equivalence*, the capacity to achieve a task through different means. Our model can achieve such motor equivalence in writing (Meulenbroek, Rosenbaum, Thomassen, Loukopoulos, & Vaughan, 1996). We are not aware of any other model that can do so.

Another ability that our model can simulate is reaching around obstacles. Getting to a target while circumventing an object is an important ability for people and animals; any model of motor planning needs to explain it. It is much harder to simulate reaching around obstacles with multiple limb segments than to simulate the motion of a single point passing around an obstacle, as has been done in several mathematically elegant models (Bullock, Bongers, Lankhorst, & Beek,1999; Fajen & Warren, 2003). Our model can coordinate its limbs to reach around obstacles by satisfying constraints that proscribe contact between body parts and the object to be missed. Computationally, the model finds the relevant movement by identifying a "bounce" posture in addition to a goal posture. The creature moves from its start posture to its goal posture and at the same time moves from the start posture to the bounce posture and back again. The series of movements from the start posture to the bounce posture and back again adds no net displacement to the compound movement, but the compound movement avoids the obstacle if an appropriate bounce posture and goal posture are specified. The simulated limb kinematics comport with observed limb kinematics produced by human participants performing analogous obstacle-avoidance tasks (Vaughan et al., 2001). Other possible models of obstacle-avoidance can be rejected with the same data (Vaughan et al., 2001).

The simulated creature can also compensate for changes in joint mobility. If a joint gets hard to turn (i.e., if the "travel cost" for the joint is elevated), a goal posture that bends that joint by a small amount is favored over a goal posture that bends that joint by a large amount. The model achieves instant compensation for changes in joint mobility, similar to what occurs in everyday life when, say, a pebble gets in your shoe and you immediately alter your gait, or if you bang your elbow and your elbow smarts. Other computational models have attempted to explain such instant compensation, but to our way of thinking they have resorted to more complicated and less effective means of doing so (Mussa-Ivaldi, Morasso, & Zaccaria, 1988).

As concerns motor disabilities, when our model is "damaged" in various ways other than elevating travel costs of individual joints, it exhibits deficits akin to those observed in the clinic. For example, apraxia, the inability to plan and carry out voluntary movements, or dyspraxia, *reduced* ability to plan and carry out voluntary movements, can be simulated in our model by restricting the number of goal postures that can be stored or accessed. Spasticity can be simulated by impairing movement generation (Meulenbroek et al., 2001). Other motor disorders can be simulated as well, though it must be emphasized that the daunting complexity of motor disabilities associated with stroke, Parkinson's disease, and other impairments is not fully captured by our model. We see this not as a problem but rather as an opportunity. A major function of modeling, in our view, is to manifest, in a structured way, one's ignorance of the system being simulated. Building complete process models in the sense that Simon and Newell advocated makes gaps in a theory salient.

With respect to learning, our posture-based model exhibits benefits from repeated testing of the same target (Rosenbaum et al., 1995). If the same target is presented repeatedly, the simulated creature takes less and less time to select and move to a goal posture because it has more and more stored postures that are sufficient for the task. In addition, the goal postures and movements that are generated become increasingly stereotyped, as is true for human participants when they reach repeatedly for the same target and "settle in" to preferred ways of performing the tasks (Fischer et al., 1997).

A penultimate point is that the model can alter the relative contributions of its limb segments depending on how quickly movements must be made. It turns out that limb segments have preferred movement times for different amplitudes they must cover, reflecting properties of their mass-spring properties. Our posture-based model can select optimal movement times or, if movement times are prescribed, can alter the relative contributions of the limb segments accordingly in ways that parallel experimental observations (Hatsopoulos & Warren, 1996; Rosenbaum, Slotta, Vaughan, & Plamondon, 1991).

Finally, our modeled creature can move smoothly through series of goal postures. This point is important vis-à-vis the way the model was introduced earlier in this chapter. As emphasized before, my colleagues and I felt it was crucial to define target states for the body to facilitate the planning of movements. Having gone on to posit such states and having found that the general approach seems workable, it is important to ask whether we inadvertently turned our model into one that transitions jerkily from one terminal state to the next. If that were the case, the outcome would be unsatisfying.

It turns out that our modeled creature can move smoothly through series of goal postures, thanks to an assumption in the model that seems reasonable given all else that is known about the time course of information processing. We assume that motor planning and motor execution can occur in parallel.

More specifically, we assume that while a movement is under way toward a goal posture, one or more future goal postures (and movements to those goal postures) can be planned. It would be counter-productive to assume that moving and planning can only occur serially (i.e., alternating between planning and moving on), for then actors would literally move, stop and plan, move, stop and plan, and so on. Sometimes it helps to stop and plan, but fluidity and continuity of performance depend on avoiding this strategy. Relying on planning for future acts while other acts are under way fits with current conceptions of information processing, which allow for, or insist upon, parallel, cascade processes (e.g., Usher & McClelland, 2001). As yet, however, we have not investigated in detail the temporal parameters of coextensive planning and moving.

Limits of the Model

Although the model has strengths, it also has weaknesses. Exposing the limits of the model is useful because the model is one of the few that has been developed from a cognitive psychological perspective. How the model still needs to be improved helps set an agenda for future cognitive psychological research on motor planning.

One limitation of our model is that, so far, it is entirely "one-sided." The modeled creature has just one leg, one arm, and one hand, all on one side of its body. As a result, the model does not have to decide between reaching or carrying out tasks with one hand or the other (or with both hands). Most people prefer to use the right hand, of course, but the basis for this preference is poorly understood (but see Sainburg, 2005). Making a two-sided animated figure will provide an opportunity to evaluate different models of laterality and dominance. If the model chooses the same hand that people do to perform various tasks and if the basis for that decision within the model is principled, that advance in modeling could help uncover the source of hand dominance.

The model is also restricted to kinematic variables. Kinematics is the description of positions in time without regard to forces or torques. Kinetics, by contrast, includes forces and torques. For the model to be taken seriously as one that can be fully implemented in mechanical robots, it must include kinetic as well as kinematic factors. Indeed, even for a cartoon creature to behave in ways that accurately reflect considerations of loads, friction, inertia, and the like, it must take into account kinetic variables. It turns out that the computations related to mechanical kinetics are very complicated, which is why we have so far refrained from modeling kinetics. We have assumed that resolution of the basic cognitive issues concerning motor planning at the kinematic level will generalize to motor planning at the kinetic level, but it remains to be seen whether that is true.

A third limitation of the model is that it has been mainly explored in two spatial dimensions rather than three. Moving in three spatial dimensions is, of course, essential for realistic motion. However, moving in 3D is harder than one might expect, at least from a computational perspective. The reason is that motions in 3D are non-commutative: The order in which movements are made matters in 3D, though it does not matter in 2D.

A variety of mathematical approaches have been developed to represent 3D motion, and we have succeeded in generating 3D motions with our simulations (Vaughan, Rosenbaum, & Meulenbroek, 2006). However, more work is needed to have full confidence in this approach. That point aside, an appealing feature of the posture-based approach is that when a goal posture is represented in advance and that goal posture, like the start posture, is treated as a point in joint space (i.e., a vector of joint angles, given a kinematic description), the movement from the start posture can be represented as a line connecting those two points. By default, the line may be straight, or to deal with obstacle avoidance or other constraints, it may be curved given an appropriate bounce posture. Because the movement is a continuous translation from the start posture to the goal posture, the non-commutativity problem is sidestepped.

A fourth limitation of the model is that the modeled creature is essentially planted in one spot in the external environment. It does not walk or otherwise change its home position in the external world. For the model to be viewed as a full simulation, it will need to be able to walk and engage in other forms of behavior that turn it into more of a "true animal" (i.e., an entity that can move from place to place) and less of a "plant" (i.e., an entity rooted to one spot). One reason to think that modeling walking should not be too hard is that walking and other forms of locomotion can be thought of in the posture-based framework as a series of transitions between two goal postures, one that has the left foot in front of the right, and one that has the right foot in front of the left. Modeling locomotion as a cyclic transition between two states is, of course, a huge simplification. Many features of locomotion would need to be added to create a more realistic model, but having a very simple underlying idea can provide a useful place from which to start.

Having the model perform other tasks besides walking and reaching is another remaining challenge. Although the model has been chiefly developed for reaching tasks, it is not intended to be just a reaching model *per se*. Rather, its core claims are meant to apply to any kind of motor activity, including eye movements, facial movements, speaking, typing, playing the violin, playing the cello, and so on. Behind this ambitious statement is the broader hypothesis that the principles on which the model relies may apply across all forms of motor behavior. An advocate of strong modularity theory (Fodor, 1983) might contest this view, possibly asserting that any given motor activity relies on its own "bag of tricks." An attraction of the posture-based model, at least for my colleagues and me, is that it affords a way of testing the idea that all motor activities are planned and controlled in essentially the same way.

BEHAVIORAL EXPERIMENTS

As mentioned earlier in this chapter, one of the motivations for simulation work is to identify areas of ignorance. Having identified those areas, modelers can push ahead with their theorizing, possibly tapping into reserves of talent and creativity they have not previously accessed. Alternatively, they may run up against limits to their own inventiveness and get stuck. Either way, they may begin to worry whether they are engaging in science or in science fiction. Are their assumptions sufficiently grounded in data?

To check already-made assumptions and to establish the basis for new ones, modelers interested in hewing closely to fact turn to experiments to learn more. My colleagues and I have followed this path. The lines of experiments we have initiated are touched on below.

Effort Estimation

One line of experiments has been concerned with the estimation of effort. The motivation has been to check whether the criteria used for preferring goal postures and movements are correct. Recall that within the model, goal postures are chosen that entail little rotation of joints with high travel costs. Movements are also chosen in the model with this criterion in mind. Other criteria may also be considered, depending on the particular task demands. Knowing which criteria people actually care about is an important challenge for validating and elaborating the model.

We wanted to have a way of estimating effort but discovered that there is no established method for doing so. The methods available include measuring oxygen consumption for different tasks, such as walking at different speeds (Hoyt & Taylor, 1981). This may be sufficient for gross motor skills like walking over long distances, but it is unlikely to be sufficient for evaluating gradations of effort for fine motor skills such as reaching for an object that is 15 inches away rather than 12.

Another approach is simply to ask people to give effort ratings (Borg, 1973). However, the resulting data turn out to be more complicated than one might expect given plausible expectations about biomechanics (Dickerson, Martin, & Chaffin, 2007). For instance, in one study in our lab (Rosenbaum & Gregory, 2002), we asked people to move the hand long or short distances to bring a computer cursor to a target. We expected long moves to be rated as more effortful than short moves, but we found the opposite. It turned out that participants' effort ratings were strongly colored by their likelihood of hitting the target, which was harder in the short-distance condition than in the long-distance condition owing to the gain of the system.

To pursue another approach, we developed a two-alternative forced choice method. Here, in each trial, we presented participants with two alternative tasks and asked them to select the one that seemed less effortful (Rosenbaum & Gaydos, 2008). In the first set of experiments, the two tasks were picking up and moving a standing bathroom plunger to either of two targets. The distances of the two targets from the start location were varied, as were their directions. Participants strongly preferred short displacements over long displacements, as would be expected from biomechanics, but they showed only a modest preference for straight-ahead directions over other directions. The data from this study therefore supported the hypothesis that long movements seem more costly than short movements and that reducing distance matters more than reducing the difference between one direction and a preferred direction, at least for the set of tasks studied. Thus, this simple method provided a way of estimating effort and provided evidence for differences in constraint weightings.

An extension of the choose-the-easier-task method showed that *reaching* some distance is judged to be more costly than *walking* the same distance (Rosenbaum, 2008). In this study, participants could walk to a near target or to a far target and could either lean over far or lean over slightly to pick up an object on the way. Crossing the leaning distances with the walking distances showed that participants were reluctant to lean far and were willing to walk relatively long distances to do so. This outcome can inform future modeling that combines walking and reaching. It is not *a priori* obvious how to assign costs to these two kinds of activities, so data like those from the task described here can help in this regard.

Another extension of the choose-the-easier-task method showed that *saying* which of two tasks would be easier does not always lead to the same choice as actually *carrying out* the task that seems easier (Walsh & Rosenbaum, 2009). The latter result challenged the view that motor imagery bears a first-order isomorphic relation to motor planning. In the early days of research on visual imagery, it was thought, or at least implicitly accepted, that visual imagery bears a first-order isomorphic relation to seeing. However, this hypothesis was exploded by Shepard and Cooper (1982). The study by Walsh and Rosenbaum (2009) made the same point about motor planning vis-à-vis motor execution.

The Hand-Path Priming Effect

Another line of experiments pertained to the hypothesis that movements and goal postures are functionally distinct. Jax and Rosenbaum (2007, 2009) asked participants to move the hand as quickly as possible to cause a cursor to move from a home position in the middle of a computer screen to any of eight targets arrayed around the home position in an imaginary circle. On some trials, an obstacle (a large dot) appeared between the home position and the target. Participants were supposed to bring the cursor to the target without letting the cursor touch the target. Participants successfully circumvented the obstacle, and this was true when, in successive trials, an obstacle always appeared between the home position and whichever target happened to appear.

Of more interest, in subsequent trials, when new targets were presented but no obstacle appeared between the home position and a target, there was a dramatic *hand-path priming* effect. Movements to the targets were curved, as if participants avoided obstacles that were no longer present. This hand-path priming effect generalized across the workspace. Even when targets were tested that had not appeared recently, the hand paths to them were needlessly curved. This result suggests that abstract properties of movements *per se* are held in working

192 DAVID A. ROSENBAUM

memory and continue to affect properties of subsequent movements. The fact that these properties are not strictly tied to goal positions is consistent with the assumption of the posture-based model that movements and goal postures are functionally distinct. In terms of the specific mechanics of the posture-based model, a way to account for the hand-path priming effect is to say that the constraints related to movement are preserved for as long as possible. Changing those constraints when they become burdensome may be computationally effective: Why plan from scratch when it suffices to use an extant method? The latter point set the stage for a review paper from our lab that was largely about this theme (Rosenbaum, Cohen, Jax, van der Wel, & Weiss, 2007). Other demonstrations of the hand-path priming effect can be found in Griffiths and Tipper (2009) and van der Wel, Fleckenstein, Jax, and Rosenbaum (2007).

The End-State Comfort Effect

A third and final line of experiments to be reported here was concerned with object manipulation. The main question was whether the way an object is grasped reflects what one plans to do with it. The posture-based model predicts, in broad terms, that object grasps should reflect anticipations. The reason is that the model says that forecasting future body states (goal postures) is central to motor planning. The model also states that a series of goal postures can be chosen in a way that reduces the effort for the entire sequence of transitions to be made. In this sense, the model incorporates hierarchical structural notions of sequential performance (Collard & Povel, 1982; Rosenbaum, Kenny, & Derr, 1983).

Consistent with this expectation, we found that object grasps showed marked signs of anticipation. When participants in one study were asked to use the right hand to pick up a horizontally suspended rod, they picked up the rod with an overhand grip if they planned to turn the rod clockwise, but they picked up the rod with an underhand grip if they planned to turn the rod counterclockwise. The opposite result held if the left hand was used. Apparently, the choice of object grasp fulfilled an unconscious desire to end the task with the thumb pointing up. Saying this another way, participants were willing to pick up the rod with a somewhat uncomfortable palm-up posture if this ensured ending the task with the forearm oriented at or near the middle of its range of rotation about its long axis (i.e., with the thumb pointing up or at approximately 1 o'clock for the left hand and up or at approximately 11 o'clock for the right hand). Having the forearm at or near the middle of its range of motion is more comfortable than having the forearm at or near an extreme of this range, as established through comfort ratings (Rosenbaum, Marchak, Barnes, Vaughan, Slotta, & Jorgensen, 1990). Having the forearm at or near the middle of its range of rotation about its long axis also affords greater sensitivity (Rossetti, Meckler, & Prablanc, 1984), power (Winters & Kleweno, 1993), and speed (Rosenbaum, van Heugten, & Caldwell, 1996), all of which are helpful for precision, as needed to complete the task we studied. In general, grabbing an object with the hand oriented one way or the other depending on how people plan to orient the hand at the end of the object transport reflects advance planning with respect to arm and hand goal postures. My colleagues and I called this the *end-state comfort* effect.

Anticipatory effects like these are well known for speech, where coarticulation effects abound—as in rounding the lips in anticipation of making an /u/ sound while saying "tulip." *Co-manipulation* effects, to coin a phrase, have been studied much less. Interestingly, children show oral coarticulation effects by age 3 (Katz, Kripke, & Tallal, 1991), but they do not reliably show the end-state comfort effect for reaching and grasping until age 9 years or so (Stoeckel, Weigelt, Beeger, & Schack, 2009; Thibaut & Toussaint, 2010). Meanwhile, cotton-tamarin monkeys (Weiss, Wark, & Rosenbaum, 2007) and lemurs (Chapman, Weiss, & Rosenbaum, 2010) show the end-state comfort effect, suggesting that the cognitive abilities underlying this effect took hold phylogenetically at least 65 million years ago.

Another manifestation of the end-state comfort effect reflects anticipation in a slightly different way. Cohen and Rosenbaum (2004) asked university students to reach out and take hold of a bathroom plunger to move it to a high target platform. When the students did this, they grasped low on the shaft. However, when we asked the same subjects to reach out and take hold of the same bathroom plunger at the same initial position to move it to a low target platform, they grasped high on the shaft. We called this inverse relation between grasp height and plunger placement height the *grasp height* effect. We believe that the source of the grasp-height effect is essentially the same as the source of other manifestations of the end-state comfort effect. Grasping the plunger low when it needs to be raised high ensures that the arm will be at or near the middle of its range of motion when the plunger is brought to its target position. Similarly, grasping the plunger high when it needs to be brought down to a low position ensures that the arm will again be at or near the middle of its range of motion when the plunger is brought to its target. Evidently, regardless of whether the dimension of control is grasp height or grasp orientation, people learn to adopt postures that afford comfortable or easy-to-control postures when precision is required.

Because the end-state comfort effect generalizes so well, its violations are informative. If precision is required at the beginning of a task rather at the end of the task, the end-state comfort effect is reduced (Rosenbaum, Halloran, & Cohen, 2006). The end-state comfort effect is also reduced when subjects reach for an object to return it to the place from which they just transported it (Cohen & Rosenbaum, 2004). In such cases, subjects are more influenced by their *memory* of where they just grasped the object than by their knowledge of where to the object will be placed next. Thus, not only are *movements* preserved (as evidenced by the hand-path priming effect, described above), but *goal postures* are also preserved. Such changes in motor behavior attest to the sensitivity of motor planning. The posture-based model is one way to simulate such sensitivity.

CONCLUSION

This chapter began with a brief homage to Bill Chase, then it turned to a domain to which Bill Chase contributed mightily, chess playing, and it turned finally to a domain that Bill Chase had little contact with, at least professionally, the planning of physical actions. Bill was an avid runner, however, so he had more than a passing interest in motor planning. I also know from the one interaction I had with Bill Chase when he interviewed me for a faculty position at Carnegie Mellon that he was very receptive to the idea that cognitive psychology needed to include physical action planning and control. Bill appreciated, I'm sure, that I was not the originator of that idea. Saul Sternberg, with whom I decided to work at Bell Laboratories though I was offered a tenure-track position at CMU, was among the few researchers who recognized that motor planning needs to be part of modern cognitive science (Sternberg, Monsell, Knoll, & Wright, 1978). Sternberg was joined in that opinion by two other cognitive psychologists who had a profound effect on me at that early stage of my career: Steven Keele (1968) and Michael Turvey (1977). My thesis adviser, Gordon Bower, was sympathetic as well to the study of motor control, perhaps because, besides being an open-minded, curious scientist and very generous person, he almost became a major league baseball pitcher before embarking on his career in science (Gluck, Anderson, & Kosslyn, 2008).

The study of motor control has never been very popular in cognitive psychology, for a number of reasons (Heuer, 2003; Rosenbaum, 2005). Not least among these is that it has had a rich history of study in neuroscience, where motorically expressed disorders have cried out for remedies and where it has been relatively easy to determine how different areas of the brain contribute to movement (Jeannerod, 1985). If neuroscientists stimulate some area of the nervous system, they can observe the effects on behavior and piece together a story for how the behavior unfolds. Cognitive psychologists have felt that they could get more bang for the buck, so to speak, by studying processes that seemed beyond the reach of neuroscientists. Still, some cognitive psychologists, my colleagues and myself included, have come to believe that understanding the assembly of behavior may also profit from the kind of functional analysis that cognitive psychologists can offer. Pursuing an algorithmic account of motor planning, which is the sort of account that most befits or benefits from cognitive psychology (Marr, 1982), may also aid the development of robotics and other applied fields such as ergonomics and skill training.

In keeping with established methods for identifying cognitive algorithms, my colleagues and I have taken a two-tiered approach to the study of motor planning. The two tiers we have pursued are computational modeling, on the one hand, and behavioral experimentation, on the other. Each approach challenges and informs the other, as summarized briefly below before this chapter reaches its conclusion.

Computational modeling of motor planning may yield a model that can be realized in robots, in instructional media (Badler, Phillips, & Webber, 1993), and, conceivably, in the entertainment industry—specifically in computer animation. When cartoon animations are generated, they are often produced by moving 3D figures and taking successive pictures of those figures (the so-called "stop-motion" method) or by having actors don reflecting markers and having them move in a motion-capture studio. Computer systems can record the motions so that artists can later add costumes or other accoutrements to the displays. Interestingly for the evaluation of the posture-based method, it turns out that the most widely used method for animation is to draw keyframes and then interpolate between those keyframes to produce desired motions. This method relates to our proposal that biological motion control entails specifying goal postures and then interpolating between those goal postures to generate movement. The success of the keyframe method for animation does not prove that a comparable method is used in biological motion systems, but the widespread reliance on the method in technology hints at its usefulness in the natural world.

Technology is a long way off from having artificial motion generation systems that are intelligent enough to receive a high-level instruction like "set up the chess board" and then go off and do just that. Ultimately, the posture-based model or a model designed with similar aims may help shift from such high-level instructions to their physical implementation. Having such a system would be a wonderful advance that could have considerable practical value. Besides doing innocuous tasks like setting up chess boards, such a system could carry out tasks that are boring or dangerous, like sewing labels on clothes for hours on end or searching for hidden landmines (Staszewski, 2007). The prospect of developing such a system is one of the main motives for the modeling work described here.

The other tier we have pursued is behavioral experiments. There is no substitute for these when it comes to testing hypotheses and, as often as not, for being humbled by the results. The study of motor control is daunting when it comes to yielding humbling behavioral data, for unlike other branches of cognitive psychology, where the behavioral measures are usually just one reaction time and accuracy score per experimental trial, motor-control studies can yield reams of data per trial. For example, with motion-capture systems like the ones used to record actor motions in movie studios, the data from even a few minutes of behavior can easily tax the memory capacities of modern computers. A challenge for behavioral scientists studying motor control is to identify subsets of data that can inform their analyses. In principle, the most critical data correspond to the data the brain also cares about when it plans movements. All the details of every upcoming movement need not be represented explicitly by the brain. In fact, a prime motivation behind virtually all theories of motor planning is avoiding the need for such "data overload."

Dealing with data overload was, of course, the problem that Chase and Ericsson (1981) so famously addressed. Bill Chase, who was a brilliant experimenter, might have endorsed the general approach taken here. From him we learned that information is most easily encoded if it is related to existing chunks.

Those chunks are formed on the basis on what is meaningful to the individual. Movements *per se* usually do not have meaning in and of themselves, but some aspects of movements are more significant than others. My colleagues and I have come to the view that something can be learned by identifying the most significant features of movements. Those features, we believe, are likely to be pivotal for motor planning and control, and those functions are no less critical for survival than are their more popular cousins in cognitive psychology: perception, attention, learning, and memory.

REFERENCES

Badler, N. I., Phillips, C. B., & Webber, B. L. (1993). *Simulating humans: Computer graphics animation and control*. New York: Oxford University Press.

Berthier, N. E. (1996). Learning to reach: A mathematical model. *Developmental Psychology, 32*, 811–823.

Bizzi, E., Mussa-Ivaldi, F. A., & Giszter, S. (1991). Computations underlying the execution of movement: A biological perspective. *Science, 253*, 287–291.

Borg, G. A. V. (1973). Perceived exertion: A note on history and methods. *Medicine and Science in Sports, 5*, 90–93.

Bullock, D., Bongers, R. M., Lankhorst, M., & Beek, P. J. (1999). A vector-integration-to-endpoint model for performance of viapoint movements. *Neural Networks, 12*, 1–29.

Chapman, K. M., Weiss, D. J., & Rosenbaum, D. A. (2010). Evolutionary roots of motor planning: The end-state comfort effect in lemurs (*Lemur catta, Eulemur mongoz, Eulemur coronatus, Eulemur collaris, Hapalemur griseus*, and *Varecia rubra*). *Journal of Comparative Psychology, 124*, 229–232.

Chase, W. G., & Ericsson, K.A. (1981). Skilled memory. In J. R. Anderson (Ed.), *Cognitive skills and their acquisition* (pp. 141–189). Hillsdale, NJ: Erlbaum.

Cohen, R. G., & Rosenbaum, D. A. (2004). Where objects are grasped reveals how grasps are planned: Generation and recall of motor plans. *Experimental Brain Research, 157*, 486–495.

Collard, R., & Povel, D-J. (1982). Theory of serial pattern production: Tree traversals. *Psychological Review, 85*, 693–707.

Dickerson, C. R., Martin, B. J., & Chaffin, D. B. (2007). Predictors of perceived effort in the shoulder during load transfer tasks. *Ergonomics, 50*, 1004–1016.

Doeringer, J. A., & Hogan, N. (1998). Intermittency in preplanned elbow movements persists in the absence of visual feedback. *Journal of Neurophysiology, 80*, 1787–1799.

Edelman, S., & Flash, T. (1987). A model of handwriting. *Biological Cybernetics, 57*, 25–36.

Fajen, B. R. & Warren, W. H. (2003). Behavioral dynamics of steering, obstacle avoidance, and route selection. *Journal of Experimental Psychology: Human Perception and Performance, 29*, 343–362.

Feldman, A., & Latash, M. L. (2005). Testing hypotheses and the advancement of science: Recent attempts to falsify the equilibrium point hypothesis. *Experimental Brain Research, 161*, 91–103.

Fischer, M. H., Rosenbaum, D. A., & Vaughan, J. (1997). Speed and sequential effects in reaching. *Journal of Experimental Psychology: Human Perception and Performance, 23*, 404–428.

Fodor, J. A. (1983). *The modularity of mind*. Cambridge, MA: MIT Press.

Gluck, M. A., Anderson, J. R., & Kosslyn, S. M. (Eds.). (2008). *Memory and mind: A Festschrift for Gordon Bower* (pp. 173–194). Mahwah, NJ: Lawrence Erlbaum Associates/Taylor & Francis Group.

Graziano, M. S., Aflalo, T. M., & Cooke, D. F. (2005). Arm movements evoked by electrical stimulation in the motor cortex of monkeys. *Journal of Neurophysiology, 94*, 4209–4223.

Graziano, M. S., Taylor, C. S. R., & Moore, T. (2002). Complex movements evoked by microstimulation of precentral cortex. *Neuron, 34*, 841–851.

Griffiths, D., & Tipper, S. A. (2009). Priming of reach trajectory when observing actions: Hand-centred effects. *Quarterly Journal of Experimental Psychology, 62*, 2450–2470.

Hatsopoulos, N. G., & Warren, W. H. (1996). Resonance tuning in rhythmic arm movements. *Journal of Motor Behavior, 28*, 3–14.

Heuer, H. (2003). Motor control. In A. Healy, & R. Proctor (Eds.), *Handbook of psychology*: vol. 4: *Experimental psychology* (pp. 317–354). Hoboken, NJ: John Wiley & Sons, Inc.

Hoyt, D. F., & Taylor, C. R. (1981). Gait and the energetics of locomotion in horses. *Nature, 292*, 239–240.

Jax, S. A., & Rosenbaum, D. A. (2007). Hand path priming in manual obstacle avoidance: Evidence that the dorsal stream does not only control visually guided actions in real time. *Journal of Experimental Psychology: Human Perception and Performance, 33*, 425–441.

Jax, S. A., & Rosenbaum, D. A. (2009). Hand path priming in manual obstacle avoidance: Rapid decay of dorsal stream information. *Neuropsychologia, 47*, 1573–1577.

Jeannerod, M. (1985). *The brain machine: The development of neurophysiological thought*. (Trans. D. Urion). Cambridge, MA: Harvard University Press.

Katz, W. F., Kripke, C., & Tallal, P. (1991). Anticipatory coarticulation in the speech of adults and young children. *Journal of Speech & Hearing Research, 34*, 1222–1232.

Keele, S. W. (1968). Movement control in skilled motor performance. *Psychological Bulletin, 70*, 387–403.

Marr, D. (1982). *Vision*. San Francisco: W. H. Freeman.

Meulenbroek, R. G. J., Rosenbaum, D. A., Thomassen, A. J. W. M., Loukopoulos, L. D., & Vaughan, J. (1996). Adaptation of a reaching model to handwriting: How different effectors can produce the same written output, and other results. *Psychological Research/Psychologische Forschung, 59*, 64–74.

Mussa-Ivaldi, F. A., Morasso, P., & Zaccaria, R. (1988). Kinematic networks: A distributed model for representing and regularizing motor redundancy. *Biological Cybernetics, 60*, 1–16.

Ore, O. (1963). *Graphs and their uses*. New York: Random House.

Piaget, J. (1952). *The origins of intelligence in children* (2nd ed.). (Trans. M. Cook). New York: International Universities Press.

Polit, A., & Bizzi, E. (1978). Processes controlling arm movements in monkeys. *Science, 201*, 1235–1237.

Rosenbaum, D. A. (2005). The Cinderella of psychology: The neglect of motor control in the science of mental life and behavior. *American Psychologist, 60*, 308–317.

Rosenbaum, D. A. (2008). Reaching and walking: Reaching distance costs more than walking distance. *Psychonomic Bulletin & Review, 15*, 1100–1104.

Rosenbaum, D. A. (2010). *Human motor control* (2nd ed.). San Diego, CA: Academic Press/Elsevier.

Rosenbaum, D. A., Carlson, R. A., & Gilmore, R. O. (2001a). Acquisition of intellectual and perceptual-motor skills. *Annual Review of Psychology, 52*, 453–470.

Rosenbaum, D. A., Cohen, R. G., Jax, S. A., van der Wel, R., & Weiss, D. J. (2007). The problem of serial order in behavior: Lashley's legacy. *Human Movement Science, 26*, 525–554.

Rosenbaum, D. A., & Gaydos, M. J. (2008). A method for obtaining psychophysical estimation of movement costs. *Journal of Motor Behavior, 40*, 11–17.

Rosenbaum, D. A., & Gregory, R. W. (2002). Development of a method for measuring moving-related effort: Biomechanical considerations and implications for Fitts' Law. *Experimental Brain Research, 142*, 365–373.

Rosenbaum, D. A., Halloran, E., & Cohen, R. G. (2006). Grasping movement plans. *Psychonomic Bulletin and Review, 13*, 918–922.

Rosenbaum, D. A., Kenny, S., & Derr, M. A. (1983). Hierarchical control of rapid movement sequences. *Journal of Experimental Psychology: Human Perception and Performance, 9*, 86–102.

Rosenbaum, D. A., Loukopoulos, L. D., Meulenbroek, R. G. M., Vaughan, J., & Engelbrecht, S. E. (1995). Planning reaches by evaluating stored postures. *Psychological Review, 102*, 28–67.

Rosenbaum, D. A., Marchak, F., Barnes, H. J., Vaughan, J., Slotta, J., & Jorgensen, M. (1990). Constraints for action selection: Overhand versus underhand grips. In M. Jeannerod (Ed.), *Attention and performance XIII: Motor representation and control* (pp. 321–342). Hillsdale, NJ: Lawrence Erlbaum Associates.

Rosenbaum, D. A., Meulenbroek, R. G., & Vaughan, J. (1999). Remembered positions: Stored locations or stored postures? *Experimental Brain Research, 124*, 503–512.

Rosenbaum, D. A., Meulenbroek, R. G., Vaughan, J., & Jansen, C. (2001b). Posture-based motion planning: Applications to grasping. *Psychological Review, 108*, 709–734.

Rosenbaum, D. A., Slotta, J. D., Vaughan, J., & Plamondon, R. J. (1991). Optimal movement selection. *Psychological Science, 2*, 86–91.

Rosenbaum, D. A., van Heugten, C., & Caldwell, G. C. (1996). From cognition to biomechanics and back: The end-state comfort effect and the middle-is-faster effect. *Acta Psychologica, 94*, 59–85.

Rossetti, Y., Meckler, C., & Prablanc, C. (1994). Is there an optimal arm posture? Deterioration of finger localization precision and comfort sensation in extreme arm-joint postures. *Experimental Brain Research, 99*, 131–136.

Sachs, J. (1967). Recognition memory for syntactic and semantic aspects of a connected discourse. *Perception & Psychophysics, 2*, 437–442.

Sainburg, R. (2005). Handedness: Differential specializations for control of trajectory and position. *Exercise and Sport Sciences Reviews, 33*, 206–213.

Schmidt, R. A., & Bjork, R. A. (1992). New conceptualizations of practice: Common principles in three paradigms suggest new concepts for training. *Psychological Science, 3*, 207–214.

Shepard, R. N., & Cooper, L. (1982). *Mental images and their transformations.* Cambridge, MA: MIT Press/Bradford Books.

Smyth, M. M. (1984). Memory for movements. In M. M. Smyth, & A. M. Wing (Eds.), *The psychology of human movement* (pp. 83–117). London: Academic Press.

Staszewski, J. (2007). Spatial thinking and the design of landmine detection training. In G. A. Allen (Ed.), *Applied spatial cognition: From research to cognitive technology* (pp. 231–265). Mahwah, NJ: Erlbaum Associates.

Sternberg, S., Monsell, S., Knoll, R. L., & Wright, C. E. (1978). The latency and duration of rapid movement sequences: Comparisons of speech and typewriting. In G. E. Stelmach (Ed.), *Information processing in motor control and learning* (pp. 117–152). New York: Academic Press.

Stoeckel, T., Weigelt, M., Beeger, H., & Schack, T. (2009, June). The developmental nature of representing comfortable end-states in long-term memory. Paper presented at the meeting of the International Society of Sport Psychology (ISSP), Marrakesh, Morocco.

Thibaut, J-P., & Toussaint, L. (2010). Developing motor planning over ages. *Journal of Experimental Child Psychology, 105*, 116–129.

Turvey, M. T. (1977). Preliminaries to a theory of action with reference to vision. In R. Shaw, & J. Bransford (Eds.), *Perceiving, acting, and knowing* (pp. 211–265). Hillsdale, NJ: Lawrence Erlbaum.

Usher, M., & McClelland, J. L. (2001). On the time course of perceptual choice: The leaky competing accumulator model. *Psychological Review, 108*, 550–592.

van der Wel, R. P., Fleckenstein, R., Jax, S., & Rosenbaum, D. A. (2007). Hand path priming in manual obstacle avoidance: Evidence for abstract spatio-temporal forms in human motor control. *Journal of Experimental Psychology: Human Perception and Performance, 33*, 1117–1126.

van der Wel, R. P., Sternad, D., & Rosenbaum, D. A. (2010). Moving the hand at different rates: Avoiding slow movements. *Journal of Motor Behavior, 42*, 29–36.

Vaughan, J., Rosenbaum, D. A., Harp, C. J., Loukopoulos, L. D., & Engelbrecht, S. E. (1998). Finding final postures. *Journal of Motor Behavior, 30*, 273–284.

Vaughan, J., Rosenbaum, D. A., & Meulenbroek, R. G. J. (2001). Planning reaching and grasping movements: The problem of obstacle avoidance. *Motor Control, 5*, 116–135.

Vaughan, J., Rosenbaum, D. A., & Meulenbroek, R. G. J. (2006). Modeling reaching and manipulating in 2- and 3-D workspaces: The posture-based model. In *Proceedings of the Fifth International Conference on Learning and Development*, Bloomington, IN, May 31–June 3.

Walsh, M. M., & Rosenbaum, D. A. (2009). Deciding how to act is not achieved by watching mental movies. *Journal of Experimental Psychology: Human Perception and Performance, 35*, 1481–1489.

Weiss, D. J., Wark, J. D., & Rosenbaum, D. A. (2007). Monkey see, monkey plan, monkey do: The end-state comfort effect in cotton-top tamarins (*Saguinus Oedipus*). *Psychological Science, 18*, 1063–1068.

Winters, J. M., & Kleweno, D. G. (1993). Effect of initial upper-limb alignment on muscle contributions to isometric strength curves. *Journal of Biomechanics, 26*, 143–153.

9

Exceptional Memory and Expert Performance[1]

From Simon and Chase's Theory of Expertise to Skilled Memory and Beyond

K. ANDERS ERICSSON

Florida State University, USA

*B*ill Chase was a remarkable person, scholar, and mentor. In this chapter I will briefly describe the collaborative research that we conducted on the acquisition of exceptional memory in unexceptional college students in the late 1970s and how this interactive research shaped and influenced me as an independent scientist. The main body of this chapter will focus on the research findings and theoretical ideas of this early research on acquired memory skill. The latter parts will describe how these ideas were later developed, extended, and generalized after Bill's sudden and unexpected death in 1983.

The chapter will contain three major sections roughly based on three historical periods. In the first shorter section, I will describe the dominant view of short-term memory and expertise when I arrived as a post-doctoral fellow at Carnegie Mellon University (CMU), which at that time was the undisputed leader of research in cognitive psychology. In the second section I will describe how I met Bill at Carnegie Mellon and how we started our research on the effects of practice on tasks measuring short-term memory. In that section I will also describe the main findings of this early research and how we later extended

1 I am grateful for the financial support provided by the FSCW/Conradi Endowment Fund of Florida State University Foundation. The author wants to thank Len Hill and Jerad Moxley for their valuable comments on earlier drafts of this chapter.

these ideas in a general theoretical proposals for cognitive mechanisms mediating exceptional memory in memorists and memory experts. In the third and last section of this chapter I will go one step further and describe my and my colleagues' subsequent research of exceptional and expert performance in many domains of expertise, such as music, chess, and sports. I will conclude with some reflections and on current and future research in understanding the prospects and limits of human performance.

THE DOMINANT VIEW OF SHORT-TERM MEMORY AND EXPERTISE IN THE LATE 1970S

My academic training in psychology was completed at the University of Stockholm in Sweden. During the 1960s and early 1970s the psychology department was famous for studies of psycho-physics and scaling (Ekman & Sjöberg, 1965) and no full professor had yet become interested in the new research on thinking and cognition. My own knowledge about how to study human thinking was therefore dramatically influenced by reading the papers by Herbert Simon and Allen Newell, and especially their book on Human Problem Solving (Newell & Simon, 1972). Their theory of human information processing was based on the assumption that human thinking can be described by elementary information processes operating within a computational environment with a central processor and memory systems, which had specified limits on storage capacity and time requirements for storage and retrieval of information. The most influential constraint on human cognitive processing and thinking was assumed to be due to the limited capacity of short-term memory (STM). George Miller's (1956) influential review showed that the capacity of STM could be described by the magical number seven plus/minus two symbols or chunks. Although extensive laboratory research has accumulated a massive body of evidence in support of this proposed limit on STM, there were some reports of potential exceptions, such as the memory performance of exceptional achievers and experts.

One of the potential exceptions to a limited capacity of STM had accrued particularly compelling empirical support. It concerned chess masters' ability to recall chess positions after a brief presentation. A chess master could accurately recall over 20 pieces from a briefly presented chess position—virtually without errors (de Groot, [1946] 1978). In a classic series of studies, Bill Chase and Herbert Simon (Chase & Simon, 1973a, 1973b) provided an account of chess masters' superior memory performance without any need to violate the general limited capacity limitations of their STM—the magical number seven plus/minus two chunks (Miller, 1956).

De Groot ([1946] 1978) had originally found that when chess masters were shown a presented chess position and picked the best move within 5–10 seconds, their memory of the locations of chess pieces was exceptional. When the chess position was removed from view, then the chess masters were able to recall virtually all of the chess pieces in the position. Conversely, less skilled players were able to recall much fewer chess pieces for the same positions. Bill

Chase and Herbert Simon replicated chess masters' memory advantage in a controlled memory experiment, where chess positions were presented only for 5 seconds, followed by an immediate recall. The time of 5 seconds was selected to eliminate storage in LTM, which was estimated to take 8 seconds (Simon, 1974). Most importantly, Chase and Simon (1973a, 1973b) also tested memory for scrambled chess positions, where chess pieces were randomly rearranged on the board. For this type of random position they found no reliable differences as a function of skill—a finding that rejects the hypothesis that chess masters had a superior memory for chess pieces in any configuration. By inference, the chess masters' superior memory for meaningful chess positions must rely on their recognition of familiar patterns and configurations of chess pieces, which in turn permitted them to recall more chess pieces. Bill and Herb also provided detailed data supporting the hypothesis that the better chess players recognized larger and more complex familiar patterns of related chess pieces (chunks) due to their larger storehouse of previously encountered patterns and configurations. In contrast, beginning chess players had not acquired these complex patterns so they had to remember the chess position by the locations of individual chess pieces, resulting in only about four or five correctly recalled pieces. Chase and Simon's (1973a, 1973b) account of the observed recall performance for both meaningful and scrambled chess positions by experts and novices implied no differences in the number of chunks stored in the STM of experts and novices (Miller, 1956).

Based on their insights into the memory of chess masters, Herb and Bill proposed the first general theory of expertise (Simon & Chase, 1973). This theory assumed that expertise depended on the accumulation of increasingly complex patterns and configurations of particular chess pieces (chunks). They estimated that "a chess master can recognize at least 50,000 different game configurations of pieces, and a grand master even more" (Simon & Chase, 1973, p. 402), and that these configurations or chunks are acquired as a function of extended experience in the activities of the corresponding domain. They argued that becoming a grandmaster in chess would require about a decade's intense preoccupation with the game and they estimated that "very roughly, that a master has spent perhaps 10,000 to 50,000 hours *staring at chess positions*, and class A player 1,000 to 5,000 hours" (Simon & Chase, 1973, p. 402, italics added). Simon and Chase (1973) proposed that the experts had relied on their large body of chunks to encode good moves associated with various combinations of patterns and thus could retrieve better moves for the patterns associated with a given chess position. They argued that "with many of these patterns are associated plausible moves that take advantage of the features represented by the patterns" (p. 402), and that chess masters often impress weaker players by their ability to notice moves at a glance. Their theory claimed that "the acquisition of chess skill depends, in large part, on building up recognition memory for many familiar chess patterns" (p. 403) and there appears to be no need for above average basic cognitive ability to reach high levels of chess skill. They did, however, hedge their claim about natural ability by saying that

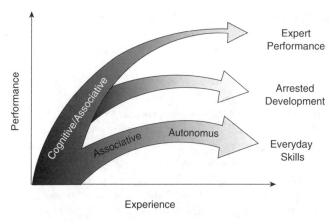

Figure 9.1   An illustration of the qualitative difference between the course of improve-ment of expert performance and of everyday activities. The goal for everyday activities is to reach as rapidly as possible a satisfactory level that is stable and "autonomous" (see the gray/white plateau at the bottom of the graph). In contrast, expert performers counteract automaticity by developing increasingly complex mental representations to attain higher levels of control of their performance and will therefore remain within the "cognitive" and "associative" phases. Some experts will at some point in their career stop engaging in deliberate practice and prematurely automate their performance.

Source: Adapted from Ericsson (1998, p. 90). Copyright ©1998 by European Council for High Ability.

"World Champion caliber grandmasters may possess truly exceptional talents along certain dimensions" (p. 403).

Although Simon and Chase (1973) did not explicitly relate their theory to earlier theoretical frameworks for the acquisition of skilled performance, there are clear parallels to earlier analyses of telegraphy (Bryan & Harter, 1897, 1899) and typing (Book, 1925). In fact, Fitts and Posner's (1967) model of skill acquisition in terms of three phases provides a good overall description. During the first phase of learning, beginners try to understand the requirements of the activity, learn rules, and focus on generating gross actions while avoiding serious mistakes—illustrated by the dark part of the lower arrow in Figure 9.1. In the second phase of learning (the shaded area on the lower arm), when people have had more experience, salient mistakes become increasingly rare, performance becomes smoother, and learners no longer need to focus as much to perform at an acceptable level. After a limited period of training and experience, an accep-table level of performance is typically attained and skills can be executed smoothly and with minimal effort. Whereas initial proficiency in everyday and professional skills may be attained within weeks and months, development to very high levels of achievement appears to require many years or even decades of experience. In fact, Bryan and Harter claimed as early as 1899 that over ten years of professional experience is necessary to become an expert.

In the years following Bill's and Herb's publications (Chase & Simon, 1973a, 1973b), their findings for experts' memories were replicated. In other domains of expertise, experts demonstrated superior memory for representative game situations, but not for recall of random, unstructured stimuli in basketball (Allard, Graham, & Paarsalu, 1980) and in games, such as chess (see Gobet & Charness, 2006, for reviews), bridge (Charness, 1979; Engle & Bukstel, 1978), and GO (Reitman, 1976). In these domains other than chess, however, the absolute size of the memory advantage for experts over novices was much smaller than that observed in chess but the differences were still significant.

In the late 1970s there were also several results that questioned some of the assumptions of Chase and Simon's (1973a, 1973b) theory. The most important finding was that chess experts are able to rapidly store information in LTM after only brief exposures (less than 8 seconds) to chess positions and thus must rely on storage in LTM for their superior performance (Charness, 1976; Frey & Adesman, 1976). Given that Neil Charness' research was a doctoral dissertation supervised by Bill Chase, Bill was very familiar with these empirical findings and their theoretical implications.

THE START OF THE RESEARCH ON EXCEPTIONAL MEMORY

I will start with a more personal section on how I, as a newly arrived post-doctoral fellow from my native Sweden, first met Bill in Pittsburgh and how we began our collaborative research on the acquisition of exceptional memory.

In late July of 1977, I arrived in Pittsburgh to work with Herb Simon on a two-year post-doctoral fellowship on the topic of protocol analysis (Ericsson & Simon, 1980, 1993), which involves an analysis of thoughts verbalized concurrently by participants while they engage in problem solving. I had arrived, one month early, to find a furnished house before my wife and my two young children arrived in late August. I found an affordable town house in Squirrel Hill, an area just north of Carnegie Mellon University, but it was not furnished and lacked a washer and dryer.

During a short visit to the department's coffee/mailroom—the social center of that department— I must have discussed my problems about finding used furniture and appliances for the town house, when Bill Chase walked in. With his warm smile, Bill spontaneously exclaimed that he loved going to garage sales and he had a station wagon that could hold most furniture. Over the next couple of weekends we bought appliances and furniture (Bill was a great bargain hunter) and moved them into my rented four-level town house. We became friends and from that time onward we would frequently have a Coke in his office and discuss issues ranging from the personal to the scientific.

After establishing my research projects with Herb Simon on the theoretical issues of protocol analysis, I thought that it would be important to start some empirical studies, where some of the insights from protocol analysis could be tested and applied. I was looking for an issue that most researchers at CMU would be interested in, and particularly Bill. The nature of the limits of short-term memory and the degree to which these limits could be changed and/or circumvented seemed to be a good topic, as long as it involved an empirical phenomenon that could be studied experimentally.

To prepare for discussions with Bill, I spent a lot of time in the library. Based on my training in Sweden, I tended to explore the history of ideas and issues more than most American graduate students, who focused primarily on the most recently published journal articles. Consequently, I was particularly interested in reading about research studies in psychology that had been published 50 to 100 years ago. I knew that any acceptable research proposal would have to satisfy Bill's interest in experimental studies of the structure of STM and it also needed to be associated with a large difference in performance that could be enlightened through verbal reports. One day I found a study that had demonstrated that immediate memory of digits could be dramatically improved through training (Martin & Fernberger, 1929). After 50 sessions of training, two students were able to increase their recall not just by one or twos digits, but their memory performance were increased from an initial state of 9 digits to 13 and from 11 digits to 15 digits, respectively. If these findings could be replicated, then it would suggest that individual differences in STM were not fixed and unmodifiable, but with training, an average student could attain an immediate memory for digits that clearly exceeded the memory of the best performing students, who could recall 9 or 10 digits correctly.

Bill was a traditional experimental psychologist and expressed clear doubts about the usefulness of verbal reports ("introspections," as he tended to call them) in permitting us to describe the mechanisms mediating increases in students' memory performance after practice. However, he felt confident that we would be able to examine the structure of the improved memory performance by testing the trainees with designed experiments. With reliance on experiments, there would be no need to have to trust the verbal reports. In fact, we would be able to test predictions and hypotheses derived from the verbal reports by designing experimental manipulations that would assess empirically the validity of the verbal reports. Bill got excited about the project and talked to a work study student, Steve Faloon (SF), who would be working for him during the summer of 1978. SF agreed to be a research participant in our study on digit span as part of his job assignment. Before starting with our replication of the memory improvement found by Martin and Fernberger (1929), we interviewed SF to make sure that he was a typical CMU student without any special cognitive abilities.

The Study of SF's Acquisition of a Memory Skill

In the summer of 1978, Bill, SF, and I would get together for an hour or so for testing every other day each week. I would read the list of digits at around 1 s per digit and Bill checked the accuracy of SF's recall before SF would give a retrospective report about his thoughts during the memory trial. If SF got all the digits correct, then I would read him a list with one more digit. If he missed any digit in the presented list, then the length of the list on the following trial would be reduced by one digit. Although our training procedure changed a bit during the more than 200 training sessions, most of the sessions were concluded by asking SF to recall as much as possible about all the digit sequences presented during the session—a typical session would involve the presentation of 200–300 digits.

The first couple of training sessions were relatively uneventful. Steve's initial memory-span performance was comparable to other college students, namely just above seven digits (Miller, 1956). His verbal reports from the memory trials were also typical for college students and he reported seeing familiar numbers, encoding patterns of digits and grouping the digits into groups of three, four or five digits. SF tried to concentrate on the first few digits and rapidly commit them to memory and then move his attention to rehearsing the following digits until he had them memorized. Then he would try to recall the first digits from memory and then continue with the digits in the rehearsal group. During the fourth practice session Steve gave a pretty lengthy report on how he had now reached his absolute limit and how no further improvements would be possible. We were satisfied that Steve's initial performance seemed to be typical of college students in all observable aspects.

In his fifth session, he showed an unexpected improvement of a couple of additional digits and was able to correctly recall an average of around ten digits—a reasonably rare performance among college students. This session was the first, where he reported encoding the first three digits as a running time for a race, that is 438 is a running time for the mile, 4 minutes and 38 seconds. From that practice session on, SF showed a relatively slow but consistent improvement for the subsequent 200 hours of practice during the next couple of years. His average running digit span, as function of number of practice sessions (typically around an hour's duration), is shown in Figure 9.2.

Encoding Digit Groups as Running Times

SF's encoding of digit groups emerged gradually. In the beginning of training he segmented the presented lists of digits into a series of 3-digit groups (see Table 9.1). Hence, Bill and I could predict even before a memory trial which groups of three digits SF would try to encode into LTM. SF tried to encode digit triplets, as running times for races of a half-mile, a mile or two miles in terms of minutes and seconds. However, a digit group such as 583 where the middle digit was greater than 5 would not be meaningful because 5 minutes and 83 seconds cannot be interpreted as mile time. In our first experiment, we compared SF's digit span for random sequences of digits to experimental lists which we had designed to satisfy additional constraints. In one session, we presented lists to SF where all of the 3-digit groups within the list (see Table 9.1) were consistent with encodings as running times. SF's digit span was reliably higher for lists where he could encode all of the 3-digit groups (average digit span = 19.5) compared to his average span of 15.3 digits for regular lists with completely random digits, where only some of the 3-digit groups could be encoded as running times.

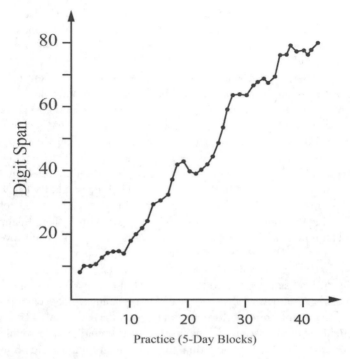

Figure 9.2   Average digit span for SF as a function of practice.

Source: Adapted from Ericsson, Chase, & Faloon (1980, p. 1181). Copyright © 1980 by American Association for the Advancement of Science (*AAAS*).

TABLE 9.1   Examples of Experimentally Manipulated Digit Sequences and the Associated Performance

Type	Mean span	Digit sequence	Recoding by SF
Random sequences	15.9, 15.3, for before and after experimental sessions	135 168 411 455 336	
Experimental session with "unencodable" digit groups	12.7	Intended grouping: 294 682 471 168 497	2 946 824 711 684 97
Experimental session with completely encodable groups	19.5	523 418 326 945 831	

In another experimental session we constructed lists that we predicted could not be encoded as running times, because the middle digit was either a 6, 7, 8, or 9. The first couple of memory trials of the session worked exactly as we planned and SF's ability to encode and later recall the digit sequences was very poor—approaching his original span before the start of training. At this point SF realized that if he removed the first digit and then grouped the remaining digits in groups of three he was able to encode several of the resulting 3-digit groups as running times (see Table 9.1). This revised encoding method led to a lower percentage of digit groups encoded as running times (only 41% of all groups compared to 68% for random lists used in a regular training session). Our experimental manipulation led to a reliably reduced digit span (average of 12.7 digits compared to his span of 15.9 digits for random sequences at that time) in a manner rather different from the one we had planned. Our attempt to reduce SF's performance uncovered the flexibility and resilience of his acquired memory skill. More importantly we showed that it is possible to design an experimental condition where the performance of a motivated expert is reliably reduced—almost to the level of untrained subjects. Theoretically derived interventions that reduce performance of skilled individuals imply that we have learned something important about the mechanisms of his/her acquired skill.

Bill and I spent hours discussing how we could design experiments that would provide compelling performance data on the mechanisms that mediated SF's acquired memory skill. One of the most fun aspects of these discussions was that Bill and I often, especially in the beginning of our studies, would predict different outcomes of the experiments. Bill was addicted to Coke (the beverage in a can) and we frequently made bets on outcomes of experiments, and whoever lost had to go to the Coke machine and buy two Cokes, one for each of us. There are several descriptions of our experiments, such as our *Science* paper (Ericsson, Chase, & Faloon, 1980), the chapters by Chase and Ericsson (1981, 1982) which are particularly detailed, as well as two articles (Ericsson, 1985; Ericsson & Chase, 1982). Therefore, I will just summarize the major findings in terms of principles of skilled memory.

Three Principles of Skilled Memory

Our fundamental discovery was that memory for rapidly presented digits could be improved dramatically and that the increased performance was based on storage in LTM—a clear rejection of Chase and Simon's (1973a, 1973b) assumption that superior memory could be explained by pre-existing chunks in LTM, that were only activated in STM with short presentation times of less than 8 seconds(Simon, 1974). One striking piece of evidence for the storage of information in LTM was that SF could recall the vast majority of the presented digit groups at the end of the testing session, where 200–300 digits had been presented as part of different memory trials. Ericsson and Kintsch (1995) discussed this and other evidence from several experiments in detail. There are several subsequent proposals for how to supplement the original Chase and Simon (1973a, 1973b) model with additional mechanisms (Gobet & Simon, 1996; Richman, Staszewski, & Simon, 1995), as well as a contentious exchange about the sufficiency of those additional mechanisms to explain the available findings (Ericsson & Kintsch, 1995; Ericsson, Patel, & Kintsch, 2000; Gobet, 2000a,

2000b). I will now turn to Bill's and my proposal for how SF was able to encode information in LTM (unlike other participants tested in the memory task) and how these mechanisms were acquired and refined during training in terms of three principles of skilled memory.

The first principle was that exceptional memory performance is mediated by mnemonic encodings, where patterns and meaningful information are accessed from long-term memory to construct an encoding in LTM of groups of the presented material, such as digits. SF acquired and refined these encoding mechanisms gradually as reflected by his gradual improvement in performance (see Figure 9.2). The experiment described above where we compared performance for digit groups that could be encoded as running times or not, was one piece of evidence supporting that claim for SF. As SF's memory performance improved, he generated additional mnemonic encodings, which allowed him to encode all the digits that did not permit a meaningful encoding as a running time. He encoded digit groups, such as 792 and 584, as ages of people, namely 79.2 years old (almost 80 years old) and 58.4 years old. Consequently, all groups of presented digits were linked to one or another mnemonic association.

The second principle we called the retrieval structure principle. According to SF's verbal reports, he would decide how to segment a sequence in digit groups before the start of the trial. For example, when presented with a list of 30 digits, SF would form four 4-digit groups and then three 3-digit groups followed by a group of five digits that he would be rehearsing at the end of the presentation, as illustrated in Figure 9.3. SF could therefore segment the presented digits into the appropriate group and encode it in LTM and then proceed to the next group and encode that one and so on until he encountered the rehearsal group. This account raises the issue of how SF was able to retrieve these encoded digits at the time of the recall of the entire list of presented digits.

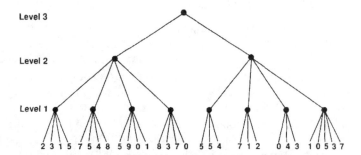

Figure 9.3 Proposed hierarchical organization of SF's memory encoding of 30 presented digits. The first level contains mnemonic encodings of digit groups, and the second level consists of supergroups in which the relative location of several digit groups is encoded.

Source: Adapted from Ericsson & Kintsch (1995, p. 217). Copyright © 1995 by American Psychological Association.

SF described that he would have a spatial position for each digit group of each type, such as the three 3-digit groups. The first 3-digit group would be at the far left of his inner eye, the second one at the middle, and the last 3-digit group at the far right. When he would recall the three 3-digit groups he would reinstate the internal cues and use them as retrieval cues to retrieve the groups of presented digits. SF's use of retrieval cues is very similar to the method of loci (see Ericsson, 1985, for a discussion). Bill and I conducted several experiments testing the existence and structure of SF's retrieval cues (retrieval structure). In one experiment we had him memorize lists of 30 digits and after the memorization of each one we tested him with designed memory probes for that particular list. For example, he was asked to recall the digit group that we pointed to in the chart of his retrieval structure (like the one in Figure 9.3, but without any numbers at the bottom). We also read a digit group to him and asked him to point where that digit group was located in the chart. We asked him to recall the digit just preceding a presented digit group, such as 426, and he would need to reply 5 (see Figure 9.3). All these findings were consistent with the existence of encoded retrieval cues organized hierarchically in a retrieval structure like the one shown in Figure 9.3 (Chase & Ericsson, 1981; Ericsson, 1985).

The third and final principle was the speed-up principle. As the result of training we found that SF improved his digit span from 7 to 82 digits. His ability to recall long sequences of digits obviously improved, but had his memory performance on a shorter list improved? After practice, SF was able to increase his memory performance even for very rapidly presented digits. For digits presented at the fastest speed possible (around 5 digits per second is the fastest speed that the digits can be read aloud), his digit span had increased to an exceptional level—around 11 digits (Chase & Ericsson, 1981). In some experimental test sessions SF memorized lists of visually presented digits using a self-paced procedure, and we found that his study times were become increasingly faster as a function of his increased digit span. In sum, these findings show that SF was able to speed up his encoding and storage of digits as a function of his training.

In sum, our original study with SF demonstrated that performance on the digit span task—generally believed to measure the fixed and limited capacity of short-term memory— could be dramatically improved, but the increases were limited to digits and did not transfer to letters (Ericsson et al., 1980). Was SF unique? As Herb Simon used to say, "Generalizability starts at two." In subsequent research, Jim Staszewski, Bill and I were able to show that three other students were able to attain exceptional levels of digit span (over 18 digits) after extended training. Their improved memory was mediated by acquired mechanisms consistent with the three principles of skilled memory (Chase & Ericsson, 1981, 1982; Richman et al., 1995). Several studies by other independent investigators have shown that memory is improvable with training (for reviews, see Ericsson, 1985; Wilding & Valentine, 1997, 2006), and a few studies showed that, with extended training, larger groups of participants could improve their memory substantially (Higbee, 1997; Wenger & Payne, 1995).

The specificity of the improved memory performance to a particular type of material made our findings different from other work on the capacity of working memory that generalized to any information that could be rehearsed, such as digits, letters, and words. The essence of our findings was that an individual could dramatically expand their working memory capacity for some type of information by acquiring memory skills based on storage in LTM and associations with retrieval cues organized in structures. In the following sections of this chapter I will explore a few issues that concern the broader generalizability of the original findings on the potential for acquiring LTWM (Ericsson & Kintsch, 1995). The first issue concerns whether the three principles are sufficient to explain the performance of many individuals alleged to have an exceptional memory—typically assumed to be qualitatively different memory system from that of normal healthy individuals. The second issue related to theoretical accounts of exceptional memory in chess masters and their relation to skilled memory that we had studied in the laboratory (Chase & Ericsson, 1982; Ericsson & Chase, 1982). This last issue and most general issue concerned the relation between the characteristics of acquiring superior memory skill and any other type of reproducibly superior skilled performance in any domain of expertise and organized activity.

DO ALL TYPES OF EXCEPTIONAL MEMORY REFLECT ACQUIRED MEMORY SKILLS?

In parallel with the research on training college students to improve their memory for digits, Bill and I started to explore the generalizability of the training effects that we had found. How would SF's memory performance compare to individuals generally believed to have exceptional memory, such as Luria's (1968) Subject S, Hunt and Love's (1972) Subject VP, Hunter's (1962) Professor Aiken, and Müller's (1911) Professor Rückle? In our first published chapter (Chase & Ericsson, 1981), Bill and I reported some data on how SF was able to perform the tasks that had been cited in support of the famous subjects' exceptionality. In fact, SF was able to match or surpass the performance of these subjects. In a subsequent paper (Ericsson & Chase, 1982), we were able to go a step further to analyze the pattern of recall times for the exceptional participants and SF for Binet's (1894) 5x5 digit matrices (see Figure 9.4) and for Luria's 50-digit matrix. SF reported encoding the matrix—as a sequence of 5 rows—and then recalled the digits in the different recall orders (see Figure 9.4) by recalling one row at a time and then rapidly extracting the relevant digits. Our analysis of the study and recall times (Ericsson & Chase, 1982) showed that our trained subjects not only could match the performance of the exceptional subjects, but there was also evidence that both trained and famous participants were relying on the same general encoding methods, storing the matrices in LTM by encoding each line of digits as digit groups.

In a subsequent review of exceptional memory performance (Ericsson, 1985), I found that truly exceptional memory performance was nearly always

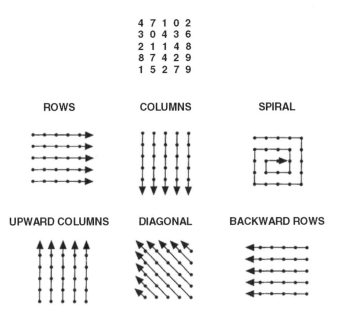

Figure 9.4   A 25-digit matrix of the type used by Binet (1894) to test his memory experts. He asked subjects to repeat the whole matrix in the various orders shown or to repeat individual rows as five-digit numbers.Source: Adapted from Ericsson & Kintsch (1995, p. 218). Copyright © 1995 by American Psychological Association.

limited to one type of material, such as digits. For example, Subject S (Luria, 1968) reported using mnemonics to remember all types of materials, such as poetry in a foreign language, with one exception and that exception was digits and numbers. For several of the exceptional individuals, there was clear evidence of relevant background experiences with numbers. Both Professors Aiken (Hunter, 1962) and Rückle (Müller, 1911) had a long history with numbers and mental calculation. They knew each number between 000 and 999 individually, so they would know if they were a prime number or their unique decomposition, such as 451 = 11 * 41. All of these exceptional individuals reported breaking up longer lists of digits into groups, where the group size was between 3 to 5 digits. Over time, skilled memory theory was going from being a curious alternative to the main contender for explaining exceptional memory performance (Wilding & Valentine, 1997, 2006). Instead of arguing that there must be exceptions for the most gifted and talented (cf. Simon and Chase's1973 exclusion of the World Class chess players), my approach was to search for even a single well-documented exception.

Recently there are several demonstrations of amazing memory performance that have been verified by the Guinness Book of World Records, such as the successful memorization and recall of the decimals of pi. Three of the top record holders for this event have been studied in the laboratory: Rajan

Mahadevan recalled the first 31,811 decimals of pi in 1981 (Ericsson, Delaney, Weaver, & Mahadevan, 2004), Tomoyori recited the first 40,000 decimals of pi in 1987 (Takahashi, Shimizu, Saito, & Tomoyori, 2006) and Chao Lu recited the first 67,890 digits of pi in 2005 (Hu, Ericsson, Yang, & Lu, 2009). It is interesting to note that Takahashi et al. (2006) found that the memory abilities of over 60-year-old Tomoyori could not be clearly distinguished from an age-matched control group. They attributed his record-breaking performance to his use of a mnemonic strategy, which involved converting 2- and 3-digit groups into words and then he formed interactive images of the words. His Guinness Book record for recalling the digits of pi was seen primarily as the result of persistent efforts. In fact, Tomoyori estimated that he had spent some 9,000–10,000 hours of daily memorization to master the 40,000 digits. Similarly, Hu et al. (2009) found no evidence for Chao Lu having a superior basic memory capacity, but rather evidence for extended intense practice and sustained effort to attain a very challenging goal. This study permitted us to describe a memorist who attained a world class memory performance in seven years, with only one year of intensive preparation. Hu et al. (2009) found that Chao Lu was significantly better than a control group of college students in memorizing a range of materials, from digits to words, under self-paced conditions at rates around 3–5 seconds per digit. From extensive verbal reports and several experiments, Hu et al. (2009) was able to describe the detailed structure of Chao Lu's memory skill which was based on converting 2-digit groups into words and then generating stories stored in LTM. In contrast to Tomoyori and Chao Lu, the third record holder of the Guiness Book of World Records, Rajan Mahadevan, seemed to violate the assumption of no differences in natural memory ability.

Rajan: A Potential Exception to Skilled Memory Theory

The most extensive and rigorous testing of Rajan's memory was conducted at Kansas State University. Thompson et al. (1991; Thompson, Cowan, & Frieman, 1993) summarized their own and earlier research on Rajan by arguing that Rajan's increased memory performance as a function of several years of testing could well be described by retrieval structures and speed-up as proposed by skilled memory theory. However, skilled memory theory could not explain Rajan's exceptional digit span, nor his 10-digit groups used to memorize lists of digits (vastly larger than any of the previously studied "exceptional" memorizers). Finally, Rajan displayed exceptional memory also for letters with a memory span of around 13 letters, which was well outside the normal range of memory span for letters. Rajan's superior memory was, however, limited to memory to two types of materials, namely digits and letters—consistent with skilled-memory theory and previously studied individuals with exceptional memory, In fact, several different investigators gave Rajan tests of spatial memory (Biederman Cooper, Fox, & Mahadevan, 1992), tests of visual recognition and recall (Baddeley, 1999) and tests for word lists, stories and complex figures (Thompson et al., 1993) and found his memory performance to be within the normal range—in some cases even below the average—for college students.

In the 1990s, Rajan's memory performance was tested at Florida State University (Ericsson et al., 2004) and these studies confirmed the earlier reported findings concerning Rajan's exceptional memory for numbers (Baddeley, 1999; Biederman et al., 1992; Thompson et al., 1991, 1993), and, in particular, his use of long "chunks" (10–15 digits long), his use of retrieval structures, and his infrequent reports of using mnemonic associations with the digits.

Our analysis on retrieval times and errors from these experiments rejected the claim that Rajan relied on superior basic memory capacity and supported a more complex internal structure for these long "chunks" (Ericsson et al., 2004). The "chunks" of digits were not uniform "chunks" but consistent with list-like structures incorporating associations between the digits within the same digit group. These associations can be viewed as a generalization of the structure of the encodings of 3-, 4- and 5-digit groups observed for trained memory-span experts (Chase & Ericsson, 1981, 1982), as later proposed in Ericsson and Kintsch's theoretical framework of long-term working memory (LTWM) (Ericsson & Kintsch, 1995; Ericsson, Patel & Kintsch, 2000). The list structure account of Rajan's encodings of digit groups can explain why the end-points of the list (especially the beginning of the lists) are accessed much more rapidly than digits in the interior of each list and that errors were more prevalent for the last half of longer chunks.

Based on our interviews with Rajan, we proposed that he acquired encoding methods for memorizing digits during the intensive period of roughly 1,000 hours, when he memorized the over 30,000 digits of pi. We proposed that Rajan's unique methods were due to the special situation and demands of memorizing the decimals of pi. The list of decimals of pi that Rajan memorized was organized in tables with ten 10-digit groups for each row (100 digits) with 50 lines on each sheet corresponding to 5,000 decimals. Rajan had engaged in memorization and mental calculation during his childhood and adolescence in India and also started memorizing the decimals of pi before coming to USA. We proposed that when he was given standardized memory tests for digits in 1980 upon his arrival in USA, he simply applied the same encoding methods that he had already acquired to memorize digits. His encoding method was based on associated digits or groups of digits within a 10-digit group with unique associations, and consequently depended on the availability of rich and varied associations between different digits.

To test this hypothesis, we presented two types of lists of digits, namely, highly redundant lists of digits, such as 83383883888338833, where there would be few unique associations between adjacent digits and the traditional type of random lists of digits, such as 61764574926576890. As we predicted, Rajan's memory performance for the redundant lists of digits was dramatically reduced and approached the performance of trained college students in studies by other experimenters. This experimentally induced reduction of Rajan's memory for digits is consistent with our hypothesis that Rajan's performance reflected the acquired skill of memorizing lists by segmenting them into 10-digit groups.

In the final experiments we tested Rajan's span for consonants and easily named symbols (!, @, #, ^, *, (, +,], \ and ?). For the list of consonants we found that Rajan segmented the list of letters into 3-letter groups, where he gave very frequent mnemonic encodings. For example, Rajan

> encoded the sequence "MSXTBTSVPCV" as "MSX", a popular license plate prefix in India (Madras State X); TBT, a sequence that was the same forwards and backwards; and finally, "SVPCV", Hunt and Love's (1972) Subject VP's Curriculum Vitae, remembering that the S came before VP instead of after.
>
> (Ericsson et al., 2004, p. 221)

Based on our analysis, we concluded that Rajan's superior memory for letter did not reflect a superior basic memory capacity for holding symbols in STM.

Our measurement of Rajan's span for easily named symbols gave even more conclusive evidence against any superior generalized capacity. In the first test session, Rajan's span for symbols was not statistically significant from the performance of a sample of college students from a pool of participants from the introduction to psychology course.

Brain Imaging and Other Recent Developments

In the first study of brain imaging of superior memory performers, Maguire, Valentine, Wilding, and Kapur (2003) conducted an experimental test of the nature and structure of superior memory in ten of the world's foremost memory performers. Most of their exceptional performers had excelled at the World Memory Championships, where the goal is to attain the best overall performance in many types of memory tests with different stimulus materials. For the purposes of comparison, Maguire et al. (2003) also identified ten control subjects whose scores on tests of spatial ability and intelligence matched those of the memory experts.

When the structural MRI images for the brains of memory experts and control subjects were compared, Maguire et al. (2003) were unable to find any significant anatomical differences. Although it is, of course, impossible to prove the complete absence of systematic differences in the size and structure of the brains of the exceptional memory performers, it is unlikely that future studies would be able to recruit a sufficiently large number of world-class memorists to conduct tests with the necessary statistical power.

Maguire et al. (2003) also recorded the brain activity (fMRI) of both groups of participants while they memorized three types of presented stimuli, namely, 3-digit numbers, faces, and snow crystals. Following the study phase, the recognition memory for the three types of stimuli were tested with all participants.

Of particular interest is that the memory experts' recognition memory for snow-flakes did not differ significantly from that of the control group. The experts showed a large advantage over controls for memory of digits, and a significant intermediate advantage for faces. After the recognition test, the participants gave detailed verbal descriptions of their encoding strategies during the memorization in the scanner. All of the memory experts reported using previously acquired memory techniques for generating associations, such as mnemonics, and all but one of the memory performers reported using "the method of loci." In sharp contrast, none of the control group reported using any of the standard mnemonic techniques. Most interestingly, the differences in brain activation between the two groups could be fully explained by the differences in their use of memory strategies (Ericsson, 2003). In short, Maguire et al. (2003) did not find any difference between the expert performers and the control group in brain anatomy or in brain activation that could not be better explained in terms of acquired memory skills.

In sum, our study of Rajan (Ericsson et al., 2004) showed that it is possible to use the methodology developed by Bill and I to analyze individuals with already acquired memory skills. By carefully reproducing their superior performance and analyzing detailed data on their performance, such as study times and collected verbal reports, it is possible to design experiments to test hypotheses about the structure of the acquired skill. These demonstrations are particularly informative when experimental changes in materials or presentation procedures lead to dramatic reductions in their performance—sometimes to the level of unexceptional control groups. If there were to emerge individuals with claims for exceptional memory, then we would argue that their performance should be studied with this type of approach before any scientific claims about truly endowed exceptional memory are published.

EXCEPTIONAL EVERYDAY SKILLS AND EXPERTISE

Bill's and my proposal for skilled memory is fundamentally different from the Simon and Chase (1973) model of expertise. The Simon–Chase (1973) theory argues that expertise is mediated by previously acquired complex patterns and chunks in LTM to retrieve plausible actions and the same pre-existing chunks to encode new chess positions in the task of recalling briefly presented chess positions. In contrast, the skilled memory model proposes that skilled individuals encode newly integrated representations in LTM that includes cues that allow the expert to retrieve that information effortlessly when it is relevant to the ongoing processing. According the Simon–Chase theory, the time to attain master level skill in chess is constrained by the necessary time required to acquire the prerequisite large body of complex chunks, much in the same way that acquiring a language is limited by one's ability to acquire a vocabulary of 10,000–50,000 words. In contrast, skilled memory theory and Ericsson and Kintsch's (1995) theoretical framework of long-term working memory

(LTWM) detail the encoding processes in LTM that permit an individual to store information with immediate accessibility based on encoding and activation of semantic or structural retrieval cues. The previously reviewed evidence on exceptional memory shows the rich variety of encoding processes and retrieval cues that different memory experts acquire. Ericsson and Chase (1982) had already shown how skilled memory could be extended to explain the expanded working memory of a mental calculator (AB, described by Chase and Ericsson, 1982) and a waiter (JC, described later by Ericsson and Polson, 1988a, 1988b). Ericsson and Kintsch (1995) later expanded and elaborated the argument and described how LTWM was an integrated part of the experts' superior performance, where encoding processes were developed to anticipate future retrieval demands by the acquisition and refinement of mental representations. The most distinctive difference between Simon and Chase's (1973) and skilled memory theory and, especially LTWM, concerns the processes of acquisition. Simon and Chase (1973) referred to the time of "staring at chess positions" and the necessary time required to form or "fixate" a new chunk in LTM (Simon, 1974). The acquisition of skilled memory involved the active construction of new mnemonic categories, new types of encodings and refined retrieval structures using trial-and-error learning and problem solving (Chase & Ericsson, 1981, 1982). In a similar manner, the acquisition of LTWM requires deliberate practice (Ericsson, Krampe, & Tesch-Römer, 1993), where the individuals work on improving particular aspects of their performance typically using training activities recommended by their teachers. The training activities are to provide immediate feedback, opportunities for evaluation and problem solving, and subsequent opportunities for repetition and refinement are available. Within the perspective of LTWM, future expert performers are not explicitly training their memory, but rather the ability to perform well on the target activity, such as selecting the best chess moves or treating sick patients to make them healthier. The superior performance on a memory task, such as recalling briefly presented chess positions, is an incidental consequence of the training and development of LTWM for planning and evaluating long sequences of potential chess moves. The transition to this new view was a long and gradual one, but it is interesting to see how many of these ideas were related to the original collaborative work between Bill and me.

Simon and Chase's (1973) theory of chess expertise argued for the mediation of acquired chunks for superior memory for chess positions and can be distinguished from accounts based on acquired memory skills by the following questions: Would it be possible for someone with essentially no knowledge of chess to attain the memory performance of chess master and how long would it take to do so?

Ericsson and Harris (1990; Ericsson & Oliver, 1989) studied a female college student (TB) with essentially no chess experience while she performed Chase and Simon's (1973a) task with 5 s presentations of meaningful chess positions for about 50, hour-long practice sessions. During this period of training TB went from recalling around 4 chess pieces to recalling 16–20 pieces—a level matching the mean of a group of chess masters. There was no significant improvement in her memory performance on randomized chess positions, thus replicating the general patterns seen in skilled chess players. Based on her retrospective reports, we found that TB was able to attain her performance by focusing on perceptually salient patterns of chess pieces, such as pawn chains, and fianchettoed defensive positions. Whereas TB virtually avoided encoding the chess pieces in the center of the chess board, our retrospective reports from a chess master showed that he focused on the center of the board, which contained the most important information for selection of the best move for the position. We concluded that TB had attained a comparable level of recall to a chess master in 50 hours, but her memory encodings were irrelevant to successful move selection. Our study showed that superior memory for meaningful chess positions can be completely dissociated from chess skill. This study also suggested that the encodings of chess positions that extract the essential structure of the chess position, as demonstrated by the chess master, must require a very different training activity for its development. The rapid trainability of memory performance by individuals not playing chess has been demonstrated in a group experiment by Gobet and Jackson (2002).

A couple of reviews (Ericsson & Kintsch, 1995; Ericsson & Lehmann, 1996) have shown that experts with extensive experience do not *always* show superior memory compared to novices when they are presented with representative stimuli from their domains of expertise, such as programmers' memory for computer programs, actors' memory for regular texts, and auditory melodies for musicians. It is also *not* the case that experts' memories for randomized and scrambled versions of representative stimuli are reduced to the level of the novices in domains such as random chess configurations, random musical notation, randomly rearranged computer programs, and nonsense sequences of ballet movements. Ericsson and Kintsch (1995; Ericsson et al., 2000) proposed that the superior memory performance of many experts should not be interpreted as a reflection of a larger number of more complex chunks, but rather as potential increases in domain-specific, working memory required for an expert's representative performance, such as selecting moves for chess players, diagnosing patients with diseases, and performing music from memory. From this perspective, the superiority of some expert performers on Chase and Simon-type memory tasks reflected to what degree their memory skills, which were acquired to support representative performance, can be used for those memory tasks. For example, the superior memory for briefly presented chess positions was attributed to chess players' ability to encode the relations between chess pieces in LTM to permit planning out consequences of alternative moves. This ability is perhaps best illustrated by chess masters' ability to play entire chess games without seeing a chess board (blindfold chess). Ericsson and Kintsch (1995) proposed that skilled performers developed encoding systems for storage of information in working memory based on storage in LTM, which they referred to as long-term working memory (LTWM). In contrast, actors have a superior ability to interpret the character of the individual, whose lines they are rendering rather than being able to memorize the lines rapidly. Similarly, a medical specialist does not recall more details of patients' data than medical students, but they are more able to extract the relevant information to make an accurate diagnosis. Hence, there are many reasons for adopting a different approach that focuses on an analysis of superior performance on representative tasks and how memory is an integrated part of the overall acquired skill mediating that performance.

THE EXPERT-PERFORMANCE APPROACH

In many domains it is difficult to clearly define what experts are able to accomplish that less accomplished individuals cannot do. The original focus on expert–novice differences (Chi, Glaser & Rees, 1982) led investigators to search for individuals who were regarded by others to be *experts*. Similarly, it was often assumed that these highly experienced and knowledgeable individuals (experts) would display superior performance on relevant tasks in their respective domains. However, researchers rapidly found that "experts" with extended experience and specialized knowledge frequently did not show a performance advantage. For example, highly experienced psychotherapists are not more successful in treatment of patients than novice therapists (Dawes, 1994). More generally, reviews of decision-making (Camerer & Johnson, 1991) and forecasting (Tetlock, 2005) show that experts' decisions and forecasts, such as financial advice on investing in stocks, do not show a reliable superiority over novices and thus do not necessarily improve with additional experience. Similar absence of improvements of experienced individuals considered experts have been documented in several other areas of expertise (Choudhry, Fletcher, & Soumerai, 2005; Ericsson, 2004; Ericsson & Lehmann, 1996). Rather, in order to establish superior performance rather than socially perceived expertise, researchers should seek *objective* measures of current performance, even when such measures may not capture all aspects of performance.

In a ground-breaking and innovative study of chess expertise, de Groot ([1946] 1978) addressed this problem by identifying challenging situations in representative games (i.e. chess positions) that required some type of action (i.e. making the next chess move). De Groot then was able to present the same game situations to all participants and could observe their thinking aloud activity while the chess players tried to find the best moves. If we can find chess players who are able to select consistently the best moves for arbitrary chess positions, then these players would be strong chess players almost by definition. Subsequent research has shown that this methodology of presenting representative situations and requiring generation of appropriate actions provides the best available measure of chess expertise as reflected in tournament skill ratings (Ericsson et al., 2000; van der Maas & Wagenmakers, 2005). A similar methodology has been applied to measure superior performance in representative situations in medical diagnosis, snooker, and a wide range of other domains (Ericsson, 2004, 2006b; Ericsson & Lehmann, 1996), including even *team* sports, such as soccer (see Williams & Ward, 2003).

Once researchers are able to identify the situations and tasks where experts exhibit their superior performance, then it is possible to design standardized tasks in the laboratory to reliably reproduce these differences. The second step of the expert-performance approach (Ericsson, 2006b) focuses directly on the analysis of the mechanisms that mediate the experts' captured superior performance. Once the processes are identified, then investigators design experimental tests that evaluate the causal role of the mechanisms that are proposed to account for the observed differences in performance.

The methodology for analyzing the mediating processes of experts is essentially similar to the methods used by Bill and me in our research on exceptional memory. The participants are performing the memory task and the times are recorded for self-paced tasks. Participants are asked to think aloud (Ericsson & Polson, 1988a) or to give retrospective reports immediately following the recall—that is, prior to getting feedback on the accuracy of their action. Based on the verbal reports, it is possible to design experiments to test hypotheses about the mediating mechanisms. In a similar manner, elite long-distance runners have been shown to run in laboratories on treadmills with superior running economy—the metabolic efficiency of maintaining their race pace—in comparison to sub-elite runners (Conley & Krahenbuhl, 1980). Interviews and field experiments show that elite long-distance runners verbally report monitoring their internal states more closely and focus more on planning their race performance during competition than less accomplished runners (Baker, Côté, & Deakin, 2005; Masters & Ogles, 1998).

In a review of similar studies of experts solving representative tasks in a wide range of domains of expertise, such as medicine, computer programming, and games, Ericsson and Lehmann (1996) found a similar pattern. When superior performers in sport are presented with representative tasks, verbal reports reveal how more advanced preparation, planning, reasoning, and evaluation mediate their superior performance in different domains of sport, such as snooker (Abernethy, Neal, & Koning, 1994), baseball (Nevett & French, 1997) and tennis (McPherson & Kernodle, 2003).

In sum, expert performance has so far been found to be primarily mediated by acquired mental representations that allow the experts to anticipate courses of action, to control those aspects that are relevant to generating their superior performance, and to evaluate alternative courses of action during performance or after the completion of the competition (Ericsson, 2006a, 2006b).

Toward Detailed Accounts of the Development of Expert Performance

The main premise of the expert-performance approach is that the development of an individual's performance occurs gradually—starting with the initial level of acceptable performance to increasingly higher levels all the way to expert levels. This assumption implies that it should be possible, at least in principle, to describe the development of *each individual's performance* as an ordered sequence of stable states with acquired mental representations and associated superior performance, as shown in Figure 9.5. Most of these states represent developed and refined mechanisms corresponding to improvements in performance over the immediately prior states. The differences correspond to specific cognitive and physiological changes in the mediating mechanisms that ultimately combine to explain the superior performance. This theoretical framework proposes that the observable reliable increases in performance have definite causes, such as developmental growth and adaptive responses to the changed structure and increased intensity or duration of training and practice activities. As illustrated by the transitions in Figure 9.5, each observable change in the performance and the associated structure of the mechanisms needs to be explained and described for each domain of expert performance. Ultimately, a complete theory should account for the development and refinement of all associated biological and cognitive changes that contribute to the acquisition of a stable reproducible expert performance.

The detailed processes and practice activities may differ from domain to domain, but the general principle remains that aspiring expert performers need to engage in training activities that are designed to improve particular aspects of performance and, once these have been mastered, direct their attention to other improvable aspects. For example, in music, a teacher listens to an intermediate music student play a piece of music and then helps the student identify mastery goals and sub-goals for improving specific aspects, along with practice

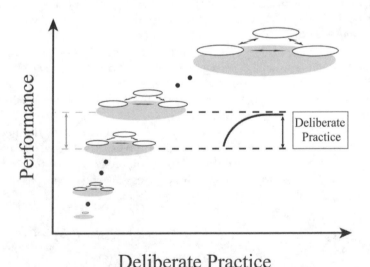

Figure 9.5   A schematic illustration of the acquisition of expert performance as a series of states with mechanisms of increasing complexity for monitoring and guiding future improvements of specific aspects of performance.

Source: Adapted from Ericsson (2009, p. 14).

techniques to achieve these goals (see Figure 9.5). Then the student images the goal states, tries to find the means to achieve this goal, monitors the sound of the attempt, and makes corrections. This type of practice with full concentration, immediate feedback and opportunities to make repetitions with gradual improvements towards the current goals, Ericsson et al. (1993) referred to as deliberate practice (see Figure 9.5). With increased levels of performance, the goals for performance improvements will change, but there are also coincidental improvements in the aspiring expert musician's representations that allow her to image the desired music experience, to translate the desired image into motor actions, and to monitor the produced sound during performance to identify areas requiring further improvement. Several recent reviews (Ericsson, 2006a, 2006b, 2007a, 2007b; Ericsson, Roring, & Nandagopal, 2007a, 2007b) have described the particular forms of deliberate practice and the associated specific representations that are increasingly refined to image, execute, and monitor performance in a wide range of domains, such as chess, medicine, music, dance, sports, games, and professions.

When I recently looked back on my work with Bill, it is interesting to see some of the precursors of deliberate practice in our training procedure with digit span. Our trainees were given tasks that were adapted to present a constant state of challenge. If they succeeded in a trial, they were given a list of digits, that were one digit longer, and if they failed, they were given an easier task with a shorter list of digits. The probability of success was kept at an average of 50% and they were given immediate feedback (just after giving the retrospective report), with a chance to repeatedly perform similar tasks after problem solving and refinement. We were able to collect some of the most extensive and validated data on the mental representations of individual participants that mediated their encoding and retrieval and their superior performance. Without that training environment, it is unlikely that we would have seen the dramatic and continued improvements that we observed.

CONCLUSION

I hope that Bill would be pleased with the direction and achievements of the current research on expert performance that is the result of the research we started together in 1978. Very early on in the research on exceptional memory, Bill was aware of differences in theoretical assumptions and mechanisms between the Simon and Chase (1973) theory of expertise and our skilled memory theory. On several occasions Bill expressed the view that theories, models, and hypotheses were primarily useful tools to discover new empirical regularities and only clear rejections of hypotheses would lead to genuine progress in our understanding. When we discovered results that did not fit the chunk-based theory of expertise, he was willing to generate and think about a theoretical framework that would account for our new findings. The next step was to attempt to extend and stretch these ideas so they could account for as many findings about exceptional memory as possible, including the original findings about the memory of chess experts.

Just before Bill's death, we had just started to make the transition from studying exceptional memory performance for a particular type of material, such as digits, to exceptional memory in different domains of activity, such as mental calculation and recalling dinner orders. A few years later it was clear that a different concept was required to study expert performance. Therefore, the emphasis on representative tasks and the essence of expertise in a domain (Ericsson & Smith, 1991) was introduced as a focus for the expert-performance approach. In traditional domains of expertise the development of superior memory is an incidental consequence of efforts to improve overall performance on representative tasks by improving the mental representations supporting planning, evaluation, reasoning, or anticipation. Consequently, domains that do not require such mechanisms do not have experts, who display exceptional memory for representative stimuli.

In this chapter I have described how the expert-performance approach differs from approaches based on the general theories of expertise. These alternative approaches rely upon simple and generalizable learning mechanisms and suggest that further experience virtually automatically leads to improvements as long as the aspiring individuals have the necessary prerequisites. The traditional theory for skill acquisition (Fitts & Posner, 1967) aptly describes how individuals tend to automate their behavior to minimize the effort required for execution of the desired performance in most types of habitual everyday activities, such as driving a car, typing, or strenuous physical work. In direct contrast, the expert-performance approach claims that acquisition of expert performance is due to an avoidance of automation and an active search for increasingly demanding tasks and standards (as is illustrated by the upper arm of Figure 9.1). The focus of this framework is on reproducible improvements in performance, where observable changes in performance reflect the longitudinal development of individual experts. The key assumption is that reliable *improvements* in performance, especially beyond the initial proficiency, require specific causes and changes in one's behavior, that is, the structure and amount of one's deliberate practice. In the process of developing a complete theory of expert and elite performance, it should be possible to better understand any limits on human achievement and to provide everyone with knowledge about their true potential and what it takes to reach it.

REFERENCES

Abernethy, B., Neal, R. J., & Koning, P. (1994). Visual-perceptual and cognitive differences between expert, intermediate, and novice snooker players. *Applied Cognitive Psychology, 18*, 185–211.

Allard, F., Graham, S., & Paarsalu, M. E. (1980). Perception in sport: Basketball. *Journal of Sport Psychology, 2*, 14–21.

Baddeley, A. D. (1999). *Essentials of human memory.* Hove, UK: Psychology Press.

Baker, J., Côté, J., & Deakin, J. (2005).Cognitive characteristics of expert, middle of the pack, and back of the pack ultra-endurance triathletes. *Psychology of Sport and Exercise, 6*, 551–558.

Biederman, I., Cooper, E. E., Fox, P. W., & Mahadevan, R. S. (1992). Unexceptional spatial memory in an exceptional memorist. *Journal of Experimental Psychology: Learning, Memory, and Cognition, 18*, 654–657.

Binet, A. (1894). *Psychologie des grands calculateurs et joueurs d'échecs* [The psychology of great calculators and chess players]. Paris: Libraire Hachette.

Book, W. F. (1925). *The psychology of skill.* New York: Gregg.

Bryan, W. L., & Harter, N. (1897). Studies in the physiology and psychology of the telegraphic language. *Psychological Review, 4*, 27–53.

Bryan, W. L., & Harter, N. (1899). Studies on the telegraphic language: The acquisition of a hierarchy of habits. *Psychological Review, 6*, 345–375.

Camerer, C. F., & Johnson, E. J. (1991). The process-performance paradox in expert judgment: How can the experts know so much and predict so badly? In K. A. Ericsson, & J. Smith (Eds.), *Towards a general theory of expertise: Prospects and limits* (pp. 195–217). Cambridge: Cambridge University Press.

Charness, N. (1976). Memory for chess positions: Resistance to interference. *Journal of Experimental Psychology: Human Learning and Memory, 2*, 641–653.

Charness, N. (1979). Components of skill in bridge. *Canadian Journal of Psychology, 33*, 1–16.

Chase, W. G., & Ericsson, K. A. (1981). Skilled memory. In J. R. Anderson (Ed.), *Cognitive skills and their acquisition* (pp. 141–189). Hillsdale, NJ: Lawrence Erlbaum Associates.

Chase, W. G., & Ericsson, K. A. (1982). Skill and working memory. In G. H. Bower (Ed.), *The psychology of learning and motivation* (Vol. 16, pp. 1–58). New York: Academic Press.

Chase, W. G., & Simon, H. A. (1973a). The mind's eye in chess. In W. G. Chase (Ed.), *Visual information processing* (pp. 215–281). New York: Academic Press.

Chase, W. G., & Simon, H. A. (1973b). Perception in chess. *Cognitive Psychology, 4*, 55–81.

Chi, M. T. H., Glaser, R., & Rees, E. (1982). Expertise in problem solving. In R. S. Sternberg (Ed.), *Advances in the psychology of human intelligence* (Vol. 1, pp. 1–75). Hillsdale, NJ: Lawrence Erlbaum Associates.

Choudhry, N. K., Fletcher, R. H., & Soumerai, S. B. (2005). Systematic review: The relationship between clinical experience and quality of health care. *Annals of Internal Medicine, 142*, 260–273.

Conley, D. L., & Krahenbuhl, G. S. (1980). Running economy and distance running performance of highly trained athletes. *Medicine and Science in Sports and Exercise, 12*, 357–360.

Dawes, R. M. (1994). *House of cards: Psychology and psychotherapy built on myth.* New York: Free Press.

de Groot, A. ([1946] 1978). *Thought and choice in chess.* The Hague: Mouton.

Ekman, G., & Sjöberg, L. (1965). Scaling. *Annual Review of Psychology, 16*, 451–474.

Engle, R. W., & Bukstel, L. H. (1978). Memory processes among bridge players of differing expertise. *American Journal of Psychology, 91*, 673–689.

Ericsson, K. A. (1985). Memory skill. *Canadian Journal of Psychology, 39*, 188–231.

Ericsson, K. A. (1998). The scientific study of expert levels of performance: General implications for optimal learning and creativity. *High Ability Studies, 9*(1), 75–100.

Ericsson, K. A. (2003). Exceptional memorizers: Made, not born. *Trends in Cognitive Sciences, 7*, 233–235.

Ericsson, K. A. (2004). Deliberate practice and the acquisition and maintenance of expert performance in medicine and related domains. *Academic Medicine, 79*, S70–S81.

Ericsson, K. A. (2006a). Protocol analysis and expert thought: Concurrent verbalizations of thinking during experts' performance on representative task. In K. A. Ericsson, N. Charness, P. Feltovich, & R. R. Hoffman (Eds.), *Cambridge handbook of expertise and expert performance* (pp. 223–242). Cambridge: Cambridge University Press.

Ericsson, K. A. (2006b). The influence of experience and deliberate practice on the development of superior expert performance. In K. A. Ericsson, N. Charness, P. Feltovich, & R. R. Hoffman (Eds.), *Cambridge handbook of expertise and expert performance* (pp. 685–706). Cambridge: Cambridge University Press.

Ericsson, K. A. (2007a). Deliberate practice and the modifiability of body and mind: Toward a science of the structure and acquisition of expert and elite performance. *International Journal of Sport Psychology, 38*, 4–34.

Ericsson, K. A. (2007b). Deliberate practice and the modifiability of body and mind: A reply to the commentaries. *International Journal of Sport Psychology, 38*, 109–123.

Ericsson, K. A. (2009). The scientific study of expert levels of performance can guide training for producing superior achievement in creative domains. In *Proceedings from international conference on the cultivation and education of creativity and innovation*. Beijing, China: Chinese Academy of Sciences.

Ericsson, K. A., & Chase, W. G. (1982). Exceptional memory. *American Scientist, 70*, 607–615.

Ericsson, K. A., Chase, W. G., & Faloon, S. (1980). Acquisition of a memory skill. *Science, 208*, 1181–1182.

Ericsson, K. A., Delaney, P. F., Weaver, G., & Mahadevan, R. (2004). Uncovering the structure of a memorist's superior "basic" memory capacity. *Cognitive Psychology, 49*, 191–237.

Ericsson, K. A., & Harris, M. S. (1990). Expert chess memory without chess knowledge: A training study. Poster presented at the 31st Annual Meeting of the Psychonomic Society, New Orleans, November 17.

Ericsson, K. A., & Kintsch, W. (1995). Long-term working memory. *Psychological Review, 102*, 211–245.

Ericsson, K. A., Krampe, R.T., & Tesch-Römer, C. (1993). The role of deliberate practice in the acquisition of expert performance. *Psychological Review, 100*, 363–406.

Ericsson, K. A., & Lehmann, A. C. (1996). Expert and exceptional performance: Evidence on maximal adaptations on task constraints. *Annual Review of Psychology, 47*, 273–305.

Ericsson, K. A., & Oliver, W. (1989). A methodology for assessing the detailed structure of memory skills. In A. Colley, & J. Beech (Eds.), *The acquisition and performance of cognitive skills* (pp. 193–215). London: Wiley.

Ericsson, K. A., Patel, V. L., & Kintsch, W. (2000). How experts' adaptations to representative task demands account for the expertise effect in memory recall: Comment on Vicente and Wang (1998). *Psychological Review, 107*, 578–592.

Ericsson, K. A., & Polson, P. G. (1988a). Memory for restaurant orders. In M. Chi, R. Glaser, & M. Farr (Eds.), *The nature of expertise* (pp. 23–70). Hillsdale, NJ: Lawrence Erlbaum Associates.

Ericsson, K. A., & Polson, P. G. (1988b). An experimental analysis of the mechanisms of a memory skill. *Journal of Experimental Psychology: Learning, Memory and Cognition, 14*, 305–316.

Ericsson, K. A., Roring, R. W., & Nandagopal, K. (2007a). Giftedness and evidence for reproducibly superior performance: An account based on the expert-performance framework. *High Ability Studies, 18*, 3–56.

Ericsson, K. A., Roring, R. W., & Nandagopal, K. (2007b). Misunderstandings, agreements, and disagreements: Toward a cumulative science of reproducibly superior aspects of giftedness. *High Ability Studies, 18,* 97–115.

Ericsson, K. A., & Simon, H. A. (1980). Verbal reports as data. *Psychological Review, 87,* 215–251.

Ericsson, K. A., & Simon, H. A. (1993). *Protocol analysis: Verbal reports as data* (rev. ed.). Cambridge, MA: Bradford Books/MIT Press.

Ericsson, K. A., & Smith, J. (1991). Prospects and limits in the empirical study of expertise: An introduction. In K. A. Ericsson, & J. Smith (Eds.), *Toward a general theory of expertise: Prospects and limits* (pp. 1–38). Cambridge: Cambridge University Press.

Fitts, P., & Posner, M. I. (1967). *Human performance.* Belmont, CA: Brooks/Cole.

Frey, P. W., & Adesman, P. (1976). Recall memory for visually presented chess positions. *Memory and Cognition, 4,* 541–547.

Gobet, F. (2000a). Some shortcomings of long-term working memory. *British Journal of Psychology, 91,* 551–570.

Gobet, F. (2000b). Retrieval structures and schemata: A brief reply to Ericsson and Kintsch. *British Journal of Psychology, 91,* 591–594.

Gobet, F., & Charness, N. (2006). Expertise in chess. In K. A Ericsson, N. Charness, P. J. Feltovich, & R. R. Hoffman (Eds.), *The Cambridge handbook of expertise and expert performance* (pp. 523–538). Cambridge: Cambridge University Press.

Gobet, F., & Jackson, S. (2002). In search of templates. *Cognitive Systems Research, 3,* 35–44.

Gobet, F., & Simon, H. A. (1996). Templates in chess memory: A mechanism for recalling several boards. *Cognitive Psychology, 31,* 1–40.

Higbee, K. L. (1997). Novices, apprentices, and mnemonists: Acquiring expertise with the phonetic mnemonic. *Applied Cognitive Psychology, 11,* 147–161.

Hu, Y., Ericsson, K. A., Yang, D., & Lu, C. (2009). Superior self-paced memorization of digits in spite of a normal digit span: The structure of a memorist's skill. *Journal of Experimental Psychology: Learning, Memory, & Cognition, 35,* 1426–1442.

Hunt, E., & Love, T. (1972). How good can memory be? In A. W. Melton, & E. Martin (Eds.), *Coding processes in human memory* (pp. 237–260). New York: Holt.

Hunter, I. M. L. (1962). An exceptional talent for calculative thinking. *British Journal of Psychology, 53,* 243–258.

Luria, A. R. (1968). *The mind of a mnemonist.* New York: Avon.

Maguire, E. A., Valentine, E. R., Wilding, J. M., & Kapur, N. (2003). Routes to remembering: the brains behind superior memory. *Nature Neuroscience, 6,* 90–95.

Martin, P. R., & Fernberger, S. W. (1929). Improvement in memory span. *American Journal of Psychology, 41,* 91–94.

Masters, K. S., & Ogles, B. M. (1998). Associative and dissociative cognitive strategies in exercise and running: 20 years later, what do we know? *The Sport Psychologist, 12,* 253–270.

McPherson, S., & Kernodle, M. W. (2003). Tactics, the neglected attribute of expertise: Problem representations and performance skills in tennis. In J. Starkes, & K. A. Ericsson (Eds.), *Expert performance in sport: Recent advances in research on sport expertise* (pp. 137–164). Champaign, IL: Human Kinetics.

Miller, G. A. (1956). The magical number seven, plus or minus two: Some limits of our capacity for processing information. *Psychological Review, 63,* 81–97.

Müller, G. E. (1911). Zur Analyse der Gedächtnistätigkeit und des Vorstellungsverlaufes: Teil I [Toward analyses of memory and imagery: Part I]. *Zeitschrift für Psychologie, Ergänzungsband, 5.*

Nevett, M. E., & French, K. E. (1997). The development of sport-specific planning, rehearsal, and updating of plans during defensive youth baseball game performance. *Research Quarterly for Exercise and Sport, 68*, 203–214.

Newell, A., & Simon, H. A. (1972). *Human problem solving*. Englewood Cliffs, NJ: Prentice-Hall.

Reitman, J. (1976). Skilled perception in GO: Deducing memory structures from inter-response times. *Cognitive Psychology, 8*, 336–356.

Richman, H. B., Staszewski, J. J., & Simon, H. A. (1995). Simulation of expert memory using EPAM IV. *Psychological Review, 102*, 305–330.

Simon, H. A. (1974). How big is a chunk? *Science, 183*, 482–488.

Simon, H. A., & Chase, W. G. (1973). Skill in chess. *American Scientist, 61*, 394–403.

Takahashi, M., Shimizu, H., Saito, S., & Tomoyori, H. (2006). One percent ability and ninety-nine percent perspiration: A study of a Japanese memorist. *Journal of Experimental Psychology: Learning, Memory, and Cognition, 32*(5), 1195–1200.

Tetlock, P. E. (2005). *Expert political judgment*. Princeton, NJ: Princeton University Press.

Thompson, C. P., Cowan, T. M., & Frieman, J. (1993). *Memory search by a memorist*. Hillsdale: NJ: Lawrence Erlbaum Associates.

Thompson, C. P., Cowan, T. M., Frieman, J., Mahadevan, R. S., Vogl, R. J., & Frieman, R. J. (1991). Rajan: A study of a memorist. *Journal of Memory and Language, 30*, 702–724.

van der Maas, H. L. J., & Wagenmakers, E. J. (2005). A psychometric analysis of chess expertise. *American Journal of Psychology, 118*, 29–60.

Wenger, M. J., & Payne, D. G. (1995). On the acquisition of mnemonic skill: Application of skilled memory theory. *Journal of Experimental Psychology: Applied, 1*, 194–215.

Wilding, J. M., & Valentine, E. R. (1997). *Superior memory*. Hove, UK: Psychology Press.

Wilding, J. M., & Valentine, E. R. (2006). Exceptional memory. In K. A. Ericsson, N. Charness, P. Feltovich, & R. R. Hoffman (Eds.), *Cambridge handbook of expertise and expert performance* (pp. 539–552). Cambridge: Cambridge University Press.

Williams, A. M., & Ward, P. (2003). Perceptual expertise: Development in sport. In J. Starkes, & K. A. Ericsson (Eds.), *Expert performance in sport: Recent advances in research on sport expertise* (pp. 219–247). Champaign, IL: Human Kinetics.

10

Commentary on Expertises
Remarks during a Symposium Honoring Bill Chase

KENNETH KOTOVSKY
Carnegie Mellon University, USA

At the 13th Carnegie Symposium in 1977, Gordon Bower was in a role he found unpalatable; he was a discussant for a portion of the symposium on the development of children's thinking, and he claimed it was the first time he had accepted such a role. His lament took the form of a contrast between being an acerbic critic who picks apart the contributions, pointing out methodological weaknesses and reasoning flaws, a role he labeled as doing a "hatchet job" that he assumed was expected in the situation, and that of being a "Cheerleader" or "Celebrator" or "Herald" who celebrates the path-breaking contributions and incisive thought of the contributors, a role he much preferred but for some reason didn't think was demanded by the task at hand. I sympathize with his dilemma in that the role of discussant does seem to be fraught with potentially challenging or uncomfortable situational demands and I too was something of a neophyte in this role and also not desirous of, in Gordon's words, "looking for possible flaws or things to take issue with or disagree about." This implicit expectation about the role of discussants is exacerbated because we work in a science that has elaborated methodological criticism to perfection, with the result that we often seem more analogous to a wrecking company than a construction company when it comes to building a cumulative science with a core of sometimes evolving but nonetheless broadly accepted theories.

My take on this dilemma of how to approach being a discussant, but not a hatchet man can be discerned in the manner in which I began my discussion of the four chapters that were my purview. I posited, somewhat tongue in cheek, that the goals of a discussant were first: to incisively summarize each of the four chapters, coupled with penetrating insights that reinforce and extend but also perhaps politely question the conclusions of the original authors, and, second, to unify them into a comprehensive overview of expertise and skill development, showing how each of the four chapters covers a portion of the space and articulates with the other three in a symbiotic way that builds to a grand theory of expertise. I further put forth that all this is to be done with great humor and wit. After thus ruining a portion of my life with a challenge that was not about to be met by me in this lifetime, I quickly abandoned it and instead, reported on the results of consulting with some very esteemed colleagues about the role of discussant. The reports of that brief empirical endeavor are reported below:

Colleague One: You should try to reinstate memory; bridge the two days across which your four papers were presented.
Colleague Two: Your primary job is to be entertaining.
Colleague Three: You're planning on presenting some of your own data? I hate people presenting their own data as discussants!

(There is some ambiguity in the interpretation of this declaration about whether the hatred is directed at the presenter or the act of presenting, but neither version is very attractive!) It is with these goals and admonitions in mind that I proceed with this discussion.

For memory bridging between the first and second day (not a challenge if you are simply turning the pages of this book), I offer the following which might, if you are particularly perspicacious, remind you of the table of contents:

Day 1

9:00	Welcome and Overview	Jim Staszewski
9:15	Expert Learners	Michelene Chi and Stephanie Touchman
10:00	Cognitive Engineering Based on Expert Skill	Jim Staszewski
11:00	Motivation and Affect in Discovery Learning	Catherine Chase
11:45	Life-Span Development of Expertise	Neil H. Charness
1:45	Discussant's Remarks	Robert S. Siegler
2:15	Chunks and Templates in Semantic Long-term Memory	Fernand Gobet
3:00	Paths to Discovery	Roger Schvaneveldt
4:00	Development of Expertise and the Control of Physical Actions	David Rosenbaum
4:45	Expert Memory Videos	

Day 2

9:00	Contributions of Automaticity and Deliberate Practice to the Acquisition of Expertise	K. Anders Ericsson
9:15	Discussant's Remarks	Kenneth Kotovsky
10:45	Genetic and Neurocognitive Foundations of Expertise	Michael I. Posner
11:30	Acquisition of Visual Skill through Video Games	Daphne Bavelier
1:30	Attentional and Memory Processes in Expert and Novice Motor Skill Performance	Sian L. Beilock
2:15	Using Neural Imaging to Investigate Learning in an Educational Task	John R. Anderson
3:00	Discussant's Remarks	Marcel Just
4:45	Expert Memory Videos	

My coverage of the above ranged from Gobet through Ericsson, two relatively related destinations, with sizable detours through Schvaneveldt's general models of relatedness-based discovery and Rosenbaum's presentation on the control of physical actions along the way; hence the pluralization in the title of this discussion.

"I know nothing about the subject,
but I'm happy to give you my expert opinion."

Figure 10.1

Figure 10.2

Being suitably bridged as per Colleague One, my next charge was to some-how meet the expectations of Colleague Two vis-à-vis being entertaining in the context of discussing the issue of expertise. To that end, I offer the following observations on expertise:

With regard to Colleague Three, things are a bit more difficult. I had some nice slides of work on "early" expertise acquired during game playing that showed people playing against AI opponents, going from hardly ever winning to winning a majority of games within about three hours of practice. The brevity of time is why I termed it "early expertise" to contrast it with more usual studies such as those described in the chapters here that occur over periods as long as ten years or more. I thought it made a nice contrast, but then images of Colleague Three arose and I inhibited myself; so it won't be mentioned even though the slides were pretty neat. It was also potentially interesting because we collected concurrent verbal protocols and they showed that our participants offered very little evidence of consciously acquiring strategies or deeper under-standing of the games (Foxes and Hounds and Abbaloney, in this instance) even as their behavior indicated very sizable and often sudden increases in profi-ciency and acquisition of specific strategies for the games. It leads to the conclu-sion that even in games that are quite strategic, their strategies can be acquired and operate non-consciously, and also suggested that the time frame for exper-tise acquisition needed to be viewed expansively to accommodate the early rapid acquisition in these types of situations, the central issue being whether expertise should be viewed exclusively as world-class performance or whether it can also include the processes involved in a large positive first derivative of skill acquisition.

But again, Colleague Three had voiced a fairly unrestrained admonition about his feelings about people who present their own data (however interesting, methodologically sound, executed with flair, and relevant), so I didn't consider it and there will be absolutely no hint or mention of it here!

FERNAND GOBET: CHUNKS AND TEMPLATES IN SEMANTIC LTM

So, where to really begin? Fernand Gobet presents some in-depth accounts of the acquisition of expertise within a well-studied domain, chess. His focus is on explaining chess expertise in terms of the formation and storage of large numbers of "chunks" and "templates" in long-term memory. A central theme of his chapter is that he presents a broad-based methodological approach that relies on both laboratory experimentation and computational modeling coupled with a focus on small n (often n = 1) studies that focus on intensive individual data modeling of individuals (IDM), an approach that contrasts somewhat with Newell-like universal theory of cognition/architectural approaches (including Soar's universal chunking–power law of practice) in its focus on the individual rather than group average or typical behavior.

The challenges of such an approach, as he points out, include dealing with between subject variability, between task variability, and between strategy variability within a given task. His approach to dealing with those challenges is to adopt an almost clinical rather than statistical approach, describing an individual and then eventually averaging over individuals rather than focusing on a particular behavior and averaging over that behavior across individuals. Some of the characteristics of his approach are that it focuses on parameters within an individual, examining how those parameters interact in a variety of tasks and describing how they develop over time (much in the spirit of Ebbinghaus ([1885] 1964), Freud (1920), Piaget (1926), Bryan and Harter (1897), and of course Bill Chase and Anders Ericsson as well.). It then constructs a detailed computational model and finally generalizes average parameters over individuals.

Within this intelligent design movement (IDM) approach, he attempts to answer central questions about expertise such as:

- To what extent is expert performance in chess due to the acquisition of specialized knowledge or memory storage?
- Do experts have better analytical abilities?
- Do experts perform more focused/deeper search?
- Do experts have different strategies from novices and from each other?
- To what extent does expertise transfer across domains or areas of specialization?

Gobet concludes from the data generated by his IDM approach that experts differ in two main ways; in memory (chunking), and in the construction and use of knowledge templates, an expansion of chunks into learned schemas. There are several major characteristic features of his approach, including showing that subjects have knowledge structures that allow them to recognize problem familiarity and quickly retrieve expert actions from LTM to resolve problems. The domain he uses in demonstrating the contributions of laboratory studies as a medium of investigation is chess, a real Carnegie Mellon and Bill Chase tradition! The domain of chess has exerted such a strong influence on the study of expertise that it behooves us to ask what might the study of expertise look like if there wasn't this unlikely marriage of chess and cognitive psychology, if instead of being so populated by chess players, the study of the cognition of expertise had been carried out by jugglers, or crossword puzzle experts, or baseball players, or gourmet chefs or pickpockets? Perhaps fortunately, we'll never know!

The strengths of his approach are that he uses powerful and combined methodologies that allow him to analyze the richness of an individual's strategy and knowledge and then combine that into a picture of overall expert performance in the area of chess. This approach provides a safeguard against washing out interesting individual differences by the more standard technique of looking at average performances. Given that the domain here is chess expertise and not an attempt to characterize broadly average performance or universal human behavior, it is a strong and fitting approach. However, it is a bit difficult to see how the "after" averaging does not introduce some of the same problems as averaging "before." There is a naïve way in which the order shouldn't matter. Characterizing and modeling average performance features across people and characterizing and modeling individuals and then averaging the results should yield the same end result, but offsetting this is the fact that the latter approach can allow an intermediate step of looking at outstanding and unique individuals before the averaging is done, thus allowing a rich description of individual differences as well as a description of overall performance features.

From a cognitive science perspective, the focus on chess is interesting and very historically appropriate to this conference honoring Bill Chase, who, along with Herb Simon, did such seminal work on chess expertise. It is an area of investigation with a long and rich history at Carnegie Mellon and elsewhere, and it has delivered a great deal of insight into the cognition of expertise. The focus on chess does raise the question, however, of how typical chess is of a wider range of human expert performance, an issue of generalizability of results. In particular, Gobet's transfer work on trying to determine the generalizability of expertise across domains of specialization relies on comparisons of people whose specialization is the Sicilian defense and the French defense, a fairly narrow range of specialization. It does seem appropriate in the context of Gobet's work to suggest that an approach that first characterizes expertise in a narrow domain (chess) and then another and another, before trying to synthesize conclusions about expertise in general seems to fit or be analogous to his overall approach to the study of chess, of developing a rich model of an individual before going on to generalize across individuals.

ROGER SCHVANEVELDT, TREVOR COHEN AND G. KERR WHITFIELD: PATHS TO DISCOVERY

This chapter takes us from the particular to the general. The authors describe the phenomenon of abductive reasoning, the formation of hypotheses on the basis of some known facts, where abduction is analogous to movement of limbs away from body. (Machines involving abduction are the machines in health clubs that really hurt—because they use small muscles in movements that tend to be rare.) It thus makes for a nice analogy for connoting lateral creative thinking which can also be all too rare and perhaps at times painful too!

The major focus of the chapter is on attempts to develop computational methods for searching vast text corpora to discover new relationships within the literature of the corpus. The Medline corpus is one such example that serves as a test bed for much of the work. It consists of over a billion terms (tokens) and four million types. A number of wordspace approaches are described, including the venerable Latent Semantic Analysis (LSA) and others, and the authors have developed a software tool, labeled "Epiphanet" to enable the discovery of new relationships in those large corpora that can form the basis for fruitful hypotheses about the area under investigation or exploration. The characteristic feature of their work is enabling the discovery of new relationships by searching not only for terms that are near neighbors of the term of interest in a search, but terms that are neighbors of neighbors of terms.

A basic assertion in this chapter is that similarity plus spreading activation yields abductive thinking, leading to possibly non-obvious or rare problem solutions. Two basic types of abductive thinking are posited: (1) search for a hypothesis (for example, the choice of a disease to explain a set of symptoms); and (2) generation of a hypothesis (for example, Newton's gravitational explanation of Kepler's square/cube law). Both of these types occur, with the latter being the more creative in that it generates new hypothesis.

While the novelty of abduction results in the generation of new hypotheses, there are challenges posed by searches in large problem spaces or corpora, even with the use of computational methods. The actual methodology involves word-space search techniques where vast databases can be searched for new relationships between terms, but under such conditions, random generation of candidate hypotheses is not viable because there is too vast a problem space of possibilities. While similarity is a useful heuristic used to generate, it still does not allow for optimization, so satisficing is used instead, whereby there is a search for a good but not necessarily best solution in the large space of possibilities. Another useful heuristic is the use of stable intermediate forms (similar to sub-goals in problem solving) that can reduce the search, and there are many others that are invoked as well. The central and particularly interesting technique for finding more distant and potentially creative solutions is to use "indirect similarity" whereby you move from terms that do not occur together but do co-occur with common other terms. One historic example that is offered in support of this approach is Swanson's discovery of fish oil as a potential treatment for Raynaud's disease through the coordination of two separate literatures via their common neighbor, blood viscosity.

These tools, using the proportion of indirectly related terms in the Medline corpus, allowed for the discovery of disease relationships that only became meaningful in later years, thus predicting in a sense, future discoveries. The relation of these abductive search techniques to expertise is that there is a possibly powerful application to cognition (do two seemingly independent ideas that have shared sets of associated ideas become meaningfully related?). It is suggested that this can be viewed as analogous to Facebook, where friends of my friends later become my friends! Alternatively, it could be viewed as a computational tool that makes us more adept thinkers through its use; another form of expertise—a kind of Excel for thought? At any rate, the contribution of this work to expertise, while somewhat conjectural and general, has the potential of providing an approach to enhancing our understanding of an important aspect of creative cognition and, when used, perhaps even enhancing cognition, even in domains beyond chess!

DAVID ROSENBAUM: DEVELOPMENT OF EXPERTISE AND THE CONTROL OF PHYSICAL ACTION

The basic argument that Rosenbaum makes is that their cognitive-planning model best accounts for data from a variety of interesting experiments investigating motion planning. The work teases out specific control mechanisms (generate vs. recall in a described plunger experiment, for example) and an overall control model that posits a hierarchy of constraints controlling motion planning with progressive elimination of candidates that fail most important constraints; a kind of satisficing model in contrast to an optimization one.

An interesting question that the author raises and addresses is, what makes this "psychology"? The answers he gives include:

- A parallel between the search for candidate goal postures and movements and problem solving search (complete with the concept of satisficing!).
- Skill development: forming deeper constraint hierarchies, finer discriminations depending on feedback from trial and error learning.
- It depends on "chunking" or increased ability to generate series of movements.
- Psychology studies behavior and movement certainly qualifies.
- As Forrest Gump might have said "Psychology is what psychology does."
- It is reflective of a more general movement within psychology toward biology and neuroscience, and more generally, a desire to be seen as more "scientific."

With regard to the latter, many of us have noticed the phenomenon of sitting taller in our airplane seats when the person next to us asks "And what do you do?" when we label ourselves "_____scientist," whether it be "cognitive scientist" or "neuroscientist" or even, "behavioral scientist." Perhaps if we could agree on replacing "psychologist" with "psychological scientist" or, for the particularly insecure, "psychological scientist scientist," we could lay this issue to rest. At any rate, the work does fit into the recent move toward biological reductionism within psychology. But having agreed that movement is central to behavior and thus part of psychology, there still remains a lingering sense that not all movements are equal in this (think peristalsis or ventricular contraction!)...while Pavlov was interested in the control of salivation, peristalsis and the rest of the digestive process, he was actually doing it as a physiologist not a psychologist—and then of course came the serendipitous discovery that gave us claim to him, but it still didn't involve claims of movement expertise! So maybe we'll leave it with Gump...and with a final word from Rosenbaum who defines "smart moves" as everyday moves and not those of the artist or athlete, making us all experts.... sort of like being from Lake Woebegone where everyone is above average!

I could, of course, point out that this view of expertise as universal skilled performance rather than outstanding performance is consistent with the viewpoint I was initially going to present about rapid increases in proficiency at game playing during the first few hours of practice being a form of expertise, despite not being world class or outstanding, but out of respect for Colleague Three, that, of course, will not be mentioned. Despite this agreement, I am left with a lingering doubt that with regard to movement, we're not all Tiger Woods or Michael Jordan, or that we can really take pride in our gastrointestinal expertise. Perhaps, even while accepting Rosenbaum's conclusion that we are all expert 'movers," there is another level of movement expertise after all!

A key element in the author's inclusiveness in bringing movement into psychology, one that mitigates the above dilemma, is treating movement not as a particular pathway of a limb through space, but rather as a meaningful and purposeful act that involves cognitive planning and the use of intermediate postural goal (or subgoal) states as well as planning for end of movement comfort in its execution. He would argue that even Skinner, the ultimate behaviorist, focused on animals' responses or operants, rather than the particularities of their movements; basically not caring whether a rat pressed a bar with its foot or its nose in exhibiting learning! He presents some very interesting experiments, showing the effect of postural goals on the initial and early stages of grasping movements, validating the view of movement as a cognitively planned and expertly executed act. The reach here (so to speak) is relating this approach to more general issues in expertise as opposed to its being an interesting but somewhat disconnected island of work on a particular domain of expert performance. Perhaps, at the very least, the fact that grasping movements are used in chess links this work to the rest of the work in this volume! The author actually makes the argument that the act of placing and moving pieces on a chess board is a harder AI challenge than playing chess, mirroring something that Herb Simon used to argue that it has turned out to be easier to create an expert chess player or medical diagnostician than to create a robot to pump gas! Nonetheless, his approach to modeling grasping behavior is a large step toward the taming of this area of behavior; the issue of average vs. expert performance, and how far the definition of expertise can be extended notwithstanding.

K. ANDERS ERICSSON: CONTRIBUTIONS OF AUTOMATICITY AND DELIBERATE PRACTICE TO THE ACQUISITION OF EXPERTISE

To continue with physiological metaphors, this chapter gets at the heart of things in a number of ways. It is focused on work on what we would all agree is expertise. It has a focus on the basic cognitive aspects of expertise, and it is rooted in work started here at CMU, with a very CMU-ish perspective originating many years ago in Anders' collaborations; first with Herb Simon and then, for the work reported here, with Bill Chase. The major focus is on STM capacity and its ability to respond to training. The major finding was that with extended practice, STM capacity could be vastly increased (from seven or eight digits to over 80). The increase was due to three factors: (1) chunking and encoding short strings as running times; (2) the formation of retrieval structures that allowed direct placement into LTM; and (3) speed-up in processing. They also found that the skill was specific to number sequences, with little or no transfer to other types of material. A significant element of this work was that the first subject, SF, did not have an exceptional memory to start with but rather developed it, with the above mechanisms during training. The findings that began with this work have been termed "skilled memory theory" that posits a core set of three principles for explaining exceptional memory performance. These include training STM for particular material using mnemonic codes that access LTM, with direct entry into LTM, via the use of a structure that provides retrieval cues for organized storage and accessing of the information and speed-up in the storage. The first of these derives from earlier work by Chase and Simon on chess experts' memory that relied on the experts' years of study and play, resulting in stored perceptual "chunks" of information that reflect their chess knowledge, although Anders endeavors to distance his work from that viewpoint for some reason; a fairly common occurrence in psychology, even outstanding psychology, whereby we all too often try to overthrow rather than build on the past, sometimes necessary, but not always the best way to build a cumulative science.

The next section of this chapter describes Anders' move, following his postdoc years at CMU, on to the study of "real" expert memory-based performance and the mechanisms mediating it, to see if skilled memory theory can account for the performance. These mechanisms include not only large amounts of practice (the 10-year rule) and in particular, focused deliberate practice, to build retrieval and control structures and assimilate feedback from errors to enable those structures to respond to increasingly complex situations. The claim is that this strategic "deliberate" practice complements and transcends a simple explanation of expert performance based on the power law of practice. His finding is that in most cases studied, in the amazing performance capabilities exhibited by memory experts (remembering, for example, the first 40,000 digits of pi (it's painful to think about the second 40,000!), skilled memory theory is consistent with most of the exhibited behavior and that some exceptional brain organization or other special mechanism explanation was not necessary. While not wanting to appear frivolous, I must admit that in my experience with playing racquetball, I've found that a few minutes spent in deliberate practice before games over time makes for a large difference in subsequent level of performance, although unfortunately, most of this experience of this effect comes from watching an opponent who must have read Anders' work.

Anders found some support for this "non-specialness" view of world-class performers in the structural and functional brain imaging studies of Maguire et al. (2003) and his colleagues that showed no structural differences between the brains of ten outstanding memory performers and "normal" brains, and no functional differences that would suggest a different brain organization other than those accounted for by the experts' use of particular strategies. An analogy would be that you cannot find out where a car has been or is going by looking at its engine structure or functioning; it is a general purpose device able to drive anywhere. Memory experts' performance would seem to be due to the driver, i.e. their prior practice and acquisition of strategy and not the particularities of brain functionality.

The impressive body of reported work is characterized by a focus on basic cognitive mechanisms and the integration of both laboratory and "real-world" empirical work with a focus on small n or single subject studies that bring together laboratory training of expert performance and the development of world-class performance-level memory expertise. The work has an audaciously wide scope, including educational implications, that, if Anders can clone himself, at some point might be expanded to include a stronger linkage between early development and differentiation that focuses on what the eventual expert looks like early on, before coming to the brink of county, country or world-class expertise, and how small influences early in life can lead to increasingly dedicated learning and performance. This goal is consistent with his idea of "translational research" between laboratory and world-class expertise studies and is an idea that has been expressed in one way or another by many of the presenters. He does make a small foray in this direction by positing an outline of a developmental trajectory that perhaps points the way to a deeper future understanding of how experts develop.

PUTTING IT ALL APART[1]

Having forsworn a grand synthesis, I will end by raising a few questions that highlight some of the implicit interactions between these four rather disparate chapters.

As should be evident by now, one question that cuts across many of these chapters concerns the definition or scope of expertise. Does expertise have to

---

1   This is an indirect reference to Allen Newell's discussion chapter, "Putting it All Together," in Klahr and Kotovsky (1989).

be world class, focal and exclusive. (Gobet's chess and Ericsson's memory experts) or more universal (David Rosenbaum's smooth, well-executed, planful movements)? Are similar issues and mechanisms involved in both?

A second question is more Vygotskian in flavor. Is reaching expertise determined by a cognitive and social cascade of events that leads people to move progressively along the path to expertise, or is it really simply describable as all being due to deliberate practice, practice that is sometimes constrained or forced by the need to operate in the world, as in Rosenbaum's expert movements, and in other cases as the result of motivation and early experience, the forces that make some musicians, for example, engage in hours and hours of deliberate and effective practice, as in some of Anders' studies? An example of one such discrete social event: Abel Prize winner (2007), Srinivasa Varadhan's comment about his own development as a mathematician "We had a very good math teacher in high school who instilled in us the idea that math didn't have to be work, you could do it for fun." How often do such events play a defining role in setting people on the path to the development of expertise and, if they are frequent, can we leave them out of the study of expertise?

In a more continuous fashion, as we examine the course of development of expertise, do early divergences in the rate of increase of some parameter or ability progressively lead to further and further divergence (power law of practice with a slightly different exponent, perhaps coupled with statistical sampling to pick off the top .000001%?) Can we detect this in the early part of the curve (the development of early expertise or the early development of expertise) and does it take the same shape for world-class and for more universal expertise?

Finally (for this discussion at least), what is the ultimate role of expertise? Is it that of a computational cognitive enhancement tool (Schvaneveldt's hypothesis generating methods for abductive thinking via similarity searches of large text corpora)? Is it an Excel for the mind? Does it allow us to jump the expertise curve and perform at a higher and more creative level? Are there analogues in other devices or strategies, or strategy shifts, such as those discussed by Staszewski (1988) or Delaney et al. (1998) that provide step functions on the generally smooth curve of development of expertise with practice and time? Fortunately, we have some real experts studying expertise from a variety of perspectives, so there is reason for great optimism. It's an optimism that is reflective of Bill's zest for life and work, an optimism and a presence that suffuse this Festschrift that both celebrates the past and anticipates the future. Having known and loved Bill, I have to say that I am thankful for these contributions that so ably honor him.

REFERENCES

Bryan, W. L., & Harter, N. (1897). Studies in the physiology and psychology of the telegraphic language. *Psychological Review, 4,* 27–53.

Delaney, P., Reder, L. M., Staszewski, J., & Ritter, F. (1998). The strategy specific nature of improvement: The power law applies by strategy within task. *Psychological Science, 9,* 1–7.

Ebbinghaus, H. ([1885] 1964). *Memory: A contribution to experimental psychology.* New York: Dover.

Freud, S. (1920). *A general introduction to psychoanalysis* (Trans. J. Riviere). New York: Boni & Liveright.

Maguire, E. A., Valentine, E. R., Wilding, J. M., & Kapur, N. (2003). Routes to remembering: The brains behind superior memory. *Nature Neuroscience, 6,* 90–95.

Newell, A. (1989). Putting it all together. In D. Klahr, & K. Kotovsky (Eds.), *Complex information processing: The impact of Herbert A. Simon.* Hillsdale, NJ: Lawrence Erlbaum Associates.

Piaget, J. (1926). *The language and thought of the child.* New York: Harcourt, Brace.

Staszewski, J. (1988). Skilled memory and expert mental calculation. In M. T. H. Chi, R. Glaser, & M. J. Farr (Eds.), *The nature of expertise* (pp. 71–128). Hillsdale, NJ: Lawrence Erlbaum Associates.

11

The Expert Brain[1]

MICHAEL I. POSNER
University of Oregon, USA

INTRODUCTION

*I*was very grateful to be at the symposium and to make this contribution to the volume celebrating the achievements of Bill Chase. Bill received his MA at the University of Wisconsin and I was fortunate enough to serve as his major adviser. His MA was a remarkable contribution to the study of visual search and he pursued these issues for his PhD after I left Wisconsin to go to Oregon. It was typical of Bill's high standards that little of this work was published at the time, although it did enter into several later papers. Bill was an empirical virtuoso capable of bringing high-level theory to test. When Bill moved to Carnegie Mellon, where Newell and Simon had done so much to bring theory to psychology, I felt strongly that important things would happen, and they did. Much of the most important work was in the field of expertise, which we examine in this volume.

This symposium is remarkably well timed. Bill Chase died in 1983 yet more than 25 years later his powerful contributions are even more at the center of the stage than they were at the time of his death.

THE PSYCHOLOGY OF CHESS

The essence of Bill's contribution can be seen in the quote below from his chapter in the 1973 volume he edited (Chase & Simon, 1973, p. 279).

1 This chapter was presented at the Chase Memorial Symposium, May 2009. The research presented in this chapter was supported by by NICHD grant 060563 to Georgia State University.

Chess skill depends in large part upon a vast, organized long-term memory of specific information about chessboard patterns. Although there clearly must be a set of specific aptitudes (e.g. aptitudes for handling spatial relations) that together comprise a talent for chess, individual differences in such aptitudes are largely over-shadowed by immense individual difference in chess experience. Hence, the overriding factor in chess skill is practice. The organization of the Master's elaborate repertoire of information takes thousands of hours to build up, and the same is true of any skilled task (e.g. football, music). That is why practice is the major independent variable in the acquisition of skill.

In 1987, I was asked to address a conference on gifted and talented children at the University of Oregon School of Education. I found that those at the meeting believed that their main job was choosing children whose individual aptitudes or abilities allowed them to achieve truly expert performance. I told them the Chase and Simon expertise story and they were truly amazed at the idea that in some sense anyone could be an expert. I used the ability to read words so quickly and expertly as an example of where widespread although not universal expertise was used. Micki Chi asked me to contribute the article from that lecture to her 1988 volume *The Nature of Expertise* which was a memorial tribute to Bill (Posner, 1988).

For much of the time between Chase's contribution (Chase & Simon, 1973) and the current period, notions that genius can be largely attributed to genetics dominated discussion of high-level performance. Currently, however, variants of the expertise story are being used by Richard Nisbett (2009) to discuss the contribution of schools to intelligence and by Malcolm Gladwell (2008) in his book to discuss how success is more than an individual achievement. Gladwell says on page 44 of his book:

> The emerging pictures from such studies is that 10,000 hours of practice is required to achieve the level of mastery associated with being a world-class expert – in anything.
> In study after study of composers, baseball players, fiction writers, ice skaters, concert pianists, chess, players, master criminals and what have you this number comes up again and again.

Even David Brooks, the noted *NY Times* conservative columnist, has adopted the idea of intelligence being caused by environmental circumstance. The embrace of the Chase and Simon idea places emphasis on the role of experience in determining individual differences in cognitive function, but does not consider the role of what Chase and Simon called the "talent for chess."

In this chapter we consider what new methods, which have developed for exploring human brain networks and individual differences in their efficiency, contribute to our understanding of how genes and experience jointly contribute to expertise. Our reasons for doing so are, first, to establish better balance between the influences of genetics and of practice on expertise. Second, it is a goal of this chapter to establish the study of expertise as a way of viewing how brain imaging might contribute to secondary and higher education. Although there is much we do not know about how the brain achieves expertise, many may be surprised that there is already knowledge of how brain networks change with experience. Although these ideas have not often been applied to the high levels of training involved in chess (but see Righi, Tarr, & Kingon, Chapter 12 in this volume), in this chapter I try to extrapolate from what is known about the development of attention and other networks to imagine how genes and experience shape high-level skills like chess.

BRAIN MECHANISMS OF EXPERTISE

This volume is primarily concerned with the study of expertise from a strictly psychological viewpoint, but it is also true that among the many things that have happened since Bill Chase's work is an enhanced understanding of brain networks. This understanding was aided by methods for examining the human brain by changes in blood flow and blood oxygenation, which together have been called neuroimaging (Posner & Raichle, 1994). The ability to localize areas of brain activity has also revitalized non-invasive electrical and magnetic methods because it is possible to relate the two approaches and thus specify brain networks in terms of both localized brain activity and the time course of their activation. As we have pointed out elsewhere, this combination has led to the specification of brain networks related to many human activities (Posner & Rothbart, 2007). Moreover, studies which image the brain before and after learning have shown that experience can lead to sharpening the efficiency of these networks by tuning the neurons at various nodes of the network to increase their ability to carry out localized computations. Experience also strengthens the connectivity between nodes of the network, which further improves their efficiency (Tang, et al., 2010).

Two aspects of these networks are somewhat more controversial. One is the issue of what is localized. I believe that the bulk of the evidence supports the idea that these networks localize computations related to the task being performed and the overall task is orchestrated through connections between these localized brain areas. This view has certainly been supported in the areas of orienting of attention (Corbetta & Shulman, 2002; Hillyard, Di Russo, & Martinez, 2004) and as an approach to the computations involved in language (Posner & Raichle, 1994). It is certainly possible and perhaps even likely that more complex reasoning and memory retrieval processes involve less specific localization (Duncan & Owen, 2000), but these differences may be more due to our weakness in correctly specifying the operations involved than they are to problems with localization. This view of localization by mental operations does not suggest that any task is local to a particular area because all tasks studied involve a limited number of widely scattered brain areas. Nor do we think there are an infinite number of mental operations, but assuming there is some localization can allow us to use both the logical methods of cognitive science and the methods of cognitive neuroscience to specify the mental operations needed to carry out even a complex task such as chess.

Common Categories

How does learning change brain networks? It is common for learning on a task to decrease the number and amount of activated brain areas (Durston & Casey, 2006). In some cases learning reorganizes the brain areas involved and in some cases it leads to enlarged areas of activation (Kelly & Garavan, 2005). Connectivity of the network can also be enhanced by practice (McNamara, Tegenthoff, Hubert et al., 2007).

Some categories are common to all members of our species and we are all experts in tasks that demand their use. An example of a natural category is faces, which can influence the infant's behavior at birth. It is believed that perception of faces in the first few months depends primarily upon subcortical structures, but by 10 months there is clear evidence that infants are dealing with faces in ways that are somewhat similar to adults (Johnson, 2004). For adults, faces activate an area of the posterior part of the fusiform gyrus, particularly on the right side, which is called the fusiform face area (Kanwisher, 2000). This brain area is part of the visual system. It probably has a role in organizing the features of the face into a whole, so that the face can be recognized through processing by more anterior areas.

A more general function of this area has been discovered, because experts in categories other than faces tend to show activation of this area for the material (e.g., dogs, birds or automobiles) in which they are expert (Gauthier, Anderson, Skudlarski, & Gore, 1999). This finding demonstrates how the function of a brain area initially associated with recognition of one particular category may through training come to be used by other categories. In this volume it is shown that an area involving the fusiform gyrus is also recruited by chess experts (Righi et al., Chapter 12 in this volume).

A similar story related to expertise underlies the visual word form area. The word form area occupies a part of the fusiform gyrus that is mainly in the left hemisphere, and has been related to chunking visual letters into a unitary whole. A good example of the importance of this brain areas is revealed by the study of a patient who, when a word was presented to the left of fixation, could only sound out the letters one by one taking many seconds to read a single word, but he could read the word fluently when presented to the right of fixation (i.e. to the left hemisphere where the word form area is located) (Cohen, et al., 2004). Imaging showed that there was interruption of the fibers that conducted information to the visual word form area from the right hemisphere occipital lobe. When words were presented to the left of fixation (i.e. directly to the right hemisphere), the patient could sound them out letter by letter although he clearly maintained his reading skills as evidenced by his performance with words presented to the right visual field (i.e. directly to the left hemisphere) so that they did reach the visual word form area. This study shows clearly that the visual word form area is a necessary condition for fluent reading.

As in the case of faces, the word form area is not used exclusively for words. There is evidence that visual objects that are involved in rapid naming tasks can use the same area. These findings suggest the importance of the operations performed by a particular brain area that move beyond any one kind of information. A particularly striking example of this plasticity is the use of the visual system in the recognition of Braille letters (Pascual-Leone & Hamilton, 2001). Although the visual system is specialized for visual stimuli, in this case, somatosensory information used in the service of language can utilize visual mechanisms.

The visual word form area is not part of an inborn category, but becomes tuned to processes that are learned with the acquisition of the skill of reading. This brain area represents a kind of learned expertise but one that is common to many people. It is reasonable to ask if newly learned arbitrary categories such as those involved in the processing of chess also involve posterior brain areas and do these area operate automatically to structure what is seen or are they part of a larger problem-solving process?

Newly Learned Categories

A number of years ago Steve Keele and I used nonsense patterns of 9 dots all derived from a single prototype by various distortions rules in order explore the learning of new categorical information (Posner & Keele, 1968). Participants learned to sort the patterns into categories represented by four different prototypes. Although the participants were never shown the prototype, they made false alarms to it, saying they had seen it before and prototypes were classified correctly as often as the learned exemplars. Many studies showed that this result might be predicted as well from storage of exemplars alone as from models based on representation of the category by the prototype. However, false alarms error in a recognition memory study suggested that prototype storage might be correct. As in many behavioral controversies, this one remained unresolved.

However, Knowlton and Squire (1993) showed that patients whose memory had been impaired by brain lesions were at a great disadvantage in remembering exemplars but dealt very well with the prototype. These studies suggested that extraction of the prototype might not involve the mid-temporal brain regions found important for explicit storage. This general idea has been confirmed by neuroimaging studies (see Smith, 2008, for a review). Newly learned categories of a variety of visual material seem to produce activation of a posterior brain area often more strongly on the right side.

The idea that new learning builds a visual representation, highly abstracted as in the case of the prototype, from the input fits very well with one idea from the Chase and Simon work. It suggests that the chess master has within the visual system a sufficiently abstract representation so that a newly seen game of chess might be analyzed in terms of already known chess positions. However, for this to work to produce the memory of the chess master, it should work quickly and automatically, that is without any conscious intent to see the material as related to prior chess games. One way of examining this issue is to compare conditions when people are asked to explicitly recall an item with situations in which they can make use of the material, but do not explicitly have to remember it. Studies using word completion presented normal people and amnesic patients with a list of words and after an interval presented a three-letter cue either taken from one of the words on the list or not. Subjects were asked either to explicitly recall the word on the list that began with the cue or to give the first associated word to the cue (Graf, Squire, & Mandler, 1984; Shimamura, 1986). Normal subjects did much better than patients with amnesia under the explicit recall task, but amnesiacs recalled as many words from the list as normals when the task was implicit. Moreover, in fMRI studies, implicit use of the primed word seemed to involve a portion of the right posterior cortex (Buckner et al., 1995).

In order to determine if this activation represented an early priming by the stored information, a high density EEG study was run (Badigaiyan & Posner, 1997). It was found that right posterior electrodes, consistent with the fMRI activation, differed between primed and unprimed words in the implicit condition during the first 150 msec after input. These data suggested that right posterior activation of information was contacted automatically and rapidly after the input cue. On the other hand, activations in the explicit condition were mostly in the hippocampal and frontal areas.

The studies cited above use rather artificial conditions of learning isolated words or nonsense patterns. One may ask if the same general mechanism is involved with more natural categories learned by experts. Tanaka and Curran (2001) used event-related electrical potentials to show that experts in dogs and birds show differences in the event-related potentials in brain areas associated with the perception of faces when viewing materials related to their expertise. An early component of the event-related potential (about 170 msec) was associated in the recognition of familiar objects for experts but not for novices. Thus there appears to be a general neural mechanism by which learning can influence posterior brain areas that can greatly improve the efficiency of handling concepts. The recent finding with chess experts shows that the same principles are involved in learning chess (Righi et al., Chapter 12, in this volume).

Another feature of the brain circuits related to expertise including faces, word form and artificial and natural categories is that they involve frontal areas in addition to the posterior area of activation. In the case of visual words, for example, frontal areas including the left ventral frontal area and the anterior cingulate are active within 150 msec after input, almost as fast as some of the posterior areas (Abdullaev & Posner, 1998). In general, the frontal and posterior areas work together over a long time interval to integrate diverse information related to the problem solution. For example, in the case of generating the use of a noun, which takes about 1100 msec, the frontal areas are in communication with posterior areas related to semantics at 450 msec (Nikolaev et al., 2001). In general, brain studies have argued that there is close communication between frontal, posterior and subcortical areas in generating the solution to problems, even those much simpler than what is involved in chess. The recent study of chess expertise also shows the importance of a number of frontal areas, suggesting that here too chess is similar to other learned categories.

Summary

Chase and Simon showed clearly that high-level skill in chess made a huge difference in the way memory for a new arrangement of chess pieces was structured. According to them, the semantics of the situation automatically structured memory for the location of the pieces, allowing the chess master to circumvent the limits of memory. The study of brain systems fully bears out these ideas and advances our knowledge of the mechanisms involved. Natural categories common to all people, such as faces, and both meaningful and meaningless categories, including those involved in chess positions, acquired by learning, whether in the laboratory or outside, all have an initial activation in posterior visual systems. This activity primes related input early in processing, thus structuring the new input in terms of past learning. Some of these findings come from studies that do not involve the complexity of chess, but they do provide insight into how the brain of the chess master works to structure the new board and to suggest possible moves. The ability to structure input has vast consequences for all types of learning. Although all our examples use visual input, we know that the same central mechanisms are involved in orienting to all sensory modalities and it seems likely that auditory and somato-sensory input would involve the same principles although the locations of stored information would be different. These mechanisms can be and have been applied to other forms of learning and problem solving, for example, in mathematics (Anderson, 2007), science, and the arts (Posner & Patoine, 2010).

INDIVIDUAL DIFFERENCES

A second goal of our chapter is to use brain research to examine the issue of whether there are individual differences which could in principle influence the ability of people to become chess masters, as suggested by Chase and Simon (1973). Since there are no reports on the genes involved in individual differences in chess, I can only summarize what we have learned about how genetic variation influences the development of brain networks in general and of attention in particular. I have worked extensively on attention networks and I believe some of what has been found can help us to understand individual differences in the ability to learn chess.

One of the major contributions of brain research is to help tie together common mechanisms of attention, learning and reasoning with differences among individuals in the same functions. For example, attention has involved three brain networks associated with alerting, orienting and executive control. We developed a test that gives a specific score for each network. We found that each of these networks has a range of scores reflecting individual differences in the efficiency of the network (Posner & Rothbart, 2007). In the case of the executive network, studies have shown that differences in the efficiency of resolving conflict from cognitive tasks correlates with parental reports of their child's ability to control their emotions and behavior, a factor called effortful control (Rothbart &

Rueda, 2005). Both executive attention and differences in effortful control among adolescents influence areas of the anterior cingulate and or mid-frontal cortex (Bush, Luu, & Posner, 2000; Whittle et al., 2008).

Each of the networks related to attention has a dominant neuromodulator (Green et al., 2008): dopamine for the executive network, acetylcholine for orienting, and norepinepherine for alerting. Because of these associations we predicted that differences in the dopamine alleles would be related to scores on executive attention, alerting scores to norepinepherine and orienting scores to cholinergic genes. Work with adults to date has largely supported this idea (Green et al., 2008).

Development of Attention Networks

The attainment of high-level skills in chess must rely upon brain plasticity to reflect the learning. Studies of human brain development have begun to reveal important changes during childhood that might provide clues to the nature of that plasticity. One of these changes involves focalization of activity during the performance of cognitive tasks (Durston & Casey, 2006). During child development, cognitive tasks come to activate fewer brain areas and those activated are smaller with advancing age. It is as though task performance is more finely tuned with development. Some of these effects are similar to what has been found in adults with practice, which also tends to reduce the number and size of brain activations. On the other hand, studies of resting fMRI in children from 9 years to adults show changes in connectivity during development, which range from predominant local connections to more global connections (Fair et al., 2009). These two effects have led to what might seem opposite views of development. The activation data suggest increasing age produces more focal activity, while connectivity studies suggest more distributed activity in older children and adults. However, these changes in activation and connectivity may work together both in development and with practice to produce more efficient networks with smaller and more tuned local activity and broader and more diffuse connectivity. This might support the findings discussed in adults, which show that high skill learning produces strong posterior regions of focal activation and rapid connections to frontal brain areas.

Recent studies have examined the brain activity of infants and young children at rest using fMRI (Fransson et al., 2007; Gao et al., 2009). These results have shown evidence of sparse connectivity between brain structures during infancy with a strong increase in connectivity at 2 years (Gao et al., 2009) and later (Fair et al., 2009). In studies of neonates, the parietal areas, prominent in the orienting of attention network, show strong connectivity to lateral and medial frontal areas. By age 2, the anterior cingulate, which has been implicated in self-regulation, shows stronger connection to frontal areas and to lateral parietal areas. These findings suggest that the control structures related to executive attention and effortful control may be present in infancy but do not exercise their full control over other networks until later. In accord with this view we have reported that error detection activates the mid-frontal and/or cingulate areas at 7 months (Berger, Tzur, & Posner, 2006), although the ability of an infant to take action based on errors seems not be present until 3–4 years of age (Jones, Rothbart, & Posner, 2003).

These studies usually examine functional connectivity between brain regions in resting fMRI. They are interpreted as being caused by improved myelination of white matter pathways over the years of development. Recently (Tang et al., 2010), we showed that white matter changes, as measured by diffusion tensor imaging, can also occur with a relatively brief period of mental practice.

Based in part on these imaging findings, we (Rothbart et al., 2011) suggested that the orienting network might play an important role in early emotional control and that caregivers might use orienting as a means of helping their child to develop self-regulation by other means. However, later in childhood and in adulthood, it appears to be the executive network that is most important in cognitive and emotional control.

There is ample evidence that as organisms develop, they produce both more focal activity in some brain areas and stronger connectivity between areas. These same mechanisms may also form the basis for what happens as expertise develops through learning. A further step would be to understand how experience and genes work together during development as a way of illuminating their potential role in expertise. The next section reviews evidence on the shaping of early networks by genes and experience.

Genetic Influences on Development

We have been conducting a longitudinal study on genetic influences on development from 7 months of age through the preschool years. We have reported on parts of this study up to 2 years of age and in this chapter review these findings together in an effort to examine how attention networks are shaped in early development (Sheese et al., 2007; Sheese et al., 2008; Voelker et al., 2009).

One goal of this work was to understand the how the early development of orienting and executive attention networks might influence control of emotions and cognition.

We used cheek swabs to extract DNA and determined the genetic variation in a dozen of the genes that had been connected to attention in the adult studies (Sheese et al., 2007). The children in this study were initially seen when they were 7 months old, but the genotyping took place when they returned to the laboratory at about 2 years of age. In addition, at age 2, we added an observation of caregiver–child interaction in which the children played with toys in the presence of one of their caregivers. Raters observed the caregiver–child interaction and rated the parents on five dimensions of parental quality according to a schedule developed by NICHD (1993). Parent dimensions scored were: support, autonomy, stimulation, lack of hostility and confidence in the child. Although all of the parents were likely concerned and caring, they did differ in their scores, and we divided them at the median into two groups. One of the groups was considered to show a higher quality of parenting, and the other a lower quality.

The 7-repeat allele of the dopamine 4 receptor gene (DRD4 gene) has been linked to attention deficit disorder and to the temperamental quality of risk taking. Adults and children with the 7-repeat allele have been shown to be higher in the temperamental quality of risk taking and to be at high risk for attention deficit disorder than those with smaller numbers of repeats (Auerbach et al., 1999; Swanson et al., 2001).

In one series of studies (Auerbach et al., 1999), it was found that the orienting of 2-month-old infants as rated by parents and observed during inspection of toys was related to the presence of the 7-repeat allele of the DRD4 gene. This allele appears to interact with a gene related to serotonin transmission (5HTT) to influence orienting.

In our longitudinal study, what we were interested in was whether parent reports of the child's impulsivity and risk taking were related to the child's carrying the 7-repeat allele of the DRD4 gene, the parent's scores on parenting quality, or an interaction of gene and parenting. We found a strong interaction effect (Sheese et al., 2007). For children without the 7-repeat polymorphism, variations in parenting within the range we examined were unrelated to the children's scores on impulsivity and risk taking. For children carrying the 7-repeat gene variant, however, variations in parenting quality made a large difference. For those children with the 7-repeat and high quality parenting, their impulsivity and risk taking were average while those with the 7-repeat and low quality parenting, impulsivity and risk taking were very much higher.

Evidence that environment can have a stronger influence in the presence of the 7-repeat alleles has been reported by others (Bakermans-Kranenburg & van IJzendoorn, 2006; van IJzendoorn & Bakermans-Kranenburg, 2006). In addition, the same group (Bakermans-Kranenburg et al., 2008) also performed a parenting training intervention and showed that the training decreased externalizing behavior, but only for those children with the DRD4 7-repeat allele. This finding is important because assignment to the training group was random, thus insuring that the result is not due to something other than the training. Three replications show that the presence of the 7-repeat allele makes parenting more influential on the behavior of the child. The parent training study suggests that the presence of the 7-repeat allele is critical to the influence of parent training but of course more evidence on this point would be important. A study with adults also illustrates the role of the 7-repeat allele in behavior (Larsen et al., 2010). In this study adults with the 7-repeat allele showed a stronger influence of their peers on alcohol consumption than adults who did not have this allele.

It seems paradoxical that the 7-repeat allele associated with developmental psychopathology (attention deficit disorder) is under positive selective pressure in recent human evolution (Ding et al., 2002). Why should an allele related to ADHD be positively selected? We think that positive selection of the 7-repeat allele could well arise from its sensitivity to environmental influences. Parenting provides training for children in the values favored by their culture in which they live. For example, Rothbart and colleagues (Ahadi, Rothbart, & Ye, 1993) found that, in Western culture, effortful control appears to regulate negative affect (sadness and anger), while in China (at least in the 1980s) it was found to regulate positive affect (outgoingness and enthusiasm). In recent years the genetic part of the nature by nurture interaction has received a lot of emphasis, but if genetic variations are selected according to the sensitivity to cultural influences that they produce in children, this could support a greater balance between genes and environment. Theories of positive selection in the DRD4 gene have stressed the role of sensation seeking in human evolution (Harpending & Cochran, 2002; Wang et al., 2004). Our new findings do not contradict this emphasis, but suggest a form of explanation that could have even wider significance. It remains to be seen whether the other 300 genes estimated to show positive selection would also increase an individual's sensitivity to variations in rearing environments. We will be examining additional longitudinal data to test these ideas further.

How could variation in genetic alleles lead to enhanced influence of cultural factors like parenting? The anterior cingulate receives input on both reward value and pain or punishment and this information is clearly important in regulating thoughts and feelings. Dopamine is the most important neuromodulator in these reward and punishment pathways. Thus changes in the availability of dopamine could enhance the influence of signals from parents related to reward and punishment. Another interaction has been reported between the serotonin transporter and parental social support on the temperamental dimension of behavioral inhibition or social fear (Fox et al., 2005). To explain this interaction, Fox, Hane and Pine (2007) argue that those children with a short form of the serotonin transporter gene, who also have lower social support from their parents, show enhanced attention to threat and greater social fear. In our study, however, we did not find that attention was the mechanism by which the genetic variation influenced the child's behavior. At two years of age there was no influence of the 7-repeat allele on executive attention, rather the gene and environment interacted to influence the child's behavior as observed by their caregiver. However, by 4 years of age when the executive attention network was better connected (Rothbart et al., 2011) there was a clear interaction between effortful control and the presence of the DRD$-7 repeat (Sheese, Rothbart, Voelker, & Posner, 2012). This finding shows the importance of considering the development of brain networks in determining the influence of genes on behavior.

An important gene X environment interaction that has been shown to work through attention in adults is the COMT gene (Blasi et al., 2005). A study of 7- to 14-year-old children (Diamond et al., 2004) found a similar effect on attention kl at this younger age. In most studies, one genotype (Val/Val) shows better performance in a variety of tasks than does the other (Met/Met). Another approach to the gene has been to construct a haplotype consisting of three different polymorphisms in the gene. Versions of this haplotype have been shown to be closely related to the perception of pain (Diatchenko et al., 2005). Executive attention and pain both have been shown to involve the anterior cingulate gyrus.

In both 7-month-old children and 2-year-olds, the genotype and the haplotypes related to the COMT gene proved to relate to aspects of performance in a task involving orienting of attention, and overall the haplotype was more strongly linked to performance. At 2 years of age it was possible to examine the relation between parenting as measured by the NICHD parent–child interaction (see last section) and variations in the COMT gene (Sheese, Voelker, Rothbart, & Posner, 2009). An interaction was found between the genetic variation and parenting quality in determining performance in the visual sequence task. In particular those 2-year-olds with higher quality parenting and the haplotype that included the Val/Val genotype were superior in the task. This provides additional support for the idea that genetic variation can influence attention networks in early development.

Parenting and the Transition

We have argued for a transition between two control networks that are active during the period of our study. According to this view, during infancy, control is principally exercised by the orienting network but by 4 years and later this control involves the executive network. If this is correct, how does the transition take place? We believe this transition is mediated through exercise of the orienting network which produces increased connectivity for the executive network. Support for this view comes in part from an adult study (Shulman et al., 2009) in which the presentation of a novel object recruits the executive network (cingulo-opercular, in their terms) to supplement the orienting network (the ventral parietal frontal network, in their terms) which is active when the objects are not sufficiently novel. If this mechanism is present in infancy, it could mean that caregivers provide impetus for the development of self-regulation when they exercise executive systems through the presentation of novel objects.

Research by Bernier, Carlson and Whipple (2010) shows that maternal sensitivity, mindfulness and autonomy-support at 15 months were correlated with their child's later executive functions at 18 to 26 months, suggesting a relationship between earlier parent– child relationship on the development of self-regulatory activities. Our data at age 2 showed that parental quality interacted with the 7-repeat allele of the DRD4 gene to influence the temperamental dimensions of impulsivity, high intensity pleasure and activity (Sheese et al., 2007) and at age 4 the same gene influenced aspects of attention and emotion although these effects no longer interacted with parenting. The COMT gene at age 2 also interacted with parenting (Voelker et al., 2009) to influence orienting tasks and at age 4 also influenced attention but did not interact with parenting quality.

These findings suggest that aspects of parenting as reported and/or observed at ages 1–2 years influences the developing child's attention networks and behavior. Although these findings are qualified by individual differences in genetic variation, they still show that parents can play a role in shaping the child's behavior.

These data suggest that both genetic and parental influences are important in the shift between orienting and executive control attention networks. We believe that the use of novel objects as instruments to soothe and interest children early in life is one tool to foster the development of self-regulation. These findings in childhood lead us to expect that in addition to long continued training, genetic variation may also play a role in who is likely to become an expert in chess and other learned skills.

Genes and Expertise

In one sense we all develop expertise in attention so the attention networks can serve as a model for understanding the role of genes and experience in any form of expertise. Despite the long training with attention, just as in other forms of expertise, there are large individual differences. It seems likely that individual differences in attention, motivation and memory may well be important determinants of who will be willing to put in the needed hours to become an expert in any particular domain.

The data clearly show that differences in attention are due in part to genetic variation, in part to experience and also to the interaction of the two. How these various causes of individuality combine may differ for any form of expertise we study. However, in accord with the position of Chase and Simon, studies of attention show that adults find it possible to improve their attention skills by various forms of training. For example, studies of target detection show that the speed and efficiency of orienting to visual targets can be improved by training in video games (Green & Bavalier, 2003). We have shown that meditation training can improve attention (Tang et al., 2007). In this case just 5 days of training are sufficient to improve some of the ability to resolve conflict as measured by the Attention Network Test (ANT). This is true even without any specific training of the network. Longer training changed the brain state by changing the efficiency of connections between the anterior cingulate and other brain areas (Tang et al., 2010). It is striking that these same mechanisms of changes in connectivity also occur during normal development. The same genes responsible for the development of the network related to attention may also play a role in their strengthening by specific training. These findings fit with the evidence of Chase and Simon that many years of practice may be important for expertise, but qualifies it to recognize that genetic and other differences may influence the effectiveness and/or the willingness to pursue the practice.

We are still a long way from understanding the biological constraints on the acquisition of expertise for high-level skills like chess, but the work to date suggests methods and results related to the argument made for what Chase and Simon called the "talent for chess."

REFERENCES

Abdullaev, Y. G., & Posner, M. I. (1998). Event-related brain potential imaging of semantic encoding during processing single words. *Neuroimage, 7*, 1–13.

Ahadi, S. A., Rothbart, M. K., & Ye, R. (1993). Children's temperament in the U.S. and China: Similarities and differences. *European Journal of Personality, 7*, 359–378.

Anderson, J. R. (2007). *How can the human mind occur in the physical universe?* New York: Oxford University Press.

Auerbach, J., Geller, V., Lezer, S., Shinwell, E., Levine, J., Belmaker, R. H., & Ebstein, R. P. (1999). Dopamine D4 receptor (D4DR) and serotonin transporter promoter (5-HTTLPR) polymorphisms in the determination of temperament in two month old infants. *Molecular Psychiatry, 4*, 369–374.

Badigaiyan, R., & Posner, M. I. (1997). Time course of cortical activations in implicit and explicit recall. *Journal of Neuroscience, 17*(12), 4904–4913.

Bakermans-Kranenburg, M. J., & van IJzendoorn, M. H. (2006). Gene–environment interaction of the dopamine D4 receptor (DRD4) and observed maternal insensitivity predicting externalizing behavior in preschoolers. *Developmental Psychobiology, 48*, 406–409.

Bakermans-Kranenburg, M. J., van IJzendoorn, M. H., Pijlman, F. T. A., Mesman, J., & Juffer, F. (2008). Experimental evidence for differential susceptibility: Dopamine D4 Receptor Polymorphism (DRD4 VNTR) moderates intervention effects on toddlers' externalizing behavior in a randomized controlled trial. *Developmental Psychology, 44*, 293–300.

Berger, A., Tzur, G., & Posner, M. I. (2006). Infant babies detect arithmetic error. *Proceedings of the National Academy of Sciences of the USA, 103*, 12649–12553.

Bernier, A., Carlson, S. M., & Whipple, N. (2010). From external regulation to self-regulation: Early parenting precursors of your children's executive functioning. *Child Development, 81*, 326–339.

Blasi, G., Mattay, G. S., Bertolino, A., Elvevåg, B., Callicott, J. H., Das, S., Kolachana, B. S., Egan, M. F., Goldberg, T. E., & Weinberger, D. R. (2005). Effect of cCatechol- O-Methyltransferase val^{158} met genotype on attentional control. *Journal of Neuroscience, 25*(20), 5038–5045.

Buckner, R. L., Petersen, S. E., Ojemann, J. G., Miezin, F. M., Squire, L. R., & Raichle, M. E. (1995). Functional anatomical studies of explicit and implicit memory retrieval tasks. *Journal of Neuroscience, 15*, 5870–5878.

Bush, G., Luu, P., & Posner, M. I. (2000). Cognitive and emotional influences in the anterior cingulate cortex. *Trends in Cognitive Science, 4/6*, 215–222.

Chase, W. G., & Simon, H. A. (1973). The mind's eye in chess. In W. G. Chase (Ed.), *Visual information processing*. New York: Academic Press.

Cohen, L. H., Dehaene, S., Martinaud, O., Lehericy, S., Lemer, C., & Ferrieux, S. (2004). The pathophysiology of letter-by-letter reading. *Neuropsychologia, 42*(13), 1768–1780.

Corbetta, M., & Shulman, G. L. (2002). Control of goal-directed and stimulus-driven attention in the brain. *Nature Neuroscience Reviews, 3*, 201–215.

Diamond, A., Briand, L., Fossella, J., & Gehlbach, L. (2004). Genetic and neurochemical modulation of prefrontal cognitive functions in children. *American Journal of Psychiatry, 161*, 125–132.

Diatchenko, L., Slade, G. D., et al. (2005). Genetic basis for individual variations in pain perception and the development of a chronic pain condition. *Human Molecular Genetics, 14*(1), 135–143.

Ding, Y. C., Chi, H. C., Grady, D. L., Morishima, A., Kidd, J. R., Kidd, K. K., et al. (2002). Evidence of positive selection acting at the human dopamine receptor D4 gene locus. *Proceedings of the National Academy of Sciences of the USA, 99*(1), 309–314.

Duncan, J., & Owen A. M. (2000). Common regions of the human frontal lobe recruited by diverse cognitive demands. *Trends in Neurosciences, 23*, 475–483.

Durston, S., & Casey, B. J. (2006). What have we learned about cognitive development from neuroimaging? *Neuropsychologia, 44*, 2149–2157.

Fair, D. A., Cohen, A. L., Power, J. D., Dosenbach, N. U. F., Church, J. A., Meizin, F. M., Schallar, B. L., & Petersen, S. E. (2009). Functional brain networks develop from a "local to distributed" organization. *PLoS Computational Biology, 5/5*, e1000381.

Fox, N. A., Hane, A. A., & Pine, D. S. (2007). Plasticity for affective neurocircuitry: How the environment affects gene expression. *Current Directions in Psychological Science, 16*, 1–5.

Fox, N. A., Nichols, K. E., Henderson, H. A., Rubin, K. H., Schmidt, L. A., Hamer, D., et al. (2005). Evidence for a gene–environment interaction in predicting behavioral inhibition in middle school children. *Psychological Science, 16/12*, 921–926.

Fransson, P., Skiold, B., Hosch, S., Nordell, A., Blennow, M., Lagercrantz, H., & Aden, U. (2007). Resting-state networks in the infant brain. *Proceedings of the National Academy of Sciences of the USA, 104*, 15531–15536.

Gao, W., Zhu, H., Giovanello, K. S., Smith, J. K., Shen, D., Gilmore, J. H., & Lin, W. (2009). Evidence on the emergence of the brain's default network from 2-week-old to 2-year-old healthy pediatric subjects. *Proceedings of the National Academy of Sciences of the USA, 106*, 6790–6795.

Gauthier, I., Tarr, M. J., Anderson, A. W., Skudlarski, P., & Gore, J. C. (1999). Activation of the middle fusiform gyrus "face area" increases with expertise in recognizing objects. *Neuron, 34*, 161–171.

Gladwell, M. (2008). *Outliers*. New York: Little, Brown.

Graf, P., Squire, L. R., & Mandler, G. (1984). The information that amnesic patents do not forget. *Journal of Experimental Psychology Learning, Memory and Cognition, 10*, 164–178.

Green, A. E., Munafo, M. R., DeYoung, C. G., Fossella, J. A., Fan, J., & Grey, J. R. (2008). Using genetic data in cognitive neuroscience: From growing pains to genuine insights. *Nature Neuroscience Reviews, 9*, 710–719.

Green, C. S., & Bavalier, D. (2003). Action video games modify visual selective attention. *Nature, 423*, 434–437.

Harpending, H., & Cochran, G. (2002). In our genes. *Proceedings of the National Academy of Sciences of the USA, 99*, 10–12.

Hillyard, S., Di Russo, F., & Martinez, A. (2004).The imaging of visual attention In N. Kanwisher, & J. Duncan (Eds.), *Attention and performance XX: Functional neuroimaging of visual cognition* (pp. 381–390). Oxford: Oxford University Press.

Johnson, M. H. (2004). Plasticity and function of brain development: The case of face processing. In N. Kanwisher, & J. Duncan (Eds.), *Attention and performance XX: Functional neuroimaging of visual cognition* (pp. 257–266). Oxford: Oxford University Press.

Jones, L., Rothbart, M. K., & Posner, M. I. (2003). Development of inhibitory control in preschool children. *Developmental Science, 6*, 498–504.

Kanwisher, N. (2000). Domain specificity in face perception. *Nature Neuroscience, 3*, 759–763.

Kelly, A. M. C., & Garavan, H. (2005). Human functional neuroimaging of brain changes associated with practice. *Cerebral Cortex, 15,* 1089–1102

Knowlton, B. J., & Squire, L. H. (1993). The learning of categories: Parallel brain systems for item memory and category knowledge. *Science, 262,* 1747–1749.

Larsen, H., van der Zwaluw, C. S., Overbeek, G., Granic, I., Franke, B., & Engels, C. M. E. (2010). A variable-number-of-tandem-repeats polymorphism in the dopamine d4 receptor gene affects social adaptation of alcohol use: investigation of a gene–environment interaction. *Psychological Science, 21,* 1064–1068.

McNamara, A., Tegenthoff, M., Hubert, D., Buchel, C., Binkofski, F., & Ragert, P. (2007). Increased functional connectivity is crucial for learning novel muscle synergies. *Neuroimage, 35,* 1211–1218.

NICHD Early Child Care Research Network. (1993). The NICHD Study of Early Child Care: A comprehensive longitudinal study of young children's lives. *ERIC Document Reproduction Service No. ED3530870.*

Nikolaev, A. R., Ivanitsky, G. A., Ivanitsky, A. M., Abdullaev, Y. G., & Posner, M. I. (2001). Short-term correlation between frontal and Wernicke's areas in word association. *Neuroscience Letters, 298,*107–110.

Nisbett, R. E. (2009). *Intelligence and how to get it.* New York: Norton.

Pascual-Leone, A., & Hamilton, R. (2001). The metamodal organization of the brain. *Progress in Brain Research, 134,* 427–445.

Posner, M. I. (1988). What is it to be an expert? In M. T. H. Chi, R. Glaser, & M. J. Farr (Eds.), *The nature of expertise* (pp. xxix–xxxvi). Hillsdale, NJ: Lawrence Erlbaum Associates.

Posner, M. I., & Keele, S. W. (1968). On the genesis of abstract ideas. *Journal of Experimental Psychology, 77,* 353–363.

Posner, M. I., & Patoine, B. (2010). How arts training improves attention and cognition. In D. Gordon (Ed.), *Cerebrum: Emerging in brain science.* Washington, DC: Dana Press.

Posner, M. I., & Raichle, M. E. (1994). *Images of mind.* New York: Scientific American Library.

Posner, M. I., & Rothbart, M. K. (2007). Research on attention networks as a model for the integration of psychological science. *Annals of the Review of Psychology, 58,* 1–23.

Rothbart, M. K., & Rueda, M. R. (2005). The development of effortful control. In U. Mayr, E. Awh, & S. W. Keele (Eds.), *Developing individuality in the human brain: A tribute to Michael I. Posner* (pp. 167–188). Washington, DC: American Psychological Association.

Rothbart, M. K., Sheese, B. E., Rueda, M. R., & Posner, M. I. (2011). Developing mechanisms of self regulation in early life. *Emotion Review, 3/2,* 207–213.

Sheese, B. E., Rothbart, M. K., Posner, M. I., White, L. K., & Fraundorf, S. H. (2008). Executive attention and self-regulation in infancy. *Infant Behavior and Development, 31,* 501–510.

Sheese, B. E., Rothbart, M. K., Voelker, P., & Posner, M. I. (2012). The dopamine receptor D4 gene 7 repeat allele interacts with parenting quality to predict Effortful Control in four-year-old children. *Child Development Research* vol 2012 ID 863242, 6 pages doi:10.1155/2012/863242

Sheese, B. E., Voelker, P. M., Posner, M. I., & Rothbart, M. K. (2009). Genetic variation influences on the early development of reactive emotions and their regulation by attention. *Cognitive Neuropsychiatry, 14*(4), 332–355.

Sheese, B. E., Voelker, P. M., Rothbart, M. K., & Posner, M. I. (2007). Parenting quality interacts with genetic variations in Dopamine Receptor D4 to influence temperament in early childhood. *Development and Psychopathology, 19,* 1039–1046.

Shimamura, A. P. (1986). Priming effect in amnesia: Evidence for a dissociable memory function. *Quarterly Journal of Experimental Psychology, 38,* 619–644.

Shulman, G. L., Astafiev, S. V., Franke, D., Pope, D. L. W., Snyder, A. Z., McAvoy, M. P., & Corbett, M. (2009). Interaction of stimulus-driven reorienting and expectation in ventral and dorsal frontoparietal and basal ganglia-cortical networks. *Journal of Neuroscience, 29,* 4392–4407.

Smith, E. E. (2008). The case for implicit category learning. *Cognitive, Affective and Behavioral Neuroscience, 8,* 3–16.

Tanaka, J. W., & Curran, T. (2001). A neural basis for expert object recognition. *Psychological Science, 12,* 43–47.

Tang, Y-Y., Lu, Q., Geng, X., Stein, E. A., Yang, Y., & Posner, M. I. (2010). Short term mental training induces white-matter changes in the anterior cingulate. *PNAS, 3/2,* 207–213.

Tang, Y-Y., Lu, O., Hu, B., Feng, S., Wang, Y., Zhao, Q., Rothbart, M. K., Tan, L-H., & Posner, M. I. (in process). Comparison of physical exercise with meditation on an aging population.

Tang, Y-Y., Ma, Y., Wang, J., Fan, Y., Feng, S., Lu, Q., Yu, K., Sui, D., Rothbart, M. K., Fan, M., & Posner, M. I. (2007). Short-term meditation training improves attention and self-regulation. *Proceedings of National Academy of Sciences of the USA, 104,* 17152–17156.

van IJzendoorn, M. H., & Bakermans-Kranenburg, M. J. (2006). DRD4 7-repeat polymorphism moderates the association between maternal unresolved loss or trauma and infant disorganization. *Attachment and Human Development, 8,* 291–307.

Voelker, P., Sheese, B. E., Rothbart, M. K., & Posner, M. I. (2009). Variations in catechol-o-methyltransferase gene interact with parenting to influence attention in early development. *Neuroscience, 16*(1), 121–130.

Wang, E. T., Ding, Y-C., Flodman, P, Kidd, J. R., Kidd, K. K., Grady, D. L. et al. (2004). The genetic architecture of selection at the human dopamine receptor D4 (DRD4) gene locus. *The American Journal of Human Genetics, 74,* 931–944.

Wang, E. T., Kodama, G., Baldi, P., & Moyzis, R. K. (2006). Global landscape of recent inferred Darwinian selection for *Homo sapiens. Proceedings of the National Academy of Sciences, 103,* 135–140.

Whittle, S. L., Yucel, M., Fornito, A., Barrett, A. B., Wood, S. J., Lubman, D. I., Simmons, J., Pantelis, D. I., & Allen, N. B. (2008). Neuroanatomical correlates of temperament in early adolescents. *Journal of American Academy of Child and Adolescent Psychiatry, 47,* 682–693.

12

Category-Selective Recruitment of the Fusiform Gyrus with Chess Expertise

GIULIA RIGHI

Children's Hospital Boston, USA

MICHAEL J. TARR

Carnegie Mellon University, USA

ASHLEY KINGON

Columbia University, NY, USA

INTRODUCTION

Chess Cognition

*T*he game of chess has been of interest to cognitive scientists for over five decades in part because proficiency at playing chess recruits both expert cognitive and perceptual knowledge (De Groot, 1978). Much of the research in chess cognition has been directed at understanding the cognitive mechanisms deployed by chess masters when faced with specific chessboard con-figurations. For example, De Groot (1978) examined differences between weak players and master players and found that both categories of players mentally search approximately the same number of possible moves, but that the experts are capable of selecting better moves more quickly. One putative mechanism for this observed difference may lie in the fact that chess masters are very accurate at reconstructing chess piece positions, even after viewing chessboards for durations as short as 5 seconds. In a seminal study, Chase and Simon (1973) investigated this phenomenon in detail. Their goal was to characterize the perceptual and cognitive strategies used by expert chess players when encoding chessboards into memory. To address this question they created two main tasks: a *perceptual* task, asking subjects to reconstruct chessboard configurations in plain view using glances as a measure of chunking, and a *memory* task, asking subjects to reconstruct chessboard configurations from memory, using the clustering and accuracy in recall as a measure of chunking. To assess the importance of previous chess knowledge/ expertise, Chase and Simon used both valid chessboard configurations, subconfigurations of which were likely to be familiar to the experienced players, and scrambled or "invalid" chessboard configurations, created by randomly placing the game pieces on a chessboard. They found that the more experienced the player, the larger the size—in terms of the number of pieces—of the encoded mental "chunks," even if the total number of chunks remained roughly consistent with the typical 7 ± 2 working memory span (Miller, 1956). Chase and Simon also observed that this experience-predicated advantage mostly disappeared with invalid chessboard configurations, presumably because the experts did not have any useful knowledge regarding the nominal game positions encountered in this condition (although later research showed that experts maintain a small but reliable advantage with random positions; Gobet & Simon, 1996a, 1996b).

To elaborate on this "chunking model hypothesis" (Chase & Simon, 1973), Gobet and Simon (1996a) explored behavioral differences between the processing of valid and invalid chess configurations, asking what sort of information is available in a chunk for it to be accurately recalled. This question provides some insight on whether chess expertise is based on perceptual and/or on conceptual knowledge. They visually manipulated chessboards by mirroring the position of the pieces along the horizontal axis, along the vertical axis, or with respect to the center-point of the chessboard. The critical question is whether the spatial location of a given "chunk" on the chessboard is necessary for the recognition of that chunk. Gobet and Simon used a position-reconstruction task. Given Chase and Simon's results (1973), one would expect experts to perform better in this task in that they should be able to rely on a fewer number of pieces in accessing full chunk templates (and consequently reconstruct the chunk correctly). Not surprisingly, they found that the stronger chess players had better recall across all conditions as compared to weaker players, and that chunk size was larger for those players with better reconstruction performance. Interestingly, Gobet and Simon also observed that subjects performed more poorly with the chessboards that were mirrored across the vertical axis or the center-point. These results suggest that the specific spatial locations of chess pieces *as a chunk* play a role in the retrieval of chunk templates, and that conceptual knowledge of the relations between pieces is not enough for successful recall. Gobet and Simon (1996a) concluded that chess knowledge encodes both the type and the precise location of each piece. In other words, chess experts view a chessboard as a collection of chunks that are defined both by the types of pieces and by the spatial relations among them, as well as their overall position in the context of a chessboard.

The importance of processing the spatial relations between elements of a complex stimulus is by no means unique to chess. Most saliently, this type of "holistic" or configural processing strategy has been implicated in face recognition (for a review, see Maurer et al., 2002). Numerous studies of face processing have found that subjects pay attention to both the specific features within a face and to the configuration of these facial features. Moreover, configural processing is critical in successful face recognition (e.g., Le Grand et al., 2001; Mondloch et al., 2002). In other words, face "experts" (most people in the world) rely on configural processing over and above the processing of individual facial features.

Gobet and Simon's findings and the extant literature on face processing, taken together, suggest that the *perceptual* processing of chess configurations in expert players may be based on some of the same "holistic" or "configural" mechanisms elucidated in face processing (Gauthier & Tarr, 2002; Rotshtein et al., 2007). As such, one might also predict that similar brain mechanisms are recruited by face processing in normal individuals and by chess processing in chess experts.

The Neural Substrates of Chess

In contrast to the many behavioral studies of expertise in chess, there are only a handful of neuroimaging studies exploring the neural bases of chess expertise. Given the ridiculously large number of studies that have used fMRI to examine face processing, one might expect somewhat greater interest in perceptual expertise within other domains (for example, see Gauthier et al., 2000). Here we review what is known about the neural bases of chess (primarily using functional magnetic resonance imaging, fMRI).

Atherton and colleagues (2003) tested subjects who had some familiarity with chess but were not experts. In a chess-related condition, they presented subjects with midgame positions on 2-D chessboards and asked them to decide what would be the best move for the "white" player; in a non-chess-related condition, they presented subjects with chessboards containing a similar number of pieces as in the chess-related condition, but in this case the pieces were randomly positioned on the chessboard and subjects were asked to simply find those pieces which were marked with a star. The comparison of these two conditions produced increased activation in the chess-related condition in several posterior brain regions, in particular, bilaterally in the inferior and superior parietal lobes, as well as left lateralized responses in the prefrontal cortex.

This study provides some general idea of which brain regions might be recruited when subjects are asked to reason about chess. However, the difference between the two conditions—one involving reasoning about a complex, rule-based domain, and one involving simple perceptual pattern recognition—leaves open the possibility that these neural substrates are generic and say little about the specific of information processing in chess. In contrast, an earlier PET study (Nichelli et al., 1994) compared four tasks, two not related directly to playing chess and two directly related to playing chess, in a group of chess players who participated in tournaments with regularity. The two non-chess tasks were: judging whether any pieces were located on either the black or white squares on a chessboard; or judging the color of a target chess piece marked with an "X." The two chess-specific tasks were: analyzing the validity of a specific move in a game position; or judging whether a checkmate could be made in a given game position. Pairwise comparisons among these four conditions reveals a network of regions that were sensitive to different aspects of chess playing, including increased activation in the left temporal lobe and hippocampus in response to the retrieval of rules of the game, and increased activation in the occipito-parietal junction and the prefrontal cortex for the checkmate judgment.

Finally, in a recent neuroimaging study using fMRI, Campitelli and colleagues (Campitelli et al., 2005) tested novices, as well as two chess experts (a grandmaster and an international chess master), in a memory task that included valid and invalid chess configurations, and also configurations in which chess pieces were replaced by symbols. For the novice subjects, they found that a comparison between chess positions and symbol positions elicited several clusters of neural activation in frontal, parietal and temporal regions, while a comparison between valid and invalid chess positions elicited relatively few clusters of activation. In contrast, the two expert chess players exhibited few differences in neural activation across the conditions employed in the study. Thus, one can reasonably conclude that although chess experts may rely on configural information, they are less sensitive than novices to the *local* appearance of the elements comprising chessboard configurations (e.g., chess pieces versus symbols). At the same time, the authors of this study take the differences between the experts and novices as evidence that "when performing a domain-specific task, experts activate different brain systems from that of novices" (Campitelli et al., 2005, p. 238). While this is almost certainly the case, their study leaves open the question as to *which brain mechanisms are recruited by chess experts within their domain of expertise?*

Two more recent studies have directly addressed this question, investigating the neural mechanisms recruited by chess experts when processing the domain of chess. First, Bilalic et al. (2010) found that chess expertise confers processing advantages for both chess-specific object recognition and chess-specific pattern recognition, with the former showing recruitment of bilateral occipitotemporal junction and the latter showing recruitment of bilateral collateral sulci. Second, Bilalic et al. (2011) found that the fusiform gyrus was more active for chess experts as compared to chess novices, but only when the stimuli were realistic chess boards. Moreover, they found that the higher fusiform gyrus response for chess experts as compared to chess novices was obtained even when the chess board stimuli were shown in control tasks that did not involve domain-specific processing. Thus, as with faces and other domains of visual expertise (Gauthier et al., 1999, 2000), category-selective neural responses appear to arise automatically when exemplars from within the expertise domain are encountered.

In this chapter we also address this question, comparing chess experts to chess novices. However, it is worth emphasizing that our study is not about chess *qua* chess, but rather about how chess expertise relates to a more general cognitive neuroscientific theory of domain-specific processing in perceptual experts (Gauthier, Tarr, & Bub, 2009).

Perceptual Expertise and Neuroimaging

For over five decades psychologists have been interested in understanding how people become "perceptual experts" at identifying exemplars within homogeneous object classes (i.e., dogs, cars, birds, X-ray films, etc.; Harley et al., 2009; Myles-Worsley, Johnston, & Simons, 1988; Palmeri, Wong, & Gauthier, 2004), akin to most individuals' ability to learn and differentiate thousands of faces. Across a wide variety of behavioral and neuroimaging studies, the acquisition of "perceptual expertise" has been associated with a number of specific changes in perception and patterns of neural activation. Of particular relevance with respect to chess is the fact that experts differ from novices in how they visually process stimuli that fall within their domain of expertise. That is, perceptual experts use not only the specific *local* features of an object, but also take into account an object's *global* configuration of those features and their spatial relations. Put another way, as with faces and with chess experts, perceptual experts across many different classes of objects appear to rely on "configural" or "holistic" mechanisms (faces, dogs, cars, novel objects known as "Greebles"; Diamond & Carey, 1986; Gauthier & Tarr, 1997; Gauthier et al., 1998; Tanaka & Taylor, 1991; Tanaka & Farah, 1993; Tanaka & Curran, 2001; Yin, 1969).

At the neural level, it is well established that there exists a "category-selective" brain region for faces within the human visual cortex sometimes referred to as the "Fusiform Face Area" or "FFA" (Kanwisher et al., 1997; Sergent & Signoret, 1992). That is, the FFA—a pea-sized subregion of visual cortex—seems to be preferentially recruited by human faces over and above the neural response seen for non-face objects (oddly, Kanwisher, 2010, has expanded this definition of FFA to include cat faces, but not animal faces more generally). Because of the apparent similarity in perceptual processing between faces and non-face objects, logic dictates that neuroimaging might reveal similarities at the neural level as well. That is, do we observe category-selective subregions within visual cortex for non-face objects in domains of perceptual expertise? Importantly, from a functional point of view, it is possible that the same cognitive principles might govern the acquisition of face and non-face expertise, but that they localize in different regions of the visual cortex (much as orientation-selective columns in V1 are spatially separable, but are governed by the same functional principles; Kamitani & Tong, 2005). Alternatively, it may be that along with sharing similar functional principles, category-selective responses for faces and non-face objects in domains of expertise co-localize to the same spatial location within the visual cortex. A finding consistent with this latter possibility would be strong evidence that face and non-face expertise rely on similar cognitive mechanisms.

Not surprisingly perhaps, tests of these alternatives have been run with somewhat discrepant results and concomitant controversy. That is, although there are several studies in which non-face domains apparently give rise to domain-specific category-selective responses *within the FFA* (Gauthier et al., 1999, 2000; Xu, 2005), there is an on-going debate as to whether such results implicate common functional and neural mechanisms for the expert recognition of faces and non-face objects (Kanwisher, 2010; Tarr & Gauthier, 2000). That being said, for the purposes of our present study, it is worth noting that Gauthier et al. (1999) found that expert-level training with novel objects—Greebles—produced increased category-selective activation in the right FFA (as measured by fMRI). Importantly, this effect was obtained using novel exemplars of Greebles that were not seen during training. Similarly, Gauthier and colleagues (2000) found that bird and car experts also show category-selective responses in the right FFA—again measured by fMRI—but that these responses were proportional to each individual subject's degree of behaviorally-measured expertise. Moreover, this effect was only true for each subject's specific domain of expertise—birds or cars—with no category-selective neural response for the non-expert domain. Finally, Xu (2005) found similar results in fMRI using bird and car images that were designed to be less "face-like" (for more on the issue of what "face-like" might mean, see Sheinberg & Tarr, 2009).

Taken together, these neuroimaging results suggest that neural selectivity in the right fusiform gyrus of human visual cortex may not be specific to one class of objects—faces—but rather may arise due to the sort of processing deployed by perceptual experts in discriminating exemplars within a homogeneous stimulus domain. As such, we hypothesize that the configural processing known to be associated with chess expertise will prompt a similar pattern of neural selectivity for chessboards in the right fusiform gyrus. Moreover, we predict that the strength of this effect will be proportional to one's level of chess expertise/experience.

The Neural Bases of Chess Expertise

The goal of our study is to investigate the neural patterns associated with chess expertise, in particular, as may result from the fact that chess experts apply configural processing in perceiving chessboards. Given the complexity of the game of chess, this question may seem somewhat narrow in scope, but what Simon and colleagues have shown in a variety of studies (Chase & Simon, 1973; Gobet & Simon, 1996a, 1996b) is that the ability to process chessboards in a configural manner is one of the fundamental differences between recreational chess players and chess experts. Moreover, a similar processing strategy has been implicated in face and expert-level object recognition. As such, examining the neural bases of this process is highly informative regarding the general neuro-cognitive mechanisms that are specifically recruited in playing chess.

We compared brain responses across two conditions which are equivalent in terms of stimulus complexity: valid game configurations versus scrambled, invalid game configurations. Moreover, we manipulated the level of expertise in our subject population by testing subjects with different levels of chess-playing experience. Given a good understanding of the neural response patterns in experts when processing objects from their domain of expertise (Gauthier et al., 1999; Gauthier et al., 2000), we expected to find similar patterns of expertise-predicated category-selectivity in chess experts, but only for valid chessboard configurations in that, as reviewed above, prior behavioral work indicates that invalid game configurations disrupt configural processing.

METHODS

Subjects

Sixteen volunteers (9 males/7 females, ranging in age from 19–26) participated in a behavioral experiment in the Tarrlab (Brown University, Providence, RI). All subjects had normal or corrected to normal vision. Subjects' chess playing experience varied from 1 year to 15 years, but none of the subjects were ranked. Nine new volunteers (5 males/4 females, ranging in age from 19–35) participated in a single-session fMRI experiment. The six novice subjects reported chess playing experience ranging from 4 months to 15 years. The three more experienced players were recruited from the local community and in the ELO system were ranked as follows: ELO 1600 (20 years of experience), ELO 1798 (21 years of experience), ELO 1800 (13 years of experience). All subjects had normal or corrected to normal vision, and no history of neurological disorders. All subjects gave informed consent before participating in the study.

Materials

In both the behavioral and scanning sessions of this study we used 3-D chessboards. All the stimuli were created using the graphics program Lightwave 3D® (NewTek, Inc., San Antonio, TX). Each chessboard we created represented a mid-game configuration with the number of pieces on the chessboard ranging from 10–20. All the chessboards were rendered in a frontal view at an angle that approximates the effect of a player looking at a chessboard from above a table (Figure 12.1(a)). The valid game positions were taken from Chess Quizzes in issues of *Chess Magazine* and *Chess Life*. The invalid game positions were created by scrambling the pieces on a chessboard randomly, thereby removing any globally meaningful patterns (Figure 12.1(a)). Critically, invalid chessboards provide a physically-matched control stimuli that falls outside the domain of chess as defined by the rules of chess. Moreover, in contrast to valid chessboards, it is unlikely that experienced chess players will have seen many of the game configurations depicted by invalid chessboards.

Both experiments were run on Apple Macintosh computers (Apple Computer, Cupertino, CA) with the behavioral experiment using PsyScript software (www.psych.lancs.ac.uk/software/psyScript.html), and the neuroimaging experiment using PsyScript (Subjects 1–6) and the Psychophysics Toolbox (psychtoolbox.org; Subjects 7–10; Brainard, 1997; Pelli, 1997) for MATLAB (Mathworks, Natick, MA). MRI Scanning sessions took place at the Brown

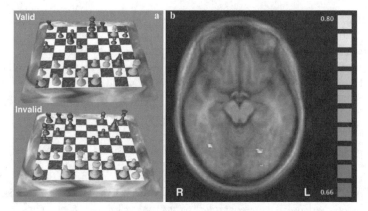

Figure 12.1   Whole-brain regression analysis across all subjects. (a) Examples of Valid and Invalid chessboard configurations used as stimuli. (b) The relationship between chess expertise and neural category selectivity in the fusiform was assessed by regressing the Valid vs. Invalid contrast against years of experience playing chess. This ANCOVA included our entire heterogeneous population of nine subjects who had between 0 and 19 years of experience. The resulting spatial map was thresholded at $p < 0.005$ and $r > 0.8$ with minimum cluster size set to 50 contiguous voxels (1 mm^3). This slice through the ventral pathway shows the only significant clusters, both of which are located within the fusiform gyrus. The right hemisphere cluster is located at: x = 35, y = –58, z = –10 (Talairach coordinates), with a mean voxel correlation of $r = 0.86$. The left hemisphere cluster is located at: x = –23, y = –65, z = –10, with a mean voxel correlation of $r = 0.88$.

MRI research facility (MRF) at the Memorial Hospital of Rhode Island (MHRI) using a 1.5T Siemens Magneton Symphony scanner. Behavioral stimuli were shown on a standard Apple CRT monitor, while the MRI stimuli were projected onto a screen that was viewed through a mirror placed in the headcoil or through MRI-safe goggles. Responses were given on a keypad strapped to the right hand of the subjects, and transmitted via fiber-optic to a response box located in the scanner control room.

Behavioral Experiment

Subjects participated in two behavioral tasks. In the first task, subjects judged the winner for a visually-presented mid-game chessboard. They were told that it was the white player's turn to move, and that they were viewing the position from the side of the white player. Eighty trials were divided into 40 valid chessboards and 40 invalid chessboards. Subjects viewed each chessboard for 7 seconds and had unlimited time to make their response on a keyboard. Although the invalid chessboards did not have a valid answer, subjects were told to provide a response even if they believed the current chessboard did not offer a valid answer. This was done to ensure that subjects carefully attended to and examined each of the chessboards regardless of whether they were valid or invalid.

Upon completing this "who is winning?" task, subjects were run in a recognition memory task in which they were presented with some of the same mid-game chessboards. In this task they decided whether or not they had seen each particular chessboard in the previous task. Eighty trials were divided into 40 old chessboards—shown during the "who is winning?" task and 40 new chessboards; for each of these two conditions, 20 chessboards were valid and 20 were invalid. Chessboards were shown for 7 seconds; subjects had unlimited time to make their response using the keyboard. Subjects were told to provide an answer for every trial, even if they had to guess. Note that prior to this second task, subjects were not aware that their memory for the chessboards shown in the first task would be tested. Following the completion of both tasks, subjects answered a questionnaire regarding their chess playing experience.

fMRI Experiment

Scanning Parameters   High-resolution volumetric MR images were acquired using a T1-weighted Siemens MPRAGE sequence (TR = 1900 ms, TE = 1.14, 4.14 ms, flipangle = 15°, 160 slices), lasting 7 min and 7 s. BOLD-contrast functional images were acquired using a T2*-weighted echoplanar sequence consisting of 48 slices with isotropic voxels of 3x3x3 mm (TR = 3840 ms, TE = 38 ms, flipangle = 90°). We also inserted four test volumes at the beginning of each scanning session, which were discarded from the analyses.

fMRI Tasks

Nine subjects participated in one MRI scanning session each. Six of the nine subjects completed the same two tasks described in the behavioral experiment, while, as detailed below, the remaining three subjects followed a slightly different design. That is, the first six subjects ran in a 1.5 hr session comprised of the "who is winning?" task followed by the recognition memory task as described above. On each trial across both tasks a chessboard appeared on the screen for 2 TRs (7680 ms) and subjects had an interval of 2 TRs to make a response once the stimulus disappeared. The "who is winning?" task comprised 100 trials divided into 5 runs, while the recognition memory task comprised 68 trials divided into 4 runs. The materials and distribution of stimuli were identical to that used in the behavioral experiment described above. Due to technical constraints, the final three subjects participated in a somewhat shorter, 45-minute MRI scanning session, in which we replaced the "who is winning?" task with two tasks that required no knowledge of chess—passive viewing of chessboards and counting white pawns on chessboards—again followed by the same recognition memory task. This was done to ensure that any novice–expert differences observed in our analysis were not simply due to the novices' inability to perform the "who is winning?" task (in that someone without knowledge regarding the rules of chess might have no basis for judging whether white or black was winning in an ongoing chess game). The passive viewing and counting pawns tasks comprised 40 trials—20 valid chessboards and 20 invalid chessboards—each divided into 2 runs, with chessboards presented in random order. For these two tasks each chessboard was presented for 2 TRs, followed by a 2 TR response interval, thus each trial lasted 15,360 ms; that is, a slow event-related design. Subjects were told to respond as quickly and as accurately as possible once the chessboard appeared on the screen. Note that no chessboards were repeated across these two tasks.

Following each MRI scanning session, all nine subjects completed a questionnaire regarding their chess playing experience.

DATA ANALYSIS

fMRI Data

Functional data were analyzed using the general linear model for event-related designs in BrainVoyager QX 1.4 (Brain Innovation B.V., The Netherlands). Before proceeding with statistical analysis, the data were motion corrected using trilinear interpolation to the first volume of each BOLD run, slice-acquisition time corrected, and temporally filtered with a high pass filter with three/cycles per point. Both anatomical and functional images were normalized to Talairach space. Each contrast hypothesis was tested by applying subtractions to the linear model for each condition, producing t-statistics for each voxel. Regions of interest (ROIs) were experimentally defined by looking at clusters of a minimum of 70 contiguous voxels with $p < 0.05$, corrected for multiple comparisons. Within these ROIs we looked at the BOLD percent signal change over time. We also performed an ANCOVA analysis (per BrainVoyager's terminology—see http://support.brainvoyager.com/functional-analysis-statistics/37-second-level-statistics/241-how-to-run-a-correlation-in-brainvoyagers-ancova-tool.html) to identify those regions where higher activation correlated with *years of chess experience*, obtaining r-value statistical maps.

RESULTS

Behavioral Results

In order to assess chess playing skill, we employed a recognition memory paradigm using chessboards. As suggested by Goldin (1979), memory for specific chessboards—as measured in an old–new recognition task—is likely to be sensitive to an individual's ability to efficiently encode in-progress games. This is presumably driven in large part by the spatial and relational complexity of chessboard configurations.

To establish baseline expertise level, for the old–new recognition task we computed three separate d-primes for each subject: sensitivity for valid chessboards, invalid chessboards, or these valid and invalid chessboards combined. We then correlated these measures with each subject's self-reported years of experience playing chess. Although it has been suggested that years of experience are not a perfect measure of expertise, the subjects who participated in our behavioral experiment did not have chess rankings, nor could we readily assess their expertise with an independent task. Indeed, one might argue that for a difficult domain such as chess, direct assessments of expertise truncate/collapse novice players in that any metric sufficiently sensitive to differentiate between high levels of skill will be insensitive to subtle differences between novices. Thus, we chose to rely on years of chess playing experience.

In the recognition memory task, individual d-primes for the valid chessboard condition ranged from -0.44 to 0.70, while d-primes for invalid chessboards ranged from -0.06 to 2.10. Overall, our subjects were actually better at remembering invalid configurations; this was true regardless of an individual's skill level in that the *difference* between valid and invalid chessboards did not correlate significantly with years of experience, $r = 0.10$, *ns*. We reasoned that this was due to the fact that our subjects, all of whom had played chess for at least one year, may have been struck by the oddity of the invalid positions and, thus, in deploying additional attention to these unusual stimuli were more likely to correctly identify invalid chessboards as old/studied independently of the number of valid subconfigurations. If the valid and invalid conditions are analyzed separately, the correlations with years of experience are $r = 0.58$, $p < .05$, for the valid chessboards, and $r = 0.42$, $p < .05$, for the invalid chessboards. Overall performance—valid and invalid chessboards combined—showed a somewhat higher correlation of $r = 0.78$, $p < 0.05$, with years of experience, most likely indicating that the greater power afforded by combining trials allowed us to better assess each individual's chess abilities. Overall we found that subjects who had more experience playing chess were better at recognizing studied chessboards, regardless of whether the chessboards were valid and invalid. This finding is in agreement with prior work showing only minimal differences between recognition memory performance on valid and invalid chessboards (Goldin 1979; Saariluoma, 1984), despite differences being observed when chessboard recall paradigms are used (Chase & Simon, 1973).

fMRI Results

Based on recent studies of face processing that have compared intact to scrambled faces (Clark et al., 1996; Puce et al., 1996), as well as earlier studies of chess expertise (Chase & Simon, 1973; Gobet & Simon, 1996a), we employed a comparison between the brain responses to valid and invalid game configurations across the "who is winning?" and counting pawns tasks.

In a first analysis, we computed statistical t maps for two groups of subjects, binned into novice (n = 4) and expert (n = 3) players based on years of experience (with means of 1.13 and 14.3 years of experience, respectively). Two players of intermediate skill level (mean of 7.5 years of experience) were excluded from this analysis because it was unclear whether they were more appropriately considered novices or experts, and as a separate group, there was insufficient power to obtain reliable results. Note that the criteria for our expert players were that they were ranked and frequently played in tournaments; the two excluded intermediate players all reported playing chess as a pastime without having actively studied the game; and our novice players knew almost nothing about chess other than the basic rules of play.

The two t maps were thresholded with $p < 0.05$ *corrected*, with the minimum cluster size of 70 mm^3 voxels. Although we were primarily interested in examining neural activation in visual areas, specifically the medial fusiform gyrus, there were a large number of other brain regions that showed a significant response in the Valid–Invalid comparison. Tables 12.1 and 12.2 show all of the clusters that met our criteria for each of the novice and expert subject groups, respectively. Critically, we did not observe any significant clusters of neural activation located within the fusiform gyrus for novices (Table 12.1). In contrast, this same analysis revealed significant regions of interest within the right fusiform gyrus for experts (Table 12.2).

TABLE 12.1   Significant Clusters for Novices. A whole-brain GLM analysis was used to compare activation for Valid versus Invalid chessboards for three chess novices. These clusters were thresholded at $p < 0.05$, with a minimum cluster size of 70 contiguous voxels (1 mm^3). t refers to the average t statistic across all voxels in a given cluster

Cortical regions (BA)	Cluster size	Talairach coordinates		
		t	x	y	z
Occipital: L Lingual gyrus (18)	101	5.49	−27	−76	−7
R Middle occipital gyrus (19)	75	5.71	39	−72	2
Temporal: R Superior temporal gyrus (13)	120	12.06	46	−42	17
Parietal: R Precuneus (7)	82	5.9	18	−60	35
R Postcentral gyrus	133	6.55	40	−19	26
L Postcentral gyrus (4)	131	6.13	−54	−15	41
Frontal: R Middle frontal gyrus (9)	225	8.19	46	7	36
L Cingulate gyrus (32)	81	4.28	−11	19	32
L Superior frontal gyrus (8)	173	5.69	−12	37	51
L Superior frontal gyrus (6)	71	4.54	−11	14	53
L Precentral gyrus (6)	105	4.01	−27	−15	59
L Medial frontal gyrus (6)	242	5.99	−1	−8	64
L Superior frontal gyrus (9)	165	5.48	−12	43	31

Note: Novices (GLM Valid – Invalid; n = 3).

TABLE 12.2   Significant Clusters for Experts. A whole-brain GLM analysis was used to compare activation for Valid versus Invalid chessboards for four chess experts. These clusters were thresholded at $p < 0.05$, with a minimum cluster size of 70 contiguous voxels (1 mm^3). t refers to the average t statistic across all voxels in a given cluster

Cortical regions (BA)	Cluster size	Talairach coordinates			
		t	x	y	z
Occipital: R Inferior Occipital gyrus (18)	291	3.99	28	− 85	− 14
R Superior Occipital gyrus	100	3.46	31	− 77	28
R Lingual gyrus	176	3.21	19	− 82	− 5
R Lingual gyrus (18)	159	2.93	21	− 80	− 2
R Middle Occipital gyrus (18)	142	3.41	34	− 81	0
L Lingual Gyrus (18)	240	3.38	− 15	− 84	− 11
L Middle Occipital gyrus	107	3.97	− 27	− 63	4
L Middle Occipital gyrus (18)	116	3.03	− 25	− 88	17
Temporal: R Fusiform gyrus	71	3.03	31	− 61	− 9
R Parahippocampal gyrus (30)	77	2.75	21	− 36	3
R Middle Temporal gyrus (21)	85	2.60	62	− 19	− 10
L Inferior Temporal gyrus (20)	137	3.37	− 50	− 55	− 13
L Middle Temporal gyrus (39)	164	3.38	− 48	− 64	24
L Middle Temporal gyrus (37)	146	3.93	− 55	− 57	− 2
L Middle Temporal gyrus	144	3.74	− 48	− 20	− 6
L Parahippocampal gyrus (37)	115	4.82	− 29	− 41	− 7
Parietal: R Precuneus (7)	379	3.86	28	− 55	48
Frontal: R Inferior Frontal gyrus (47)	97	3.16	32	29	− 10
R Medial Frontal gyrus	243	2.92	10	44	− 10
R Medial Frontal gyrus	209	2.95	11	43	− 10
R Superior Frontal gyrus (9)	200	3.64	11	55	21
R Superior frontal gyrus (9)	88	3.91	31	44	26
R Middle Frontal gyrus (9)	309	3.15	50	17	34
L Inferior Frontal gyrus (47)	138	3.36	− 43	22	− 2
L Superior Frontal gyrus (8)	375	3.28	− 4	43	47
L Medial Frontal gyrus (6)	92	3.24	− 14	3	62

Note: Experts (GLM Valid − Invalid; n = 4).

Given the heterogeneity of our subjects with respect to their chess playing skills, a more sensitive analysis—that also includes players of intermediate skill level—may be realized by employing a whole-brain regression analysis (referred to as an ANCOVA in BrainVoyager) to identify those voxels in which individual subjects' BOLD activations for Valid–Invalid contrast are significantly correlated with their individual years of chess playing experience. That is, in an assumption-free manner, this analysis identifies the brain regions—across the entire brain—in which the neural response to valid chessboards relative to invalid chessboards is strongly correlated with expertise (Table 12.3). Again, we were primarily interested in regions located within the ventral visual pathway. As shown in Figure 12.1(b), this whole-brain regression reveals significant clusters in the right medial fusiform, $r = .86$, $p < 0.003$, and the left medial fusiform, $r = 0.88$, $p < 0.002$.

TABLE 12.3   Whole-Brain Regression Analysis across All Subjects. The relationship between chess expertise and neural category selectivity in the fusiform was assessed by regressing the Valid versus Invalid contrast against years of experience playing chess. This ANCOVA included our entire heterogeneous population of nine subjects who had between 0 and 19 years of experience. These clusters were thresholded at $p < 0.005$ and $r > 0.8$ with minimum cluster size set to 50 contiguous voxels (1 mm^3). r refers to the average r value across all voxels in a given cluster

Cortical regions (BA)	Cluster size	t	Talairach coordinates		
			x	y	z
Occipital: L Middle occipital gyrus (18)	183	0.89	− 33	− 92	1
L Lingual gyrus	79	0.89	− 6	− 65	1
L Cuneus (18)	86	0.93	− 5	− 71	18
Temporal: R Fusiform gyrus (37)	56	0.86	35	− 58	− 10
R Inferior temporal (20)	65	0.92	59	− 24	− 19
L Fusiform gyrus (19)	56	0.88	− 23	− 65	− 10
L Superior temporal (13)	113	0.92	− 39	− 45	23
Parietal: R Precuneus (7)	91	0.81	22	− 56	51
R Postcentral gyrus (43)	67	0.87	54	− 13	14
R Postcentral gyrus (2)	81	0.92	37	− 29	39
R Inferior parietal lobule (39)	284	0.92	37	− 61	41
L Precuneus (7)	399	0.85	− 3	− 62	47
L Inferior parietal lobule (40)	159	0.86	− 33	− 49	42
Frontal: R Cingulate gyrus (31)	104	0.89	2	− 32	36
R Cingulate gyrus (32)	83	0.84	5	19	34
R Precentral gyrus (6)	202	0.89	47	− 6	60
R Superior frontal gyrus (6)	245	0.88	22	8	54
R Medial frontal gyrus (9)	124	0.85	25	37	15
L Cingulate gyrus (24)	81	0.80	− 17	− 18	44

Note: Valid –Invalid Regressed Against Years of Experience.

DISCUSSION

The study of expert-level cognitive processing has a long tradition within the field of cognitive science. The advent of modern neuroimaging methods—notably, fMRI—has sparked renewed interest in this topic, in large part because of the expertise framework's potential to account for category-selective neural responses in ventral visual areas (Bukach et al., 2006; Gauthier et al., 2009; Tarr & Gauthier, 2000). Here we build on the idea that the ability to discriminate between exemplars within a homogeneous object category recruits a network of neural and functional processes also implicated in face individuation. Of note, it is not expertise *per se* that is considered the common thread here, but rather the fact that perceptual expertise of this sort—with both faces and non-face objects—recruits configural/holistic mechanisms in which local perceptual features are spatially related to one another to form a larger whole. Based on the extant body of work on chess, we posited that similar configural/holistic processing is recruited by chess experts when processing (valid) chessboards. That is, skilled chess players relate the spatial positions of local features—chess pieces—to one another in order to discriminate between the complex game configurations depicted by chessboards.

Here we investigated the neural bases of these perceptual processes and related the obtained neural response patterns to each individual player's level of chess expertise, much as other researchers have related behaviorally-measured bird or car expertise to category-selective neural responses within the ventral visual pathway (Gauthier et al., 2000; Xu, 2005). For all these domains of perceptual expertise the underlying functional assumption is that greater skill within the domain leads to more configural/holistic processing—a connection often made within the domain of face recognition (Yin, 1969; Tanaka, 2001). From a theoretical standpoint, our study also leverages the established link between configural processing elicited by perceptual expertise and focal activation in fusiform gyrus (Gauthier & Tarr, 2002; Rotshtein et al., 2007). In that skillfully playing chess requires identifying complex spatial relationships between pieces, we hypothesized that processing chessboards would recruit the right fusiform gyrus of the human ventral visual pathway, and that this category-selective effect would be modulated by an individual's level of chess expertise.[1] Moreover, we postulated that such effects should manifest more in valid game configurations in that the global configural properties of chessboards become meaningless for invalid, scrambled chessboards (much as scrambling a face disrupts configural processing). To reiterate, our predictions are based on the extensive perceptual expertise literature suggesting that activation in the fusiform gyrus is triggered by processing strategies that develop with expertise,

---

1 It is worth noting that although the subjects in our study showed a very wide range of chess playing abilities, we were unable to recruit and test players at the master and grandmaster level; we expect that such highly proficient players would show even more pronounced expertise-modulated neural effects.

rather than by the class of stimuli *per se* (Gauthier et al., 1999; Gauthier et al., 2009). Here we simply extended this model by investigating category selectivity for a class of stimuli—chessboards—that have little in common, from the standpoint of object shape, with the object classes used in earlier studies.

Our results support these conjectures. In particular, when the valid versus invalid chessboard comparison in fMRI is regressed against each individual subject's years of chess playing experience, we find focal regions of neural activation within the fusiform gyrus bilaterally, with the magnitude of activation driven by an individual's level of expertise. First and foremost, this result is consistent with the idea that experienced chess players recruit different perceptual mechanisms when compared to less experienced players. Second, that this pattern emerges from a valid versus invalid comparison—analogous to the oft-used intact versus scrambled faces comparison—also supports our hypothesis that chess expertise recruits configural perceptual and neural mechanisms.

It is worth noting that differential sensitivity to valid and invalid chessboards was observed also in the middle occipital region, which has also been previously associated with category-selective responses (Rossion et al., 2003). In our study, activation in the middle occipital region also seems to be modulated by the level of expertise. More specifically, novices show only one small significant cluster in this region, while experts, both in the standard GLM (Table 12.2) and in the regression analysis (Table 12.3), show a somewhat broader occipital response. One possibility is that these category-selective occipital responses are associated with the early visual detection of expert objects domains and facilitate rapid, specialized processing (e.g., deployment of configural mechanisms).

Turning away from the narrow question of category-selectivity in the ventral visual pathway of human cortex, one of the many reasons why chess is an interesting domain of study is that it is a complex game that recruits both perceptual and cognitive skills (de Groot, 1978). Thus, we should consider some of the other significant clusters of activation beyond those found in ventral temporal cortex (see Tables 12.1, 12.2 and 12.3). Previous studies examining the neural substrates recruited for chess have also observed recruitment of parietal and frontal regions in a variety of tasks (Atherton et al., 2003; Campitelli et al., 2005; Campitelli et al., 2007).

In the present study we found increased activation in several portions of the parietal lobe, including the inferior parietal lobule (IPL) and the precuneus. Increased activation in these regions was observed in both the traditional GLM analysis, showing more extensive clusters of activations for experts compared to novices, and in our regression analysis. Similar patterns of activation in these regions have also been observed by Atherton and colleagues (2003) and by Campitelli and colleagues (2005). These regions may be recruited because of the demands placed on spatial working memory by chess—encoding the locations of many chess pieces (Atherton et al., 2003; Chafee & Goldman-Rakic, 1998). Finally, the recruitment of the IPL may be related to the maintenance of chess configurations in working memory (Chafee & Goldman-Rakic, 1998):

although our subjects were not explicitly asked to memorize the chessboards during the scanning session, it is plausible that they may have tried to maintain each chessboard in working memory in order to perform the tasks presented to them.

Studies investigating the neural substrates of chess have also highlighted activation in the prefrontal cortex. Campitelli and colleagues (2005) found clusters of activation in the superior frontal gyrus (SFG) and the medial frontal gyrus (MFG) when comparing valid chess positions to scrambled chess positions during a match-to-sample task. In our study we observe significant recruitment of the SFG and MFG by both novices and experts, but with slightly different patterns of responses. In our novice subjects these clusters are almost all left lateralized. This may be the result of processing strategies that rely on verbalization (Campitelli et al., 2005). In contrast, our expert subjects showed significant left *and* right activity in prefrontal cortex (Table 12.2), which may be the result of experts recruiting more complex processing strategies that rely on both verbalization but also possibly on more abstract encoding (Tulving et al., 1994). Moreover, when neural responses are regressed against years of experience, thereby partialing out those regions that are active regardless of expertise, we find recruitment of almost exclusively right frontal regions by experts (Table 12.3).

Finally, our results are very consistent with those of Bilalić et al. (2010, 2011). In particular, much as we report here, Bilalić et al. (2011) found that the fusiform gyrus was selectivity recruited when viewing chess boards – regardless of task – but only for chess experts and not for chess novices. Similarly, they likewise conclude that this region of human visual cortex mediates the "automatic holistic processing of any highly familiar multipart visual input" (Bilalić et al., 2011).

To summarize, consistent with behavioral data indicating both perceptual and cognitive components to chess expertise, fMRI reveals chess-related BOLD responses in the human ventral object pathway, in parietal regions, and in the frontal lobes, all of which are correlated with our subjects' years of experience playing chess. Returning to our main point, classic studies of chess experts have found that these experts rely on configural processes. As such, we hypothesized that the category-selective region of the middle fusiform gyrus associated with configural processing in other domains of perceptual expertise would be recruited to a greater or lesser extent depending on a subject's level of chess expertise, that is, more in chess experts than in chess novices. This prediction is consistent with other studies of non-face expertise in which configural processes seem to be required in order to attain expert-level performance (Gauthier et al., 1998). Our results bear out this prediction, revealing expertise-correlated focal responses in the medial fusiform gyrus, bilaterally, as well as in occipital regions also implicated in expert-level processing. More generally, these findings lend further support to the idea that category-selectivity in the human ventral visual pathway arises because of task demands rather than stimulus geometry (Gauthier et al., 2009). Interpretation of significant expertise-correlated clusters in both parietal and frontal lobes is somewhat less obvious in that few studies of perceptual expertise and category-selectivity have focused on these regions. Moreover, chess is a rather unique domain in that it recruits both rule-based knowledge and perceptual components. Thus, other domains of expertise may share perceptual processing with chess, but not all or any of the putative expertise-related cognitive mechanisms that may exist.

REFERENCES

Atherton, M., Zhuang, J., Bart, W. M., Hu, X., & He, S. (2003). A functional MRI study of high level cognition: The game of chess. *Cognitive Brain Research, 16,* 26–31.

Brainard, D. H. (1997). The psychophysics toolbox. *Spatial Vision, 10,* 433–436.

Bilalić, M., Langner, R., Erb, M., & Grodd, W. (2010). Mechanisms and neural basis of object and pattern recognition: A study with chess experts. *Journal of Experimental Psychology. General, 139*(4), 728–742. doi:10.1037/a0020756

Bilalić, M., Langner, R., Ulrich, R., & Grodd, W. (2011). Many faces of expertise: Fusiform face area in chess experts and novices. *The Journal of Neuroscience, 31*(28), 10206–10214.

Bukach, C. M., Gauthier, I., & Tarr, M. J. (2006). Beyond faces and modularity: The power of an expertise framework. *Trends in Cognitive Science, 10*(4), 159–166.

Campitelli, G. J., Gobet, F., Head, K., Buckley, M., & Parker, A. (2007). Brain localization of memory chunks in chess players. *International Journal of Neuroscience, 117,* 1641–1659.

Campitelli, G. J, Gobet, F., & Parker, A. (2005). Structure and stimulus familiarity: A study of memory in chess-players with functional magnetic resonance imaging. *Spanish Journal of Psychology, 8,* 238–245.

Chafee, M. V., & Goldman-Rakic, P. S. (1998). Matching patterns of activity in primate prefrontal area 8a and parietal area 7ip neurons during a spatial working memory task. *Journal of Neurophysiology, 79*(6), 2919–2940.

Chase, W. G., & Simon, H. A. (1973). Recall of rapidly presented random chess positions is a function of skill. *Psychonomic Bulletin and Review, 3*(2), 159–163.

Clark, V. P., Keil, K., Maisog, J. M., Courtney, S., Ungerleider, L. G., & Haxby, J. V. (1996). Functional magnetic resonance imaging of human visual cortex during face matching: A comparison with positron emission tomography. *Neuroimage, 4*(1), 1–15.

De Groot, A. D. (1978). *Thought and choice in chess* (2nd ed.). The Hague: Mouton.

Diamond, R., & Carey, S. (1986). Why faces are and are not special: An effect of expertise. *Journal of Experimental Psychology: General, 115*(2), 107–117.

Gauthier, I., Skudlarski P., Gore, J. C., & Anderson, A. W. (2000). Expertise for cars and birds recruits brain areas involved in face recognition. *Nature neuroscience, 3*(2), 191–197.

Gauthier, I., & Tarr, M. J. (1997). Becoming a "Greeble" expert: Exploring mechanisms for face recognition. *Vision Research, 37*(12), 1673–1682.

Gauthier, I., & Tarr, M. J. (2002). Unraveling mechanisms for expert object recognition: Bridging brain activity and behavior. *Journal of Experimental Psychology, 28*(2), 431–446.

Gauthier, I., Tarr, M. J., Anderson, A. W., Skudlarski, P., & Gore, J. C. (1999). Activation of the middle fusiform "face area" increases with expertise in recognizing novel objects. *Nature Neuroscience, 2*(6), 568–573.

Gauthier, I., Tarr, M. J., & Bub, D. (2009). *Perceptual expertise: Bridging brain and behavior.* New York, NY: Oxford University Press.

Gauthier, I., Williams, P., Tarr, M. J., & Tanaka, J. (1998). Training "Greeble" experts: A framework for studying expert object recognition processes. *Vision Research, 38*(15–16), 2401–2428.

Gobet, F., & Simon, H. A. (1996a). Recall of random and distorted chess positions: Implications for the theory of expertise. *Memory and Cognition, 24*(4), 493–503.

Gobet, F., & Simon, H. A. (1996b). Templates in chess memory: A mechanism for recalling several boards. *Cognitive Psychology, 31,* 1–40.

Goldin, S. E. (1979). Recognition memory for chess positions: Some preliminary research. *American Journal of Psychology, 92,* 19–31.

Harley, E. M., Pope, W. B., Villablanca, J. P., Mumford, J., Suh, R., Mazziotta, J. C., et al. (2009). Engagement of fusiform cortex and disengagement of lateral occipital cortex in the acquisition of radiological expertise. *Cerebral Cortex, 19*(11), 2746–2754.

Kamitani, Y., & Tong, F. (2005). Decoding the visual and subjective contents of the human brain. *Nature Neuroscience, 8*(5), 679–685.

Kanwisher, N. (2010). Functional specificity in the human brain: A window into the functional architecture of the mind. *Proceedings of the National Academy of Sciences of the USA, 107*(25), 11163–11170.

Kanwisher, N., McDermott, J., & Chun, M. M. (1997). The fusiform face area: A module in human extrastriate cortex specialized for face perception. *The Journal of Neuroscience, 17*(11), 4302–4311.

Le Grand, R., Mondloch, C. J., Maurer, D., & Brent, H. P. (2001). Neuroperception. Early visual experience and face processing. *Nature, 410*(6831), 890.

Maurer, D., Le Grand. R., & Mondloch, C. J. (2002). The many faces of configural processing. *Trends in Cognitive Science, 6*(6), 255–260.

Miller, G. A. (1956). The magical number seven, plus or minus two: Some limits on our capacity for processing information. *Psychological Review, 63,* 81–97.

Mondloch, C. J., Le Grand, R., & Maurer, D. (2002). Configural face processing develops more slowly than featural face processing. *Perception, 31*(5), 553–566.

Myles-Worsley, M., Johnston, W. A., & Simons, M. A. (1988). The influence of expertise on x-ray image processing. *Journal of Experimental Psychology. Learning, Memory, and Cognition, 14*(3), 553–557.

Nichelli, P., Grafman, J., Pietrini, P., Alway, D., Carton, J. C., & Miletich, R. (1994). Brain activity in chess playing. *Nature, 369,* 191.

Palmeri, T. J., Wong, A. C., & Gauthier, I. (2004). Computational approaches to the development of perceptual expertise. *Trends in Cognitive Sciences, 8*(8), 378–386.

Pelli, D. G. (1997). The VideoToolbox software for visual psychophysics: Transforming numbers into movies. *Spatial Vision, 10,* 437–442.

Puce, A., Allison, T., Gore, J. C., & McCarthy, G. (1996). Face-sensitive regions in human extrastriate cortex studied by functional MRI. *Journal of Neurophysiology, 74*(3), 1192–1200.

Rossion, B., Caldara, R., Seghier, M., Schuller, A. M., Lazeyras, F., & Mayer, E. (2003). A network of occipito-temporal face-sensitive areas besides the right middle fusiform gyrus is necessary for normal face processing. *Brain, 126*(Pt 11), 2381–2395.

Rotshtein, P., Geng, J. J., Driver, J., & Dolan, R. J. (2007). Role of features and second-order spatial relations in face discrimination, face recognition, and individual face skills: Behavioral and functional magnetic resonance imaging data. *Journal of Cognitive Neuroscience, 19*(9), 1435–1452.

Saariluoma, P. (1984). *Coding problem spaces in chess: A psychological study.* Turku: Societas Scientiarum Fennica.

Sergent, J., & Signoret, J. (1992). Varieties of functional deficits in prosopagnosia. *Cerebral Cortex, 2,* 375–388.

Sheinberg, D., & Tarr, M. J. (2009). Objects of expertise. In I. Gauthier, M. J. Tarr, & D. Bub (Eds.), *Perceptual expertise: Bridging brain and behavior.* New York, NY: Oxford University Press.

Tanaka, J. J., & Taylor, M. (1991). Object categories and expertise: Is the basic level in the eye of the beholder? *Cognitive Psychology, 23,* 457–482.

Tanaka, J. W. (2001). The entry point of face recognition: Evidence for face expertise. *Journal of Experimental Psychology: General, 130*(3), 534–543.

Tanaka, J. W., & Curran, T. (2001). A neural basis for expert object recognition. *Psychological Science, 12,* 43–47.

Tanaka, J. W., & Farah, M. J. (1993). Parts and wholes in face recognition. *Quarterly Journal of Experimental Psychology, Section A, Human Experimental Psychology, 46*(2), 225–245.

Tanaka, J. W., & Gauthier, I. (1997). Expertise in object and face recognition. In R. L. Goldstone, D. L. Medin, & P. G. Schyns (Eds.), *Perceptual mechanisms of learning* (vol. 36, pp. 83–125). San Diego, CA: Academic Press.

Tarr, M. J., & Gauthier, I. (2000). FFA: A flexible fusiform area for subordinate-level visual processing automatized by expertise. *Nature Neuroscience, 3*(8), 764–769.

Tulving, E., Kapur, S., Craik, F. I., Moscovitch, M., & Houle, S. (1994). Hemispheric encoding/retrieval asymmetry in episodic memory: Positron emission tomography findings. *Proceeding of the National Academy of Sciences of the USA, 91,* 2016–2020.

Xu, Y. (2005). Revisiting the role of the fusiform face area in visual expertise. *Cerebral Cortex, 15,* 1234–1242.

Yin, R. K. (1969). Looking at upside down faces. *Journal of Experimental Psychology, 81,* 141–145.

13

Expert Performance[1]
From Action to Perception to Understanding

SIAN L. BEILOCK

University of Chicago, USA

What makes novice and expert performance so different? At first glance, one might suggest that the answer is simple. It is the quality of overt behavior that separates exceptional performers from those less skilled. We can all point to many real-world examples of such performance differences—just try comparing any professional athlete to his or her recreational counterparts. However, although actual performance is one component that differentiates novice from well-learned execution, researchers who approach skill acquisition from a cognitive perspective believe that these overt performance distinctions are only part of the picture. Indeed, these distinctions are viewed as merely the surface-level manifestation of skill level differences. The cognitive control structures that drive performance are what is thought to truly distinguish beginners from more advanced performers (Chase & Simon, 1973). More specifically, experts' ability to organize their knowledge in meaningful ways and to be able to access this knowledge on demand sets highly-skilled performers apart from others (Ericsson & Polson, 1988; Richman, Staszewski, & Simon, 1995).

Yet, skill-level differences are not only reflected in one's *on-line* task performance (by this I mean the real-time unfolding of performance and its corresponding outcomes); they are also reflected *off-line* (i.e., in situations in which individuals are not overtly acting). In the current chapter I focus on these off-line situations in an attempt to shed light on how sensorimotor skill expertise

---

1 This research was supported by Spencer Foundation Grant 201000085 to Sian L. Beilock.

impacts individuals' perception and understanding of action. The research I review not only informs the question of what makes an expert different from his or her novice counterpart; it also makes salient the robust and widespread influence that one's action experience has on one's understanding and representation of the information one encounters—even when there is overt intention to act.

This chapter draws heavily on theories of embodied cognition, which has its roots in ecological psychology's questioning of a distinction between perception and action (Gibson, 1979). Broadly speaking, the embodied viewpoint suggests that our ability to represent objects, events, and even abstract concepts (e.g., metaphor) is subserved by the sensorimotor systems we rely on to navigate throughout the world (e.g., Barsalou, 1999; Gallese & Lakoff, 2005; Glenberg; 1997; Wilson, 2002; Zwaan, 1999). In this chapter I explore how experience operating in particular environments modulates this cognition–action link.

THE EMBODIED VIEWPOINT

Traditional views of cognition suggest that conscious experience gives rise to abstract codes that are arbitrarily related to the objects or concepts they represent (Newell & Simon, 1972; Pylyshyn, 1986). An individual's knowledge is conceptualized as a network of connected nodes or concepts in the form of amodal propositions (e.g., Collins & Quillian, 1969). Recent embodied approaches, however, propose that amodal propositions are not the only manner in which knowledge is represented.

Theories of embodied cognition such as perceptual symbols systems (PSS; Barsalou, 1999), for example, suggest that our representations of objects and events are built on a system of activations based on the brain states that were active during the actual perception and interaction with the objects and events one encounters. That is, our cognitive representations of a particular action, item, or event are subserved by perceptual symbols that are analogically related to the states that produced these experiences. Perceptual symbols are believed to be multimodal traces of neural activity that contain at least some of the features and motor information present during actual sensorimotor experience (Barsalou, 1999; for embodied cognition reviews, see Garbarini & Adenzato, 2004; Glenberg, 1997; Niedenthal et al., 2005; Wilson, 2002; Zwaan, 1999).

In an attempt to capture how individuals understand and process the information they encounter, PSS and the embodied viewpoint, more generally, have been used to predict behavior across a number of diverse domains, ranging from language comprehension (e.g., Stanfield & Zwaan, 2001) to social interactions (for a review, see Niedenthal et al., 2005). Yet there is little work examining how embodied representations might arise. If our knowledge is undergirded by neural operations that embody previous actions and experiences, then those with extensive motor skill experience in a particular domain should represent information in that domain quite differently than those without such experiences—even when there is no intention to act.

In this chapter I review work demonstrating that variations in individuals' motor skill repertoires carry implications for: (1) the ability to perceive and predict the actions of others; (2) the ability to comprehend action-related language; and (3) the judgments individuals make about objects and events in their environment. On the surface, cognitive operations ranging from language comprehension to making preference judgments appear unrelated to the body and previous motor skill experience, but here I will present research demonstrating that this is not the case. In doing so, I will suggest that only by taking into account one's previous action experiences can we gain a full understanding of how individuals represent and comprehend information in their environment—whether they are on the playing field attempting to anticipate an opponent's move or in a classroom attempting to comprehend action-related language.

ACTION PERCEPTION, UNDERSTANDING, AND PREDICTION

When we observe others performing actions, how do we understand their movements and their intended outcomes? Recent work demonstrates that one means by which we understand the actions we encounter is by calling upon some of the same cognitive and neural operations that drive our own overt skill execution. Such recruitment is largely dependent on one's experience performing the actions in question.

To understand this phenomenon, consider a study by Calvo-Merino et al. (2005), who used functional magnetic resonance imaging (fMRI) to explore brain activity patterns when individuals watched an action they were skilled in performing versus one they were not. Experts in classical ballet and Capoeira watched videos of ballet or Capoeira (a Brazilian martial arts dance) while their brains were being scanned. When brain activity while individuals watched their own dance style was compared to activity when individuals watched the other dance style (e.g., ballet dancers watching ballet versus ballet dancers watching Capoeira), greater activation was seen in a network of brain regions (e.g., bilateral activation in premotor cortex and intraparietal sulcus, right superior parietal lobe, and left posterior superior temporal sulcus) thought to support both the observation and production of action (Rizzolatti, Fogassi, & Gallese, 2001).

A follow-up study suggested that it is the influence of motor experience on action observation, above and beyond visual experience, that drives such effects. Calvo-Merino et al. (2006) examined brain activation while male and female ballet dancers observed dancers performing moves specific to the observer's gender versus moves specific to the opposite gender. Calvo-Merino et al. (2006) found greater premotor, parietal, and cerebellar activity when dancers viewed moves from their own motor skill repertoire compared to moves performed by dancers of the opposite gender (moves dances had watched on countless occasions, but did not routinely perform). These results suggest that action perception is subserved by the systems involved in action production and the more experience one has performing the actions being observed, the more strongly this relation holds.

Such motor experience-driven effects go beyond the mere observation of action (for a review, see Wilson & Knoblich, 2004). Recent work by Calise and Giese (2006) demonstrates that motor experience can actually have an impact on individuals' ability to make perceptual discriminations among different actions they observe. In their study, Calise and Giese trained individuals to perform an unusual gait pattern. Typical human gait patterns are characterized by a phase difference of approximately 180° between the two opposite arms and the two opposite legs. Calise and Giese trained participants to produce arm movements that matched a phase difference of 270° (rather than the typical 180°). Participants were trained blindfolded with only minimal verbal and haptic feedback from the experimenter.

Both before and after training, participants performed a visual discrimination task in which they were presented with two point-light walkers. Participants were asked to determine whether the gait patterns of the point-light walkers were the same or different. In the display, one of the walkers' gait pattern always corresponded to phase differences of 180°, 225°, or 270° (the phase difference participants were trained to perform). The other point-light walker was manipulated to have a phase difference either slightly lower or higher than one of these three prototypes.

Overall, individuals improved in their perceptual description performance as a function of nonvisual motor training. However, such improvement was limited to the discrimination of point-light walkers from the 270° prototype participants had learned to perform. This result suggests a direct influence of learning motor sequences on visual recognition of such sequences—an influence that is independent of visual learning as individuals were blindfolded during motor skill acquisition. Further support for this conclusion comes from the fact that individual differences in the learning of the 270° phase pattern predicted visual discrimination performance after training. That is, the better participants learned to perform the 270° gait pattern, the better their perceptual discrimination performance after learning (but not before).

Thus, experience performing motor skills not only carries implications for individuals' success in performing such actions; it also affects the cognitive and neural substrates recruited during action observation. This in turn has implications for individuals' ability to discriminate between actions they observe. If similar cognitive and neural operations are involved in the planning, execution, and perception of actions, then it follows that predicting the outcomes of self-produced actions should be easier than predicting the outcomes of actions produced by others. In essence, predictions should be best when the systems used to predict and produce reside in the same individual. This is exactly what has been found.

When watching videos of people throwing darts at targets, individuals are better at judging where the darts they have thrown will land, as opposed to darts thrown by others (Knoblich & Flach, 2001). Moreover, Repp and Knoblich

(2004) found that expert pianists, who played unfamiliar musical excerpts on a soundless keyboard, were later able to distinguish their own playing from that of others, even when tempo and dynamic information were removed from the recordings and the differences could be judged only on the basis of expressive aspects of the playing. Similarly, non-musicians can recognize the sound of their own clapping, even when the clapping stimuli are stripped of all information except for temporal information (Flach, Knoblich, & Prinz, 2004). Finally, although people have more experience watching the actions of friends, individuals are actually better at recognizing their own movements from point-light displays than that of close companions (Loula, Prasad, Harber, & Shiffrar, 2005). These results are best explained by the idea that much of the way we understand the actions we perceive (visually or auditorily) is through simulation by our own motor system. If that system is the same one that created the action to begin with, it is easier for us to recognize. One possible function of this overlap is that, if we represent others' actions just as our own, it is easier to coordinate movement with them (see Knoblich & Sebanz, 2006, for a review).

LANGUAGE COMPREHENSION

Rather than our representations of the objects and events we encounter being limited to amodal or propositional code that is arbitrarily related to the concepts it represents, our understanding appears to rely on previous and related sensorimotor experiences. This is true in the language we read about or hear spoken too. For example, when individuals make sensibility judgments about sentences by pushing a button that is either close to or far away from their bodies, the sentence's implied action direction interacts with the direction of the response (Glenberg & Kaschak, 2002). For instance, reading the sentence "Close the drawer" increases the time needed to respond with a movement directed toward the body (the opposite direction of the implied action) relative to a response involving movement directed away from the body (the same direction as the implied action). Similarly, sensibility judgments of sentences such as "Can you squeeze a tomato?" are facilitated when participants are primed with an associated hand shape (a clenched hand) compared to an inconsistent hand shape (a pointed finger; Klatzky, Pellegrino, McCloskey, & Doherty, 1989). Reading about performing a motion-directed act (e.g., "Eric turned down the volume") has also been shown to activate motor plans associated with actually producing this action (a counter-clockwise hand movement; Zwaan & Taylor, 2006). This interaction between the actions implied by language and motor behavior performed concurrently with comprehension has been taken to suggest that language comprehension is interconnected with the systems involved in the understanding and planning of actions (Barsalou, 1999; Glenberg & Kaschak, 2002).

Converging evidence from cognitive neuroscience supports this idea. For example, reading action words associated with the leg and arm (e.g., "kick," "pick") activates brain areas implicated in the movements of these body parts (Hauk, Johnsrude, & Pulvermüller, 2004), and reading action-related sentences such as "I bit the apple" or "I kick the ball" activates the same areas of premotor cortex as those involved during the actual movement of mouth and leg effectors, respectively (Tettamanti et al., 2005). A recent study using transcranial magnetic stimulation (TMS) suggests that activation of the motor substrates governing the actions one reads about is actually an important component of comprehension, rather than a superficial by-product. Pulvermüller, Hauk, Nikolin, and Ilmoniemi (2005) found that when stimulation was applied to arm or leg cortical areas in the left hemisphere, lexical decisions to words denoting arm or leg actions, respectively, were facilitated. This finding suggests that these motor-related cortical areas contribute to our understanding of linguistic descriptions of body-relevant actions.

To the extent that our comprehension of action-related language is grounded in the systems that support action execution, people who have experience interacting with the objects and performing the actions they read about may represent this information very differently than those who do not have such experience. Despite demonstrations of motor involvement in language comprehension, little work has explored whether differences in motor skill expertise augment or attenuate these effects. In a series of studies, we have been exploring this issue by examining differences in how novice and expert athletes represent both everyday and sport-specific objects and actions they read about.

In a first experiment, Holt and Beilock (2006) had ice-hockey experts (Division 1 college-level players or individuals who had at least two years of high-school varsity playing experience and played organized ice-hockey in college) and novices read sentences describing hockey and non-hockey situations. The non-hockey situations depicted everyday objects and individuals (e.g., "The child saw the balloon in the air"). The hockey situations were hockey-specific (e.g., "The referee saw the hockey helmet on the bench"). A picture of a target object was presented after each sentence. Participants were asked to judge whether the target was mentioned in the preceding sentence and to offer the judgment as quickly as possible. The target either matched the action implied in the sentence (match) or did not (mismatch) (see Figure 13.1). The correct response to all target items, whether matches or mismatches, was always "yes." Filler items that were not mentioned in the preceding sentence required a "no" response and were used to equate the number of "yes" and "no" responses across the experiment. Although the correct response to all target items was always "yes," the action orientation of some items (i.e., matches) corresponded more closely to the action implied in the sentence that preceded these items than the action orientation of other items (i.e., mismatches). Building on the initial logic and work of Zwaan and colleagues (see Stanfield & Zwaan, 2001), we hypothesized that if individuals mentally represent perceptual qualities and action possibilities of the information they comprehend linguistically, then responses should be facilitated for matches relative to mismatches.

We predicted that both novice and expert hockey players would show the match–mismatch effect (i.e., responding faster to items that matched the action implied in the preceding sentence versus items that did not) for pictures of

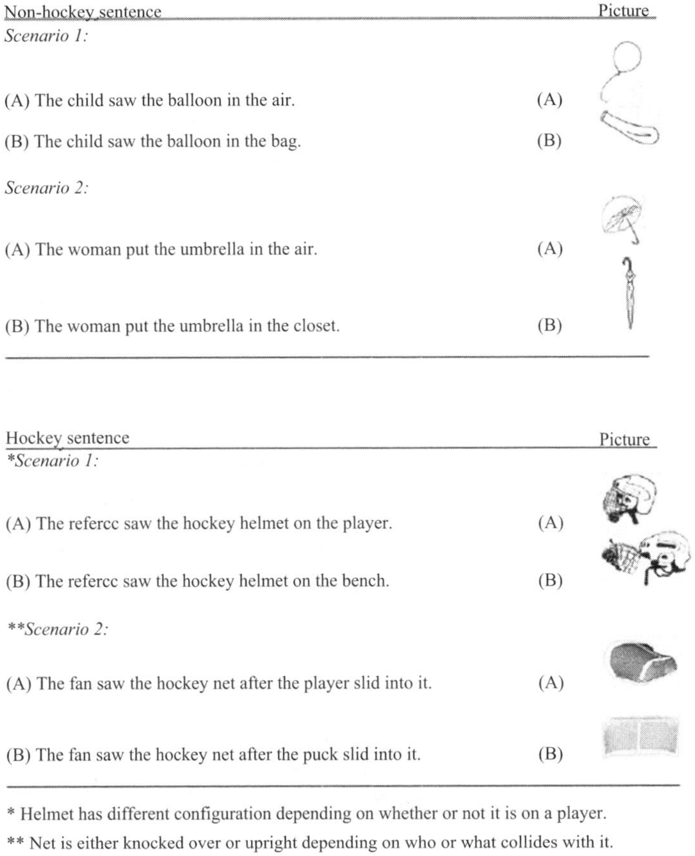

Non-hockey sentence		Picture
Scenario 1:		
(A) The child saw the balloon in the air.	(A)	
(B) The child saw the balloon in the bag.	(B)	
Scenario 2:		
(A) The woman put the umbrella in the air.	(A)	
(B) The woman put the umbrella in the closet.	(B)	

Hockey sentence		Picture
Scenario 1:		
(A) The refercc saw the hockey helmet on the player.	(A)	
(B) The refercc saw the hockey helmet on the bench.	(B)	
**Scenario 2:*		
(A) The fan saw the hockey net after the player slid into it.	(A)	
(B) The fan saw the hockey net after the puck slid into it.	(B)	

* Helmet has different configuration depending on whether or not it is on a player.

** Net is either knocked over or upright depending on who or what collides with it.

Figure 13.1 Examples of experimental stimuli. Picture A serves as a "match" for Sentence A and a "mismatch" for Sentence B. Picture B serves as a "match" for Sentence B and a "mismatch" for Sentence A.

Source: Reprinted from Holt and Beilock (2006).

common objects and activities unrelated to hockey because both novices and experts presumably have the same amount of knowledge and experience interacting with such everyday items. However, if experience impacts the mental simulation of actions one reads about, then individuals with hockey expertise should show the match–mismatch effect for the hockey-specific items, while hockey novices should not.

Both novice and expert hockey players were able to understand the sentences they read (as indicated by high accuracy levels). Additionally, participants responded more quickly to everyday items that matched the action implied in the preceding sentence than those that did not—suggesting that participants' representations contained information about the sensorimotor qualities of the objects and individuals they read about. However, only those with hockey knowledge and

TABLE 13.1   Accuracy and Reaction Time Data for Hockey and Non-Hockey Items

| | Accuracy (% Correct) | | | | Reaction Time (msec) | | | |
| | Match | | Mismatch | | Match | | Mismatch | |
Expertise	M	SE	M	SE	M	SE	M	SE
Hockey								
Novice	93.8	1.00	87.0	1.30	813.0	26.8	825.2	25.0
Expert	96.7	0.67	87.5	1.70	726.7	24.5	811.2	31.7
Nonhockey								
Novice	97.6	0.56	91.2	1.40	663.8	20.2	746.8	25.8
Expert	95.0	0.93	90.6	1.70	706.5	22.3	762.8	25.0

experience showed this effect for the hockey scenarios (see Table 13.1). This finding is consistent with the hypothesis that a highly specific set of motoric experiences (e.g., athletic expertise) plays an important role in mediating the effect of the mental simulation of action on language comprehension.

In a second experiment, Holt and Beilock (2006) presented novice and expert football players (Division 1 college-level players or individuals who had at least two years of high-school varsity playing experience and played organized football in college) with pictures of football players performing actions that either matched or did not match actions implied in preceding sentences. Critically, we manipulated the extent to which the action implied in the sentence was football-specific (an action one would only perform were one a football player, e.g., a quarterback handing off to a receiver) versus non-football-specific (an action performed by a football player, but that everyone should have performed in the past, e.g., a football player sitting down on a bench). Embedding both football-specific actions and non-football-specific (everyday) actions within the domain of football provides a stronger test of the prediction that knowledge and experience performing an action leads to covert action simulation when reading about that action. This is because even novices in a given domain should show evidence of this type of representation, provided they have experience performing the action in question. Under this view, both novices and experts should respond faster to a picture of a football player performing an everyday action that matches the action implied in a preceding sentence relative to a picture of an action that does not. In contrast, for football-specific actions, only those who have knowledge and experience performing the action should show the effect. This is exactly what was found (see Table 13.2; as in Experiment 1, note accuracy is high and does not significantly differ across expertise or sentence type). Thus, the ability to differentiate action orientations (suggesting one is representing sensorimotor information associated with the objects and individuals one is reading about) is not just a function of general domain knowledge, but is dependent on specific experience one has performing the actions and interacting with the objects in question.

TABLE 13.2   Accuracy and Reaction Time Data for Football-Specific Action Items and Everyday Action Items

Expertise	Accuracy (% Correct)				Reaction Time (msec)			
	Match		Mismatch		Match		Mismatch	
	M	SE	M	SE	M	SE	M	SE
Football Action								
Novice	95.8	1.1	93.8	1.6	920.7	38.3	931.7	40.7
Expert	96.6	1.3	89.7	3.3	763.4	32.7	888.4	47.6
Everyday Action								
Novice	93.7	1.5	91.5	1.6	961.9	37.3	1,016.1	42.3
Expert	94.7	1.6	89.6	3.1	793.7	31.2	856.5	36.1

The above findings are consistent with the idea that motor plans to act are activated when individuals perceive specific objects or events, with the type of plan and the link dependent on the extent to which one has experience performing such actions. However, it should be noted that these results could be explained by a purely perceptual representation or simulation of the sentences that involves no contribution from the motor system. We have recently turned to functional magnetic resonance imaging (fMRI) to address this issue.

When listening to hockey-related action sentences, if hockey experts are mentally simulating the actions in question, they might show greater activation in motor-related regions of cortex relative to non-action sentences. Novices would not be expected to show this pattern of activity. The specific pattern of neural activation obtained would therefore help to elucidate precisely which components of the motor system underlie an experience-dependent influence on language comprehension (or if the motor system is involved at all).

In a study aimed at addressing these issues, we (Beilock et al., 2008) recruited hockey novices (who had neither hockey-playing nor hockey-watching experience) and hockey experts (Division I intercollegiate hockey athletes and professional players). During functional MRI scan acquisition, all subjects listened to sentences describing hockey actions (e.g., "The hockey player received the pass") and non-hockey actions (e.g., "The individual pushed the door bell"). No overt behavioral task was performed in the scanner to prevent contaminating activation patterns related to comprehending the sentences with activation corresponding to stimulus-driven responses.

After exiting the scanner, individuals performed a version of the behavioral task used by Holt and Beilock (2006) described above. Specifically, participants were presented with the same hockey and non-hockey action sentences they had listened to during scanning followed by pictures of individuals performing actions that either did or did not match those implied in the sentence. We were interested in whether the match–mismatch effect found in Holt and Beilock (2006) for hockey stimuli varied as a function of hockey experience (i.e., experts, novices) and how it related to neural activation when merely listening to hockey-action sentences.

All participants responded more quickly to pictures that matched the everyday actions implied in the sentences than to pictures that did not (i.e., the match–mismatch effect)—replicating Holt and Beilock's (2006) results. This was not the case for the hockey actions. Only hockey players showed a match–mismatch effect for hockey-related sentences. Novices showed no difference in their response times for hockey action pictures that matched the action implied in the sentence versus those that did not.

To further elucidate the role of expertise in language understanding, it is necessary to relate the neural activation observed while participants listened to hockey-action sentences with the aforementioned behavioral results. Interestingly, ice-hockey experts showed greater activation for hockey-action relative to non-hockey-action sentences in a premotor region devoted to the planning and selection of actions (left dorsal lateral pre-motor cortex, PMd). Novices did not show this pattern of activation, and activation for novices in this region while listening to hockey-action sentences was significantly less than the hockey players. Moreover, left PMd activity during hockey-action sentences positively related with the post-scan sentence comprehension task (i.e., the difference in RT to pictures that matched the hockey action implied in the sentence versus those that mismatched). Specifically, those individuals showing the greatest match–mismatch effect for hockey-related sentences showed the greatest amount of activation in the PMd region specifically for hockey-action sentences. These individuals also happened to be the expert players, suggesting that when individuals with hockey expertise listen to domain-relevant action sentences, they recruit premotor regions involved in the planning and coordination of action.

Together, these findings suggest that we represent our surroundings, at least in part, by calling upon multimodal traces of neural activity (Barsalou, 1999) related to how we might execute an observed behavior or act on the objects we encounter and, importantly, that this activation differs as a function of one's action experience in a particular domain. Nonetheless, can we broaden this conception of bodily influence to include more than just the representation of action? The answer appears to be "yes." Below I consider work showing that action-based processes can influence one's preferences for stimuli in one's environment and, again, I show that this is related to one's previous experiences interacting with the objects or stimuli in question.

EXPLICIT JUDGMENTS

Fluency, defined as the subjective ease with which an item is processed, is thought to lead individuals to have a feeling of remembering which can often serve as a useful heuristic in recognition. However, fluency does not always result in accurate memory judgments because it can arise independently of whether one has actually seen the item they are judging before. For example, a word such as "test" presented in a semantically predictive sentence (e.g., "the anxious student took a test") is more likely to be recognized as old (i.e., having been seen or studied previously) than when this same word it is presented in a non-predictive sentence (e.g., "later in the afternoon she took a test"). This is because semantic expectancy increases the conceptual fluency of this word (Whittlesea, Jacoby, & Girard, 1990). Similarly, manipulating an item's visual clarity alters its perceptual fluency. The easier an item is to visually process, the more likely individuals are to say they have seen it before (Whittlesea et al., 1990).

In a recent series of studies, Yang, Gallo, and Beilock (2009) asked whether memory errors might arise from a source rather different from the semantic or visual context of a given stimulus. Specifically, we examined whether fluency effects might be tied to motor plans that are automatically activated in association with the items individuals encounter—even in situations where there is no intention to act.

As mentioned above, recent behavioral and neurophysiological work suggests that we represent our surroundings, at least in part, by activating motor processes related to how we might execute an observed behavior or act on the objects around us. Yang et al. (2009) reasoned that if such activation gives rise to information about ease or fluency of planning and executing an action, then this may in turn impact memory judgments for these items. In other words, fluency might not only arise from the conceptual context in which an item is viewed or the visual qualities of the item itself, but also from the automatic activation of motor plans for action associated with the stimuli one is making memory judgments about.

To test this idea, we turned to the domain of typing. Recent work has shown that an integral part of letter processing—at least for experienced typists—is the motor simulation of typing the letters themselves. Specifically, in a Stroop-like task, Rieger (2004, 2007) found that typing experts' manual responses were faster when the finger used to indicate the color of a presented letter was congruent with the finger typically used to type the letter. Such work suggests that when typing experts perceive letters, they automatically activate motor plans for typing them. If this motor simulation carries information about how easy it would be to produce such letters, then individuals' propensity to recognize letters as previously studied items in a memory judgment task might be a function of how easy it would be to actually type the letters. This would be the case despite the fact that the individuals have no intention to type while viewing the letters.

In Yang et al. (209), expert and novice typists were presented with a series of letter dyads. To ensure that participants were attending to the presented dyads, we instructed individuals to indicate, using their first impression, whether they liked each dyad with a verbal "yes" or "no" response. Everyone then took a subsequent recognition memory test. To manipulate the typing ease of the dyads, we varied whether the presented letter dyads would be typed, using standard touch-typing methods, with the same finger (e.g., FV) or different fingers (e.g., FK). The interval between typing consecutive letters using the same finger is longer than the interval between typing consecutive letters with different fingers (Viviani & Laissard, 1996). This is because typing is a parallel process in which consecutive letters are programmed simultaneously and a given finger can only be in one place at a time. Thus, letter dyads typed by the same finger should cause more motor interference or be harder to type than dyads typed with different fingers because the latter case can be planned and performed more so in parallel than the former case (Rosenbaum, 2010; Rumelhart & Norman, 1982).

If dyad recognition memory judgments are driven by motor fluency, individuals' propensity to incorrectly recognize a dyad as old should be higher for those dyads that would be easier to type (i.e. different-finger dyads) than harder to type (i.e., same-finger dyads). However, this should only hold for skilled typists who have extensive typing experience and have thus formed consistent mappings between specific letters and the fingers used to type them. This is exactly what Yang et al. (2009) found. Skilled typists made more false recognition errors (i.e., indicating they had studied a dyad when in fact they had not) for same-finger dyads in comparison to different-finger dyads (see Figure 13.2).

The above findings suggest that explicit memory judgments can be influenced by the motor associations individuals have with the items being judged. But can we take this a step further? If (1) individuals activate motor plans for acting on the objects they perceive in their environment, and (2) if this mental simulation of action differs as a function of skill level, and (3) if people prefer to act in ways that create less motor interference (i.e., are more fluent), then individuals should report higher ratings of liking for objects that are easier to act on than for objects that are harder to act on—even though these individuals have

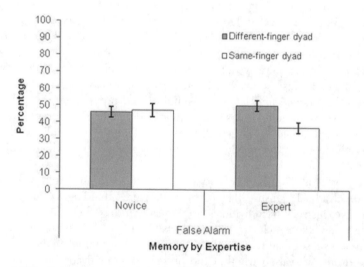

Figure 13.2   Recognition responses for letter dyads for typing novices and experts. Error bars represent 95% confidence intervals.

Source: Adapted from Yang, Gallo, & Beilock (2009).

no intention to act. In other words, the fluency associated with typing letter dyads may not only impact one's memory judgments; they may also affect one's preferences for one dyad over another.

To explore this idea, we (Holt & Beilock, 2006) again turned to the domain of typing. Expert and novice typists were simultaneously presented with two separate letter dyads on a screen and asked to indicate the dyad they preferred. Specifically, participants were informed that they would see two letter dyads and that they should verbally indicate which of the two dyads they preferred, using their first impressions of the letters while avoiding choosing dyads based on their associations with any initials or abbreviations. As in the memory judgment study, the dyads fell into one of two categories: Dyads that would be typed with the same finger using standard typing methods (e.g., FV) or dyads that would be typed with different fingers (e.g., FJ). Each dyad pair presented to participants always involved one dyad from each category—a paradigm first introduced by Van den Bergh, Vrana and Eelen (1990). As mentioned above, because typing is thought to involve the overlap of successive key strokes (Rumelhart & Norman, 1982), typing two letters with the same finger should result in more motor interference than typing two letters with different fingers, as the former case requires that the same digit essentially be in two places at once (or in very close succession).

Results demonstrated that skilled typists preferred dyads typed with different fingers (i.e., dyads that would be easier to type) significantly more than chance. Novices showed no preference. Importantly, participants were recruited for a study examining "cognitive task performance" to minimize associations with the study and typing. It was only when the study was completed that individuals were categorized as skilled or novice typists. As a result, participants were unaware of the link between the study and typing, and when asked, could not explicate how the letter dyads typed with the same versus different finger differed.

To explicitly test how closely related these preference judgments were to motor system activation, in another part of the study, while making their preference judgments on some trials, participants held a finger press pattern in memory that involved the same fingers that would be used to type the presented dyads. If holding this pattern utilizes motor system resources that could otherwise be used to inform typists' preference judgments, such preferences should disappear—exactly what occurred. A second experiment showed that this motor interference was specific to the digits actually involved in typing the dyads. When expert typists held a motor pattern in memory involving fingers not used to type the dyads, the preference remained. Thus, covert mental simulation of acting on the information one is presented with not only impacts preference judgments, but this influence is limited to information motorically resonant with the specific effectors involved in the simulated action.

Together, the work presented in this chapter suggests that a complete understanding of high-level performance not only requires consideration of physical (or *on-line*) execution and the cognitive processes used to govern this performance, but also consideration of skill-level differences in more *off-line* processes. Specifically, one's motor skill expertise carries implications for how one understands the action of others, how one comprehends language about action in their domain of skill specialization, and even the preferences one has for the items and events one encounters when there is no immediate intention to act.

IMPLICATIONS FOR THE ACQUISITION OF EXPERTISE

The findings presented so far suggest that we represent our surroundings, at least in part, via the activation of sensorimotor processes associated with how we might execute an observed behavior or act on the objects we encounter. By considering the influence of motor skill expertise, we see that these cognition–action links are experience-driven. These findings have implications for understanding what makes an expert performer different from his or her novice counterpart. They also shed light on how best to teach complex skills (with and without overt motor components) to others.

As an example, motor imagery has been widely used as a rehabilitation technique for stroke and other patients who wish to regain finer motor control in certain tasks (for a review, see Dickstein & Deutsch, 2007). Motor imagery has also been used to train surgeons in complex surgical procedures (Hall, 2002; Rogers, 2006), to promote the learning and retention of complex athletic tasks (Driskell, Copper, & Moran, 1994; Feltz & Landers, 1983), and the transfer of motor skills. For example, Gentili, Papaxanthis, and Pozzo (2006) demonstrated that imagery training using one arm can transfer to improved performance using the opposite arm. Mentally simulating an action is thought to activate the neural substrates involved in action production. It is perhaps not surprising, then, that simulation of certain actions benefits subsequent performance. Nonetheless, the full potential of this finding has yet to be exploited, not only as a rehabilitation or motor-learning technique, but also as a potential means of acquiring more complex cognitive skills that do not necessarily involve overt action, such as reading or spatial reasoning.

Interestingly, it is not just the explicit mental simulation of action that can improve performance. Action observation can result in improved performance as well. Vogt (1995) found that either observing or performing sequential arm movements resulted in similar improvement in the temporal consistency of executing such movements—suggesting that, in some cases, action observation facilitates subsequent motor performance as much as action production itself. In terms of higher-level cognitive skill learning, Glenberg and Robertson (1999) showed that individuals more readily learned to operate a compass if they read about its operation and watched an actor physically enact the operation than if they only read about the actions. Although both groups gained similar levels of knowledge concerning compass operation, the group that watched the individual act on the object ultimately performed at the highest level on a subsequent novel compass navigation task. If watching an individual operate a compass results in the mental simulation of action in the perceiver that captures the action possibilities the compass affords, subsequent performance should be facilitated in comparison to conditions in which such action possibilities are not made salient. This is exactly what was found.

Finally, the above-mentioned observation and imagery learning effects not only apply to skills with explicit action components (e.g., athletic tasks or operating a compass), but may carry implications for the learning of skills that involve no overt action at all. For instance, many physics concepts, like torque and angular momentum, can be hard to grasp. However, the structure and framework of physics lead us to believe that alternatives to traditional lecture and book learning may produce the highest level of physics understanding. In particular, students can actually feel some of the effects of physics concepts, as opposed to just reading about them or seeing them. Based on the above findings, it seems likely that providing students with specific motor experiences exemplifying particular physics concepts will lead to the activation of the neural substrates that are involved in performing and experiencing these physics concepts—activation that provides an elaborate and robust situational representation that aids in understanding and retention. In other words, we hypothesize that being able to experience a physics concept like momentum will recruit brain areas involved in sensing and executing movement (during the experience itself and even when one reads about the concept later in a book or hears about it from one's teacher). As reviewed above, when these sensorimotor areas are involved in thinking and reasoning tasks, people's understanding of the concepts in question is improved.

Of course, it is also important to mention that many physics concepts are counterintuitive and, therefore, students may develop alternative conceptions after interactions with physical phenomena rather than conceptions aligned with the scientific explanation. It is likely that directed motor experience specifically designed to correctly reinforce physics concepts will readily contribute to learning about these concepts when students do not have a lot of experience with them and thus do not have misconceptions about them. Moreover, it is also the case that one may be able to use the sensorimotor system as leverage to help alleviate misconceptions that students walk into the classroom with. Work in our lab is currently focused on such issues. In sum, by providing people with action experience, we hope to advance performance in school.

REFERENCES

Barsalou, L. W. (1999). Perceptual symbol systems. *Behavioral and Brain Sciences, 22,* 577–660.

Beilock, S. L., & Holt, L. E. (2007). Embodied preference judgments: Can likeability be driven by the motor system? *Psychological Science, 18,* 51–57.

Beilock, S. L., Lyons, I. M., Mattarella-Micke, A., Nusbaum, H. C., & Small, S. L. (2008). Sports experience changes the neural processing of action language. *Proceedings of the National Academy of Sciences of the USA, 105*, 13269–13273.

Calise, A., & Giese, M. A. (2006). Nonvisual motor training influences biological motion perception. *Current Biology, 16*, 69–74.

Calvo-Merino, B., Glaser, D. E., Grezes, J., Passingham, R. E., & Haggard, P. (2005). Action observation and acquired motor skills: An fMRI study with expert dancers. *Cerebral Cortex, 15*, 1243–1249.

Calvo-Merino, B., Grezes, J., Glaser, D. E., Passingham, R. E., & Haggard, P. (2006). Seeing or doing? Influence of visual and motor familiarity on action observation. *Current Biology, 16*, 1905–1910.

Chase, W. G., & Simon, H. A. (1973). Perception in chess. *Cognitive Psychology, 4*, 55–81.

Collins, A. M., & Quillian, M. R. (1969). Retrieval time from semantic memory. *Journal of Verbal Learning and Verbal Behavior, 8*, 240–247.

Dickstein, R., & Deutsch, J. E. (2007). Motor imagery in physical therapist practice. *Physical Therapy, 87*, 942–953.

Driskell, J. E., Copper, C., & Moran, A. (1994). Does mental practice enhance performance? *Journal of Applied Psychology, 79*, 481–492.

Ericsson, K. A., & Polson, P. G. (1988). An experimental analysis of the mechanisms of a memory skill. *Journal of Experimental Psychology: Learning, Memory, & Cognition, 14*, 305–316.

Feltz, D. L., & Landers, D. M. (1983). The effects of mental practice on motor skill learning and performance: A meta-analysis. *Journal of Sport Psychology, 5*, 25–57.

Flach, R., Knoblich, G., & Prinz, W. (2004). Recognizing one's own clapping: The role of temporal cues in self-recognition. *Psychological Research, 11*, 147–156.

Gallese V., & Lakoff, G. (2005). The brain's concepts: The role of the sensory-motor system in reason and language. *Cognitive Neuropsychology, 22*, 455–479.

Garbarini, F., & Adenzato, M. (2004). At the root of embodied cognition: Cognitive science meets neurophysiology. *Brain and Cognition, 56*, 100–106.

Gentili, R., Papaxanthis, C., & Pozzo, T. (2006). Improvement and generalization of arm motor performance through motor imagery practice. *Neuroscience, 137*, 761–772.

Gibson, J. J. (1979). *The ecological approach to visual perception*. London: Erlbaum.

Glenberg, A. M. (1997). What memory is for. *Behavioral and Brain Sciences, 20*, 1–55.

Glenberg, A. M., & Kaschak, M. P. (2002). Grounding language in action. *Psychonomic Bulletin & Review, 9*, 558–565.

Glenberg, A. M., & Robertson, D. A. (1999). Indexical understanding of instructions. *Discourse Processes, 28*, 1–26.

Hall, J. C. (2002). Imagery practice and the development of surgical skills. *American Journal of Surgery, 184*, 465–470.

Hauk, O., Johnsrude, I., & Pulvermüller, F. (2004). Somatotopic representation of action words in the motor and premotor cortex. *Neuron, 41*, 301–307.

Holt, L. E., & Beilock, S. (2006). Expertise and its embodiment: Examining the impact of sensorimotor skill expertise on the representation of action-related text. *Psychonomic Bulletin & Review, 13*, 694–701.

Klatzky, R., Pellegrino, J., McCloskey, B., & Doherty, S. (1989). Can you squeeze a tomato? The role of motor representations in semantic sensibility judgments. *Journal of Memory and Language, 28*(1), 56–77.

Knoblich, G., & Flach, R. (2001). Predicting the effects of actions: Interactions of perception and action. *Psychological Science, 12*, 467–472.

Knoblich, G., & Sebanz, N. (2006). The social nature of perception and action. *Current Directions in Psychological Science, 15*(3), 99–104.

Loula, F., Prasad, S., Harber, K., & Shiffrar, M. (2005). Recognizing people from their movement. *Journal of Experimental Psychology: Human Perception and Performance, 31*, 210–220.

Newell, A., & Simon, H. A. (1972). *Human problem solving.* Englewood Cliffs, NJ: Prentice-Hall.

Niedenthal, P. M., Barsalou, L. W., Winkielman, P., Krauth-Gruber, S., & Ric, F. (2005). Embodiment in attitudes, social perception, and emotion. *Personality and Social Psychology Review, 9*, 184–211.

Pulvermüller, F., Hauk, O., Nikolin, V. V., & Ilmoniemi, R. J. (2005). Functional links between motor and language systems. *European Journal of Neuroscience, 21*, 793–797.

Pylyshyn, Z. W. (1986). *Computational cognition: Toward a foundation for cognitive science.* Cambridge, MA: MIT Press.

Repp, B. H., & Knoblich, G. (2004). Perceiving action identity: How pianists recognize their own performances. *Psychological Science, 15*, 604–609.

Richman, H. B., Staszewski, J., & Simon, H. A. (1995). Simulation of expert memory using EPAM IV. *Psychological Review, 102*, 305–330.

Rieger, M. (2004). Automatic keypress activation in skilled typing. *Journal of Experimental Psychology: Human Perception and Performance, 30*, 555–565.

Rieger, M. (2007). Letters as visual action-effects in skilled typing. *Acta Psychologica, 126*(2), 138–153.

Rizzolatti, G., Fogassi, L., & Gallese, V. (2001). Neurophysiological mechanisms underlying understanding and imitation of action. *Nature Reviews Neuroscience, 2*, 661–670.

Rogers, R. G. (2006). Mental practice and acquisition of motor skills: Examples from sports training and surgical education. *Obstetrics & Gynecology Clinics of North America, 33*, 297–304.

Rosenbaum, D. A. (2010). *Human motor control* (2nd ed.). San Diego: Academic Press/ Elsevier.

Rumelhart, D. E., & Norman, D. A. (1982). Simulating a skilled typist: A study of skilled cognitive-motor performance. *Cognitive Science, 6*, 1–36.

Stanfield, R. A., & Zwaan, R. A. (2001). The effect of implied orientation derived from verbal context on picture recognition. *Psychological Science, 12*, 153–156.

Tettamanti, M., Buccino, G., Saccuman, M. C., Gallese, V., Danna, M., Scifo, P., Fazio, F., Rizzolatti, G., Cappa, S. F., & Perani, D. (2005). Listening to action-related sentences activates fronto-parietal motor circuits. *Journal of Cognitive Neurosciences, 17*, 273–281.

Van den Bergh, O., Vrana, S., & Eelen, P. (1990). Letters from the heart: Affective categorization of letter combinations in typists and nontypists. *Journal of Experimental Psychology: Learning, Memory, Cognition, 16*, 1153–1161.

Viviani, P., & Laissard, G. (1996). Motor templates in typing. *Journal of Experimental Psychology: Human Perception and Performance, 22*, 417–445.

Vogt, S. (1995). On relations between perceiving, imagining and performing in the learning of cyclical movement sequences. *British Journal of Psychology, 86*, 191–216.

Whittlesea, B. W. A., Jacoby, L. L., & Girard, K. (1990). Illusions of immediate memory: Evidence of an attributional basis for feelings of familiarity and perceptual quality. *Journal of Memory & Language, 29*, 716–732.

Wilson, M. (2002). Six views of embodied cognition. *Psychonomic Bulletin & Review, 9*, 625–636.

Wilson, M., & Knoblich, G. (2004). The case for motor involvement in perceiving conspecifics. *Psychological Bulletin, 131,* 460–473.

Yang, S., Gallo, D., & Beilock, S. L. (2009). Embodied memory judgments: A case of motor fluency. *Journal of Experimental Psychology: Learning, Memory, & Cognition, 35,* 1359–1365.

Zwaan, R. A. (1999). Embodied cognition, perceptual symbols, and situation models. *Discourse Processes, 28,* 81–88.

Zwaan, R. A., & Taylor, L. J. (2006). Seeing, acting, understanding: Motor resonance in language comprehension. *Journal of Experimental Psychology: General, 135,* 1–11.

14

Can Neural Imaging Be Used to Investigate Learning in an Educational Task?[1]

JOHN R. ANDERSON
Carnegie Mellon University, USA

SHAWN BETTS
Carnegie Mellon University, USA

JENNIFER L. FERRIS
Carnegie Mellon University, USA

JON M. FINCHAM
Carnegie Mellon University, USA

INTRODUCTION

*T*his chapter is concerned with how neural imaging might inform the development of an intelligent tutoring system. Bill Chase was one of the subjects in the research on development of programming skills in LISP (Anderson, Farrell, & Sauers, 1984) that led to the development of cognitive tutors (Anderson, Conrad, & Corbett, 1989; Anderson et al., 1995). During this early work on skill acquisition the first author (JRA) remembers many conversations with Bill about what the neural basis might be of skill acquisition. It would have been great to still have him as a colleague to discuss the current research.

1 This research was supported by NSF award REC-0087396 and DARPA grant AFOSR-FA9550-07-1-0359. We would like to thank Jared Danker, Yulin Qin, and Darryl Schneider for their comments on this chapter.

Neural imaging has contributed to the understanding of many forms of learning (e.g., Buckner & Wheeler, 2001; Chein & Schneider, 2005; Nomura & Reber, 2008; Poldrack, 2000). Most of this research has used relatively simple laboratory tasks such as word memory (e.g., Wagner et al., 1998), perceptual priming (e.g., Wiggs & Martin, 1998) or simple skill acquisition (e.g., Hill & Schneider, 2006). The question of interest in this chapter is whether neural imaging can inform an understanding of the kind of learning that takes place in school. Studies of school learning tend to use data sources such as final test performance that are both very summary in nature and much delayed in time from the learning episodes. Imaging data from the performance of an actual school task might provide information that would be informative about the critical learning events.

We created a learning environment that reproduced the essential aspects of a Cognitive Tutor, an intelligent computer-based instructional system that has been shown to have success in teaching high school mathematics (Anderson et al., 1995; Koedinger et al., 1997). These systems are deployed in over 1000 schools nationwide and interact with over 500,000 students in the United States (Koedinger & Corbett, 2006; Ritter et al., 2007, in press). These tutors interact with students as they solve problems providing instruction on an as-needed basis. The simplified system in this chapter was designed to enable use in a functional magnetic resonance imaging (fMRI) scanner and to interact with a simulation of a cognitive model. Figure 14.1(a) illustrates its interface. The student selects parts of an equation by pointing and clicking with a mouse. As illustrated in Figure 14.1(a), the selected portion is highlighted in gray and the student picks operations to perform on the selection by using the menu buttons below. When the student needs to enter information, a keypad appears, as in Figure 14.1, and the student clicks the keys with a mouse. Figure 14.1(a) captures the student at the point where they are about to begin entry. In this case the student has chosen the two x-terms, selected "Collect" (this option is hidden by the keypad), and is ready to enter 3 + 4 and * into the shaded boxes. Simple help options are available should a student become stuck. The curriculum sequence is based on the material in the first four chapters of Foerster's (1990) classic algebra text. The first one or two problems in a section will contain instruction explaining the new transformations in that section. Note that all interaction with this system involves mouse actions and this is the only input device that the student needs in the scanner.

We have been cautious in exposing children to this system because we do not want to cause any interference with their classroom learning of algebra. Therefore, we created an isomorph of algebra, a data-flow representation, for piloting the system with adults. Figures 14.2(a) and 14.2(b) show data-flow equivalents of a relatively simple equation and a relatively complex equation in this system. Part (a) is the isomorph of the equation $5x + 4 = 39$ and part (b) is an isomorph of the equation $(2x - 5x) + 13 + 9x = 67$. Students are told that a number comes in the top box, flows through a set of arithmetic operations, and the result is the number that appears in the bottom. They are taught a set of graph transformations, isomorphic to the transformations with the linear

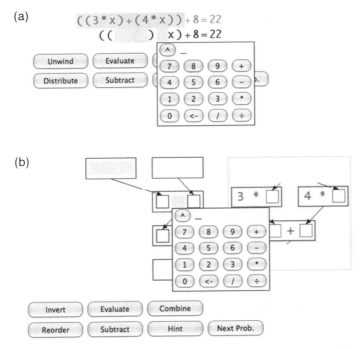

Figure 14.1   Illustration of the interface for the algebra tutor during a transformation: (a) the linear representation; (b) the data-flow representation.

equations, that enables them to determine which number appears in the top box. Figure 14.2(b) illustrates the data-flow interface for a comparable point to Figure 14.2(a). Students point to boxes in this graph, select operations, and key in results from a keypad. The motor actions are isomorphic to the actions for a linear equation and in many cases physically identical. Anderson (2007, Chapter 5) reports a behavioral comparison of adults working with the data-flow tutor and children working with linear equations. Children are a bit more error-prone than adults (CMU students) but show nearly identical learning trajectories.

The current imaging study was performed with adults using the data-flow representation and looked for the effect of six days of practice with this instructional system. We will focus on six predefined regions that past research has repeatedly found to be involved in algebra problem solving (for a review, see Anderson, 2007). Figure 14.3 illustrates these regions and their association with components of a model that will be described later in the chapter. These regions can be grouped into three pairs of regions for the current task:

1. There is the motor region where the hand is represented and a region of the fusiform gyrus that has been found to play a critical role in the recognition of visual objects (e.g., Grill-Spector, Knouf, & Kanwisher, 2004;

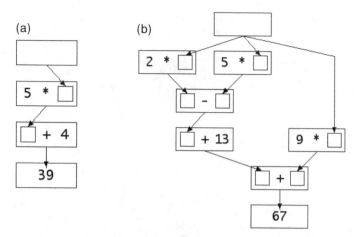

Figure 14.2   The data-flow equivalents of (a) 5x + 4 = 39 and (b) (2x – 5x) + 13 + 9x = 67.

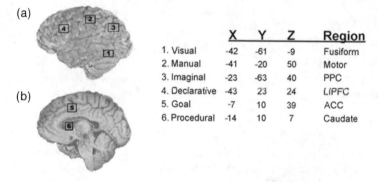

	X	Y	Z	Region
1. Visual	-42	-61	-9	Fusiform
2. Manual	-41	-20	50	Motor
3. Imaginal	-23	-63	40	PPC
4. Declarative	-43	23	24	LIPFC
5. Goal	-7	10	39	ACC
6. Procedural	-14	10	7	Caudate

Figure 14.3   An illustration of the locations of the six brain regions associated with ACT-R modules. In part (a) are the regions close to the surface of the cortex and in part (b) are the regions deeper in the brain. The Talairach coordinates are for the left side; all data will be reported from this hemisphere. Most of the regions are cubes 5 voxels long, 5 voxels wide, and 4 voxels high. The exceptions are the procedural (caudate), which is 4 × 4 × 4 the goal (ACC), which is 5 × 3 × 4, and the fusiform which is 5 × 5 × 3. A voxel in our research is 3.125 mm long and wide and 3.2 mm high.

McCandliss, Cohen, & Dehaene, 2003). These regions will track the perceptual-motor aspects of the task. While the data-flow representation is different than standard algebra and the motor actions in the tutor are different than those in typical paper and pencil algebra, regular algebra equation solving does involve significant perceptual-motor components. While we expected these regions to be heavily involved in the task, we did not expect any learning to occur in these regions.

2. There are two prefrontal regions that we have found to be critical in the control of the information processing. First, a portion of the lateral

inferior prefrontal cortex (LIPFC) has been found to play a critical role in controlling the recall of declarative information (e.g., Buckner, Kelley, & Petersen, 1999; Cabeza et al., 2002; Danker, Gunn, & Anderson, 2008; Dobbins & Wagner, 2005; Fletcher & Henson, 2001; Sohn et al., 2003, 2005). Second, we think that a region of the anterior cingulate cortex (ACC) holds the subgoal representations that determine how the information-processing progresses (at the end of the chapter we will discuss other views of the ACC). We predicted decreased activation in the LIPFC with practice because retrieval of task-relevant information gets faster as it is practiced, but no change in the ACC because the control demands remain constant.

3. There are two regions that are responsible for the cohesion of the information being represented and the procedures being executed. First, with respect to data representation, the posterior parietal cortex (PPC) appears to hold a representation of information relevant to the problem. Others have found this and nearby regions to be involved spatial processing (e.g., Dehaene et al., 2003; Reichle, Carpenter, & Just, 2000) and verbal encoding (Clark & Wagner, 2003; Davachi, Maril, & Wagner, 2001). Second, with respect to procedural execution, there is the head of the caudate which is part of the basal ganglia system that some (e.g., Amos, 2000; Frank, Loughry, & O'Reilly, 2001; Wise, Murray, & Gerfen, 1996) have speculated serves the function of pattern recognition and selection of cognitive actions. We have sometimes found decreases in activation in these regions if the information processing is reorganized to be more efficient but we have not always found learning-related effects (see Anderson, 2007, for a review). We do not predict learning-related changes in these regions because both the representational and procedural components of the task are driven by the need to interact with the tutoring interface and the interface does not change with learning.

THE IMAGING STUDY

The full experiment involved 12 participants (Carnegie Mellon undergraduates) who went through the following 6-day procedure:

- Day 0: Participants received some general instruction on the tutor and did the isomorphs of Sections 1-1 and Section 1-2 from the Foerster text. This material involves a familiarization with algebraic expressions and their evaluation.
- Day 1: Participants did Sections 1-7 (on the invert operation to solve 1-step equations), 2-6 (on collection of constants), and 2-7 (on 2-step equations) in the scanner. Figure 14.1(b) is an example of a problem from Section 2.6 and Figure 14.2(a) is an example of a problem from Section 2-7.
- Days 2–4: Participants did three sections from Chapter 3 that involved more advanced collection and distribution and three sections from Chapter

4 that involved solving more complex diagrams like Figure 14.2(b). The diagrams included the invert, combine, and evaluate operations from the Day 1 material as steps in their solution, along with other more advanced transformations.

- Day 5: They repeated the same sections as Day 1 with different problems but the same operations.

Before the repetition on Day 5, participants completed 181 problems from 11 sections in the Foerster text. Except for the Day 1 and Day 5 problems, the problems were all the odd problems in the Foerster sections. For half of the participants, the problems on Day 1 were the odd problems from the Foerster sections and the problems on Day 5 were the even problems and this was reversed for the other half of the participants.

The analysis of the imaging data will focus on Sections 1-7 and 2-6. The problems in Section 2-7 were fewer and more heterogeneous and will be ignored in this report (although performance on these was similar). The solution of all problems in both Sections 1-7 and 2-6 can be divided up into two analogous episodes. Figure 14.4 illustrates the transitions that define these episodes. During the first episode (the *transformation phase*, between states (a) and (b) or between states (d) and (e) in Figure 14.4) participants selected one or two boxes to operate on, selected the transformation ("Invert" in Section 1-7 or "Combine" in Section 2-6), entered information into answer boxes through the keypad with a mouse, and then performed a 12-second 1-back task (Owen, Laird, & Bullmore, 2005) to allow the blood oxygen level dependent (BOLD) responses to return to a common baseline and prevent rehearsal. During the

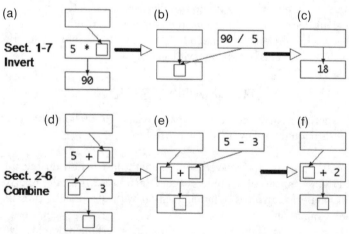

Figure 14.4   The invert problem (analogous to 5x = 90) in Section 1.7 going through two episodes: first State (a), is transformed to achieve State (b) and then this is evaluated to achieve State (c). The combine problem (analogous to (5 + x) − 3) in Section 2.6 similarly goes through two episodes: first State (d) is transformed to achieve State (e) and then this is evaluated to achieve State (f).

1-back the screen went blank and participants saw a sequence of letters presented at the rate of one per 1.25 seconds. They were to simply press the mouse if the same letter occurred twice in succession (which happened one-third of the time). During the second episode (the *evaluation phase*, between states (b) and (c) or between states (e) and (f) in Figure 14.4), participants selected a box with an arithmetic expression that had been created in the first episode, selected "Evaluate," entered the value of the expression using the keypad, and then performed another 12-second 1-back task.

RESULTS

We performed repeated-measures ANOVAs on the error rates and latencies using day (1 or 5) and problem type (invert or combine) as factors. The average error rates were 15.0% for invert-day-1, 22.1% for combine-day-1, 14.4% for invert-day-5, and 21.8% for combine-day-5. The effect for problem type was significant ($F(1,10) = 12.34$; $p < .01$) but not the effects of days ($F(1,10) = 0.03$) nor the interaction ($F(1,10) = 0.002$). We suspect the majority of the errors reflect slips on the students' part, which explains why they did not decrease with learning. In subsequent work with children we have found higher error rates on Day 1 which decreased substantially by Day 5.

We only analyzed the latencies and imaging data for the correct trials. The average latencies were 53.2 seconds for invert-day-1, 55.5 seconds for combine-day-1, 46.4 seconds for invert-day-5, and 49.8 seconds for combine-day-5. The effect of problem type was significant ($F(1,10) = 9.56$; $p < .05$) as was the effect of days ($F(1,10) = 45.84$; $p < .0001$) but the interaction was not ($F(1,10) = 0.90$). The significant decrease in latency combined with a lack of a learning effect on accuracy suggests most of the learning gain reflects an increased proficiency in interacting with the system.

Figure 14.5 displays the variability in solution times for the invert problems (Part a) and the combine problems (Part b). This is plotted in 2-second scans. The minimum number of scans possible is 17 (12 scans for 1-back, 1 scan for the transformation, 1 for the evaluation, 1 scan to indicate done, 2 scans between indicating done and the next problem). The number of scans varied from 19 to 38. This wide temporal variability creates a considerable challenge with respect to aggregating imaging data from individual trials. To deal with these long latencies and high variability, we used event-locked averaging (Anderson et al., 200a). The method takes advantage of the interface interactions that occur as a natural part of a problem-solving episode with these tutors. The event-locked averaging used the 8 intervals defined by the interactions between the tutor and student such as the selection of a transformation or the end of the 1-back. Event-locked averaging is a scheme for averaging the BOLD signals from trials consisting of intervals of varying length to obtain a BOLD response for a template that has intervals of mean length. It assigns the scans from the intervals for particular trials to positions in the template for purposes

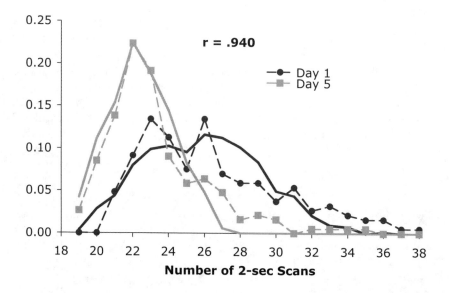

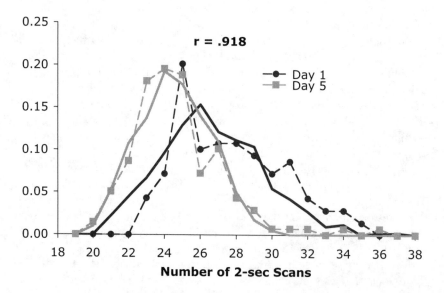

Figure 14.5   Distribution of number of scans to solve problems: Part (a) shows the distribution for invert problems and part (b) shows the distribution for combine problems. Dotted lines connect the observed proportions of solutions of various lengths and solid lines show the predictions of the ACT-R model.

of averaging. Figure 14.6 illustrates how it would choose scans from a trial (represented above) and assign them to positions in the template (represented below). The assignment procedure depends on the length n of the interval in that trial relative to the length m of the interval in the template:

1. If n is greater than or equal to m, the procedure creates a sequence of length m by taking $m/2$ scans from the beginning and $m/2$ from the end. If m is odd, it selects one more from the beginning. This means just deleting the $n-m$ scans in the middle.
2. If n is less than m, the procedure creates a beginning sequence of length $m/2$ by taking the first $n/2$ scans and padding with the last scan in this first $n/2$. It constructs the end similarly. If either n or m is odd, the extra scan is from the beginning.

The averaging of trials according to this event-locked method creates scan sequences that preserve the temporal structure of the beginning and end of the sequences but just represent the approximate average activity in their middle. When there is a rich density of behavioral markers, there is little loss of information in the middle of these intervals. This results in an articulate representation of how the activity in a region changes as problem solving progresses. For a more detailed discussion of this method, see Anderson et al. (2008a).

(a) Day 1 Invert

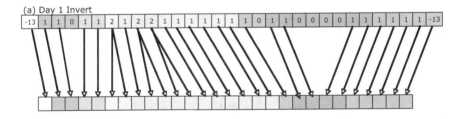

(b) Day 5 Invert

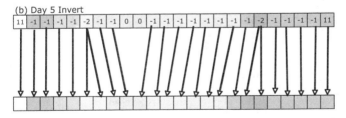

Figure 14.6   How the scans from the 8 intervals in particular trials might be assigned to the template for invert problems on Day 1 and Day 5 for the purpose of averaging. The first scan is the baseline from the last scan of the 1-back. The numbers associated with the scans on the trial are used in the statistical contrast that looks for an effect of learning in the exploratory analyses.

Analysis of Predefined Regions

The introduction to the chapter set out six predefined regions (see Figure 14.3), organized into three pairs that have been found to be related to phases of solving algebra equations. Figures 14.7–14.9 show the results for these pairs of regions that offer interesting contrasts. The vertical lines in these figures reflect the eight behaviorally defined boundaries in the data used for event-locked averaging. We discuss these figures below.

1. Analysis of Activity in the Fusiform Gyrus and the Motor Region Figure 14.7 displays the data for the fusiform and motor regions. These regions respond both to the execution of a transformation and the evaluation of the result with the BOLD response going down to baseline in the intervals during which the participants are performing the 1-back task. The first and last scans for a problem constitute the two baseline scans. To eliminate any linear drift over these relatively long intervals, we performed a linear correction so both would have the value of 0. Qualitatively, these data show some other trends beyond the overall response to the task structure of transformations followed by evaluations. First, the fusiform shows a marked decrease from Day 1 to Day 5. Second, the response in the motor area rises more rapidly than does the response in the fusiform.

To determine the significance of such trends we performed two analyses of variance (ANOVA) on the areas under the curves: one for the transform part of

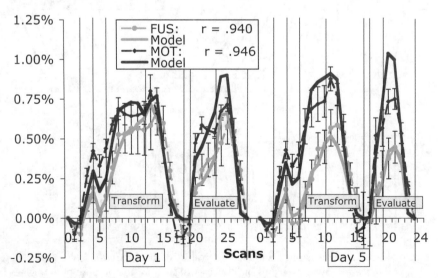

Figure 14.7   A comparison of the BOLD response in the fusiform and motor regions. The vertical lines are the boundaries of the intervals. The solid curve gives the predictions of the ACT-R model. The dotted lines display the data and the standard errors of the mean for each data point.

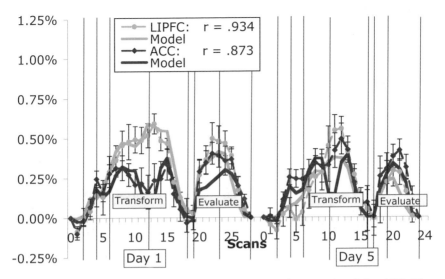

Figure 14.8   A comparison of the BOLD response in the LIPFC and the ACC. The vertical lines are the boundaries of the intervals. The solid curve gives the predictions of the ACT-R model. The dotted lines display the data and the standard errors of the mean for each data point.

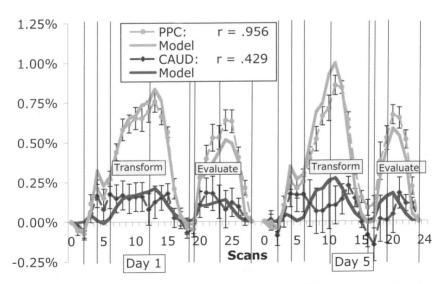

Figure 14.9   A comparison of the BOLD response in the PPC and the caudate. The vertical lines are the boundaries of the intervals. The solid curve gives the predictions of the ACT-R model. The dotted lines display the data and the standard errors of the mean for each data point.

the problem and the other for the evaluate part of the problem. We analyzed these two portions of the curve separately because the transformation phase involves more actions (mouse clicks) than the evaluation phase and it is not meaningful to compare them. To get some idea of differential time course, both the transformation scans and evaluation scans were divided into two halves. The factors in the ANOVA were region (fusiform versus motor), day (1 versus 5), and half (first versus second). The dependent measure was the area under the curve during each half of the transformation phase or each half of the evaluation phase.

With respect to the transformation phase, the two significant main effects were region (F(1,10) = 8.61; $p < .05$, reflecting the greater activity in the motor region) and half (F(1,10) = 39.92; $p < .0001$, reflecting greater activity in the second half). These two factors participate in a marginally significant interaction (F(1,10) = 4.85, $p = .052$) such that the difference between halves is greater in the case of the fusiform (areas under the curve are 0.6% versus 3.3%) than in the case of the motor region (2.5% versus 4.3%). This is consistent with the observation of a slower rise in the fusiform region. The final significant effect is a day-by-region interaction (F(1,10) = 5.53; $p < .05$) such that the fusiform shows a decrease in activation as function of days (2.5% on Day 1 versus 1.4% on Day 5) while the motor does not (3.3% on Day 1 versus 3.5% on Day 5).[2] The effect of practice in the fusiform is significant by a simple t-test ($t(10) = 2.25, p < .05$)[3] confirming the apparent decrease in activity.

With respect to the evaluation phase, the only significant main effect was region (F(1,10) = 10.33; $p < .01$), again reflecting the greater activity in the motor region. The interaction between region and half is highly significant (F(1,10) = 55.88; $p < .0001$), in the same direction as the more marginal interaction for the transformations. The activity actually decreased over halves in the motor (2.1% to 1.8%) but increased in the fusiform (0.8% to 1.3%). The day-by-region interaction, which had been significant in the transformation phase, is now marginal (F(1,10) = 3.79; $p < .15$) but in the same direction—the fusiform shows a decrease as function of days (1.3% on Day 1 versus 0.8% on Day 5) while the motor does not (2.0% on Day 1 versus 1.9% on Day 5). The effect of practice in the fusiform is significant by a simple t-test ($t(10) = 2.41, p < .05$).

Absolute differences in response magnitude between the two regions are not particularly interesting but the interactions with regions are. The region-by-day interaction confirms the apparent trend in Figure 14.7 that the fusiform is decreasing in activation with practice—an unpredicted outcome. The other region by half interaction confirms that the fusiform shows relatively greater activity later than the motor region. We will describe a model that attributes the interaction with halves to the fact that visual processing is more involved in the 1-back task than motor processing. The visual system has to encode each element while the motor system has only to occasionally generate a simple repetitive press.

2 Since there are fewer scans on Day 5, the peak response is actually greater in the motor region, which is consistent with the same number of actions happening in a shorter time span.
3 All t-tests are two-tailed.

2. Analysis of Activity in the LIPFC and ACC   Figure 14.8 compares the activity of the LIPFC and ACC. To assess the various trends separate ANOVAs were again performed on the transformation and evaluation phases. With respect to the transformation phase, the only significant main effect was half $(F(1,10) = 21.46; p < .001)$, reflecting greater activity in the second half. This is modulated by a highly significant interaction with region $(F(1,10) = 28.88; p < .001)$, such that the difference is much greater in the LIPFC (0.9% in the first half and 3.1% in the second half) than in the ACC (1.0% in first half and 1.5% in the second half). The other significant interaction is between day and region $(F(1,10) = 10.24; p < .01)$, such that the activity decreases in the LIPFC over days (2.4% to 1.5% but increases in the ACC (1.0% versus 1.5%). The effect of practice in the LIPFC is significant by a simple t-test $(t(10) = 2.44, p < .05)$ while the reverse effect in the ACC is marginal $(t(10) = -1.91, p < .10)$. With respect to the evaluation phase, the significant main effects were operation $(F(1,10) = 22.75; p < .001)$ and day $(F(1,10) = 8.02; p < .05)$. The effect of day is modulated by a marginally significant day-by-region interaction $(F(1,10) = 3.48; p < .10)$, such that the reduction with practice is greater for the LIPFC (from 1.0% to 0.5%) than the ACC (from 0.9% to 0.7%). The effect in LIPFC is significant $(t(10) = 2.98, p < .05)$ while the effect in the ACC is not significant $(t(10) = 0.96)$.

Probably the most significant result is that the LIPFC shows strong learning effects while the ACC does not. As noted in the Introduction, we would predict this on the basis of reduced retrieval demands on the LIPFC and constant sub-goaling demands in the ACC. The other interaction with region was that the ACC became active earlier than the LIPFC.

3. Analysis of Activity in the PPC and the Caudate   Figure 14.9 compares the activity for the parietal and caudate regions. These two regions have often behaved similarly in past experiments (for a review see Anderson, 2007), but appear to behave quite differently in this experiment. With respect to the transformation phase, the two significant main effects were region $(F(1,10) = 29.49; p < .001$, reflecting the low activity in the caudate) and half $(F(1,10) = 51.48; p < .0001$, reflecting greater activity in the second half). These two factors participate in a highly significant interaction $(F(1,10) = 78.82; p < .0001)$ reflecting the fact that activity increased greatly in the second half in the parietal (1.6% to 4.6%) while it decreased in the caudate (0.5% to 0.4%). With respect to the evaluation phase, there is only a significant main effect of region $(F(1,10) = 24.84; p < .001)$. The factor of days did not participate in any significant effects in either analysis.

The two noteworthy results in these analyses are the lack of effects of practice and the interaction between region and half. As in the case of the ACC, the caudate is distinguished by relatively high early activation. Its activation is particularly low throughout the evaluation phase. The average area under the curves in Figure 14.9 during the evaluation phase in the caudate is 0.

Summary

Four of the six predefined regions showed the predicted relationship to the task structure and the learning manipulation (Day 1 versus Day 5). As predicted, the Motor, ACC, and PPC all showed a response to task structure but did not show an effect of learning. Also as predicted, the LIPFC showed a response to task structure and a decrease with experience. The fusiform showed the predicted response to task structure but unexpectedly also showed learning-related decreases. The caudate showed only a weak response and, as will become clear when we get to modeling it, the caudate showed some unexpected effects in its temporal time course. Besides their differential response to the learning manipulation, the regions differed in their degree of involvement early in an operation. Some regions (motor, ACC, and caudate) showed about as much activation late as early whereas others (fusiform, LIPFC, PPC) showed more than twice as much activation late than early.

TESTING A COGNITIVE MODEL

Figure 14.5 shows the behavioral predictions of a cognitive model[4] developed in the ACT-R architecture (Anderson, 2007; Anderson et al., 2004). ACT-R has been used to model people's behaviors in a great variety of tasks including categorization, learning algebra and geometry, driving while talking on a cell phone, and air traffic control (see http://act-r.psy.cmu.edu/ for the variety of tasks researchers have modeled). By specifying behavioral models within such a framework, one is forced to make the theory computationally explicit, thus allowing for true evaluation of the theory as well as allowing for predictions in novel circumstances. According to the ACT-R theory, cognition emerges through the interaction of a number of relatively independent modules. Each of these modules reflects a set of assumptions derived from the empirical literature. By using the same modules for a wide range of tasks one can test the generality of these assumptions

Six of the ACT-R modules are involved in interacting with the algebra tutor. These six modules correspond to the six predefined brain regions discussed earlier and this correspondence is shown in Figure 14.3. Figure 14.10 illustrates the activity of these modules in the solution of a problem in Section 1-7 on Day 1. Figure 14.10 is broken into two panels, each spanning about 25 seconds going down the panel. The first panel begins at the end of 1-back for the previous problem and the second panel stops in the middle of the second 1-back; so the two panels reflect slightly less than a full problem. Each panel has

---

4 The model, which runs with the ACT-R software in Macintosh Common Lisp (MCL), can be downloaded at the ACT-R models website (http://act-r.psy.cmu.edu/models/) under the title of the chapter. Running instructions are in the file read&start.lisp. This download also contains the version of the experimental algebra tutor that was used in this research. This model is basically the same model as reported in Anderson (2007), only modified to deal with the changes to the tutor interface.

Figure 14.10   Representation of (left-to-right) the visual, procedural, goal, retrieval, imaginal, and manual modules in the solution of an invert (Section 1.7) problem (see Figure 14.4a) by ACT-R on Day 1. Each of the two columns represents 25 seconds of problem solving. The box labeled 1 reflects retrieval of an algebraic fact (in this case that / is the inverse of *) while the box labeled 2 reflects retrieval of the arithmetic fact (in this case that 40 / 5 = 8) that will be required in the evaluation step. The number steps correspond to the points listed on the top of Figure 14.9.

marked the events that are used to break the imaging data into intervals (see Figure 14.7). The six columns in each panel represent the activity of the six modules and the lengths of the boxes in the columns reflect the durations of the module engagements. Below we review these modules in left-to-right order as they appear in Figure 14.10:

1. *Visual Module*: In ACT-R, a visual module is responsible for encoding visual information from the environment. The visual module is active throughout the performance of the task. It takes a time uniformly distributed between 100 and 300 milliseconds to encode a box or button and a time uniformly distributed between 25 and 75 milliseconds to encode the letters. This accounts for the difference in the size of the visual boxes in Figure 14.10 when working on the problem and when working on the 1-back.

2. *Procedural Module*: The procedural module is responsible for the execution of productions that control the solution of the equation and performance of other aspects of the task. Production rules are pieces of procedural memory that specify how to respond to the contents of various modules with additional requests. So, for instance, one production rule might respond to the appearance of "3 + 4" in the visual module with a request to the retrieval module for an arithmetic fact. Each of the thin boxes in the procedural column represents 50 milliseconds to fire a production (a fixed parameter of the ACT-R theory). These productions fire throughout the task, but vary in their frequency of firing in different parts of the task reflecting the different amounts of cognitive engagement at those points.

3. *Goal Module*: The goal module holds the various subgoals that control the solution. For instance, the production mentioned above that requests retrieval of an arithmetic fact would only fire when the goal was to evaluate the contents of a box in the data flow diagram. The changes between subgoals are instantaneous in ACT-R and are reflected in Figure 14.10 by lines. As a general rule, a subgoal is associated with executing each action (i.e., click a box, select an operator, enter a result) and monitoring that the correct change has taken place with the interface. In addition, a single subgoal is associated with the 1-back task and with bridging the delay between problems.

4. *Retrieval Module*: The retrieval module is responsible for maintaining cues that drive an activation-based retrieval from declarative memory. In this task, the module is occupied retrieving task instructions about what to do next and retrieving various algebraic and arithmetic facts. The smaller boxes reflect retrieval of information about what to do next while the larger two boxes reflect retrieval of general facts. The retrieval of task information is represented as faster than the retrieval of algebraic and arithmetic facts because the task information repeats every problem and so should be highly active. The box labeled 1 reflects retrieval of an algebraic fact (in this case, that / is the inverse of *) while the box labeled 2 reflects retrieval of the arithmetic fact (in this case that 40/5 = 8) that will be required in the evaluation step.

5. *Imaginal Module*: The imaginal module stores and manipulates intermediate problem representations that must be held in mind between what is given and the solution. In this task the imaginal module builds up representations of the contents of the various boxes attended. The time for the imaginal module to update such representations is .2 seconds, which is the default value in ACT-R and has been used in many of our previous modeling efforts.

6. *Manual Module*: The manual module is responsible for controlling and planning hand movements. In this task it is being called up to control mouse movement. Based on the model in Anderson (2007), we used the following estimates for motor time: 100 milliseconds for a simple click during the 1-back, 400 milliseconds to move to and click a box, 800

milliseconds to move and click an operator (because of the longer distance movements), and 400 milliseconds per character entered into the pop-up menu. These times vary uniformly trial to trial from half to one-and-a-half times these mean values.

A number of values were estimated in fitting these latencies. These include the mean visual, retrieval, and manual times and their variability. These were estimated to fit the distribution of latencies in Figure 14.5. In addition, to fit the speed-up from Day 1 to Day 5 we assumed that practice had decreased the retrieval times by a factor of .5 and the visual encoding times by a factor of .667. ACT-R predicts the decrease in retrieval times because declarative facts increase in speed with practice. However, the decrease in visual encoding times was a post hoc assumption based on the decrease in the fusiform. The ACT-R architecture does not have any mechanism yet to produce such a perceptual learning effect. Given that many parameters were estimated, the match between theory and latency data in Figure 14.5 is not very compelling evidence for the model. The more demanding tests concern the ability to predict the BOLD responses in the associated regions given these latency estimates.

Predicting the BOLD Response

The patterns of activity of the modules in Figure 14.10 lead to predictions for the patterns of activity that should be seen in associated brain regions as in Figures 14.7–14.9 (Anderson, 2007; Anderson et al., 2008a). These predictions are derived by treating the activity in Figure 14.10 as a 0-1 boxcar function (much like a design matrix in a typical SPM analysis, Friston et al., 2006) and convolving this with a standard hemodynamic response represented as a gamma function (e.g., Glover, 1999):

$$H(t) = m(t/s)^a e^{-(t/s)}$$

The parameter m is the magnitude parameter and determines the height of the function, the parameter s is the scale parameter and determines the temporal spread, and the parameter a is the shape parameter and determines the narrowness of the function. In this chapter, a is fixed to be 6, s to be 0.75 seconds, and m is estimated to fit the magnitude of response in a brain region.[5] The fits of the model predictions to the six predefined regions are displayed in Figures 14.7, 14.8 and 14.9. These predictions were obtained by applying the same event-locked averaging to individual trials of the model that were applied to individual subject trials. The figures give the correlations between the pattern predicted

5 The setting of the parameters a and s come from another experiment (Kao et al., submitted) where we had participants press a finger to a visual signal and tried to model the response in the motor area. Handwerker, Ollinger, and D'Esposito (2004) present data indicating that the variability in the BOLD response across regions is small relative to the variability across participants.

by the module and the observed data. These correlations do not depend on the estimation of the magnitude parameter.

The magnitude of the predicted BOLD response depends on estimating a magnitude parameter for each region. This parameter was set to minimize the following measure of deviation Sum of Squared Standard Errors of Prediction (SSSEP):

$$\sum_i \frac{(\hat{B}_i - \overline{B}_i)^2}{s_{B_i}^2}$$

which sums the squares of the deviations between the predicted and the mean BOLD responses for scan i divided by the standard errors of the means. Under the null hypothesis that these are just random deviations, this statistic has an expected value equal to the number of data points fit minus the number of parameters estimated. Anderson et al. (2008a) advocate estimating the magnitude parameter to fit one curve and then testing its predictions for another curve without further parameter estimation. For this experiment, we estimated the magnitude parameter to fit the Day 1 data and predicted the Day 5 data. Given 27 non-zero BOLD values for Day 1 and 23 for Day 5, the expected values for the SSSEP measures are 26 (since one parameter is estimated to fit that data) for Day 1 and 23 for Day 5. Values much larger than this would indicate significant deviations. Anderson et al. (2008a) show that under the null hypothesis the SSSEP statistic has a gamma distribution and gives a formula (from Kotz & Adams, 1964) for calculating the parameters of the gamma distribution that deals with the non-independence of successive points on the BOLD response. A gamma distribution can be characterized by an index α and a scale β and these can be calculated as:

$$\alpha = n/2S(n,r)$$
$$\beta = 2*S(n,r)$$
$$S(n,r) = 1 + \frac{2r^2}{1-r^2}\left(1 - \frac{1-r^{2n}}{n(1-r^2)}\right)$$

where r is the correlation of the error of measurement between adjacent points on the BOLD response[6] and n is the expected value of the SSSEP statistic. Given an estimate of .837 from our data for r, the gamma distribution for n = 26

---

6 Let x_{rij} be the difference in the rth region between the value for the ith subject for scan j and the mean for that scan for that region. Then r can be calculated:

$$r = \frac{\sum_r \sum_i \sum_{j=0}^{n-1} x_{rij} * x_{rij+1}}{\sqrt{\left(\sum_r \sum_i \sum_{j=0}^{n-1} x_{rij}^2\right) * \left(\sum_r \sum_i \sum_{j=1}^{n} x_{rij}^2\right)}}$$

has index 2.56 and scale 10.14 while for n = 23 the index is 2.30 and the scale is 9.98. With these parameters, the .05 critical values are 57.2 for the Day 1 deviations and 53.2 for the Day 5 deviations.

Anderson et al. (2008a) note that testing for critical values has the undesirable consequence of rewarding noise in the data. If the measurement of the data is noisy, it is unlikely that models that have serious problems will exceed the critical value. On the other hand, with enough precision in measurement, any model will produce a critical value because there always will be some small and unimportant deviation. Therefore, it is also useful to compare the relative goodness of fit of a model with that of alternative models. We will do this by trying to fit each of the six modules to each of the six predefined regions. Table 14.1 provides the SSSEPs obtained by fitting each module to each region for Day 1 in part (a) and for Day 5 in part (b). As can be seen, most of the sums exceed their critical values, but different modules show different degrees of fit to different regions. Part (c) adds the log likelihood for the two sums given the assumed gamma distributions to find an overall measure of how well a module fits a region. Below we will discuss the fits to each of the regions (columns in Table 14.1). In a comparison of two modules (rows) as fits to a region, it is

TABLE 14.1   Results of Fitting Different Modules to Different Predefined Regions (critical values of SSSEPs are 57.2 for Day 1 and 53.2 for Day 5)

	Fusiform	Motor	LIPFC	ACC	PPC	Caudate
(a)						
Day 1 SSSEPs						
Visual	104.91	104.20	78.76	82.48	42.67	35.53
Manual	143.58	56.42	48.39	76.34	49.53	29.52
Retrieval	288.06	177.39	29.44	79.68	123.74	24.01
Goal	198.65	157.40	66.66	44.03	126.22	17.18
Imaginal	122,58	75.90	40.83	78.47	37.25	23.11
Procedural	998.80	362.11	335.88	266.31	486.24	85.68
(b)						
Day 5 SSSEPS						
Visual	51.48	103.85	25.67	80.23	119.75	62.32
Manual	122.57	42.60	133.96	40.08	92.20	82.95
Retrieval	143.90	205.04	41.60	114.90	241.12	67.61
Goal	128.01	95.38	129.87	28.30	83.13	48.03
Imaginal	135.17	47.32	102.20	32.78	60.99	66.83
Procedural	167.83	111.96	126.26	65.81	133.85	95.08
(c)						
Log Likelihood						
Visual	− 14.80	− 19.07	− 11.00	− 15.27	− 15.82	− 10.50
Manual	− 24.10	− 10.36	− 17.47	− 11.67	− 13.85	− 11.90
Retrieval	− 39.14	− 34.69	− 8.65	− 18.06	− 33.38	− 10.40
Goal	− 29.50	− 22.92	− 18.40	− 8.63	− 19.15	− 8.74
Imaginal	− 23.42	− 12.15	− 14.16	− 11.37	− 10.49	− 10.31
Procedural	− 109.22	− 43.19	− 42.00	− 30.32	− 56.88	− 16.79

useful to keep in mind for each 2.3 units that one of the log likelihoods is less negative if it is 10 times more likely.

- *Fusiform.* The visual module produces the best fit to the fusiform, as hypothesized, but with significant deviations. The deviations, however, are rather technical in character—the observed BOLD response returns to baseline during the 1-back one scan later than predicted. Removing these next-to-last scans in the 1-back from the SSSEP statistic removes the significant deviations. This may reflect a slightly faster decaying BOLD response than the one we have assumed.
- *Motor.* The manual module produces the best fit to the motor region, as hypothesized. The closest competing module is the imaginal which is one-sixth as likely. The significant deviations in the fit of the manual module to the Day 1 motor profile reflect a failure to predict the dip below baseline during the first 1-back and the slow return to baseline during the second 1-back. Again, these seem rather technical difficulties that do not challenge the fundamental correspondence between module and region. If we elaborated our assumed BOLD function to include an undershoot we might have been able to capture this.
- *LIPFC.* There are no significant deviations in the fit of the retrieval module to the LIPFC and it fits 10 times better than the closest competitor (the visual module). While the deviation is not significant, the module does somewhat overpredict the reduction in activation from Day 1 to Day 5—empirically, the area under the curve on Day 5 is 52% of the area on Day 1 whereas 45% is predicted.
- *ACC.* There are no significant deviations in the fit of the goal module to the ACC and it fits 15 times better than the closest competitor (the imaginal module). While not significant, there is a qualitative mismatch in the predictions of the goal module. The goal module predicts a double peak in the ACC on both Days 1 and Day 5 during the transformation phase. The source of this can be seen in bottom half of the left side of Figure 14.10: a single subgoal controls the keying of the expression (e.g., 90/5) which takes a long time allowing the BOLD response to drop off. That predicted dip occurs on Day 1 but not Day 5.
- *PCC.* The PPC is best fit by the hypothesized imaginal module but there are significant deviations on Day 5. The model again predicts the BOLD response goes down to baseline one scan sooner than it does. Without the last non-zero point the SSSEP statistics would be 18.17 for Day 1 and 34.54 for Day 5. Thus, again the model predicts a more rapid drop to baseline at the end than is empirically observed.
- *Caudate.* In contrast to the relatively good fits for the other modules, the procedural module gives the worst fit of the 6 modules to the activity in the caudate (see Table 14.1(c)). As Figure 14.10 illustrates, relatively few productions fire early because of the 4 seconds of dead time inserted between the keying of the next problem operation for the previous

problem and the presentation of the next problem. However, the beginning is the period of greatest caudate activity. Unfortunately, as is apparent in Figure 14.9, the noise is high relative to the magnitude of the caudate response, making it hard to ascertain the actual pattern of activity in this region. However, it clearly does not match the predictions of the procedural module.

We were surprised, given the strong influence of the task structure, how discriminative these results were. The 6-modules-to-regions mapping proposed for the ACT-R theory is more than 170 times more likely than the nearest alternative 1-1 mapping (which involves assigning the imaginal module to the motor region and the manual module to the parietal region). If we consider the assignments of the visual to the fusiform and the manual to the motor as established beyond question, and only consider various assignments of retrieval, goal, and imaginal, procedural to LIPFC, ACC, PPC, and caudate, the ACT-R assignment is over 90,000 times more likely than the next best 1-1 mapping (which involves assigning goal to PPC and imaginal to ACC). Except for the caudate-procedural, the mappings lead to good predictions. They usually only differ by an undershoot or the speed of final drop-off in the BOLD response (retrieval to LIPFC, imaginal to PPC). The one qualitative failure for these regions was that the ACC did not show the predicted mid-transformation drop on Day 5.

DISCUSSION

While all the six regions showed a rise during the algebraic task (transformation or evaluation) and a drop-off during the 1-back task, they differed in the pattern of activation during the periods of engagement. All regions except the caudate showed more activation in the second half of these intervals than the first half, but that ratio varied from 3.3 times greater in the fusiform to just 1.2 times greater in the ACC. The reason for the heavy late activity in the fusiform was that this region was engaged in encoding the results of the transformations and the elements of the 1-back. The reason for the relatively higher early activity in the ACC was that it was heavily engaged early in setting up the goal structure for solving the particular kind of problem at hand.

In addition to these effects of task structure, we did find the predicted learning-related reduction of activity in LIPFC region, reflecting the reduced retrieval effort with practice and that reduction in activity correlated with the reduction in latency. Anderson (2007) reviews the many studies of cognitive skill where practice reduced activity in this region. However, we also found an unexpected learning-related reduction in the fusiform region that was of equivalent proportional magnitude. This surprising result suggests that an important ingredient in the learning was an increased facility to parse the data-flow representations. It remains to be seen whether children will show a comparable decrease when they practice with regular algebraic expressions. The learning-related decreases in the fusiform are consistent with other reports of priming (e.g., McCandliss et al., 2003) and reports of training-induced decreases (e.g., Xue et al., 2006).

While the fits of most modules were relatively good, we have never done an experiment that so definitely indicated a mismatch between the procedural module and the caudate. We have found satisfactory fits to the caudate in some experiments that are of short duration (e.g., Anderson, 2005). In experiments with more extended tasks (e.g., Anderson et al., 2008a; Anderson & Qin, 2008) we have tended to find the same early rise in caudate activity. The procedural module provided such a bad fit in the current experiment because this early caudate rise occurred during a period where the module predicted no activity at all. This region of the caudate is known to also reflect reward activities (e.g., Breiter et al., 2001; Delgado et al., 2003) and to respond to eye movements (e.g., Gerardin et al., 2003). Perhaps the initial activity there may reflect the reward-related activity or reflect eye movements. Increased caudate firing at episode boundaries has also been found in rats (Barnes et al., 2005) and in monkeys (Fujii & Graybiel, 2005).

To conclude by addressing the title of this article, this chapter has shown that imaging can help identify the components that are undergoing change in an educational task. The richness of interaction with a tutor creates many behavioral markers for segmenting the interactions into short sequences of scans. Event-locked averaging allows extraction of a meaningful time course of processing.

REFERENCES

Amos, A. (2000). A computational model of information processing in the frontal cortex and basal ganglia. *Journal of Cognitive Neuroscience, 12*, 505–519.

Anderson, J. R. (2005). Human symbol manipulation within an integrated cognitive architecture. *Cognitive Science, 29*, 313–342.

Anderson, J. R. (2007). *How can the human mind occur in the physical universe?* New York: Oxford University Press.

Anderson, J. R., Bothell, D., Byrne, M. D., Douglass, S., Lebiere, C., & Qin, Y. (2004). An integrated theory of mind. *Psychological Review, 111*, 1036–1060.

Anderson, J. R., Byrne, D., Fincham, J. M., & Gunn, P. (2008). Role of prefrontal and parietal cortices in associative learning. *Cerebral Cortex, 18*, 904–914.

Anderson, J. R., Carter, C. S., Fincham, J. M., Ravizza, S. M., & Rosenberg-Lee, M. (2008). Using fMRI to test models of complex cognition. *Cognitive Science, 32*, 1323–1348.

Anderson, J. R., Conrad, F. G., & Corbett, A. T. (1989). Skill acquisition and the LISP Tutor. *Cognitive Science, 13*, 467–506.

Anderson, J. R., Corbett, A. T., Koedinger, K., & Pelletier, R. (1995). Cognitive tutors: Lessons learned. *The Journal of Learning Sciences, 4*, 167–207.

Anderson, J. R., Farrell, R., & Sauers, R. (1984). Learning to program in LISP. *Cognitive Science, 8*, 87–130.

Anderson, J. R., & Qin, Y. (2008). Using brain imaging to extract the structure of complex events at the rational time band. *Journal of Cognitive Neuroscience, 20*(9),1624–1636.

Barnes, T., Kubota, Y., Hu, D., Jin, D. Z., & Graybiel, A. M. (2005). Activity of striatal neurons reflects dynamic encoding and recoding of procedural memories. *Nature, 437*, 1158–1161.

Breiter, H. C., Aharon, I., Kahneman, D., Dale, A., & Shizgal, P. (2001). Functional imaging of neural responses to expectancy and experience of monetary gains and losses. *Neuron, 30*, 619–639.

Buckner, R. L., Kelley, W. M., & Petersen, S. E. (1999). Frontal cortex contributes to human memory formation. *Nature Neuroscience, 2*, 311–314.

Buckner, R. L., & Wheeler, M. E. (2001). The cognitive neuroscience of remembering. *Nature Reviews Neuroscience, 2*, 624–634.

Cabeza, R., Dolcos, F., Graham, R., & Nyberg, L. (2002). Similarities and differences in the neural correlates of episodic memory retrieval and working memory. *Neuroimage, 16*, 317–330.

Chein, J. M., & Schneider W. (2005). Neuroimaging studies of practice-related change: fMRI and meta-analytic evidence of a domain-general control network for learning. *Cognitive Brain Research, 25*(3), 607–623.

Clark, D., & Wagner, A. D. (2003). Assembling and encoding word representations: fMRI subsequent memory effects implicate a role for phonological control. *Neuropsychologia, 41*, 304–317.

Danker, J. F., Gunn, P., & Anderson, J. R. (2008). A rational account of memory predicts left prefrontal activation during controlled retrieval. *Cerebral Cortex, 18*, 2674–2685.

Davachi, L., Maril, A., & Wagner, A. D. (2001). When keeping in mind supports later bringing to mind: Neural markers of phonological rehearsal predict subsequent remembering. *Journal of Cognitive Neuroscience, 13*, 1059–1070.

Dehaene, S., Piazza, M., Pinel, P., & Cohen, L. (2003). Three parietal circuits for number processing. *Cognitive Neuropsychology, 20*, 487–506.

Delgado, M. R., Locke, H. M., Stenger, V. A., & Fiez, J. A. (2003). Dorsal striatum responses to reward and punishment: Effects of valence and magnitude manipulations. *Cognitive, Affective, & Behavioral Neuroscience, 3*, 27–38.

Dobbins, I. G., & Wagner A. D. (2005). Domain-general and domain-sensitive prefrontal mechanisms for recollecting events and detecting novelty. *Cerebral Cortex, 15*, 1768–1778.

Fletcher, P. C., & Henson, R. N. A. (2001). Frontal lobes and human memory: Insights from functional neuroimaging. *Brain, 124*, 849–881.

Foerster, P. A. (1990). *Algebra I* (2nd ed.). Menlo Park, CA: Addison-Wesley.

Frank, M. J., Loughry, B., & O'Reilly, R. C. (2001). Interactions between the frontal cortex and basal ganglia in working memory: A computational model. *Cognitive, Affective, and Behavioral Neuroscience, 1*, 137–160.

Friston, K., Ashburner, J., Kiebel, S., Nichols, T., & Penny, W. (Eds.). (2006). *Statistical parametric mapping: The analysis of functional brain images*. London: Elsevier.

Fujii, N., & Graybiel, A. M. (2005). Time-varying covariance of neural activities recorded in striatum and frontal cortex as monkeys perform sequential-saccade tasks. *Proceedings of the National Academy of Sciences of the USA, 102*, 9032–9037.

Gerardin, E., Lehericy, S., Pochon, J. B., Tezenas du Montcel, S., Mangin, J. F., Poupon, F., Agid, Y., Le Bihan, D., & Marsault, C. (2003). Foot, hand, face and eye representation in the human striatum. *Cerebral Cortex, 13*, 162–169.

Glover, G. H. (1999). Deconvolution of impulse response in event-related BOLD fMRI. *NeuroImage, 9*, 416–429.

Grill-Spector, K., Knouf, N., & Kanwisher, N. (2004). The fusiform face area subserves face perception, not generic within-category identification. *Nature Neuroscience, 7*, 555–562.

Handwerker, D. A., Ollinger, J. M., & D'Esposito, M. (2004). Variation of BOLD hemo-dynamic responses across participants and brain regions and their effects on statistical analyses. *Neuroimage, 21*, 1639–1651.

Hill, N. M., & Schneider, W. (2006). Brain changes in the development of expertise: Neurological evidence on skill-based adaptations. In K. A. Ericsson, N. Charness, P. Feltovich, & R. Hoffman (Eds.), *Cambridge handbook of expertise and expert performance* (pp. 653–682). New York: Cambridge University Press.

Koedinger, K. R., Anderson, J. R., Hadley, W. H., & Mark, M. (1997). Intelligent tutoring goes to school in the big city. *International Journal of Artificial Intelligence in Education, 8*, 30–43.

Koedinger, K. R., & Corbett, A. T. (2006). Cognitive Tutors: Technology bringing learning science to the classroom. In R. K. Sawyer (Ed.), *Handbook of the learning sciences* (pp. 61–78). New York: Cambridge University Press.

Kotz, S., & Adams, J. W. (1964). Distribution of sum of identically distributed exponentially correlated gamma-variables. *The Annals of Mathematical Statistics, 35*, 277–283.

McCandliss, B. D., Cohen, L., & Dehaene, S. (2003). The visual word form area: Expertise for reading in the fusiform gyrus. *Trends in Cognitive Sciences, 7*, 293–299.

Nomura, E. M., & Reber, P. J. (2008). A review of medial temporal lobe and caudate contributions to visual category learning. *Neuroscience & Behavioral Reviews, 32*, 279–291.

Owen, A., Laird, A., & Bullmore, E. (2005). N-back working memory paradigm: A meta-analysis of normative functional neuroimaging studies. *Human Brain Mapping, 25*, 46–59.

Poldrack, R. A. (2000). Imaging brain plasticity: Conceptual and methodological issues. *NeuroImage, 12*, 1–13.

Reichle, E. D., Carpenter, P. A., & Just, M. A. (2000). The neural basis of strategy and skill in sentence-picture verification. *Cognitive Psychology, 40*, 261–295.

Ritter, S., Anderson, J. R., Koedinger, K. R., & Corbett, A. (2007). Cognitive Tutor: Applied research in mathematics education. *Psychonomic Bulletin & Review, 14*, 249–255.

Ritter, S., Haverty, L., Koedinger, K., Hadley, W., & Corbett, A. (in press). Integrating intelligent software tutors with the mathematics classroom. In K. Heid, & G. Blum (Eds.), *Research on technology and the teaching and learning of mathematics: Syntheses, cases, and perspectives.* Greenwich, CT: Information Age Publishing.

Sohn, M-H., Goode, A., Stenger, V. A., Carter, C. S., & Anderson, J. R. (2003). Competition and representation during memory retrieval: Roles of prefrontal cortex and posterior parietal cortex. *Proceedings of the National Academy of Sciences of the USA, 100*, 7412–7417.

Sohn, M-H., Goode, A., Stenger, V. A., Carter, C. S., & Anderson, J. R. (2005). An information-processing model of three cortical regions: Evidence in episodic memory retrieval. *NeuroImage, 25*, 21–33.

Wagner, A. D., Schacter, D. L., Rotte, M., Koutstaal, W., Maril, A., Dale, A. M., Rosen, B. R., & Buckner, R. L. (1998). Building memories: Remembering and forgetting of verbal experiences as predicted by brain activity. *Science, 281*, 1188–1191.

Wiggs, C. L., & Martin, A. (1998). Properties and mechanisms of perceptual priming. *Current Opinion in Neurobiology, 8*, 227–233.

Wise, S. P., Murray, E. A., & Gerfen, C. R. (1996). The frontal cortex-basal ganglia system in primates. *Critical Reviews in Neurobiology, 10*, 317–356.

Xue, G., Chen, C., Jin, Z., & Dong, Q. (2006). Cerebral asymmetry in the fusiform areas predicted the efficiency of learning a new writing system, *Journal of Cognitive Neuroscience, 18*, 923–931.

15

Commentary
The Emergence of a Multi-Level Approach to the Study of Skill Acquisition and Expertise

DANIEL ANSARI[1]

Department of Psychology, University of Western Ontario, Canada

The present volume contains four chapters from leading experts and their collaborators in the study of expertise and skill acquisitions. The four papers are the product of the 36th Carnegie Symposium on Cognition entitled: "Expertise and Skill Acquisition: The Impact of William G. Chase." Two of these contributions are theoretical perspectives (Posner, Chapter 11, and Beilock, Chapter 13), while the other two chapters (Anderson et al., Chapter 14, and Righi, Tarr, & Kingon, Chapter 12, in this volume) report empirical neuroimaging data investigating the neural correlates of skill acquisition.

At a macro-level of description what ties these chapters together is that they all show that the development of expertise and skill acquisition involves multiple factors and interacting levels of description (e.g. cognitive, sensorimotor, neuronal, developmental and genetic). In this vein, the contributions demonstrate that, while traditional, purely cognitive, accounts which explain expertise in terms of practice-related changes in the organization of information that is relevant to the domain of expertise (i.e. chess playing) still hold much water, much is now known about other factors and processes at multiple levels of description (including neuronal and genetic) that further constrain our understanding of expertise and skill acquisition. Thereby widening both the theories and models we have at our disposal to explain the processes we observe as well

1 Daniel Ansari is supported by operating grants from the Natural Sciences and Engineering Research Council of Canada (NSERC), the Canadian Institutes of Health Research (CIHR) and the Canada Research Chairs Program (CRC).

as the methodological toolbox to investigate them. In other words, the present set of chapters clearly illustrate that since the seminal work of Bill Chase, new theoretical models and methodological approaches have been developed, building on his seminal advances, that allow for a broader approach to the study of expertise.

In this commentary, I will discuss each of these contributions, highlighting what I perceive to be some of the central theoretical contentions made as well as empirical data reported. In doing so, I will discuss the ways in which the theoretical approaches as well as data described in the contributions may inform one another to provide a richer characterization of expertise and skill acquisition. I will conclude this commentary by highlighting a set of factors that I perceive as additional important aspects that should feature prominently in the future study of skill acquisition and expertise.

In his theoretical perspective, Michael Posner raises the important question concerning the role played by individual differences in the emergence of expertise and acquisition of skills. Specifically, he considers what factors can explain why some individuals become experts in a given domain, while others do not? To account for such individual differences, Posner highlights the potential role of attention and individual differences in the efficiency of attentional mechanisms in constraining the acquisition of skills and expertise. Through decades of empirical research on attention, Posner and his colleagues have established that attention can be broadly fractionated into three different networks (alerting, orienting and executive control). These networks can be tested independently using behavioral measures such as the Attentional Network Task. Furthermore, as he reviews, each of these networks has been shown to have distinct neuronal correlates, each of which is thought to be associated with different neurotransmitter systems. Moreover, variability in the efficiency of these three attentional networks has linked to different genetic variants. In view of these findings, which are described in detail in Posner's chapter, it can therefore be hypothesized that individual differences in attentional networks constrain skill acquisition and the emergence of expertise (Posner & Rothbart, 2007). In other words, individual differences in the integrity and efficiency of attentional networks (as measured by both neuroimaging and behavioral methods) may be associated with variability in the degree to which individuals are likely to devote the effort and time necessary to organize their knowledge about a particular domain in such a way to allow them to become experts.

Against the background of Posner's description of the Attentional Networks, one could imagine that the executive control network, in particular, facilitates individuals' ability to focus on information processing in a given domain and thus provides a gateway towards the acquisition of expertise. Moreover, individual differences in attentional network function is, as Posner discusses in his chapter, constrained by genetic variability in the genes that code for neurotransmitters which modulate the functioning of attentional networks. Thus, one of the factors that should be considered in expertise research is how individual differences in genetic variability influence the functioning of attentional networks, which serve as a gateway to information processing and therefore the development of skills and expertise. Importantly, as Posner highlights, genes do not exert their influence in a vacuum, but their effects on brain networks and thus cognitive functions are influenced by environmental factors, such as parenting. Acquisition of expert skills, such as, for example, virtuoso musical skills, requires the availability of instruments and environmental support. How differences in these environmental influences interact with genetic variability to influence skill acquisition and expertise represents a major frontier for future research in this field.

The chapter by Beilock provides a novel perspective on the factors that underlie skill acquisition which differs significantly from dominant, cognitive, information processing-based approaches that view changes in knowledge representations in memory to be the driving factor behind skill acquisition and expertise. In stark contrast to such "disembodied" perspectives on cognition and the acquisition of expertise, Beilock discussed an "embodied" view of expertise. Specifically, through a systematic review of empirical evidence, Beilock demonstrates that knowledge representations are embodied, and presents evidence demonstrating that experts in a particular domain will activate representations related to their physical interactions with domain-relevant objects during the processing of information relevant to their domain of expertise. In other words, prior motor experiences and the reactivation of these "embodied" experiences are thought to play a role in modulating the processing of expertise-related information, whether it is during the observation of other experts or during the actual execution of expertise-related behaviors.

For example, while experts observe other experts, they activate their own sensorimotor experiences with the objects of expertise. One powerful example that Beilock discusses is the case of hockey players. In a neuroimaging study (Beilock et al., 2008), the functional brain activation patterns of both hockey players (experts) and non-hockey players (novices) were examined while these individual listened to hockey-action-related and non-hockey-action-related sentences. In this task, greater activation of regions of the brain associated with selecting and planning motor actions were found for the hockey-related sentences in the hockey players compared to the novices. For the non-hockey-related sentences, no group differences were observed. This finding demonstrates that merely observing (or listening) to information relevant to the domain of expertise leads to activations in brain regions typically associated with actions. In other words, while hockey players (experts) listen to information relevant to their domain, they are activating representations that are related to the actions relevant to that domain. Thus, expert knowledge may not always be represented in abstract, "disembodied" codes in long-term memory but the access to this knowledge may involve a reactivation of the bodily, sensorimotor experiences and motor acts associated with that knowledge. This is just one of many examples that Beilock discusses in her chapter to convincingly show that the activation of sensorimotor processes is intimately tied to both the observation of other experts and the execution of expertise-related behavior.

What Beilock does not discuss is how this might relate to the acquisition in the domain of chess playing, which formed a central part of Chase's work on expertise. If one thinks about chess playing, it is abundantly clear that it involves the complex sequencing of actions. If the "embodied" perspective on cognition and expertise is correct, then for an expert chess player, the opening move must trigger a series of "embodied" representations of both their own future actions and those of their opponents. Critically, there must exist, at some level, a dynamic process of simulating one's own actions and how these will change as a function of the opponent's moves (actions). In many ways, therefore, it is entirely possible that chess expertise is, at least, partially embodied.

The "embodied" perspective has important implications for research in the acquisition of chess expertise. One example is the study by Righi, Tarr, and Kingon in the present volume. To investigate the neural correlates of chess expertise, Righi, Tarr and Kingon using fMRI to measure correlates of brain activity while chess players of various levels of expertise viewed chessboard configurations and had to judge whether the player with the white or black chess pieces was winning. They viewed chessboards that either had a valid or an invalid configuration of chess pieces. The key result of their study is a correlation between the years of experience playing chess and brain activation when viewing the chessboard configurations. In their chapter, the authors focus on the correlation between chess expertise and the fusiform gyrus and interpret this expertise-related activation as reflecting perceptual expertise in the representation of chessboard configurations that is similar to perceptual expertise in other domains such as object and face expertise, which has consistently been associated with activation in ventral stream regions such as the fusiforum gyrus. Specifically, it is contended that this expertise-related correlation with activation in the fusiform gyrus for valid compared to invalid configurations of the chessboard is reflective of greater configural processing of chessboards in relative experts compared to chess novices.

While this is indeed a central part of their findings, Table 12.3 of their chapter suggests that there were also correlations in areas typically associated with sensorimotor tasks, such as the post-central and pre-central gyri. Given the perspective provided by Beilock, one might speculate that these correlations between expertise and brain activation during viewing valid chess configurations represent action simulations, such as the activation of "embodied" representations of the moves that lead to the particular configuration that is being viewed and/or an activation of the actions (moves) that either the observer or the opponent might take next. In other words, it is possible that part of the neuronal processes that go into evaluating the plausibility of a particular chessboard configuration involve the "embodied" simulation of chess movements that occurred in the past (leading up to the configuration observed) and/or future moves.

The findings presented by Righi, Tarr, and Kingon are one of the few neuroimaging studies of chess expertise and nicely demonstrate how modern, cognitive neuroscience tools such as the fMRI can be used to further constrain our understanding of the differences between experts and non-experts. While methods such as the fMRI to image the neural correlates of cognitive processes are certainly powerful, they also have many limitations. One key shortcoming in the context of using neuroimaging to study skill acquisition and expertise is the constraints placed by these methods on the type of tasks that can be used to study such processes.

The absence of ecological validity associated with present-day methods for the functional imaging of the brain is succinctly discussed by Anderson et al. in their contribution to this present volume. Moreover, Anderson et al. show how this limitation may be overcome. As Anderson and colleagues describe in their present chapter, they have been developing tutor systems to teach children algebra. Here they use a slightly modified version to train adults and measure the effect of brain function. Thus they combine a program that has already found widespread application in classrooms with modern neuroimaging methods. In addition, Anderson and his colleagues have developed a powerful and widely used computational modeling tool: 'Adaptive Control of Thought-Rational' (ACT-R) for constraining data on human cognition, which has been previously applied to understand, for example, the mechanisms underlying algebraic problem solving (Anderson, 2005). In the study described in the present volume, Anderson and colleague combine their ecologically valid tutoring in algebra with neuroimaging and evaluate it using the ACT-R computational architecture. Thus, Anderson and colleagues used a truly multi-method approach to the study of skill acquisition. The methods and data described by Anderson and his colleagues are extremely exciting, as they suggest that the time has come when we can use cognitive neuroscience to inform our understanding of learning and skill acquisition and, most importantly, that we can do so by using tasks that resemble those that are used in the classroom, rather than experiments that are severely stripped down from the kinds of tasks that children are given to learn in classrooms. In a similar vein, neuroimaging has been applied to studying how the application of educational remediation changes the brains of children with difficulties in domains such as reading and arithmetic (Kucian et al., 2011; Temple et al., 2003).

In addition to the factors that contribute to skill acquisition and expertise highlighted in this volume, there are a few variables that I believe are important to consider in the future study of skill acquisition and expertise. First of all, it seems of particular importance to take development seriously in the study of skill acquisition and the development of expertise. Questions such as whether there are age-related changes in the mechanisms that underlie skill acquisition and expertise and, relatedly, whether sensitive periods exist and what developmental biases might be identified early on to predict who might become an expert in a particular domain need to be addressed. A developmental perspective on skill acquisition and expertise is not only important from a scientific perspective, but will have implications for instruction and the fostering of expertise in different age groups. Taking development seriously in research on expertise and skill acquisition will also be important when considering the interactions between genes and environment which might give rise to expertise (as discussed by Posner), as such interactions are modulated by development (Karmiloff-Smith, 1998; Scarr & McCarney, 1983).

A related factor concerns how the strategies change over the course of skill acquisition, leading either to expertise or lack thereof in the course of learning and developmental time. Research on strategies suggests that children use multiple strategies adaptively (Siegler, 1999), raising the question of which pattern of strategy development is most predictive of the emergence of expertise (Rosenberg-Lee, Lovett, & Anderson, 2009; Staszewski, 1988). Identifying the strategies (or mosaic of strategies) that foster skill acquisition and the development of expertise will have important educational implications.

The final issue that I would like to draw attention to that receives comparatively little attention in the present set of chapters is the degree of transfer from a domain of expertise to other cognitive functions. To what extent does training in one domain lead to transfer effects in another (Kimball & Holyoak, 2000)? In addition, if individual differences in attention, through their interactions with genes and development, are predictors of skill acquisition and expertise, this raises the question of whether training in attention leads to transfer effects that enhance skill acquisition. This question is currently hotly pursued in the domains of attention and working memory research (Klingberg, 2010; Rueda et al., 2005). Whether such training truly leads to far-transfer effects (as opposed to mere near transfer effects, such as making individuals better at problems and tasks closely related to their domain of expertise) is still largely unknown.

Taken together, the above-discussed contributions provide novel perspectives on skill acquisition and expertise and introduce new methods that will help to further our understanding of these processes. In this way, they provide a roadmap to future, multidisciplinary investigations of skill acquisition and expertise.

REFERENCES

Anderson, J. R. (2005). Human symbol manipulation within an integrated cognitive architecture. *Cognitive Science, 29*(3), 313–341. doi: 10.1207/s15516709cog0000_22.

Beilock, S. L., Lyons, I. M., Mattarella-Micke, A., Nusbaum, H. C., & Small, S. L. (2008). Sports experience changes the neural processing of action language. [Research Support, Non-U.S. Gov't Research Support, U.S. Gov't, Non-P.H.S.]. *Proceedings of the National Academy of Sciences of the USA, 105*(36), 13269–13273. doi: 10.1073/pnas.0803424105.

Karmiloff-Smith, A. (1998). Development itself is the key to understanding developmental disorders. *Trends in Cognitive Science, 2*(10), 389–398.

Kimball, D. R., & Holyoak, K. J. (2000). Transfer and expertise. In E. Tulving, & F. I. M. Craik (Eds.), *The Oxford handbook of memory*. Oxford: Oxford University Press.

Klingberg, T. (2010). Training and plasticity of working memory. *Trends in Cognitive Science, 14*(7), 317–324. doi: S1364-6613(10)00093-8 [pii] 10.1016/j.tics.2010.05.002.

Kucian, K., Grond, U., Rotzer, S., Henzi, B., Schonmann, C., Plangger, F.,... von Aster, M. (2011). Mental number line training in children with developmental dyscalculia. *NeuroImage, 57*(3), 782–795. doi: 10.1016/j.neuroimage.2011.01.070.

Posner, M. I., & Rothbart, M. K. (2007). Research on attention networks as a model for the integration of psychological science. *Annual Review of Psychology, 58,* 1–23. doi: 10.1146/annurev.psych.58.110405.085516.

Rosenberg-Lee, M., Lovett, M. C., & Anderson, J. R. (2009). Neural correlates of arithmetic calculation strategies. [Research Support, Non-U.S. Gov't Research Support, U.S. Gov't, Non-P.H.S.]. *Cognitive, affective & behavioral neuroscience, 9*(3), 270–285. doi: 10.3758/CABN.9.3.270.

Rueda, M. R., Rothbart, M. K., McCandliss, B. D., Saccomanno, L., & Posner, M. I. (2005). Training, maturation, and genetic influences on the development of executive attention. *Proceedings of the National Academy of Sciences of the USA, 102*(41), 14931–14936.

Scarr, S., & McCarney, K. (1983). How people make their own environments: A theory of genotype greater than environment effects. *Child Development, 54*(2), 424–435.

Siegler, R. S. (1999). Strategic development. *Trends in Cognitive Science, 3*(11), 430–435. doi: S1364-6613(99)01372-8.

Staszewski, J. J. (1988). Skilled memory and expert mental calculation. In M. T. H. Chi, R. Glaser, & M. J. Farr (Eds.), *The nature of expertise*. Hillsdale, NJ: Lawrence Erlbaum Associates.

Temple, E., Deutsch, G. K., Poldrack, R. A., Miller, S. L., Tallal, P., Merzenich, M. M., & Gabrieli, J. D. (2003). Neural deficits in children with dyslexia ameliorated by behavioral remediation: Evidence from functional MRI. *Proceedings of the National Academy of Sciences of the USA, 100*(5), 2860–2865.

Index

Note: page numbers in *italic* type refer to Figures; those in **bold** type refer to Tables.

Taylor & Francis

eBooks

FOR LIBRARIES

ORDER YOUR FREE 30 DAY INSTITUTIONAL TRIAL TODAY!

Over 23,000 eBook titles in the Humanities, Social Sciences, STM and Law from some of the world's leading imprints.

Choose from a range of subject packages or create your own!

Benefits for you
▶ Free MARC records
▶ COUNTER-compliant usage statistics
▶ Flexible purchase and pricing options

Benefits for your user
▶ Off-site, anytime access via Athens or referring URL
▶ Print or copy pages or chapters
▶ Full content search
▶ Bookmark, highlight and annotate text
▶ Access to thousands of pages of quality research at the click of a button

For more information, pricing enquiries or to order a free trial, contact your local online sales team.

UK and Rest of World: **online.sales@tandf.co.uk**

US, Canada and Latin America: **e-reference@taylorandfrancis.com**

www.ebooksubscriptions.com

ALPSP Award for BEST eBOOK PUBLISHER 2009 Finalist
sponsored by

Taylor & Francis eBooks
Taylor & Francis Group

A flexible and dynamic resource for teaching, learning and research.

0 1341 1526132 0

RECEIVED

SEP 1 0 2013

GUELPH HUMBER LIBRARY
205 Humber College Blvd
Toronto, ON   M9W 5L7